Dionysus and Rome

Trends in Classics –
Supplementary Volumes

Edited by
Franco Montanari and Antonios Rengakos

Associate Editors
Stavros Frangoulidis · Fausto Montana · Lara Pagani
Serena Perrone · Evina Sistakou · Christos Tsagalis

Scientific Committee
Alberto Bernabé · Margarethe Billerbeck
Claude Calame · Jonas Grethlein · Philip R. Hardie
Stephen J. Harrison · Richard Hunter · Christina Kraus
Giuseppe Mastromarco · Gregory Nagy
Theodore D. Papanghelis · Giusto Picone
Tim Whitmarsh · Bernhard Zimmermann

Volume 93

Dionysus and Rome

Religion and Literature

Edited by
Fiachra Mac Góráin

DE GRUYTER

ISBN 978-3-11-077776-5
e-ISBN (PDF) 978-3-11-067223-7
e-ISBN (EPUB) 978-3-11-067231-2
ISSN 1868-4785

Library of Congress Control Number: 2019953924

Bibliographic information published by the Deutsche Nationalbibliothek
The Deutsche Nationalbibliothek lists this publication in the Deutsche Nationalbibliografie; detailed bibliographic data are available on the internet at http://dnb.dnb.de.

© 2021 Walter de Gruyter GmbH, Berlin/Boston
This volume is text- and page-identical with the hardback published in 2020.
Editorial Office: Alessia Ferreccio and Katerina Zianna
Logo: Christopher Schneider, Laufen
Printing and binding: CPI books GmbH, Leck

www.degruyter.com

Preface

This volume grew out of a conference on 'Dionysus and Rome,' held at University College London on 3–4 September 2015, which was generously funded by the Classical Association, the Institute of Classical Studies, the Jowett Copyright Trust, the A.G. Leventis Foundation, and the Department of Greek and Latin at UCL. Heartfelt thanks go to all those who spoke at the conference, and to those who helped, especially Gesine Manuwald and Liz McKnight.

Sincere thanks are due to the series editors Franco Montanari and Antonios Rengakos, who accepted the book for publication, and to a number of expert readers. For help with production I warmly thank Jana Fritsche, Marco Acquafredda, and Katerina Zianna at De Gruyter. Last but not least, I am very grateful to Amélie von Kuhlberg for preparing the index.

Fiachra Mac Góráin
London, August 2019

Contents

Preface —— V
List of illustrations —— IX
List of contributors —— XI

Fiachra Mac Góráin
Introduction. Dionysus in Rome: accommodation and resistance —— 1

Simon Perris and Fiachra Mac Góráin
The ancient reception of Euripides' *Bacchae* from Athens to Byzantium —— 39

Stéphanie Wyler
Images of Dionysus in Rome: the archaic and Augustan periods —— 85

Daniele Miano
Liber, Fufluns and the others: rethinking Dionysus in Italy between the fifth and the third centuries BCE —— 111

Julietta Steinhauer
Dionysian associations and the Bacchanalian affair —— 133

Gesine Manuwald
Dionysus / Bacchus / Liber in Cicero —— 157

John F. Miller
Bacchus and the exiled Ovid (*Tristia* 5.3) —— 177

Alessandro Schiesaro
Alius furor. Statius' *Thebaid* and the metamorphoses of Bacchus —— 193

Francesco Massa
The shadow of Bacchus:
Liber and Dionysus in Christian Latin literature (2nd–4th centuries) —— 219

Index rerum et nominum —— 239
Index locorum —— 245
Index of inscriptions and visual artefacts —— 247

List of illustrations

Fig. 1: Graphic reconstruction of the terracotta group with Liber and Libera on the roof of the Sant'Omobono temple. 530–520 BCE. Design P. Lulof and G. Pala. After Mura Sommella 2011: fig. 16. —— **88**

Fig. 2: Bearded Liber on a bronze *cista* from Praeneste. Third century BCE. Design after *MonInst* 9. Pl. 58–9. —— **92**

Fig. 3: Bifrontic Herm of Liber from the Palatine. Rome, Museo Palatino, inv. 614 and 601. With permission of the Ministero dei beni e delle attività culturali e del turismo, Soprintendenza Speciale per il Colosseo, il Museo Nazionale Romano e l'area archeologica di Roma. Augustan. Photo S. Wyler. —— **95**

Fig. 4: Handle of the cista Ficoroni, Rome, Museo Nazionale Etrusco di Villa Giulia, inv. 24787. 350–30 BCE. Licence CC-BY-SA 4.0, (Creative Commons Attribution-Share Alike 4.0 International). Photo Sailko. —— **96**

Fig. 5: Fresco fragment from Lanuvium, Museo civico di Lanuvio. With permission of the Soprintendenza del Lazio e dell'Etruria Meridionale. Photo S. Wyler. —— **99**

Fig. 6: Mosaic from the House of the Centaur, Pompeii VI, 9, 12, Naples, Museo Archeologico Nazionale, inv. 100019, late-second century BCE. With permission of the Soprintendenza per i beni archeologici di Napoli. Photo S. Wyler. —— **100**

Fig. 7: Fresco from a columbarium in the Villa Doria Pamphili, 20–10 BCE. Rome, Museo Nazionale Romano (Palazzo Massimo). With permission of the Ministero per i beni e le attività culturali – Museo Nazionale Romano. Photo S. Wyler. —— **104**

Fig. 8. Mirror with Fufluns embracing Semla, Vulci (from *ES* 83) —— **119**

Fig. 9. Mirror with Fufluns, Menerva, Artamis and Esia, Praeneste (from *ES* 87) —— **121**

Fig. 10. Mirror with Hiaco, Menerva and Fortuna, Praeneste (from Matthies 1912) —— **124**

Fig. 11. Cista with a meeting of gods, Praeneste (from *Mon. Inst.* 1873) —— **126**

List of Contributors

Fiachra Mac Góráin is Associate Professor of Classics at University College London. His research interests include Virgil and the Virgilian tradition, Augustan poetry more broadly, and the representation of religion in literature. He has co-edited (with Charles Martindale) *The Cambridge Companion to Virgil (Second Edition)*, and is writing a book to be entitled *Virgil's Dionysus*.

Gesine Manuwald is Professor of Latin at University College London. Her research interests include Cicero's speeches, Roman drama, Roman epic and the reception of the classical world especially in Neo-Latin literature. She has published widely on all these areas.

Francesco Massa is an historian of religions specializing in religious interactions in the Roman Empire. After a PhD at the École Pratique des Hautes Études in Paris and at the Fondazione San Carlo in Modena, he worked in Paris, Aix-Marseille, Toulouse, and Geneva. At present, he is Assistant Professor at the University of Fribourg where he is leading a research project on 'Religious competition in Late Antiquity' founded by the Swiss National Science Foundation (2019–2023). He is author of *Tra la vigna e la croce. Dioniso nei discorsi letterari e figurativi cristiani (II-IV secolo)* (Stuttgart, 2014).

Daniele Miano is Lecturer in Ancient History at the University of Sheffield. He has worked extensively on the history and the historiography of Pre-Roman and Roman Italy, and on ancient polytheism. His most recent book is Fortuna. *Deity and Concept in Archaic and Republican Italy* (OUP 2018).

John F. Miller is Arthur F. and Marian W. Stocker Professor of Classics at the University of Virginia. His recent research chiefly explores interactions between Latin literature and Roman religion; he has also published widely on Ovid in the Renaissance. He is author of *Ovid's Elegiac Festivals: Studies in the Fasti* (1991) and *Apollo, Augustus, and the Poets* (2009), and is co-editor of five collaborative volumes on Greek and Latin literature and culture, most recently (with Jenny Strauss Clay) *Tracking Hermes, Pursuing Mercury* (2019).

Simon Perris is Associate Professor of Classics at Victoria University of Wellington. His main research interests are Greek tragedy and classical reception. He is the author of *The Gentle, Jealous God: Reading Euripides' Bacchae in English* (2016) and co-editor of *Athens to Aotearoa: Greece and Rome in New Zealand Literature and Society* (2017). He is currently writing a book on classical influences on Maori literature.

Alessandro Schiesaro is Professor of Classics at the University of Manchester. His research focuses on the intersection between Latin poetry, literary theory and Roman cultural history. He has written on didactic poetry, Roman theatre, and several Roman authors and their reception.

Julietta Steinhauer is a Senior Teaching Fellow at University College London and Research Associate at the Institute of Classical Studies in London. Her main research interests are in the history of religion and migration in the Hellenistic and early Roman periods. Publications include a monograph, *Religious Associations in the Post-classical Polis* (2014), and several articles on related topics. Her current project focuses on the interplay of religion and migration in the Mediterranean in the second and first centuries BCE.

Stéphanie Wyler is Associate Professor of History and Anthropology of the Roman worlds at the University of Paris and researcher at the Anhima centre (Anthropologie et Histoire des Mondes Antiques). Her main research interests are images, archaeology and texts on religions in classical Rome. Her PhD was on the images of Dionysus in Rome. A list of her publications may be viewed at: http://www.anhima.fr/spip.php?article558&lang=fr

Fiachra Mac Góráin
Introduction. Dionysus in Rome: accommodation and resistance

Abstract: This introductory chapter provides a wide-angle history of the presence of Dionysus/Bacchus/Liber on Italian soil from the archaic to the early Christian periods, covering archaeological and literary sources. In parallel, it surveys the main scholarly trends on the Italian versions of Dionysus, and emplots the contributions to this volume in a history of scholarship. The main focus of the chapter, which is programmatic for the volume, is the interface of Greek and Roman cultures, and whether it is possible to identify and define (an) Italian version(s) of Dionysus. It posits two aspects to the Romans' reception of Bacchus, which may be termed 'accommodation' and 'resistance'. The interplay between these two levels of response will inform an analytic narrative that assesses the relationship between the Greek Dionysus and the Roman Liber, embracing *interpretatio* and religious polymorphism, and addressing some of the most important Dionysian manifestations in Roman culture: the founding of the temple of Ceres, Liber and Libera; the Bacchanalia; the Liberalia; Roman leaders' uses of Dionysus; the poets' references to Bacchus; and a brief glance at the Bacchic-Christian interface.

As 'our oldest living symbol',[1] Dionysus/Bacchus has evolved over many different forms. Until relatively recently, scholars believed that he was an import from the East, and a late addition to the Greek pantheon. Rohde, Nilsson, Wilamowitz and Otto all subscribed to different versions of the Nietzschean myth that an ecstatic Dionysus cult was assimilated from Thrace and tamed by the influence of Apollo.[2] This view was based on the god's slight role in the Homeric poems, coupled with

---

For discussion of Dionysus in Rome and bibliographical advice, I wish to thank Clifford Ando, Andreas Bendlin, Tom Carpenter, Michael Crawford, Elena Giusti, Dan Hogg, Duncan MacRae, John North, Donncha O'Rourke, Richard Seaford, and Peter Wiseman. This Introduction has benefited enormously from exchanges with the contributors to this volume.

1 Seaford 2006, 3. In this Introduction I develop some material from Mac Góráin 2017.
2 Rohde 1950 [1890–94], 282–303, esp. 287–8; Nilsson 1925 [1922], 194 and 208–9; Cumont [1929] 2006, 315–16; Wilamowitz 1931-2, II.74; Otto 1965 [1933], 202–8. Nietzsche popularized this view, but it had been expressed pointedly before him, and in more historical terms; see Creuzer 1820, 3.156.

https://doi.org/10.1515/9783110672237-001

the persistent mythical motif of his arrival and reception, which is central to Euripides' *Bacchae*. Not until the decipherment of the god's name on Linear B tablets from Pylos and Chania did it emerge that he belonged to the earliest-attested stratum of Hellenic culture, and so the mythical motif of the god's epiphany was reassessed as a structural feature of his myth, rather than a dim historical reminiscence of his integration.[3] This was already implicit in Hölderlin's phrase 'der kommende Gott' ('the god who comes', 'Brod und Wein'), coined around 1800. Indeed, Dionysus was always arriving from elsewhere, Marcel Detienne's 'étrange étranger',[4] a stranger through-and-through, even when returning to his Theban homeland, victorious from his Eastern conquests.

Though he is the most widely-studied of the Graeco-Roman divinities, the version that dominates popular and scholarly perceptions is the one that became current in Athens in the archaic and classical ages: Dionysus as the god of wine and poetic inspiration, fertility and nature, theatre and ritual madness, rebirth and the afterlife. His Roman and Italian manifestations are often neglected or considered secondary, their local inflections left unappreciated. E.R. Dodds' judgement was not untypical:

> It was the Alexandrines, and above all the Romans—with their tidy functionalism and their cheerful obtuseness in all matters of the spirit—who departmentalized Dionysus as 'jolly Bacchus' the wine-god with his riotous crew of nymphs and satyrs. As such he was taken over from the Romans by Renaissance painters and poets; and it was they in turn who shaped the image in which the modern world pictures him.[5]

Studies of the reception of Dionysus, which now themselves make up a small scholarly industry, have shown how much modern perceptions of Dionysus owe to German Romanticism and Nietzsche (who privileged Greek over Roman source materials), as well as to Renaissance painters and poets.[6] Dodds did, however, concede – albeit in a footnote – the honourable exception of Horace, whose *Odes* 2.19 and 3.25 'show a deeper understanding of the god's true nature'. But how exceptional among the Romans was Horace's understanding of Bacchus?[7] And what does it mean anyway to speak of a 'god's true nature' in view of an evolving continuum of forms and identities?

---

3 See Eliade 1978, 359.
4 The title of one of the essays in Detienne 1986, not present in the English translation, Detienne 1989. The idea is already in the eastward-looking Cumont [1929] 2006, 317; see also Wyler 2011.
5 Dodds 1960, xii.
6 McGinty 1978; Frank 1982; Henrichs 1984; Emmerling-Skala 1994; Detienne 2001; Baeumer 2006; Konaris 2011; Mariño Sánchez 2014; Morel 2015; Bohrer 2015.
7 On Horace's Bacchic poetics, see Schiesaro 2009.

This volume contributes to the study of what Robert Parker has recently dubbed the 'divine diaspora', the Greek gods abroad.[8] It focuses on Dionysus in Rome and Italy, but draws on a wide range of evidence from the literary and mythical to the epigraphic and visual, but also brings together specialists in different sub-disciplines of classics and ancient history, including art history, ancient reception, history of religions, literary history, and rhetoric and oratory. The contributors attempt to synthesize literary and archaeological sources when and where our evidence allows this. We thus follow in the footsteps of Denis Feeney's *Religion and Literature at Rome*, a book which is often cited, though rarely equalled in its integration of literature and ritual.[9] As will emerge, the story told by this ensemble of essays sees a close relationship between myth and ritual in Dionysian media. Literary or rhetorical descriptions of ritual are not simply an epiphenomenon of religious worship, but can profoundly affect and inform a person's participation in and attitude to ritual.

The 'Rome' of our title is broadly defined, encompassing a range of Latin literature and also territories which came under the sway of Rome, including Italy. Far from aiming at comprehensiveness, we offer broad coverage through a series of in-depth case studies from archaic Italy through the Roman republic and empire, and including early Christianity. We give due attention to under-studied treatments of Bacchus, such as those by Cicero, Ovid in the *Tristia*, Statius in the *Thebaid*, Christian writers' perspectives on Latin Liber, or give a fresh perspective on relatively well-known Dionysian events or media, such as the Bacchanalia, or the epigraphic or pictorial record for Dionysus, or the reception of Euripides' *Bacchae*. Roman and Italian versions of Dionysus are worthy of attention, not only because of their mediating influence on later ages, but because they serve as a test-case of cultural relations in the ancient Mediterranean, especially along the Greek and Roman cultural continuum.[10] All contributors to the volume reflect on the Greek-Roman interface and on the ways in which Dionysus exhibits local traits in Latin literature or in Roman or Italian media.

A significant and revealing topic which animates our collection and which forms the core argument of this introduction is the Romans' split-level attitude in their receptions of Dionysus, which may be classified under 'accommodation' and 'resistance'. A large body of evidence attests to organic seepage of Dionysian media from the Greek world to Rome. The material record suggests that Dionysus

---

8 Parker 2017, 1.
9 Feeney 1998. Following Feeney, see Barchiesi, Rüpke and Stephens 2004; Bendlin and Rüpke 2009; Rüpke and Spickermann 2010, and the essays which follow in that volume of *ARG*.
10 On this general phenomenon see Veyne 2005.

was extensively cultivated in Italy, and that Dionysian artefacts were in high consumer demand. On the other hand, there are strands of hostility in the Roman discourse of the Republican era: Dionysus features in Roman narratives of decline in the face of foreign, especially Greek, influence, of which the Bacchanalian affair of 186 BCE provides the most pointed example. Though each chapter in the volume advances its own argument with its own focus, each of them shows its subjects operating between these two poles of accommodating and resisting Dionysus.

The volume thus adds to the growing body of scholarship on Dionysus and Rome, still a minority interest in Dionysian studies, which tend to focus on Greek media, or sometimes to see the Italian evidence with Greek lenses without adequate attention to local colouring.[11] What unites and distinguishes our volume is the sustained focus on the *interface* between Greek and Roman elements, while we still acknowledge that they exist on a continuum. The major monographs on Dionysus have tended to marginalize Italian evidence in favour of Greek.[12] Nonetheless, several monographs have touched on Roman and Italian sources. Shortly before the decipherment of Linear B, Henri Jeanmaire gave relatively brief coverage to the Roman versions of Dionysus in his five-hundred-page history of the cult of Dionysus/Bacchus, and was agnostic as to whether the cult title 'Pater Liber' (more often 'Liber Pater') indicated identification with an Italic deity or was a translation of an epithet of the Greek god.[13] Adrien Bruhl devoted a wide-ranging monograph to Liber Pater, which stretched from the archaic period through to the high empire, covering literary and archaeological evidence from Italy and the Roman imperial provinces. He posited a pre-Greek, but irrecoverable, Italic Liber, and attempted to isolate what was distinctively Roman or Italian about the god, but was criticized for his too rigid insistence on a division between 'Greek' and 'Roman'.[14] Martin Nilsson surveyed the Dionysian mysteries of the Hellenistic and Roman age, seeing the Roman material alongside the Greek.[15] More recently, following up on his gargantuan study of the Bacchanalia, Jean-Marie

---

11 For a brief and useful overview of Dionysus/Liber in Rome and Italy see Isler-Kerényi 2010. For some local Italic evidence see Casadio 1994a, organized by region, as are his works on Dionysus in the Greek world, Casadio 1994b and 1999. See also the doctoral dissertations of Niafas 1998 and Serignolli 2017.
12 Ivanov [1923] 2012; Otto [1933] 1965; Kerényi 1976; Daraki 1985.
13 Jeanmaire 1951, 453–82.
14 Bruhl 1953; Boyd 1955.
15 Nilsson 1957; see also Matz 1963; for Dionysian mysteries in the Roman era see recently Bremmer 2014, 100–9.

Pailler has contributed a book of essays on Dionysian ritual in Italy.[16] The most recent monograph on Dionysus in Rome is in Polish, by Danuta Musiał; its chapters cover the evidence for Dionysian worship across poetry, historiography, and the history of art.[17]

Dionysus' multi-faceted nature lends itself to treatment in multi-authored collections of essays that, like the present volume, aim to offer a rounded picture by combining different specialities. A landmark collection of essays about Dionysian associations edited by Olivier de Cazanove gave considerable coverage to the Italian evidence, with a mostly archaeological focus, including the temple of Mater Matuta at Satricum in Latium and the Torre Nova inscription.[18] An exhibition entitled 'Dionysos. Mito e Mistero' was held at Comacchio in the province of Ferrara in Emilia Romagna in 1989, and focussed on the Dionysian imaginary in the Greek and Etruscan worlds. The exhibition is commemorated by a richly illustrated and documented catalogue, and a collection of essays which contains many chapters on the reception of Dionysus in Italy.[19] A 1993 collection edited by Thomas Carpenter and Christopher Faraone entitled *Masks of Dionysus* gave some coverage to the Italian evidence alongside Greek sources, but for the most part, did not thematize the local inflections of the Italian sources.[20] More recently, two prodigious collections of essays have devoted a moderate if still significant amount of space to Italian evidence. The Berlin collection, *Dionysos. A Different God? Dionysos and Ancient Polytheism*, edited by Renate Schlesier, contains some four essays on headline Roman topics, though the book's ample indices allow the reader to trace discussion of sources by textual passage, personal name, or geographical location.[21] Finally, the Madrid collection, *Redefining Dionysos*, edited by Alberto Bernabé, Miguel Herrero de Jáuregui, Ana Isabel Jiménez San Cristóbal, and Raquel Martín Hernández contains some five (of thirty) essays on Roman culture, including Nonnus and Christianity.[22]

There are also clusters of scholarship on specific local cults. Some evidence for cultic worship points clearly to migration of Greek mystery cult, whether the fifth-century inscription from Cuma that designates a cemetery as reserved for

---

16 Pailler 1998 and 1995.
17 Musiał 2009, with summary in French at 277–79.
18 Cazanove 1986.
19 Berti and Gasparri 1989; Berti 1991.
20 Carpenter and Faraone 1993; the exception is Bonfante 1993 on Fufluns.
21 Schlesier 2011; see in particular Burkert 2011; Carpenter 2011; Fuhrer 2011; Heinemann 2011; and Sabetai 2011.
22 Bernabé *et al.* 2013; see in particular Alonso Fernández 2013; Cabrera 2013; Hernández de la Fuente 2013; Meilán Jácome 2013; Wyler 2013a.

those who have been initiated into Bacchic cult,[23] or the so called 'Orphic' golden leaves, some of which mention 'bakkhoi', including the earliest-dated, from about 400 BCE, found at Hipponion in Calabria.[24] Earlier epigraphic finds have also been interpreted as evidence for Dionysian worship, though with much less certainty, including a pot dating from around 800 BCE with the earliest Greek inscription in Italy, which may read 'euoin', the Dionysian ritual cry, found at a cemetery near Gabii in Latium.[25]

Foundational studies of early Roman religion, which aimed to assess it in its own right rather than as a poor cousin of Greek religion,[26] gave significant attention to Liber Pater, often discussing his ethnic and cultural origins, and there was considerable disagreement between those who posited an Italic origin, those who saw the god as essentially a Greek import, and those who saw Dionysus and the Italic versions as derived from a common source, perhaps in Illyria.[27] Ultimately, as John Scheid points out, the attempt to prise apart Greek and Roman elements is misguided, since they were mixed from the beginning.[28]

In between these possibilities are various gradations of approximation or translation, which we might call *interpretatio romana*, a phrase coined by Tacitus but adopted by historians of religions to denote different kinds of syncretism or equivalence between deities from different cultures.[29] As far as 'interpreting' Liber as Dionysus is concerned, the debate implicates divine attributes and iconography, nomenclature, spheres of competency, and forms of worship. Unlike the Athenian Dionysus, for example, Italian Liber was not officially a theatre god

---

[23] *SEG* 4.92; see Pailler 1995, 111–26; Casadio 2009.
[24] See Graf and Johnston 2013.
[25] Osteria dell'Osa, tomb 482; see Peruzzi 1992, 465; Wiseman 2004, 13–14; *contra* Colonna 2004, 481–83; Wilson 2009, 550; see also Boffa 2015. The 'Ceres inscription' (*CIE* 8079), from a fragmentary pot found at Civita Castellana in Viterbo, may allude to Dionysus via a mention of wine or the ritual cry (even if the reading 'Loufir' is now discredited); see Radke 1965, 180; Joseph and Klein 1981; Cazanove 1991; Bakkum 2009, 398. On both these examples see Watkins 1995.
[26] See Feeney 1998, 2–8 for scholarly paradigms in the study of Roman as against Greek religion.
[27] Fowler 1911, 255; Wissowa 1912, 297–304 (with further literature, on the subject as then constituted; Schur 1926; Altheim 1931, 17–48; Latte 1960, 70, 161–2, 270–72; Radke 1965, 175–83; Dumézil [1966] 1970, 377–78, 512–22.
[28] Scheid 1995; Feeney 1998, 4–5, 50–52. See also Fowler 1911, 255–56; Cumont [1929] 2006, 320, and Altheim 1931.
[29] On the meaning and history of this phrase in the study of religion see Bettini 2016. See also Ando 2008, 43–58; Miano, and Massa in this volume.

(though Ovid and other authors do recall that there were once games at the Liberalia, which are thought to have merged with the games of the Cerealia).[30] Sure enough, 'jolly Bacchus' is indeed a wine god, but early Roman religion has Jupiter preside over the Vinalia, which has led some scholars to believe that Liber was a hypostasis of Jupiter;[31] in any case, here, the Greek paradigm comes to overwrite the indigenous one. And as Francesco Massa has recently pointed out, Liber is worshipped in cultic forms which mark a departure from worship of Dionysus, such as the joint cult with Libera and the enhanced association with the triumph (to which we shall return shortly).[32] In the present volume, Daniele Miano considers the relationship between Dionysus and local Italian gods – Liber and Fufluns – with regard to the phenomenon of divine polymorphism, drawing on the theories of Jan Assmann, Homi Bhabha and others about religious and cultural translation.[33]

The establishment of the temple of Ceres, Liber, and Libera has given rise to some notable treatments, which debate, among other things, the god's political associations and putative connection with the plebs.[34] Enrico Montanari and Peter Wiseman have contributed significant studies of the cult of Liber and its political resonances, with particular emphasis on the god's association with liberty.[35] A prodigious body of work has sprung up around the Bacchanalian affair of 186 BCE.[36] A recent volume of papers examines the art and archaeology of the sanctuary of Bacchus at Sant'Abbondio outside Pompeii, and includes a contribution by Stéphanie Wyler on the statues of Bacchus/Liber/Loufir and his divine consort on the pediment of the temple.[37] There are many scattered treatments of the worship of Dionysus in the provinces of the Roman empire.[38]

---

30 *F.* 3.783–5 with Heyworth 2019 *ad loc.* Further attestations to games for Liber in Degrassi 1963, 425–26 on Liberalia (March 17th). See Lipka 2009, 43. For (largely political) connections between Liber and the theatre see Montanari 1998, 148–52.

31 Jupiter, Liber and vinalia: Meuli 1955, 213; Radke 1965, 175–83; Montanari 1984, 250–52; Cazanove 1988; Cazanove 1991; Scheid 2005; Musiał 2013. Liber as 'Jovian hypostasis': Lipka 2009, 140.

32 Massa 2016.

33 See also Miano 2018 and Miano and Bispham, Forthcoming.

34 See below on the temple of Ceres, Liber and Libera.

35 Montanari 1984; Montanari 1988, 103–36; Montanari 1998; Wiseman 1998, 35–51; Wiseman 2000; Wiseman 2004, 32–36, 63–86. Petronius' Trimalchio puns on the *Liber-liber* link at *Sat.* 41; see Housman 1918, 164.

36 See below on the Bacchanalia.

37 Van Andringa 2013; Wyler 2013b; see also De Simone 2011, 301.

38 Cumont [1929] 2006, 325–37; Bruhl 1953, 212–48; Foucher 1981; Hutchinson 1986; Tassignon 1996; Fiedler 2005; Tomas 2015; Jeličić-Radonić 2015; Nikoloska 2015; Mayer-Olivé 2017.

Though nearly all of the scholarship detailed in previous paragraphs draws on visual evidence, it is worth pointing out that art historians have produced some of the most significant contributions on Dionysus in Rome and Italy. On the most basic level, the evidence attests to a vogue for Dionysus in decorative art, whether in private or public spaces. As well as depicting mythical scenes, visual and plastic media challenge the modern viewer to reconstruct the social and religious practices in which the artefacts were used, or which they suggest, whether the symposium, or ritual that implies beliefs or hopes, for example for an afterlife. Dionysian images often have a ritual point of reference, but the language of art has its own autonomy, and can mean different things depending on the context. Since pots and iconographic schemes travelled from Greece to Italy, much of the work on Greek ceramics is relevant to our brief, and it ranges from the iconographic to the interpretative.[39] There have been many individual discussions of the Etruscan visual evidence, in which Fufluns appears to be identified with the Greek Dionysus, as discussed by Daniele Miano in this volume.[40] Dionysian subjects are prominent in Roman and Campanian wall painting, the subject of a recent monograph by Marianna Scapini.[41] Stéphanie Wyler, who contributes a chapter on archaic and Augustan images of Dionysus to this volume, has had an influential voice in the debate on the visual imaginary of Bacchus, and her own monograph, *Les images de Liber: perceptions du dionysisme dans la Rome républicaine*, is eagerly awaited.[42] One of the most intriguing documents for Dionsyian cult in Italy is the megalographic frieze at the Villa of Mysteries in Pompeii, which has given rise to vigorous scholarly debate as to whether or not it depicts Dionysian mystery ritual.[43] Sculptural reliefs deserve a separate mention; apart from the Dionysian motifs on the Ara Pacis Augustae, the imperial sarcophagi which depict banqueting scenes are often read as evidence for belief in Dionysus' connection with a blessed afterlife.[44]

Literary evidence for Italian interest in Dionysus emerges with the earliest Latin literature in the third century BCE. Naevius' *Lycurgus*, insofar as it may be

---

39 Gasparri 1986a and Gasparri 1986a; Carpenter 1986 and 1997; Moraw 1998; Isler-Kerényi 2007 and 2015.
40 Bomati 1983; Berti/Gasparri 1989; Berti 1991; Bonfante 1993; Werner 2005; Palethodoros 2007; Maras 2009; Riva 2018.
41 Scapini 2016; on Campania see also Zanker 1998.
42 See various items by Wyler in the bibliography.
43 See Seaford 1981; Veyne 1998; Sauron 1988; Henderson 1996; Gazda 2000; Scapini 2016. On Dionysus in the area around Vesuvius see De Simone 2011.
44 On the Ara Pacis see Castriota 1995 and Sauron 2000. On the sarcophagi see Turcan 1966 and Matz 1968–75.

reconstructed from the surviving fragments, dramatizes a clash in which Liber defeats the resistance of the eponymous king. Even though, as noted above, myths of Dionysus' arrival are no longer thought of as historical reminiscences of the god's installation in Greece, nonetheless Latin tragedies on Dionysian subjects continue to be read as thematizing Roman receptions of foreign cults, and Greek and Eastern influences more generally. It has even been suggested that the negative portrayal of Bacchic religion in early Roman drama conditioned the Senate into clamping down on the Bacchanalia.[45] Predictable though the allegorical interpretation is, it is difficult to completely exclude reading Lycurgus' hostility to Dionysus as a futile struggle before inevitable capitulation. In the event, all of the major Republican Latin tragedians composed plays that encompassed Dionysian themes, from Ennius' *Athamas* through Pacuvius' *Pentheus* to Accius' *Bacchae* and *Stasiastae* (or *Tropaeum Liberi*).[46] A number of Plautus' comedies give humorous perspectives on the stereotypical motifs of Bacchic cult and its votaries.[47] It remains, however, difficult to determine how these references should be interpreted in relation to the Bacchanalian affair.

From the archaeological record we can infer a story of the unproblematic integration and incorporation of Dionysus from Magna Graecia and Etruria into Roman culture.[48] In contrast to these material sources, which are for the most part non-discursive,[49] literary sources provide us with narratives about how Dionysus was received at Rome. There are several notable cases beyond Naevius' *Lycurgus* in which myths of hospitality – extended or denied – seem to reflect on the god's transition from Greek to Roman (though never quite nativized) divinity. This is perhaps not surprising when we consider that scholars have been apt to read Euripides' *Bacchae* as a meditation on the influx to Athens of foreign deities such as Bendis, Attis, Isodaites, and Sabazios.[50] The *Bacchae* itself fits into a wider pattern of hospitality stories involving Dionysus' arrival followed by welcome and reward, or rejection and punishment, or a combination of both, sometimes with additional motifs such as the god's disguise or epiphany, and a contrast between

---

45 Rousselle 1987.
46 One these plays see Pastorino 1955 with Mariotti 1957; Rousselle 1987; Flower 2000, 28; Manuwald 2011, 200–1, 224, and discussion of Accius' *Bacchae* in the next chapter (Perris and Mac Góráin).
47 See Gruen 1990, 50–51; Flower 2000, 25–27; and Schiesaro 2016, 28–30.
48 See Wyler in this volume, and Mura Sommella 2017 for an argument about the earliest evidence for a Dionysian sanctuary in Rome itself.
49 Epigraphic evidence is a significant exception to this, such as the Fufluns Paxies inscriptions which Miano discusses in this volume.
50 Dodds 1960, xx–xxv; Versnel, 1990, 103–23.

those who recognize Dionysus' divinity and would welcome him, and those who wish to exclude him.[51] The persecution of Dionysus by Lycurgus at *Iliad* 6.123–32 fits loosely into this pattern, but more clear-cut examples are the seventh Homeric hymn, and various stories narrated by Hyginus, Nonnus, and in other epic and mythographic sources.[52]

The incorporation of foreign cults in Rome can easily be thought of as a kind of hospitality, whatever the mechanism of introduction, be it *evocatio*[53] (as in the case of Juno Regina from Veii to Rome in 396 BC), or propitiatory importation (as in the case of Aesculapius or the Magna Mater).[54] Dionysius of Halicarnassus, who sees Rome as a Greek city, and who sees all things Roman with Greek eyes,[55] records a tradition (how historically reliable, it is impossible to know) that Dionysus was embedded into the Roman civic calendar in the 490s, along with Demeter and Koré.[56] Livy does not record the founding of the temple; at this point in his history he is focussed on narrating the struggle of the orders, and it is apparent that the plebs adopt the temple as their headquarters; he does, however, often mention it, usually with reference to dedications, and calling it either Aedes Cereris or Aedes Cereris Liberi Liberaeque.[57] Rome was at war with the Etruscans after the expulsion of the Tarquins. During a food shortage before the battle of Lake Regillus the consul Aulus Postumius Albus (soon to be *cognomin*ated 'Regillensis') ordered the guardians of the Sibylline books to consult their oracles. He learned that he should propitiate these three divinities, and so as he was about to lead out his army, vowed a temple and annual festivities to them, if the food supply should be restored. As Dionysius says, 'these gods, hearing his prayer, caused the land to produce rich crops, not only of grain but also of fruits, and all imported provisions to be more plentiful than before; and when Postumius saw

---

[51] On the arrivals and receptions of Dionysus in myth and literature cf. Dodds 1960, xxv; Kerényi 1976, 122–188, esp. 175–88; Otto 1965, 79–85, and Weaver 2004, 29–63.

[52] See Hyg. *Fab*. 129 (Oeneus), 130 (Icarius and Erigone), 131 (Nysus), 132 (Lycurgus), 133 (Ammon), 134 (Tuscan pirates). See also Apoll. *Bibl*. 3.5; Diod. Sic. 3.65.4–6; and the Falernus episode of Sil. *Pun*. 7.162–211. For a reworking of this story-pattern in the *Aeneid* see Mac Góráin 2013.

[53] Ando 2008, 128–48.

[54] On foreign gods at Rome see Orlin 2010; for a recent perspective on foreign gods at Rome, see Rolle 2017 on Cybele, Isis and Serapis in the works of Varro.

[55] On Dionysius' Hellenocentrism see Cornell 1995, 37–41; Schultze 1995; Schultze 2004.

[56] DH *Rom. Ant*. 6.17.2, Δήμητρι καὶ Διονύσῳ καὶ Κόρῃ. On the temple and its cult see Bruhl 1953, 30–45; Le Bonniec 1958; Cazanove 1983; Coarelli 1993; Scheid 1995; Spaeth 1996; Orlin 1997, 100–101; and Mignone 2016, esp. 205–11, who disputes the evidence locating the temple on the Aventine.

[57] 3.55.7; 41.28.2 etc.

this, he himself caused a vote to be passed for the building of these temples.'⁵⁸ The temple was dedicated by the consul Cassius in 493. Dionysius seems to be using the memoirs of Aulus Postumius Albinus (consul in 151), written in Greek.⁵⁹ The trio of gods is recognizable as a version of the Eleusinian gods, even though there is no Triptolemus equivalent, and even though it is not certain what role Iacchus had in the Eleusinian ritual as early as the 490s.⁶⁰ In all likelihood worship of the three gods was already common in Rome, having spread from Sicily and southern Italy.⁶¹ The incorporation may well have involved a taming or sanitization of the cult's ecstatic elements to accommodate it to Roman religious norms. Nonetheless, Cicero tells us (*Balb.* 55) that the ritual was Greek in form and language, and that the priestesses were of Campanian-Greek origin.⁶²

The temple of Ceres, Liber, and Libera itself is among the evidence discussed by Stéphanie Wyler in this volume, though with slightly different emphases to the present paragraph. Vitruvius (*Arch.* 3.3.5) tells us that its pediments were ornamented in the Etruscan fashion with statues of terracotta or gilt bronze; and Pliny the Elder (*NH* 35.45.154) reports (on the authority of Varro) that everything was Etruscan in the temples *until* the temple of Ceres, Liber, and Libera was built, and he tells us of the signatures of two Greek craftsmen, Damophilos and Gorgasos, who provided the temple with statues and paintings. We hear also of a painting of Liber and possibly Ariadne, a renowned work by Aristides, which was brought to Rome by Lucius Mummius after the sack of Corinth, and which was placed in this temple and survived there until the temple burned down in 31 BCE, to be restored later, and dedicated by Tiberius in 17 CE.⁶³ Interestingly Pliny the Elder considers this the first Greek painting to have been exhibited at Rome, though in his day they had become common in the forum.⁶⁴ The combination of Greek and native elements in the temple suggest Dionysus as a fitting emblem of cultural fusion.

We might have expected this temple to be the cult site of the Liberalia, but in fact none of our sources confirm this, and the celebration there of the Cerealia in

---

58 6.17, tr. Cary.
59 Wiseman 1998, 35.
60 On Iacchus at Eleusis see Clinton 1992, 64–71.
61 See Cornell 1995, 263–64 and Beard-North-Price 1998, I, 64–66.
62 *Balb.* 55; see Lipka 2009, 67.
63 Plin. *NH* 35.24; Strabo 8.6.23; for the fire and restoration, see Dio. 50.10 (fire), Strabo 8.341 (painting and fire), and Tac. *Ann.* 2.49 (restoration); Tacitus tells us that Augustus had begun the restoration. See further Miller, pp. 177–78, in this volume.
64 35.24 *quam primam arbitror picturam externam Romae publicatam, deinde video et in foro positas volgo.*

April may even rule it out.[65] Danuta Musiał has argued that the worship of Ceres at Rome eclipsed that of Liber, and that this facilitated the coalescence of Liber with Dionysus.[66] Sources for the Liberalia suggest rural agrarian rites that combine Greek and indigenous elements, but also urban rites. Ovid records that young men assumed the *toga libera* on this day, and puns on the connection between Liber and *libertas*, an etymology which looks to Dionysus' Athenian cult title 'Eleuthereus', and to parallel etymological links between Dionysus Lysios/Lyaeus and Greek λύειν.[67] A fragment of Naevius from an unknown context suggests that free speech was enjoyed at the Liberalia: 'Libera lingua loquemur ludis Liberalibus' ('We will speak with a free tongue at the games of the Liberalia', Naev. *com.* 112 Ribbeck².) Varro records that priestesses of Liber garlanded their heads with ivy and roasted cakes (*liba*) for celebrants.[68] Augustine gives a slanted version of Varro's account, from the *Divine Antiquities*, of phallic processions that took place in Italian villages. The passage is worth quoting in full:

> Inter cetera, quae praetermittere, quoniam multa sunt, cogor, in Italiae compitis quaedam dicit sacra Liberi celebrata cum tanta licentia turpitudinis, ut in eius honorem pudenda virilia colerentur, non saltem aliquantum verecundiore secreto, sed in propatulo exultante nequitia. Nam hoc turpe membrum per Liberi dies festos cum honore magno plostellis inpositum prius rure in compitis et usque in urbem postea vectabatur. In oppido autem Lavinio unus Libero totus mensis tribuebatur, cuius diebus omnes verbis flagitiosissimis uterentur, donec illud membrum per forum transvectum esset atque in loco suo quiesceret. Cui membro inhonesto matrem familias honestissimam palam coronam necesse erat inponere. Sic videlicet Liber deus placandus fuerat pro eventibus seminum, sic ab agris fascinatio repellenda...

> Among other rites which I am compelled to pass over due to their sheer number, there are certain rites of Liber that [Varro] says are celebrated at Italian crossroads with such shameful abandon that the private parts of the male are worshipped in the god's honour, and not even in secret, out of some deference to modesty, but openly and with wantonness running riot. Yes indeed, during Liber's festal days this disgusting member would be exhibited on a waggon with great honour, and carried first around the crossroads in the countryside, and then brought all the way into the city. In the town of Lavinium they even dedicated a whole month to Liber, and during these days they all used such disgraceful language until that member had been carried through the forum and come to rest in its own place. Then the

---

65 On the festival see Musiał 2013; see Miller 2002; Kovács 2015; and Heyworth 2019 on Ovid's *Liberalia*.
66 Musiał 2007.
67 *Fasti* 3.771–78; see Hor. *Ep.* 9.38 *Lyaeo soluere*; and Sen. *Tranq. An.* 9.17.8 (with Giusti 2017); parallels in Leinieks 1996, 302–25 and Seaford 1996, 190.
68 Varro, *LL* 6.14; cf. Ov. *F.* 3.726–36.

most respectable woman, a mother of a family, had to place a garland on said dishonourable member. In this way, supposedly, the god Liber was to be propitiated so that all would turn out well with the seeds; in this way the hex needed to be warded off the fields... (*City of God* 7.21.2–4; Varro *ARD* 262 [42] Cardauns)

The satiric tone in describing Pagan religious ritual is something that Augustine inherits from his Church Father predecessors, who are discussed in Francesco Massa's contribution on Christian Latin authors in the final chapter of this volume. Despite Augustine's polemical rhetoric, which makes it difficult to extract what Varro actually said, it does seem that this rite may have been both urban and rural: there is mention of a procession into the city (*usque in urbem*), which may be Rome, and also Lavinium. In addition, the Italian phallophoria resembles the phallic procession of the Athenian Dionysia, which celebrates fertility and plenitude.[69] For Augustine, the phallic rite exemplifies Liber's dominion over the liquid seeds, which he mentions several times beyond the passage quoted (*civ.* 6.9, 7.2, 7.21). It is easy to connect this with Greek sources which see Dionysus as god of liquid life, especially in nature,[70] a motif which in Statius' *Thebaid* is repurposed to metapoetic ends as Bacchus, god of poetic inspiration, presides over the provision or withholding of water, as discussed by Alessandro Schiesaro in this volume.

Whatever the origins of, and Romans' attitudes to, the Liberalia, if our sources for the temple of Ceres, Liber and Libera suggest a hospitable incorporation, this view is counterbalanced by the evidence for the senate's repression of the Bacchanalia in 186 BCE.[71] An inscription found at Tiriolo in 1640 gives an account of the senate's decision to restrict and regulate group worship of the Bacchanalia, and we have a lurid account of the affair in Livy's history.[72] The severe clampdown, which reportedly detained both consuls at Rome, and involved the

---

69 On the Athenian ritual see Csapo 2013.
70 See Tiresias' speech at Eur. *Ba.* 278–85. Plutarch is most explicit; see *De Iside et Osiride* 365A. ὅτι δ' οὐ μόνον τοῦ οἴνου Διόνυσον, ἀλλὰ καὶ πάσης ὑγρᾶς φύσεως Ἕλληνες ἡγοῦνται κύριον καὶ ἀρχηγόν, ἀρκεῖ Πίνδαρος μάρτυς εἶναι λέγων (fr. 153) 'δενδρέων δὲ νομὸν Διόνυσος πολυγαθὴς αὐξάνοι, ἁγνὸν φέγγος ὀπώρας·' διὸ καὶ τοῖς τὸν Ὄσιριν σεβομένοις ἀπαγορεύεται δένδρον ἥμερον ἀπολλύναι καὶ πηγὴν ὕδατος ἐμφράττειν. On Dionysus and moisture see Otto 1965, 160–170.
71 On the episode see especially North 1979; Pailler 1988; Gruen 1990; Granet 1990 (a response to Pailler 1988); Cancik-Lindemaier 1996; Turcan 1996, 300–306; Beard-North-Price 1998, I, 90–96; Pailler 1998; Takács 2000; Davies 2004, 79–81; Pagán 2004, 50–67; Rüpke 2007, 31–33; Wyler 2008; Briscoe 2008, esp. 330; Nousek 2010; Riedl 2012.
72 *CIL* 1 2, 581 = *ILLRP* 511 = *ILS* 18; Livy 39.8–18.

execution of thousands of Bacchants, is often thought of as an atypical intervention on the part of the Roman authorities, who were usually very hospitable to foreign gods, and so the episode calls for explanation. One is that the senate's real target was not Bacchus himself – indeed the god is not mentioned in the inscription, which only mentions Bacchanals and Bacchants – but rather the organizational structures of the cult, which had drawn to itself quasi-civic functions such as witnessing seals and oaths, and keeping a common fund, and therefore came close to threatening the authority of the state.[73] One of the main themes in the episode is the (regulation of the) role of women in cult and indeed in society, including their relations with young men, and the senatorial clampdown may be read as an expression of patriarchal norms.[74] Julietta Steinhauer revisits the question of the structures and social makeup of worship in her contribution to the present volume, reading Livy's history and the *Senatus consultum de bacchanalibus* against one another, and emphasizing how much latitude the senatorial legislation appears to concede to female participants. Another explanation is that the senate wished to tighten its legal and administrative grip on territories in southern Italy, especially after losses incurred during the Hannibalic war.[75] One may agree that the remit of the senate's decision was more limited than might at first appear to have been the case,[76] and also with the argument that rather than expressing xenophobic conservatism, the senate wished to define traditional Roman modes of worship in a way that had not been done before.[77]

Though Aulus Postumius P. f. Albus Regillensis (consul 496) had been responsible for welcoming Liber to Rome, according to Livy, it was his descendant Spurius Postumius L. f. A. n. Albinus (consul 186) who presided over the investigation, and persuaded the senate to legislate in favour of dismantling the cult of the Bacchanalia and prosecuting its votaries with capital punishment. Livy's account is stranger than fiction, and scholars have often detected in it a dramatic substrate, whether comedy or *fabula praetexta*.[78] Euripides' *Bacchae* has been suggested as background and/or illuminating comparand.[79] The repression of the

---

[73] North 1979; Turcan 1996, 303.
[74] Montanari 1984, 249, 257; Pailler 1988, 523–96; Scheid 1991; Pailler 1995, 171–82; Cancik-Lindemaier 1996; Flower 2002; Schultz 2006, 82–92; Panoussi 2019, 120–39.
[75] Gruen 1990.
[76] Cazanove 2000a (with Rüpke 2007, 261, n. 64), and Cazanove 2000b.
[77] Orlin 2010, 163–75.
[78] Comedy: Scafuro 1989; Walsh 1996; *fabula praetexta*: Wiseman 1998.
[79] Cazanove 1983, 106–13 (but mainly Lycurgus tragedies); Heslin 2005, 247–54; Riedl 2012; Schiesaro 2016, 31.

Bacchanalia is a moralizing re-run of Euripides' play. This claim of *Bacchae* intertextuality helps us to see the 'affair' against the background of the mythical pattern of the god's arrival followed by welcome or rejection. In this case, as Alessandro Schiesaro has pointed out, the 'sacrificulus et vates' who peddles Bacchic rites recalls the Lydian stranger whom Pentheus derides as a γόης ἐπῳδός (*Ba.* 234). Similarly, the rhetoric of the consul Postumius echoes that of Euripides' Pentheus in its obsession with sexual decorum: Pentheus accuses the Theban women of preferring Aphrodite to Dionysus (*Ba.* 225), while Postumius asks the senators whether these effeminized males (*simillimi feminis mares*) can be made into soldiers (39.15). Livy's description of the ἀρχὴ κακῶν echoes a few more details from the play:

> Graecus ignobilis in Etruriam primum uenit nulla cum arte earum, quas multas ad animorum corporumque cultum nobis eruditissima omnium gens inuexit, sacrificulus et uates; nec is qui aperta religione, propalam et quaestum et disciplinam profitendo, animos errore imbueret, sed occultorum et nocturnorum antistes sacrorum. (39.8.3)

> A low-born Greek went into Etruria first of all, but did not bring with him any of the numerous arts which that most accomplished of all nations has introduced amongst us for the cultivation of mind and body. He was a hedge-priest and wizard, not one of those who imbue men's minds with error by professing to teach their superstitions openly for money, but a hierophant of secret nocturnal mysteries. (tr. Roberts)

The mention of money echoes Pentheus' taunts to Tiresias that he wishes to profit from the new cult (*Ba.* 257), while the charge of nocturnal license, closely followed by accusations of sexual depravity (39.8.6), echoes Pentheus' exchange with the Lydian stranger in which the two disagree as to whether darkness invests the rites with reverence or lechery (*Ba.* 485–88). Tellingly, however, Livy refers to this Greek's arrival, via Etruria, as a beginning of things (*primum uenit*), but he can hardly have been anywhere near the first, given the prevalence of Bacchic religion, which the consul Postumius acknowledges all of Italy has known about for a long time, even if not everyone understood its true nature (39.15.6). The emphasis on Hellenic origins is sustained in the second ἀρχὴ κακῶν in Livy's narrative in that Paculla Annia, a priestess from Campania in Magna Graecia, instituted reforms that led to the growth of the cult and its descent into scandal: she allowed men to be initiated, increased the number of initiation ceremonies from three per year to five per month, and changed it from a diurnal to a nocturnal rite.[80] But she seems not to have lacked for popular interest.

---

[80] Cf. Liv. 39.13.8, *tum Hispala originem sacrorum expromit. primo sacrarium id feminarum fuisse, nec quemquam eo uirum admitti solitum. tres in anno statos dies habuisse, quibus interdiu*

How can we account for the apparent inconsistency between the Romans' embrace of the cult of Liber and their clampdown on the Bacchanalia, or how can we make sense of their schizophrenic rejection-of-cum-fascination-with Dionysus, discernible also in the Bacchanalian affair? One clue may be found in Livy's distinction between 'good' and 'bad' Greeks, which may suggest an alignment between on the one hand, good and bad Greeks, and on the other, good and bad Bacchism. It is hard not to see parallels between the Romans' complex attitudes to Greek culture,[81] and their attitude to Dionysus, which, in the Bacchanalian affair, at least, involves surface-level regulation or disapproval that is undermined by continuing pervasive interest.[82] Beyond this, should we pursue comparisons with the Romans' complex attitudes to other foreign deities, such as the Magna Mater, who is often found in close proximity to Dionysus, including in the *Bacchae* itself (*Ba.* 78–82)? Indeed, scholars have argued that the Magna Mater also enjoyed a 'double cult', one more 'Roman' and domesticated, the other Phrygian and ecstatic.[83] Mary Beard has written that 'there was a constant tension between, on the one hand, Roman rejection of the cult of Magna Mater as something dangerously foreign and, on the other, the incorporation of the cult in the symbolic forms of state power.'[84] On one level, it would easy to claim that there is no contradiction at all, in that Liberalia and Bacchanalia are simply two different cults.[85] Sure enough, Livy mentions the temple of Ceres, Liber, and Libera several times in fairly close proximity to his Bacchanalian narrative without appearing to feel

---

Bacchis initiarentur; sacerdotes in uicem matronas creari solitas. Pacullam Anniam Campanam sacerdotem omnia, tamquam deum monitu, immutasse: nam et uiros eam primam filios suos initiasse, Minium et Herennium Cerrinios; et nocturnum sacrum ex diurno, et pro tribus in anno diebus quinos singulis mensibus dies initiorum fecisse.

81 Gruen 1992 is fundamental for the second century BCE. In later times, Juvenal's Umbricius embodies the Romans' paradoxical attitude to the Greeks. For overviews see Henrichs 1995; and Wallace-Hadrill 1998. On Bacchus in Italy amid the 'second Hellenization of Rome' in the second and first centuries BCE, see also Wyler in this volume.

82 For 'good' and 'bad' Greeks in Roman receptions of Dionysus, see Wyler 2011, 194.

83 See Graillot 1912, esp. 70–107; Borgeaud 1996, 95–104. 2004, 66.

84 Beard 1994, 166; she continues. 'By emphasizing the unresolved tension between the incorporation of the cult and its rejection, I am distancing myself from the conventional scholarly approach to this material —which either stresses the flagrant incompatibility of the Eastern rituals of Magna Mater with Roman tradition or constructs a linear narrative history in which a "tamed" version of the cult is gradually incorporated into the mainstream of Roman state religion.' For a similar argument about the Magna Mater / Cybele across the oeuvre of Varro, see Rolle 2017, esp. 117–22.

85 Montanari 1988, 119–22.

any contradiction.[86] And it is notable that both the inscribed letter about the *SC de Bacchanalibus* and Livy's narrative make allowance for continued worship of ancestral religion, which raises a clear distinction between old and new forms of worship, even of gods that can in other circumstances be aligned or identified with one another. The *senatus consultum* prescribes procedure for continuing worship, with which Livy's account largely agrees.[87] Legislation of cultic form partly *creates* the distinction between legitimate and illicit worship. Livy's Postumius distinguishes twice between established (legitimate) and new (illicit) religion.[88] When the consuls are tasked with destroying the places of worship ('Bacchanalia' denotes shrines as well as the rites),[89] they are supposed to destroy all 'Bacchanalia', first at Rome, then throughout all of Italy, *except* where there is an old altar or consecrated statue,[90] pointing once again to a distinction between old and new Bacchism. But on another level clearly in some sense the god of the Bacchanalia is to be identified with the god of the Liberalia and the different forms of Dionysus/Bacchus/Liber that were worshipped throughout Italy. Here we are in the realm of religious polymorphism: as Henk Versnel has asked, is Dionysus one god or many? The question may be asked of other gods too, but does not appear to have troubled the ancients in the way that it troubles us, even on the relatively rare occasions that they acknowledged it.[91]

There is a close parallel in Cicero's *Laws* for the apparent contradiction, that reflects and indeed perhaps resolves the accommodation/resistance tension. The following exchange occurs while Cicero and Atticus are legislating for the nocturnal rites of Ceres (2.35–36):

> **Marcus:** But if we suppress the nocturnal sacrifices, what will become of the august mysteries of Iacchus, and the Eumolpidæ? For we are constructing laws, not for the Romans only, but for all just and valiant nations.
> **Atticus:** I think it is but courteous to except these mysteries likewise, especially as we ourselves happen to have been initiated in them.
> **Marcus:** With all my heart, let us except them. For it seems to me that among the many admirable and divine things your Athenians have established to the advantage of human

---

86 Temple of Ceres at 40.2; Temple of Ceres, Liber and Libera at 41.28.
87 39.18.8–9.
88 39.15.2–3 and 39.16.8–11.
89 Pailler 1995, 159–68.
90 39.18.7, *datum deinde consulibus negotium est, ut omnia Bacchanalia Romae primum, deinde per totam Italiam diruerent, extra quam si qua ibi uetusta ara aut signum consecratum esset*. It used to be believed that a shrine at Bolsena had been destroyed, but Olivier de Cazanove (2000c) has argued, persuasively in my view, that this structure was a cistern rather than a Bacchanal.
91 On Dionysus see Versnel 2011b, 23; in general see also Versnel 2011a, 239–308.

society, there is nothing better than the mysteries by which we are polished and softened into politeness, from the rude austerities of barbarism. Justly indeed are they called initiations, for by them we especially learn the grand principles of philosophic life, and gain, not only the art of living agreeably, but of dying with a better hope. But what displeases me in the nocturnal mysteries, is what the comic poets hold up to ridicule. If such licence was allowed at Rome, what abominations might be committed by the man who should carry premeditated debauchery into the mysteries, in which even a stolen glance was in ancient times a crime? (tr. Barham)[92]

Just a few lines later (2.37), Cicero cites with apparent approbation the *severitas* of the senate in repressing the Bacchanalia,[93] and the result of their discussion will be restrictive legislation that outlaws women's nocturnal rites except in limited circumstances. The passage contains a number of significant features that bear on the apparent inconsistency at issue.[94] First, the different attitudes that can be had in relation to the nocturnal mysteries – Cicero and Atticus enthusiastically approve of them, but Cicero acknowledges, citing the comic poets, that one could equally disapprove of them on the grounds of the potential for debauchery under cover of darkness. The split-level attitude is entirely reminiscent of the different attitudes to Dionysian cult in Euripides' *Bacchae*: the chorus lyrically embrace the beatific experience of Dionysian ecstasy; Tiresias acknowledges the god's greatness on philosophical and theological grounds, and Cadmus on politically pragmatic ones; opposed to these is Pentheus' suspicious prurience.[95] So Cicero can channel his inner Tiresias in one breath and his inner Pentheus in the next.

---

92 Latin from de Plinval (1968): {MARCVS} *Quid ergo aget Iacchus Eumolpidaeque uostri et augusta illa mysteria, si quidem sacra nocturna tollimus? Non enim populo Romano, sed omnibus bonis firmisque populis leges damus.* {ATTICVS} *Excipis credo illa, quibus ipsi initiati sumus.* {MARCVS} *Ego uero excipiam. Nam mihi cum multa eximia diuinaque uide<a>ntur Athenae tuae peperisse atque in uitam hominum attulisse, tum nihil melius illis mysteriis, quibus ex agresti immanique uita exculti ad humanitatem et mitigati sumus, initiaque, ut appellantur, ita re uera principia uitae cognouimus, neque solum cum laetitia uiuendi rationem accepimus, sed etiam cum spe meliore moriendi. Quid autem mihi displiceat in noct<ur>n<is>, poetae indicant comici. Qua licentia Romae data quidnam egisset ille qui in sacrificium cogitatam libidinem intulit, quo ne inprudentiam quidem oculorum adici <f>as fuit?*
93 2.37.5, *Quo in genere seueritatem maiorum senatus uetus auctoritas de Bacchanalibus et consulum exercitu adhibito quaestio animaduersio<que> declarat.*
94 On this section of the *Laws* see Bendlin 2002, 67–68; Dyck 2004 *ad loc.*; and Rolle 2017, 129–39 (a discussion of nocturnal initiatory rites at Rome).
95 Pentheus: 215–47; Chorus: e.g. 72–167; Tiresias: 266–327; Cadmus: 330–42.

Secondly, hidden within Cicero's qualification and citation of the comic poets[96] is an acknowledgement of the power or relevance of poetic expression to inform one's attitude to religious ritual: it is not that comedy is probative – rather, even though it is a stylized literary genre, Cicero does not dismiss it as trivial or consider it extraneous to religious experience, but uses it to form and express his attitude to the realities of the nocturnal mysteries; indeed the restrictive legislation responds to the attitude expressed by an allusion to the comic poets. This should hardly surprise us, since Cicero frequently uses quotation of or reference to drama to support all kinds of arguments.

The third issue is the possible contradiction between (on the one hand) praise of Iacchus and the mysteries and (on the other hand) endorsement of the senate's clampdown on the Bacchanalia, which seems to be a local version of the contradiction that we see writ large in the Romans' complex attitude to Dionysus. The contradiction would depend, of course, on some degree of identification or identifiability between Iacchus and Bacchus. There are indeed many contexts in which Iacchus and Bacchus are aligned or straightforwardly identified with one another.[97] In other contexts, even at Eleusis, the distinction between Iacchus and Dionysus is clear-cut.[98] In her discussion of these adjacent passages in Ch. 6 of the present volume, Gesine Manuwald expresses caution as to whether Cicero is implying an identification of the Iacchus of the Eleusinian mysteries and the Bacchus of the Bacchanalia, and it is indeed obvious that Cicero is thinking of two different cults. On the other hand, twice in *De natura deorum*, Cicero formulates the polymorphism of Dionysus, in passages which Manuwald also discusses. The Stoic Balbus distinguishes between Liber the son of Semele and Liber the son of Ceres, 'whom our ancestors solemnly and piously deified with Ceres and Libera, the nature of whose worship can be gathered from the mysteries'.[99] As Francesco Massa has pointed out recently, the distinction here is not one between a Latin Liber and a Greek Dionysus, but one between a god of Greek myth and ancestral Roman ritual practice.[100]

---

96 See Dyck 2004, 353: 'Here Cic. alludes to the comic plot in which a young man has impregnated a woman at an all-night festival, with complications upon the birth of the child; cf. Pl. *Aul* 35–36; *adulescentis illius ... qui illam stupravit noctu Cereris vigiliis* [and other sources].'
97 Soph. *Ant.* 1152; Virg. *Ecl.* 6.15, and see further Kern 1916, 619.
98 Clinton 1992, 66 on the possible distinction between the two gods in an Eleusinian setting.
99 Cic. ND 2.62, *hunc dico Liberum Semela natum, non eum quem nostri maiores auguste sancteque Liberum cum Cerere et Libera consecraverunt, quod quale sit ex mysteriis intellegi potest*.
100 Massa 2016, 120–21. See also Manuwald, pp. 160–61, and Massa 2016, 120 on Cic. *ND* 3.35, where Cotta enumerates five different Dionysi on the basis of genealogy.

In the event, Aristides' painting of Bacchus, brought to Rome after the sack of Corinth in 146 BCE, was a harbinger of the flood of Greek wealth that was to engulf Rome after the conquest of Greece. Of course, 'Greek culture leaves its mark on Roman at every moment we can document,'[101] but there is a pervasive narrative of 'Hellenization' in the late republic, summed up by Horace's quip *Graecia capta ferum victorem cepit* (*Ep.* 2.1.156), that conquered Greece Greekified Rome. From this point on, there was no question of clampdown or even resistance: Dionysus became the poster-boy for Hellenism. This itself seems ironic, given the god's 'Eastern' credentials and supposed Egyptian origins, which could still be activated in Roman contexts.[102] His increasingly pervasive presence is expressed in several overlapping registers that we might term politics, art, and literature, though of course the divisions between these three are artificial.[103] The Alexander historians have it that the king of kings imitated Dionysus' triumph in the East; and whether or not the relationship with Dionysus actually goes back to the time of Alexander himself, certainly Dionysus featured very heavily in the religious propaganda of the Hellenistic kingdoms, with a number of rulers taking the title 'Dionysos' or 'Neos Dionysos'.[104] He seems to have been a symbol for charismatic power based on a combination of military might and his sponsorship of fertility. He featured also in Roman politics at least from the Social War onwards.[105] There was a tradition that Dionysus had invented the triumph.[106] Several Roman generals (and later, emperors) came to imitate Dionysus, which was not

---

[101] Wallace-Hadrill 1998, 79.
[102] Said (1977, 170 = 2005, 77) called Euripides' *Bacchae* 'perhaps the most Asiatic of all the Attic dramas'; see further Perris 2016, 126. Diodorus Siculus (3.74) writes of a Dionysus born in Egypt. Herodotus (2.42) and Plutarch (*De Iside et Osiride* 364e) record traditions that identify Dionysus with Osiris; the connection recurs in Tibullus 1.7, and also in the Egyptianizing paintings at the Villa della Farnesina; see Wyler 2005. Dionysus' eastern roots are the target of xenophobic comedy in Lucian's *Concilium Deorum*.
[103] For Apollo operating on and across the same three levels in Augustan poetry, politics and art, see Miller 2009.
[104] For Alexander and Dionysus see Nock 1928; Goukowsky 1981; Bosworth 1988a, 1988b, 1996; Koulakiotis 2017. For Dionysus and the Hellenistic kingdoms see Rice 1983; Dunand 1986; Fuhrer 2011; Isler-Kerényi 2011. On the guilds of the 'artists of Dionysus' see Le Guen 2001 and Aneziri 2003.
[105] Mannsperger 1973; Castriota 1995, 91–94.
[106] Versnel 1970, 235–252; Rutherford 2013, 419–20. On the visual and literary sources for Dionysus triumphant see Buccino 2013; Catania 2014; and Catania 2015.

always well received at Rome.[107] Pliny the Elder tells us in neutral terms that Marius used to drink from a *cantharus* in imitation of Dionysus, but Valerius Maximus puts the same story in more censorious terms, implying *hybris* on the part of Marius.[108] The most famous case of Dionysus-*imitatio* backfiring[109] is the career of Mark Antony. No doubt it was to curry favour in the East that he adopted the persona – though the beginnings of it are already visible if implicit in Antony's fondness for wine, often mentioned in Cicero's *Philippics* – but even upon his entry into Ephesus in 41 BCE, Plutarch reports, styled as a 'Neos Dionysos' and accompanied by a Bacchic entourage, some of the Ephesians hailed him as Dionysus the Giver of Joy and the Gentle (Χαριδότην καὶ Μειλίχιον), while to most, victims of his corrupt governance, he was Dionysus the Raw-Eater and the Savage (Ὠμηστὴς καὶ Ἀγριώνιος).[110] He even seems to have attempted a defence of his own drunkenness: at any rate Pliny the Elder records that he 'vomited up' a pamphlet *De sua ebrietate*.[111] Cassius Dio reports that Octavian exhorted his troops before the Battle of Actium by denouncing Antony's Dionysian persona.[112] Again it is Plutarch who records a tradition of rumours that on the night before the battle of Actium a Bacchic thiasos was heard tumultuously leaving Alexandria, and that this was interpreted as a sign that the god was deserting Antony (*Ant.* 75.3). Nonetheless, it was probably because of Antony's close association with Bacchus that Augustus was hesitant in embracing the god too overtly; for example, he neglected to restore the temple of Ceres, Liber, and Libera promptly, despite his claim in the *Res gestae* that he had restored eighty-two temples, and omitted none that was in need of repair. It seems a remarkable omission; and yet, recent scholars have renewed efforts to expose the rehabilitation of Bacchus and his reappropriation by Augustus from Antony, often with reference to the poetry of Virgil and Horace, and to Roman wall painting and some numismatic evidence.[113]

---

107 Turcan 1977; Wacht/Rickert 2010, 76–78; Fuhrer 2011; Kopij 2014; Scapini 2016, 54–56. The motif was to have a fertile afterlife after the imperial period; see Gesing 1988; and Emmerling-Skala 1994, esp. 148–77.
108 Plin. HN 33, 150; cf. Val. Max. 3.6.6 *iam C. Marii* **paene insolens factum**: *nam post Iugurthinum Cimbricumque et Teutonicum triumphum cantharo semper potauit, quod Liber pater Indicum ex Asia deducens triumphum hoc usus poculi genere ferebatur, <ut> inter ipsum haustum uini **uictoriae eius suas uictorias conpararet.***
109 See Emmerling-Skala 1994, 115–32.
110 Plut. *Ant.* 24.4–5.
111 Plin. *HN* 14.148; see esp. Scott 1929; Marasco 1992; and Freyburger-Galland 2009.
112 50.25.4.
113 *RG* 20. On Octavian/Augustus and Bacchus see Mannsperger 1973; Becher 1976; Castriota 1995; Batinski 1990–91; Schiesaro 2009; Cucchiarelli 2011a and 2011b; Mac Góráin 2014; Kovács 2015; Miller 2002 is circumspect, and see his contribution to this volume.

Nestled among these historical events between Marius-as-Dionysus and Antony-as-Dionysus we find Cicero, himself a polymorph whose *obiter dicta* on the god are very revealing, precisely because we encounter Cicero operating in so many different modes. His references to the god look backwards to poetic and intellectual traditions – Cicero is our source for some of the major scenes of Dionysian madness in early Roman tragedy, for example – as well as giving a contemporary perspective on attitudes to the god and indeed on many other matters from rhetoric to politics, precisely by invoking Dionysus. Gesine Manuwald's chapter in this volume explores these resonances, which occur in a wide range of texts across his philosophical, oratorical, rhetorical and epistolographic works. As Manuwald discusses, this same figure can disapprove of statues of maenads as unbefitting for his library, while still punning on the link between *Liber* and *libertas* in a letter to Atticus in the aftermath of Julius Caesar's assassination.[114]

In what seems like another iteration of the accommodation-and-resistance pattern, despite Roman castigations of Marius' or Antony's Dionysian pretensions, and despite Cicero's disapproval of the maenad statues, it would be difficult to overestimate the proliferation of Dionysian imagery in the visual and plastic arts of the period: wall painting, sculpture, campana plaques, gems, silverware, and ceramics, in which Dionysus appears (alongside other divinities) as a god of luxury, *tryphe*, ritual, and Hellenism itself.[115] As Stéphanie Wyler discusses in this volume, there are parallels between the poetry and the painting, notably in the sacro-idyllic landscapes of painting and relief sculpture that allude to the world to which Dionysian ritual gives access, and the pastoral and rural poetry of Virgil, Tibullus and Horace.[116]

Alongside this aesthetic, Bacchus was also a god of inspiration for the poets, itself a legacy of classical Greek and Hellenistic traditions. Even Lucretius the rationalist experienced poetic inspiration as Dionysian ecstasy: the god came to stand as a figure for the irrational, as explored recently by several contributions in a collection of essays on Augustan poetry and the irrational.[117] But poetic pos-

---

[114] *Fam.* 7.23; *Att.* 14.14.
[115] See Castriota 1995; Zanker 1998; Wyler 2005; Wyler 2006a; Wyler 2008; Wyler 2013a; Scapini 2016.
[116] See Wyler 2006a and Wyler 2006b.
[117] Hardie 2016, esp. 14–22; see especially Gowers 2016. See also Schiesaro 2009 and Giusti 2016.

tures can themselves be politically charged. Dionysus could be an attractive figure for a drop-out elegist to dally with,[118] but for the same elegist, several revolutions later, he could assist Apollo in hymning Augustus' victory at the Battle of Actium.[119] Likewise for Horace, Bacchus is the god of the symposium and thus of civilization, of the whole atmosphere of the lighter genres of poetry and even of the *recusatio*; but he also comes to inspire the poet to sing the glories of Augustus, guarantor of peace and leisure after generations of civil war.[120] Virgil draws on different aspects of Bacchus: as god of poetry and landscape in the *Eclogues*, of fertility and mystery-cult in the *Georgics*, and of tragedy, madness, resistance to Fate, but also of triumph, in the *Aeneid*.[121] It is notable that the Augustan poets do their best to tame Bacchus, to accommodate him to the needs of the regime. Alden Smith has written about the 'rehabilitation' of Bacchus in the *Georgics*, though I believe that a sense of danger subsists under the cheerful exterior.[122] Aspects of the Dionysian are divided between different characters in the *Aeneid*: it is the women opposed to Fate, Dido and Amata, who experience Dionysian madness and rave as maenads; while Dionysus' triumphal aspect devolves to Augustus in Anchises' Parade of Heroes.[123] And yet, Aeneas too is a Dionysus-figure, as Clifford Weber so convincingly demonstrated.[124]

It is against this pervasive presence of Dionysus in politics and the literary and visual arts that several of the more literary contributions to this volume may be positioned. As we have seen from the example of Livy, literary texts can have their own rhetoric of the Dionysian, which may point to a cultic experience either through derision and distortion, or precisely by taking flight from reality in a way that serves a distinct literary function. The following chapter (by Simon Perris and Fiachra Mac Góráin) offers a reception history of Euripides' *Bacchae* from its early classic status through to Christianizing Byzantine reworkings in John Malalas' *Chronography* and the *Christus Patiens*. Its temporal span, from the classical

---

118 Propertius 1.3.14, *hac Amor hac Liber, durus uterque deus*; cf. Propertius 3.17 with Miller 1991; Heyworth and Morwood 2011 *ad loc.*; and Wallis 2018, 131–63.
119 Propertius 4.6.76, *Bacche, soles Phoebo fertilis esse tuo*. A comprehensive treatment of Bacchus in the lighter genres of Latin poetry would be desirable; see Serignolli 2017. See Tib. 1.7 and 2.1. On the poets see also Bruhl 1953, 133–44; Hunter 2006, 40–82; Fabre-Serris 2009; and Freyburger 2013.
120 Batinski 1990-91; Schiesaro 2009; Serignolli 2019.
121 Mac Góráin 2013; Mac Góráin 2013–14; Mac Góráin 2014.
122 Smith 2007; Mac Góráin 2014.
123 Krummen 2004; Bocciolini Palagi 2007; Giusti 2018, esp. 88–147. On Roman maenads see Alonso Fernández 2013 and Bremmer 2017.
124 Weber 2002; see also Mac Góráin 2013.

period to the Christian era, is also programmatic for the scope of the volume. For completeness and comparison we consider both Greek and Latin receptions, and so (for example) among 'narratives' we include Theocritus and ps-Oppian as well as Ovid and Nonnus, and our contention is that receptions of the *Bacchae* often reveal cultural or religious attitudes to Dionysus that are typical of their time and place; that in limited cases, *Bacchae* receptions suggests a discourse about ritual, and that the contrast and interplay between Greek and Roman receptions is itself illuminating.

John Miller analyzes an elegiac hymn to Bacchus written from exile (*Tr.* 5.3), composed on the occasion of the Liberalia, when poets have gathered in Ovid's absence to worship Bacchus at a shrine. The poem looks to other Bacchic movements in Ovid's oeuvre, notably the Theban history of *Metamorphoses* 3 and 4, and the Liberalia of *Fasti* 3. At a basic level Bacchus stands as a god of poetic inspiration and patronage. We might have expected Ovid to link Bacchus with Augustus as Virgil did in the *Aeneid*, but instead he pursues analogies between Bacchus and himself: the god's eastern sojourn is refigured from triumph to exile narrative, and on this basis Ovid appeals to him to intercede with his fellow-god Augustus on the poet's behalf. By preventing Ovid from worshipping Liber, Augustus is cast in the role of Pentheus. Will he meet a fate like that of Pentheus? And will Bacchus get to return to his city? Interwoven in this poem are references to Augustus' patron-god Apollo, which expose the interplay of Apollo and Bacchus in the discourse of the age.[125] Ovid seems to make it quite clear that Augustus is trying to appropriate Bacchus, while also marginalizing him.

Bacchus in Statius' *Thebaid* is the subject of the next paper, by Alessandro Schiesaro. By the time Statius comes to write this epic, there have already been so many refigurations of Bacchus in Roman literature, including the adaptations and reworkings of Euripides' *Bacchae*.[126] How was Statius supposed to find an untrodden path between Virgil's great tragic scenes of Dionysian madness, Ovid's grotesquely comic rewriting of the death of Pentheus, the sublime *furor* of Lucan, the machinations of Atreus in Seneca, not to mention the lighter versions of Bacchus in lyric and elegy? It is perhaps not surprising, though entirely in line with his reinvention of the epic's godscape, that he demotes Bacchus to an inef-

---

125 See Cucchiarelli 2011a and Cucchiarelli 2011b; Mac Góráin 2012–13.
126 On Bacchic ritual in Latin literature see Panoussi 2009, esp. 115–44 and Panoussi 2019, 117–67. On Statius' *Achilleid* see Heslin 2005, esp. 193–256; Panoussi 2019, 203–17. Massa and Nelis (forthcoming) will examine the representation of the mysteries in Latin literature.

fectual ephebe, no longer in the confidence of Jupiter, who had ordained the pitiless dénouement of the *Bacchae*,[127] but has now fallen foul of *Thebes*, engulfed in civil war. As if to confirm Pentheus' suspicions that bacchic women are more interested in Aphrodite than Dionysus,[128] Venus stages a Bacchanal on Lemnos to punish the women who neglected her rites. A sense of Dionysian danger subsists, however, when Statius' *matrona* channels Lucan's Sibyl in a maenadic frenzy to utter a dire prophecy of civil war. Clearly Statius' construct is built on so many layers of literary treatment that it has moved far away from real Dionysian ritual, and yet it retains political bite in view of its convergence on the poetics of civil war, which had been a feature of Virgil's and Ovid's Dionysian dynamics.

We might diagnose Statius' mannered and hyper-literary construction of Dionysus as symptomatic of an absolute divergence between literary myth and 'real' ritual, and sure enough for the imperial period it can sometimes be difficult to see links between the two bodies of evidence. It is difficult, for example, to see Juvenal's 'Bacchanalia' – a byword for debauchery – corresponding to any contemporary cultic reality, though we might not expect any more of satire.[129] On the other hand, inscriptions and sarcophagi (and some literary texts) from the imperial period give us every reason to believe that Dionysian cultic worship continued unabated.[130] One of the most remarkable features of the epigraphic record for maenadism and Dionysian associations is the perfusion of cultic terminology from the mythical to the ritual sphere.[131] Equally striking is the *gulf* between colourful literary rhetoric and epigraphically attested cultic forms: the notion of Dionysus as a god of transgression turns out to be a myth when tested against a body of epigraphic data.[132]

Ultimately Dionysian myth and cult came to coexist alongside and compete and even conflict with Christianity.[133] One register of opposition is allusion and

---

127 Eur. *Ba.* 1349.
128 Eur. *Ba.* 225.
129 Juv. Sat. 2.1-3 *Vltra Sauromatas fugere hinc libet et glacialem | Oceanum, quotiens aliquid de moribus audent | qui Curios simulant et Bacchanalia uiuunt*, with Pailler 1988, 757–58.
130 For the epigraphic evidence, Jaccottet 2003 is fundamental; see also Turcan 2003. On the sarcophagi see Turcan 1966 and Matz 1968–75.
131 See Henrichs 1978, 122 on maenadism; Jaccottet 2003, I, 17–30 on the thiasos; and in general Massa 2014, 69–70. For analytic discussion of historical versus mythical maenadism see Bremmer 1984. We return to this point in the next chapter.
132 Jaccottet 2003, I, 66–100 on the Bacchant and the evidence for the gender of participants and gender mixing in Dionysian worship.
133 See Wacht/Rickert 2010, esp. 91–95, 'Adaption und Abgrenzung' and 'Koexistenz und Konflikt.'

reference to the Bacchanalia in Christian discourse.[134] Another is reception of Euripides' *Bacchae* in Christian texts, such as Clement of Alexandria's *Protrepticus*. Our concluding chapter, by Francesco Massa, builds on his large body of work about Dionysus and Christianity, and Christianity and pagan religions more generally.[135] Much of Massa's previously published work shows how Greek Christian sources appropriated the motifs of Dionysian cult – from recognition and denial of similarities between Christianity and the Dionysian religion through the influence of Dionysian motifs on the construction of the literary and visual Christian imaginary, to Christianizing interpretations of Dionysian texts. Here he selects case studies from Christian authors writing in Latin: Tertullian, Arnobius, Lactantius and Firmicus Maternus, who are engaging in similar debates. A prominent motif in the Christian discourse is the resurgence of the rhetoric of resistance, to the extent that we may draw a line from Euripides' Pentheus through Livy's Postumius to these Latin authors. Since all Christian authors operate mainly with the received *koine* of the Dionysian imaginary, only occasionally is it possible to discern a distinction in their point of view between the Greek Dionysus and the Latin Liber. Not the least fascinating of Massa's findings is Firmicus Maternus' use of Dionysian motifs to describe the Devil.

Beyond the scope of our volume is the phenomenon of Dionysian Christianity, whose beginnings may already be apparent in the earliest Christian texts, which grow out of different sources, from the Jewish to the Graeco-Roman.[136] Dionysian motifs and Christianity remain intertwined in literary and visual media throughout late antiquity,[137] and often, if sporadically thereafter: in medieval Christian allegorical interpretation,[138] in Rabelais' *Gargantua and Pantagruel*,[139] and in Renaissance painting.[140] Not the least fascinating chapter in the afterlife of Dionysus would tell more fully than has been done how Nietzsche, a founding father of modern Dionysian studies, himself substituted Dionysus for Christ as a guiding light and object of veneration, concluding his *Ecce Homo* with 'Dionysus versus the Crucified'.[141]

---

[134] Pailler 1988, 759–76.
[135] See, esp. Massa 2014.
[136] See pp. 61–62 (ch. 2) on the gospels.
[137] See Hernández de la Fuente 2013; Massa 2014; and Friesen 2015. For critique of the alignment between Christ and Dionysus see Edwards 2004, 39–40.
[138] Emmerling-Skala 1994.
[139] Weinberg 1972.
[140] Morel 2015.
[141] This figure, which overwrites the Apollo-Dionysus polarity of *The Birth of Tragedy* (see Smith 2000, xxv) occurs also in *The Will to Power*, §1052; for the figure in Nietzsche's thought see

Bibliography

Alonso Fernández, Z. 2013. 'Maenadic ecstasy in Rome: fact or fiction?' In Bernabé et al., 185–99.
Altheim, F. 1931. *Terra Mater: Untersuchungen zur altitalischen Religionsgeschichte*. Giessen.
Ando, C. ed. 2003. *Roman Religion*. Edinburgh.
Ando, C. 2008, *The Matter of the Gods. Religion and the Roman Empire*. Berkeley/Los Angeles.
Aneziri, S. 2003. *Die Vereine der dionysischen Techniten im Kontext der hellenistischen Gesellschaft: Untersuchungen zur Geschichte, Organisation und Wirkung der hellenistischen Technitenvereine*. Stuttgart.
Baeumer, M.L. 2006. *Dionysos und das Dionysische in der antiken und deutschen Literatur*. Darmstadt.
Bakkum, G.C.L.M. 2009. *The Latin Dialect of the Ager Faliscus*. Amsterdam.
Barchiesi, A., J. Rüpke, and S. Stephens, eds. 2004. *Rituals in Ink. A Conference on Religion and Literary Production in Ancient Rome*. Stuttgart.
Batinski, E.E. 1990–91. 'Horace's rehabilitation of Bacchus', *CW* 84, 361–78.
Beard, M. 1994. 'The Roman and the foreign: the cult of the 'Great Mother' in imperial Rome.' In *Shamanism, History and the State*, edited by N. Thomas and C. Humphrey. Ann Arbor, MI, 164–90.
Beard, M., J.A. North, and S. Price. 1998. *Religions of Rome*. 2 vols. Cambridge.
Becher, I. 1976. 'Augustus und Dionysos – ein Feindverhältnis?' *Zeitschrift für ägyptische Sprache und Altertumskunde*, Berlin Akad.-Verl. 103, 88–101.
Bendlin, A. 2002. '*Mundus Cereris*: Eine kultische Institution zwischen Mythos und Realität.' In Ἐπιτομὴ τῆς οἰκουμένης: *Studien zur römischen Religion in Antike und Neuzeit*, edited by C. Auffarth and J. Rüpke. Stuttgart, 37–73.
Bendlin, A. and J. Rüpke, eds. 2009. *Römische Religion im historischen Wandel. Diskursentwicklung von Plautus bis Ovid*. Stuttgart.
Bernabé, A., M. Herrero de Jáuregui, A.I. Jiménez San Cristóbal, R.M. Hernández, eds. 2013. *Redefining Dionysos*. Berlin/Boston.
Berti, F. and C. Gasparri, eds. 1989. *Dionysos. Mito e mistero*. Bologna.
Berti, F. ed., 1991. Dionysos. *Mito e mistero. Atti del convegno internazionale*. Comacchio 3–5 novembre 1989. Comacchio.
Bettini, M. 2016. '*Interpretatio romana*: category or conjecture?' In Bonnet, Pirenne-Delforge and Pironti, 17–36.
Bispham, E. and C.S. Smith, eds. 2000. *Religion in Archaic and Republican Rome: Evidence and Experience*. Edinburgh.
Bocciolini Palagi, L. 2007. *La trottola di Dioniso. Motivi dionisiaci nel vii libro dell'Eneide*. Bologna.
Boffa, G. 2015. 'Il vaso ben levigato. Una proposta di lettura per l'iscrizione più antica dalla necropoli di Osteria dell'Osa.' *La parola del passato* 70, 76–98.

Girard 1984 and Leonard 2012, 162–76. On Nietzsche and antiquity, see the sources listed in Mac Góráin 2012–13, 193 n. 6.

Bohrer, K.H. 2015. *Das Erscheinen des Dionysos. Antike Mythologie und moderne Metapher.* Berlin.
Bomati, Y. 1983. 'Les légendes dionysiaques en Étrurie.' *REL* 61, 87–107.
Bonfante, L. 1993. 'Fufluns Pacha: the Etruscan Dionysus.' In Carpenter and Faraone, 221–35.
Bonnet, C., V. Pirenne-Delforge and G. Pironti, eds. 2016. *Dieux des Grecs, dieux des Romains. Panthéons en dialogue à travers l'histoire et l'historiographie.* Rome.
Borgeaud, P. 1996. *La mère des dieux. De Cybele à la Vierge Marie.* Paris.
Bosworth, A.B. 1988a. *From Arrian to Alexander. Studies in Historical Interpretation.* Oxford.
Bosworth, A.B. 1988b. *Conquest and Empire. The Reign of Alexander the Great.* Cambridge.
Bosworth, A.B. 1996. *Alexander and the East. The Tragedy of Triumph.* Oxford.
Boyd, M.J. 1955 Review of Bruhl 1953. *CR* 5, 95–96.
Bremmer, J. 1984. 'Greek maenadism reconsidered.' *ZPE* 55, 267–86.
Bremmer, J.N. 2014. *Initiation into the Mysteries of the Ancient World.* Berlin.
Bremmer, J.N. 2017. 'Roman maenads.' In *Albert's Anthology.* Loeb Classical Monographs 17. Cambridge, MA, 23–25.
Briscoe, J. 2008. *A Commentary on Livy, books 38–40.* Oxford.
Bruhl, A. 1953. *Liber Pater. Origine et expansion du culte dionysiaque à Rome et dans le monde romain.* Paris.
Buccino, L. 2013. *Dioniso trionfatore. Percorsi e interpretazione del mito del trionfo indiano nelle fonti e nell'iconografia antiche.* Rome.
Burkert, W. 2011. 'Dionysos – "different" im Wandel der Zeiten. Eine Skizze.' In Schlesier, 15–22.
Cabrera, P. 2013. 'The gifts of Dionysos.' In Bernabé et al., 488–503.
Cancik-Lindemaier, H. 1996. 'Der Diskurs Religion im Senatsbeschluß über die Bacchanalia von 186 v. Chr. und bei Livius (B. XXXIX).' In *Geschichte – Tradition – Reflexion. Festschrift für Martin Hengel zum 70. Geburtstag, Vol. II Griechische und römische Religion*, edited by H. Cancik, H. Lichtenberger, and P. Schäfer. Tübingen, 77–96.
Cardauns, B. ed. 1976. *M. Terentius Varro. Antiquitates Rerum Divinarum.* Teil I: *Die Fragmente.* Wiesbaden.
Carpenter, T.H. 1986. *Dionysian Imagery in Archaic Greek Art: Its Development in Black-Figure Vase Painting.* Oxford.
Carpenter, T.H. 1997. *Dionysian Imagery in Fifth-Century Athens.* Oxford.
Carpenter, T.H. 2011. 'Dionysos and the blessed on Apulian red-figured vases.' In Schlesier, 253–61.
Carpenter, T.H. and C.A. Faraone, eds., 1993. *Masks of Dionysus.* Cornell, NY.
Casadio, G. 1994a. 'Dioniso italiota: Un dio Greco in Italia meridionale.' In *Forme de religiosità e tradizioni sapienzali in Magna Grecia.* Atti del convegno Napoli 14–15 dicembre 1993 a cura di A.C. Cassio e P. Poccetti. *AION* 16, 79–107.
Casadio, G. 1994b. *Storia del culto di Dioniso in Argolide.* Rome.
Casadio, G. 1999. *Il vino dell'anima. Storia del culto di Dioniso a Corinto, Sicione,* Trezene. Rome.
Casadio, G. 2009. 'Dionysus in Campania: Cumae.' In Casadio and Johnston, 33–45.
Casadio, G. and Johnston, P. eds., 2009. *Mystic Cults in Magna Graecia.* Austin, TX.
Castriota, D. 1995. *The Ara Pacis Augustae and the Imagery of Abundance in Later Greek and Early Roman Imperial art.* Princeton.

Catania, A. 2014. 'The transformation of imperial triumphal imagery on Roman sarcophagi.' In *Formkonstanz und Bedeutungswandel*, edited by D. Boschung and L. Jäger. Paderborn, 207–27.
Catania, A. 2015. 'Representations of victory in a Dionysian context on Campanian sarcophagi.' In *Römische Sarkophage: Akten des internationalen Werkstattgesprächs, 11.–13. Oktober 2012*, edited by B. Porod and G. Koiner. Graz, 44–53.
Cazanove, O. de. 1983. 'Lucus Stimulae. Les aiguillons des Bacchanales.' *Mélanges de l'École française de Rome. Antiquité* 95, 55–113.
Cazanove, O. de, ed. 1986. *L'association dionysiaque dans les sociétés anciennes. Collection de l'École française de Rome – 89*. Actes de la table ronde organisée par l'École française de Rome (Rome 24–25 mai 1984). Rome.
Cazanove, O. de. 1988. 'Jupiter, Liber, et le vin latin.' *Revue de l'histoire des religions* 205, 245–65.
Cazanove, O. de. 1991. 'θεὸς ἐν ἀσκῷ. Osservazioni sui meccanismi di trasmissione della figura di Dionysos all'Italia centrale arcaica.' In Berti 171–84.
Cazanove, O. de 2000a. 'I destinatari dell'iscrizione di Tiriolo e la questione del campo di applicazione del Senatoconsulto *De Bacchanalibus*.' *Athenaeum* 88, 59–69.
Cazanove, O. de. 2000b. 'Some thoughts on the 'religious romanisation [sic]' of Italy before the social war.' In *Religion in Archaic and Republican Rome and Italy*, edited by E. Bispham and C. Smith. Edinburgh, 71–76.
Cazanove, O. de. 2000c. 'Bacanal ou citerne? À propos des salles souterraines de la *Domus* II à Bolsena et de leur interprétation comme lieux de culte dionysiaque.' *L'Antiquité classique* 69, 237–53.
Clinton, K. 1992. *Myth and Cult. The Iconography of the Eleusinian Mysteries*. Stockholm.
Coarelli, F. 1993. 'Ceres, Liber, Liberaque, Aedes; Aedes Cereris.' *LTUR* I, 260–61.
Colonna, G. 2004. 'Discussione e interventi.' In *Oriente e occidente: metodi e discipline a confronto. Riflessioni sulla cronologia dell'età del ferro in Italia*. Atti dell'incontro di studi. Roma, 30–31 ottobre 2003, a cura di G. Bartolini e F. Delpino. Mediterranea I, 478–83.
Cornell, T.J. 1995. *The Beginnings of Rome: Italy and Rome from the Bronze Age to the Punic Wars (c. 1000–264 BC)*. London/New York.
Creuzer, F. 1820. *Symbolik und Mythologie der alten Völker, besonders der Griechen, zweite völlig umgearbeitete Ausgabe*. Leipzig/Darmstadt.
Csapo, E. 2013. 'Comedy and the *pompe*: Dionysian genre-crossing.' In *Greek Comedy and the Discourse of Genres*, edited by E. Bakola, L. Prauscello, M. Telò. Cambridge, 40–80.
Cucchiarelli, A. 2011a. 'Virgilio e l'invenzione dell''età augustea' (Modelli divini e linguaggio politico dalle 'Bucoliche' alle 'Georgiche').' *Lexis* 29, 229–74.
Cucchiarelli, A. 2011b. 'Ivy and laurel. Divine models in Virgil's *Eclogues*.' *HSCP* 106, 155–78.
Cumont 2006 [1929]. *Les religions orientales dans le paganisme romain*. Volume édité par Corinne Bonnet & Françoise Van Haeperen avec la collaboration de Bastien Toune. Rome.
Daraki, M. 1985. *Dionysos*. Paris.
Davies, J.P. 2004. *Rome's Religious History: Livy, Tacitus and Ammianus on their Gods*. Cambridge.
Degrassi, A. 1963. *Inscriptiones Italiae. Volumen XIII – Fasti et Elogia. Fasciculus II – Fasti Anni Numani et Iuliani. Accedunt Ferialia, Menologia Rustica, Parapegmata*. Rome.
De Simone, G.F. 2011. 'Con Dioniso fra i vigneti del vaporifero Vesuvio.' *Cronache ercolanesi* 41, 289–310.
Detienne, M. 1986. *Dionysos à ciel ouvert*. Paris.

Detienne, M. 1989. *Dionysus at Large*, tr. A. Goldhammer. Boston/London.
Detienne, M. 2001. 'Forgetting Delphi between Apollo and Dionysus.' *CPh* 96, 147–58.
Dodds, E.R. 1960. *Euripides Bacchae* (2nd ed.). Oxford.
Dumézil, G. 1970 [1966]. *Archaic Roman Religion. With an Appendix on the Religion of the Etruscans*. Trans. P. Krapp. Foreword by M. Eliade. Chicago/London.
Dunand, F. 1986. 'Les associations dionysiaques au service du pouvoir lagide (IIIe s. av. J.-C.).' In Cazanove, 85–104.
Dyck, A.R. ed. 2004. *A Commentary on Cicero*, De Legibus. Ann Arbor, MI.
Edwards, M. 2004. *John*. Oxford.
Eliade, M. 1978 [1976]. *A History of Religious Ideas*. Volume 1. *From the Stone Age to the Eleusinian Mysteries*, tr. W.R. Trask. Chicago.
Emmerling-Skala, A. 1994. *Bacchus in der Renaissance*. 2 vols. Hildesheim.
Fabre-Serris, J. 2009. 'Figures romaines de Dionysos à la fin du Ier siècle av. J.-C.' In *Images of the Pagan Gods. Papers of a Conference in Memory of Jean Seznec, Warburg Institute Colloquia* 14, edited by R. Duits and F. Quiviger 281–96.
Feeney, D. 1998. *Literature and Religion at Rome*. Cambridge.
Fiedler, M. 2005. 'Kultgruben eines Liber Pater-Heiligtums im römischen Apulum (Dakien). Ein Vorbericht.' *Germania: Anzeiger der römisch-germanischen Komission des deutschen archaeologischen Instituts* 83, 95–125.
Flower, H.I. 2000. 'Fabula de Bacchanalibus: the Bacchanalian cult of the second century BC and Roman drama.' In *Identität und Alterität in der frührömischen Tragödie*, edited by G. Manuwald. Würzburg, 23–36.
Flower, H.I. 2002. 'Rereading the Senatus consultum de Bacchanalibus of 186 BC: Gender roles in the middle Roman republic.' In *Oikistes: Studies in Constitutions, Colonies, and Military Power in the Ancient World, Offered in Honor of A.J. Graham*, edited by V.B. Gorman and E.W. Robinson. Leiden/Boston, 79–98.
Foucher, L. 1981. 'Le culte de Bacchus sous l'empire romain.' *ANrW*, II 17.2, 685–702.
Fowler, W.W. 1911. *The Religious Experience of the Roman People from the Earliest Times to the Age of Augustus*. London.
Frank, M. 1982. *Der kommende Gott. Vorlesungen über die neue Mythologie*. Frankfurt am Main.
Freyburger, G. 2013. 'Liber-Bacchus dans la poésie augustéenne: du passé de Rome au temps d'Auguste.' In *Poésie augustéenne et mémoires du passé de Rome: en hommage au professeur Lucienne Deschamps / textes réunis par Olivier Devillers & Guillaume Flamerie de Lachapelle*. Paris/Bordeaux, 93–99.
Freyburger-Galland, M.-L. 2009. 'Political and religious propaganda between 44 and 27 BC.' *Vergilius* 55, 17–30.
Friesen, C.J.P. 2015. *Reading Dionysus: Euripides' Bacchae and the cultural contestations of Greeks, Jews, Romans and Christians*. Tübingen.
Fuhrer, T. 2011. 'Inszenierungen von Göttlichkeit: die politische Rolle von Dionysos/Bacchus in der römischen Literatur.' In Schlesier, 373–89.
Gasparri, C. 1986a. 'Dionysos.' In *LIMC* 3.1, 414–514.
Gasparri, C. 1986b. 'Dionysos/Bacchus.' In *LIMC* 3.1, 540–66.
Gazda, E.K. ed. (with the assistance of C. Hammer, B. Longfellow, and M. Swetnam-Burland). 2000. *The Villa of the Mysteries in Pompeii: Ancient Ritual, Modern Muse*. Ann Arbor, MI.
Gesing, P. 1988. *Triumph des Bacchus. Triumphidee und bacchische Darstellungen in der italienischen Renaissance im Spiegel der Antikenrezeption*. Frankfurt am Main.
Girard, R. 1984. 'Dionysus versus the Crucified.' *MLN* 99, 816–35.

Giusti, E. 2016. 'Dithyrambic iambics: *Epode* 9 and its general(s') confusion.' In *Horace's Epodes. Contexts, Intertexts, and Reception*, edited by P. Bather and C. Stocks. Oxford, 131–51.

Giusti, E. 2017. 'The metapoetics of liber-ty. Horace's Bacchic ship in Seneca's *De Tranquillitate Animi*.' In *Horace and Seneca: Interactions, Intertexts, Interpretations*, edited by M. Stöckinger, K. Winter and T. Zanker. Berlin, 239–63.

Giusti, E. 2018. *Carthage in Virgil's Aeneid. Staging the Enemy under Augustus*. Cambridge.

Goukowsky, P. 1981. *Essai sur les origines du mythe d'Alexandre (336-270 av. J.-C.)*, Nancy, 1981, 2 vols., I *Les origines politiques*, II *Alexandre et Dionysos*.

Gowers, E. 2016. 'Under the influence: Maecenas and Bacchus in *Georgics* 2.' In Hardie, 134–52.

Graf, F., and S.I. Johnston. 2013[2] *Ritual Texts for the Afterlife: Orpheus and the Bacchic Gold Tablets*. London.

Graillot, H. 1912. *Le culte de Cybèle, mère des dieux, à Rome et dans l'Empire romain*. Paris.

Granet, J. 1990. 'Dionysos contre Rome.' *Pallas* 36, 53–70.

Gruen, E.S. 1992. *Culture and National Identity in Republican Rome*. Cornell, NY.

Gruen, E.S. 1990. *Studies in Greek Culture and Roman Policy*, Berkeley/Los Angeles/London.

Hardie, P. ed. 2016. *Augustan Poetry and the Irrational*. Oxford.

Heinemann, A. 2011. 'Ein dekorativer Gott? Bilder für Dionysos zwischen griechischer Votivpraxis und römischem Decorum.' In Schlesier, 391–412.

Henderson, J. 1996. 'Footnote: representation in the Villa of Mysteries.' In *Art and Text in Roman Culture*, edited by J. Elsner. Cambridge, 235–76.

Henrichs, A. 1978. 'Greek maenadism from Olympias to Messalina.' *HSCPh* 82, 121–60.

Henrichs, A. 1984. 'Loss of self, suffering, violence: the modern view of Dionysus from Nietzsche to Girard.' *HSCPh* 88, 205–40.

Henrichs, A. 1995. '*Graecia capta*: Roman views of Greek culture.' *HSCP* 97, 243–61.

Hernández de la Fuente, D. 2013. 'Parallels between Dionysos and Christ in late antiquity: miraculous healings in Nonnus' Dionysiaca.' In Bernabé et al., 464–87.

Heslin, P.J. 2005. *The Transvestite Achilles. Gender and Genre in Statius'* Achilleid. Cambridge.

Heyworth, S.J. ed. 2019. *Ovid. Fasti Book III*. Cambridge.

Heyworth, S.J. and J. Morwood, eds. 2011. *A Commentary on Propertius, Book 3*. Oxford.

Housman, A.E. 1918. 'Jests of Plautus, Cicero, and Trimalchio.' *CR* 32, 162–64.

Hunter, R. 2006. *The Shadow of Callimachus*. Cambridge.

Hutchinson, V.F. 1986. *Bacchus in Roman Britain: The Evidence for his Cult*. Oxford.

Isler-Kerényi, C. 2007. *Dionysos in Archaic Greece: An Understanding through Images*. Translated by W.G.E. Watson. Leiden/Boston.

Isler-Kerényi, C. 2010. 'Il culto di Liber/Bacco nel mondo romano. – The Cult of Liber/Bacchus in the Roman World.' In *Il sorriso di Dioniso/The Smile of Dionysus*, edited by E. La Rocca. Turin/London/Venice/New York, 27–44.

Isler-Kerényi, C. 2011. 'Dionysos in Pergamon. Ein polytheistisches Phänomen.' In Schlesier, 433–46.

Isler-Kerényi, C. 2015. *Dionysos in Classical Athens. An Understanding through Images*. Translated by Anna Beerens. Leiden/Boston.

Ivanov, V.I. 2012. *Dionysos und die vordionysischen Kulte*. Introduction and appendices by M. Wachtel and Chr. Wildberg. Tübingen.

Jaccottet, A.-F. 2003. *Choisir Dionysos. Les associations dionysiaques ou la face cachée du dionysisme*. 2 volumes, Zurich.

Jeanmaire, H. 1951. *Dionysos. Histoire du culte de Bacchus*. Paris.
Jeličić-Radonic, J. 2015. 'The cult of Dionysus or Liber – votive monuments in Salona.' In *Cult and Votive Monuments in the Provinces*. Proceedings of the 13th International Colloquium on Roman Provincial Art, edited by C.-G. Alexandrescu. Cluj-Napoca, 23–32.
Joseph, L.S., and J.S. Klein, 1981. 'A new restoration in the Faliscan Ceres-inscription with notes on Latin *molere* and its Italian cognates.' *HSCP* 85, 293–300.
Kerényi, C. 1976. *Dionysos. Archetypal Image of Indestructible Life*. Translated from the German by R. Mannheim. London.
Kern, O. 1916. 'Iakchos.' In *RE 9* (edited by Pauly-Wissowa), 613–22.
Konaris, M. 2011. 'Dionysos in nineteenth-century scholarship.' In Schlesier, 467–478.
Kovács, D. 2015. 'Liberalia in Ovid – Liber in the Roman religion.' In *Sapiens Ubique Civis*. Proceedings of International Conference on Classical Studies (Szeged, Hungary, 2013), edited by J. Nagyillés, A. Hajdú, G. Gellérfi, A. Horn Baroody, and S. Baroody. Budapest, 306–19.
Kopij, K. 2014. 'Was Pompey the Great regarded as Neos Dionysos? Some evidence from coins.' In *Proceedings of the 7th International Numismatic Congress in Croatia, Opatija, September 27–28, 2013*, edited by J. Dobrinić. Rijeka, 119–26.
Koulakiotis, E. 2017. 'Plutarch's *Alexander*, Dionysos and the metaphysics of power.' In *Greek Historians on War and Kingship*, edited by T. Howe, R. Stoneman and S. Müller. Oxford, 226–49.
Krummen, E. 2004. 'Dido als Mänade und tragische Heroine: Dionysische Thematik und Tragödientradition in Vergils Didoerzählung.' *Poetica* 36, 25–69.
Latte, K. 1960. *Römische Religionsgeschichte*. Munich.
Le Bonniec, H. 1958. *Le culte de Cérès à Rome*. Paris.
Le Guen, B. 2001. *Les associations de technites dionysiaques à l'époque hellénistique*. 2 vols. Nancy.
Leinieks, V. 1996. *The City of Dionysos: A Study of Euripides' Bakchai*. Stuttgart.
Leonard, M. 2012. *Socrates and the Jews. Hellenism and Hebraism from Moses Mendelssohn to Sigmund Freud*. Chicago, IL.
Lipka, M. 2009. *Roman Gods. A Conceptual Approach*. Leiden/Boston.
Mac Góráin, F. 2012–13. 'Apollo and Dionysus in Virgil.' *Incontri di filologia classica* 12, 191–238.
Mac Góráin, F. 2013. 'Virgil's Bacchus and the Roman republic.' In *Augustan Poetry and the Roman Republic*, edited by J. Farrell and D.P. Nelis. Oxford, 124–45.
Mac Góráin, F. 2014. 'The mixed blessings of Bacchus in Virgil's *Georgics*.' *Dictynna* 11.
Mac Góráin, F. 2017. 'Dionysus in Rome.' In *A Handbook to the Reception of Classical Mythology*, edited by V. Zajko and H. Hoyle. Malden/Oxford, 323–36.
Mannsperger, D. 1973. 'Apollon gegen Dionysos: Numismatische Beiträge zu Octavians Rolle als Vindex Libertatis.' *Gymnasium* 80, 381–404.
Manuwald, G. 2011. *Roman Republican Theatre*. Cambridge.
Maras, D.F. 2009. *Il dono votivo, gli dei e il sacro nelle iscrizioni etrusche di culto*. Rome.
Marasco, G. 1992. 'Marco Antonio "Nuovo Dioniso" e il *De sua ebrietate*.' *Latomus* 51, 538–48.
Mariño Sánchez, D. 2014. *Injertando a Dioniso. Las interpretaciones del dios, de nuestros días a la antigüedad*. Madrid.
Mariotti, S. 1957. Review of Pastorino 1955. *Gnomon* 29, 315–17.
Massa, F. 2014. *Tra la vigna e la croce. Dioniso nei discorsi letterari e figurativi cristiani (ii–iv secolo)*. Stuttgart.

Massa, F. 2016. 'Liber face à Dionysos: une assimilation sans écarts? *Koinè* dionysiaque et pratiques rituelles romaines.' In Bonnet, Pirenne-Delforge, and Pironti, 117–29.
Massa, F. and D. Nelis, eds. (forthcoming) *Dire les mystères en latin. Mnemosyne* special issue.
Matz, F. 1963. 'DIONYSIAKH TELETH: Archäologische Untersuchungen zum Dionysoskult in hellenistischer and römischer Zeit.' In *Abhandlungen der Geistes- und Sozialwissenschaftlichen Klasse, Akademie der Wissenschaft u Literatur* 16. Mainz, 1395–1453.
Matz, F. 1968-75. Die *Dionysischen Sarkophage*. 4 vols. Berlin.
Mayer-Olivé, M. 2017. 'Aproximación al estudio de la presencia del culto de Liber Pater en las provincias romanas danubianas a través de las inscripciones latinas.' *Euphrosyne* 45, 517–37.
McGinty, P. 1978. *Interpretation and Dionysos. Method in the Study of a God*. The Hague.
Meilán Jácome, P. 2013. 'Bacchus and felines in Roman iconography: issues of gender and species.' In Bernabé *et al.*, 526–40.
Meuli, K. 1955. 'Altrömischer Maskenbrauch.' *MH* 12, 206–35.
Miano, D. 2018. *Fortuna. Deity and Concept in Archaic and Republican Italy*. Oxford.
Miano, D. and E. Bispham, eds. Forthcoming. *Gods and Goddesses in Ancient Italy*. London.
Miller, J.F. 1991. 'Propertius' hymn to Bacchus and contemporary poetry.' *AJP* 112, 77–86.
Miller, J.F. 2002. 'Ovid's Liberalia.' In *Ovid's Fasti: Historical Readings at its Bimillennium*, edited by G. Herbert-Brown. Oxford, 199–224.
Miller, J.F. 2009. *Apollo, Augustus, and the Poets*. Cambridge.
Mignone, L.M. 2016. *The Republican Aventine and Rome's Social Order*. Ann Arbor, MI.
Montanari, E. 1984. '"Figura" e "funzione" di Liber Pater nell'età repubblicana.' *Studi e materiali di storia delle religioni* 8, 245–64.
Montanari, E. 1988. *Identità culturale e conflitti religiosi nella Roma repubblicana*. Rome.
Montanari, E. 1998. 'Il dinamismo della tradizione: Roma e la ricezione del dionisismo.' In *Il potere dei ricordi: studi sulla tradizione come problema di storia*, edited by M. Mastrogregori (Storiografia 2), 139–57.
Moraw, S. 1998. *Die Mänade in der attischen Vasenmalerei des 6. und 5. Jahrhunderts v. Chr.: Rezeptionsästhetische Analyse eines antiken Weiblichkeitsentwurfs*. Mainz.
Morel, P. 2015. *Renaissance dionysiaque. Inspiration bachique, imaginaire du vin et de la vigne dans l'art européen (1430–1630)*. Paris.
Mura Sommella, A. 2017. 'Arianna ritrovata! Un nuovo gruppo acroteriale dall'Area Sacra del Foro Boario.' In *The Age of Tarquinius Superbus. Central Italy in the Late 6th Century BC. Proceedings of the Conference The Age of Tarquinius Superbus, A Paradigm Shift?* Rome, 7–9 November, 2013, edited by P.S. Lulof and C.J. Smith. Louvain, 107–12.
Musiał, D. 2007. 'La triade plébéienne et la déesse Cérès.' In *Society and Religions. Greek and Roman History*, edited by D. Musiał. Vol. 2, 47–54.
Musiał, D. 2009. *Dionizos w Rzymie*. Kraków.
Musiał, D. 2013. 'Divinities of the Roman Liberalia.' *Przegląd Humanistyczny* 2, 95–100.
Niafas, K. 1998. *Liber Pater and His Cult in Latin Literature until the End of the Augustan Period*. PhD dissertation, Exeter.
Nikoloska, A. 2015. 'The world of Dionysos on monuments from the Republic of Macedonia.' In *Cult and Votive Monuments in the Provinces. Proceedings of the 13th International Colloquium on Roman Provincial Art*, edited by C.-G. Alexandrescu. Cluj-Napoca, 87–96.
Nock, A.D. 1928. 'Notes on ruler-cult, I–IV.' *JHS* 48, 21–43.
North, J.A. 1979. 'Religious toleration in Republican Rome.' *PCPS* 25, 85–103, reprinted in Ando 2003, 199–219.

Nousek, D. 2010. 'Echoes of Cicero in Livy's Bacchanalian narrative.' *CQ* 60, 156–66.
Nilsson, M.P. 1925 [1921]. *A History of Greek Religion*. Oxford.
Nilsson, M.P. 1957. *The Dionysiac Mysteries of the Hellenistic and Roman Age*. Lund.
Orlin, E.M. 1997. *Temples, Religion and Politics in the Roman Republic*. Leiden/New York/Cologne.
Orlin, E.M. 2010. *Foreign Cults in Rome. Creating a Roman Empire*. Oxford.
Otto, W.F. 1965 [1933]. *Dionysus. Myth and Cult*. Bloomington, IN.
Pagán, V.E. 2004. *Conspiracy Narratives in Roman History*. Austin, TX.
Pailler, J.-M. 1988. *Bacchanalia. La répression de 186 av. J.-C. à Rome et en Italie: vestiges, images, tradition*. Rome.
Pailler, J.-M. 1995. *Bacchus. Figures et pouvoirs*. Paris.
Palethodoros, D. 2007. 'Dionysiac imagery in archaic Etruria.' *Etruscan Studies* 10, 187–201.
Panoussi, V. 2009. *Greek Tragedy in Vergil's "Aeneid." Ritual, Empire, and Intertext*. Cambridge.
Panoussi, V. 2019. *Brides, Mourners, Bacchae. Women's Rituals in Roman Literature*. Baltimore, MD.
Parker, R. 2017. *Greek Gods Abroad. Names, Natures, and Transformations*. Berkeley, CA.
Pastorino, A. 1955. *Tropaum Liberi. Saggio sul Lucurgus de Nevio e sui motivi dionisiaci nella tragedia latina arcaica*. Varese.
Perris, S. 2016. *The Gentle, Jealous God. Reading Euripides'* Bacchae *in English*. London.
Peruzzi, E. 1992. 'Cultura greca a Gabii nel secolo VIII.' *La Parola del passato* 47, 459–68.
Plinval, G. de 1968. *Cicéron. Traité des lois*. Paris.
Radke, G. 1965. *Die Götter Altitaliens*. Münster.
Rice, E.E. ed. 1983. *The Grand Procession of Ptolemy Philadelphus*. Oxford.
Riedl, M. 2012. 'The containment of Dionysos: religion and politics in the Bacchanalia affair of 186 BCE.' *International Political Anthropology* 5, 113–33.
Riva, C. 2018. 'Wine production and exchange and the value of wine consumption in sixth-century BC Etruria.' *JMA* 30, 237–61.
Rohde, E. 1925. [1890–94] *Psyche. The Cult of Souls and Belief in Immortality among the Ancient Greeks* (translation from the German 8th ed., rep. 1987). London.
Rolle, A. 2017. *Dall'Oriente a Rome. Cibele, Iside e Serapide nell'opera di Varrone*. Pisa.
Rousselle, R. 1987. 'Liber-Dionysus in early Roman drama.' *CJ* 82, 193–98.
Rüpke, J. [2001] 2007. *Religion of the Romans*. Cambridge/Malden, MA.
Rüpke, J. and W. Spickermann, eds. 2010. 'Religion and literature.' *Archiv für Religionsgeschichte* 11, 121–22.
Rutherford, I. 2013. 'Dithyrambos, thriambos, triumphus. Dionysiac discourse at Rome.' In *Dithyramb in Context*, edited by P. Wilson and B. Kowalzig. Oxford, 409–23.
Sabetai, V. 2011. 'Eros reigns supreme: Dionysos' wedding on a new krater by the Dinos painter.' In Schlesier, 137–60.
Said, E.W. 1977. 'Orientalism.' The *Georgia Review* 31, 162–206.
Said, E.W. 2005 [1978]. *Orientalism* [with 2003 Preface]. London.
Sauron, G. 1998. *La grande fresque de la Villa des Mystères*. Paris.
Sauron, G. 2000. *L'histoire végétalisée. Ornement et politique à Rome*. Paris.
Scafuro, A.C. 1989. 'Livy's comic narrative of the Bacchanalia.' *Helios* 16, 119–42.
Scapini, M. 2015. 'Augustus and Dionysus's triumph: a non-existent paradox.' *Acta. Ant. Hung.* 55, 185–209.

Scapini, M. 2016. *Le stanze di Dioniso. Contenuti rituali e committenti delle scene dionisiache domestiche tra Roma e Pompei*. Madrid.

Scheid, J. 1991. 'D'indispensables étrangères. Les rôles religieux des femmes à Rome.' In *Histoire des femmes en Occident*, edited by P. Schmitt Pantel. Rome, Vol. 1, 405–37.

Scheid, J. 1995. 'Graeco ritu: a typically Roman way of honoring the gods.' *HSCP* 97, 15–31.

Scheid, J. 2005. 'Les dieux du Capitole: un exemple des structures théologiques des sanctuaires romains.' In *Théorie et pratique de l'architecture romaine. La norme et l'expérimentation*, edited by X. Lafon and G. Sauron. Aix-en-Provence, 93–100.

Schiesaro, A. 2009, 'Horace's Bacchic poetics.' In *Perceptions of Horace*, edited by L.B.T. Houghton and M. Wyke. Cambridge, 61–79.

Schiesaro, A. 2016. 'Bacchus in Roman drama.' In *Roman Drama and its Contexts*, edited by S. Frangoulidis, S.J. Harrison and G. Manuwald. Berlin/New York, 25–41.

Schlesier, R., ed. 2011. *Dionysos: A Different God? Dionysos and Ancient Polytheism*. Berlin/New York.

Schultze, C.E. 1995. 'Dionysius of Halicarnassus and Roman chronology.' *PCPhS* 41, 192–214.

Schultze, C.E. 2004. 'Dionysius of Halicarnassus: Greek origins and Roman games (*AR* 7.70–73).' In *Games and Festivals in Classical Antiquity*, edited by S. Bell and G.M. Davies. Oxford, 93–105.

Schultz, C.E. 2006. *Women's Religious Activity in the Roman Republic*. Chapel Hill, NC.

Schur, W. 1926. 'Liber Pater.' *RE* (Pauly-Wissowa), 13.1.68–76.

Scott, K. 1929. 'Octavian's propaganda and Antony's *De sua ebrietate*.' *CPh* 24, 133–41.

Seaford, R.A.S. 1981. 'The mysteries of Dionysos at Pompeii.' In *Pegasus: Classical Essays from the University of Exeter*, edited by H.W. Stubbs. Exeter, 52–67.

Seaford, R.A.S. 1996. *Euripides* Bacchae. Warminster.

Seaford, R. 2006. *Dionysos*. London.

Serignolli, L.V.G. 2017. *Baco, o Simpósio, e o poeta*. PhD dissertation, São Paolo.

Serignolli, L.V.G. 2019. 'Bacchus, Augustus, and the poet in Horace *Odes* 3.25.' In *Augustan Poetry. New Trends and Revaluations*, edited by P. Martins, A.P. Hasegawa, and J.A. Oliva Neto. São Paolo, 275–306.

Smith, D. trans. 2000. *Friedrich Nietzsche. The Birth of Tragedy. A New Translation by Douglas Smith*. Oxford.

Smith, R.A. 2007. '*In vino civitas*: the rehabilitation of Bacchus in Vergil's *Georgics*.' *Vergilius* 53, 52–86.

Spaeth, B.S. 1996. *The Roman Goddess Ceres*. Austin, TX.

Takács, S.A. 2000. 'Politics and religion in the Bacchanalian Affair of 186 B.C.' *HSCP* 100, 301–10.

Tassignon, I. 1996. *Iconographie et religion dionysiaques en Gaule Belgique et dans les deux Germanies*. Geneva.

Tomas, A. 2015. 'Liber Pater or Dionysus? The evidence of the Bacchic cult at Novae (*castra et canabae legionis*) and in its hinterland.' In *Ad fines imperii romani: Studia Thaddaeo Sarnowski septuagenario ab amicis, collegis disciplisque dedicata*, edited by A. Tomas. Warsaw, 257–76.

Turcan, R. 1966. *Les sarcophages romains à représentations dionysiaques. Essai de chronologie et d'histoire religieuse*. Paris.

Turcan, R. 1977. 'César et Dionysos.' In *Hommage à la mémoire de J. Carcopino*. Paris, 317–25.

Turcan, R. 1996 [1992]. *The Cults of the Roman Empire*, tr. A. Nevill. Malden, MA/Oxford.

Turcan, R. 2003. *Liturgies de l'initiation bacchique à l'époque romaine (Liber). Documentation littéraire, inscrite et figurée*. Paris.
Van Andringa, W., ed. 2013. *Archéologie et religion: le sanctuaire dionysiaque de S. Abbondio à Pompéi – Varia. Mélanges de l'École française de Rome – Antiquité*. 125-1.
Versnel, H.S. 1970. *Triumphus: An Inquiry into the Origin, Development, and Meaning of the Roman Triumph*. Leiden.
Versnel, H.S. 1990. *Ter Unus. Isis, Dionysos, Hermes: Three Studies in Henotheism*. Leiden: E.J. Brill.
Versnel, H.S. 2011a. *Coping with the Gods*. Leiden/Boston.
Versnel, H.S. 2011b. 'Heis Dionysos! One Dionysos? A polytheistic perspective.' In Schlesier, 23–46.
Veyne, P. 1998. 'La fresque dite des Mystères à Pompeii', in *Les mystères du gynécée*. Paris, 13–153.
Veyne, P. 2005. *L'empire gréco-romain*. Paris.
Wacht, M. and Rickert, F. 2010 'Liber (Dionysos).' In *RAC* 13, 67–99.
Wallace-Hadrill, A. 1998. 'To be Roman, go Greek. Thoughts on Hellenization at Rome.' In *Modus Operandi, Essays in Honour of Geoffrey Rickman*, edited by M. Austin, J. Harries, and C. Smith. London, 79–91.
Wallis, J. 2018. *Introspection and Engagement in Propertius: A Study of Book 3*. Cambridge.
Walsh, P.G. 1996. 'Making a drama out of a crisis: Livy on the Bacchanalia.' *G&R* 43, 188–203.
Watkins, C. 1995. 'Greece in Italy outside Rome.' *HSCP* 97, 35–50.
Weaver, J.B. 2004. *Plots of Epiphany: Prison-Escape in Acts of the Apostles*. Berlin.
Weber, C. 2002. 'The Dionysus in Aeneas.' *CPh* 97, 322–43.
Weinberg, F.M. 1972. *The Wine and the Will. Rabelais's Dionysian Christianity*. Detroit, MI.
Werner, I. 2005. *Dionysos in Etruria: The Ivy Leaf Group*. Stockholm.
Wilamowitz, U. von Moellendorf. 1931–2. *Der Glaube der Hellenen*. 2 vols. Berlin.
Wilson, J.-P. 2009. 'Literacy.' In *A Companion to Archaic Greece*, edited by K.A. Raaflaub and H. van Wees. Malden, MA, 542–63.
Wiseman, T.P. 1998. 'Two plays for the Liberalia.' In *Roman Drama and Roman History*. Exeter, 35–51.
Wiseman, T.P. 2004. *Myths of Rome*. Exeter.
Wiseman, T.P. 2000. 'Liber. Myth, drama and ideology in republican Rome.' In *The Roman Middle Republic: Politics, Religion, and Historiography, c. 400–133 B.C.* (Papers from a Conference at the Institutum Romanum Finlandiae, September 11–12, 1998), edited by C. Bruun. Rome, 265–99, repr. in id. *Unwritten Rome*. Exeter, 84–139.
Wissowa, G. 1912². *Religion und Kultus der Römer*. Munich.
Wyler, S. 2004. '"Dionysos domesticus." Les motifs dionysiaques dans les maisons pompéiennes et romaines (IIe s. av.-1er s. ap. J.-C.).' *MEFRA* 116, 933–51.
Wyler, S. 2005. 'Le décor dionysiaque de la villa de la Farnésine, ou l'art de faire grec à Rome.' *Métis (N. S.)* 3, 101–29.
Wyler, S. 2006a. 'Roman replications of Greek art at the Villa della Farnesina.' *Art History* 29, 213–32.
Wyler, S. 2006b. 'Images dionysiaques à Rome: à propos d'une fresque méconnue de Lanuvium.' In *Religions orientales, culti misterici. Neue Perspektiven, nouvelles perspectives, prospettive nuove*, edited by C. Bonnet, P. Scarpi and J. Rüpke. Stuttgart, 135–45.

Wyler, S. 2008. 'Réhabilitation de Liber: ambiguïtés de la condamnation des images dionysiaques, de "l'affaire" des Bacchanales à Actium.' In *Un discours en images de la condamnation de mémoire*, edited by S. Benoist and A. Daguet-Gagey. Metz, 229–44.

Wyler, S. 2011. 'L'acculturation dionysiaque à Rome: l'invention d'une alterité.' In *Identités romaines. Conscience de soi, et représentation de l'autre dans le Rome antique*, edited by M. Simon. Paris, 191–201.

Wyler, S. 2013a. 'An Augustan trend toward Dionysos: around the 'Auditorium of Maecenas."' In Bernabé *et al*. 2013, 541–53.

Wyler, S. 2013b. 'Dionysos/*Loufir*/*Liber* et sa parèdre. Le fronton du temple et le culte de S. Abbondio.' *MEFR* 125–1 (online).

Zanker, P. 1998. *Eine Kunst für die Sinne: zur Bilderwelt des Dionysos und der Aphrodite*. Berlin.

Simon Perris and Fiachra Mac Góráin
The ancient reception of Euripides' *Bacchae* from Athens to Byzantium

Abstract: This chapter offers a reception history of Euripides' *Bacchae* from its original production until its intertextual transformation in the Byzantine *Christus Patiens*. It traces a broad arc from Classical Athens through the Roman Empire, taking in also Hellenistic Alexandria, the Greek-speaking East, Christianity, and Byzantine literature. By examining the cultural contexts and inflections of the different receptions of one poetic text – Greek, Roman and Italian, 'Eastern', and Christian – it exposes distinctions between religious or cultural attitudes to Bacchus/Dionysus across a broad range of Greek and Latin sources. The discussion is divided into four thematic sections, within which receptions are mostly presented in chronological order: Classic *Bacchae*; Performances; Narratives; and Christian discourse. These sections encompass drama, epic, didactic, epyllion, historiography, biography, epigram, scholarly citations, and theological texts. A selection of the most significant case studies receive in-depth discussion in the body of the chapter; for completeness, the reception history of *Bacchae* is filled out by listing additional receptions in summary form in an appendix.

Introduction

Euripides' *Bacchae* was undoubtedly the single most influential literary text for constructions of Dionysus throughout Greco-Roman antiquity. In this chapter, we examine how receptions of the play across the spectrum of Greek and Roman literature act as a barometer for cultural attitudes to Dionysus. Many of the most significant and revealing receptions occur in Latin texts or in Greek texts that deal with Roman subjects, whether Plutarch's *Antony*, Greek epigrams about Italian pantomime performances, or Christian writings polemicizing against Greek and Roman cults. Accordingly, many of the Greek literary receptions bear directly on the Roman focus of this volume. Though not all of the receptions that we discuss are directly relevant to Roman affairs, nonetheless we have decided to aim at a detailed reception history of the play from Athens to Byzantium for two reasons. First, because the contrast and interplay between Greek and Roman receptions help to give definition to what is distinctly Roman or otherwise about specifically

Roman receptions. And second, because a comprehensive reception history of Euripides' *Bacchae* is a desideratum in its own right.[1]

Euripides' *Bacchae* is good to think with when examining the close relationship between Dionysian myth and ritual, and thus between literature and religion. The play itself already thematizes attitudes to the god, and is suffused with ritual motifs and language,[2] but the dramatic presentation puts these at a remove from lived experience. The play's reception history plays out in particular two main positions or sets of positions, pro- and anti-Dionysian. Interestingly, there are patterns or clusters of pro- and anti-Dionysian positions across the Greek-Roman divide: Roman receptions of the play tend to manifest censoriousness about Dionysus as against their Greek counterparts, in ways that can only be appreciated if both sets of sources are viewed as a whole. The pro- and anti-Dionysian positions are themselves dramatically elaborated within the *Bacchae* itself, and so the reception history engages with a tension at the heart of the play. The chorus and the disguised stranger express a beatific vision of the Dionysian experience, which draws on the language of mystery cult; Tiresias puts forwards philosophical arguments for worshipping Dionysus, and Cadmus politically pragmatic ones. On the other hand Pentheus supplies a dissenting voice – censorious, cynical, rational, yet still curious to the point of prurience – but his anti-Dionysian rhetoric will echo throughout the ages from Livy's consul Postumius through to Christian apologetics. As far as the Greek evidence is concerned, it has been argued that Euripides' play exercised a significant influence on historical ritual practices, at least as far as maenadism and the thiasos were concerned.[3] On the Roman side, descriptions of Bacchic worship often echo motifs from the *Bacchae*. With reference to the Bacchanalian affair of 186 BCE, Peter Heslin argues that the '*Bacchae* was revised by the Roman Senate from the perspective of Pentheus, con-

---

The authors would like to thank each other, as well as Joel Gordon, Francesco Massa, Chris Pelling, Richard Seaford, Tim Smith, James Watson, Ruth Webb, Rosie Wyles, and audiences in Canterbury, Durham and Athens.

1 On the ancient reception of the *Bacchae* see Sandys 1900, lxxxii–lxxxviii; Dodds 1960, xxix; Funke 1966; Roux 1970, 72–77; Seaford 1996, 52–54; Mills 2006, 103–5; Sauron 2007; Massa 2014, esp. 69–72, 167–80; Friesen 2015; Perris 2015, 508–11. On the play's modern reception see Radke 2003 and Billings 2018 (scholarly reception); Fischer-Lichte 2014; Perris 2016 (literary and dramatic reception).
2 Versnel 1990, 167–69; Seaford 1996, *passim*, but see esp. 35–44.
3 See Henrichs 1978, 122 on maenadism; Jaccottet 2003, I, 17–30 on the thiasos; and in general Massa 2014, 69–70. For analytic discussion of historical versus mythical maenadism see Bremmer 1984.

sidered not as an impious and feckless tyrant, but as a dutiful Roman magistrate.'[4] And Alessandro Schiesaro has suggested that Hispala's lurid imaginings that she would be ripped apart by the Bacchants if she were to disclose their secrets is based on the sparagmos in Euripides' play, in which Pentheus is torn limb from limb by his mother and aunts.[5] It would seem that even though Euripides' *Bacchae* by no means defined the historical Dionysian cult, which varied across time and space,[6] it affected perceptions, and could be drawn on to articulate a position for or against Dionysus. It evolved from being a poetic manifestation of cult and historical practices to being used as a quasi-historical record of ritual practices, instantiating them anew.

We begin by sketching the contours of the survey and establishing the classic status of the *Bacchae*; we then order the material into three partly overlapping categories: (i) performances, (ii) narrative retellings, and (iii) the place of the *Bacchae* in Christian discourse, looking in each case at how the receiving source may be read as an interpretation of the *Bacchae*, and at what it tells us about ancient views of Dionysus. We discuss the most interesting and dynamic receptions in the present pages, and summarize the remaining evidence in an appendix. But first a methodological question: what distinguishes a reception of the *Bacchae* from a treatment of or allusion to its myth? The question is resonant of the 'intertextuality wars' of the long 1990s.[7] Indeed, what is an allusion, a reception, or a literary adaptation?[8] These questions are also complicated by the fact that poetic and visual versions of the story predate Euripides' play; indeed, some receiving sources seem conversant with both *Bacchae* and parallel traditions. We focus as far as possible on specific reminiscences of the play, as determined by verbal echoes such as direct quotation, or other similarities such as structural imitation. Some of the sources which we examine respond to Euripides' *Bacchae* by modifying or inverting some feature, often as part of a dynamic debate on the meaning of the *Bacchae*.

---

4 Heslin 2005, 247.
5 Schiesaro 2016, 31.
6 Wyler 2011, 191 cautions against making Eur. *Ba.* definitive in our understanding of Dionysus and his cult.
7 See, e.g., Thomas 1986; Hinds 1998; Edmunds 2001; and now Conte 2017. With reference to the reception of *Bacchae* see Friesen 2016, 66–69.
8 Martindale 1993; Irwin 2001; Irwin 2004; Hutcheon 2006; Sanders 2006.

Classic *Bacchae*

There is a tradition (albeit impugned)[9] that Euripides composed *Bacchae* in Macedonia before dying there in 406 BCE. Perhaps in 405 BCE, a tetralogy comprising *Bacchae*, *Iphigenia at Aulis*, *Alcmeon*, and (presumably) an unnamed satyr play, produced by 'Euripides the Younger' at the City Dionysia, won the tragic poet a fifth, posthumous victory in the city's premier dramatic competition.[10] The play was successful from its first production. Indeed, it has been suggested that it provoked a response in Aristophanes' *Frogs* even before it was staged.[11]

As well as being widely performed and read in educational contexts, *Bacchae* also prompted responses in Greek and Roman drama; some of these are difficult to pin on the *Bacchae* specifically, since the play itself was but one of several on Dionysian subjects with which it may have shared structures, themes, motifs and language.[12] As Dodds surmised, 'The πάθη of Dionysus, the patron god of drama, may well be the oldest of all dramatic subjects.'[13] *Bacchae* was thus only one entry in a series of tragedies about Pentheus, unfolding within a broader series of tragedies about Dionysus. Most notable of all the earlier plays on Dionysian themes were Aeschylus' *Lycurgeia* and so-called 'Theban tetralogy', both of which offer some parallels to the *Bacchae*.[14] Euripides clearly drew on the *Lycurgeia* in a number of ways.[15] At the same time, *Bacchae* also departs significantly, and influentially, from Aeschylus' treatment of the Pentheus episode in *Pentheus* and, more generally, from the 'standard' myth. In particular, the standard account prior to *Bacchae* appears to have had Pentheus losing a military engagement on Cithaeron; Euripides certainly bolstered Agave's role in the dramatic plot, and

---

9 Scullion 2003.
10 Σ Ar. *Ran.* 67; *Suda*, 'Euripides'; see Hall 2016 on audience reception of the first performance of *Bacchae* in Athens.
11 See Friesen 2015, 63–64; Kuch 1993, 548 (*Frogs* as post 404).
12 Greek tragedy in the fourth century and beyond, Kuch 1993; Easterling 1997; Gildenhard and Revermann 2010; Csapo *et al.* 2014; Kotlińska-Toma 2015. Dionysus and Greek drama, Dodds 1960, xxviii–xxxiii; Oranje 1984, 124–30; Bierl 1991; Dover 1993, 39–40. Euripides' influence in the fourth century, Xanthakis-Karamanos 1980, 28–34.
13 Dodds 1960, xxviii.
14 Dodds 1960, xxviii–xxxiii; Sommerstein 2016. See also Jouan 1992; Sommerstein 2008, 60–67 (*Edonians*), 18–23 (*Bassarids*), 126–29 (*Lycurgus*), 152–55 (*Youths*), 170–74 (*Wool-Carders*), 188–91 (*Pentheus*), 224–33 (*Semele*), 244–49 (*Archeresses*), 248–49 (*The Nurses of Dionysus*); and Sommerstein 2013.
15 Dodds 1960, xxxi–xxxii; Sommerstein 2008, 61; Sommerstein 2016 outlines the similarities and differences.

may well have introduced the cross-dressing theme.[16] But Euripides' play comes to eclipse all the other plays on the same subject, and its innovations characterize the standard version to which later ones respond.

Looking back half a millennium to the Golden Age of Athens, Plutarch mentions *Bacchae* in his assertion that the Athenians spent more money putting on dramatic performances than defending their liberty from the barbarians.[17] A beneficiary of the Macedonian defeat of Athens, Alexander is reputed to have quoted Tiresias' claim that 'on a fine subject it is no great task to speak well' (*Ba.* 266) in reply to Callisthenes who had just eulogized the Macedonians in an after-dinner speech.[18] Although tradition records that Alexander quoted other lines from Euripides, it is perhaps not surprising that he quoted from *Bacchae*: one biographical tradition holds that Euripides had spent the last years of his life at the Macedonian court, and Alexander's mother Olympias was famously a maenad.[19] Moreover, this quotation may be seen in the context of Alexander's Dionysian behaviour while on campaign.[20] Later in Hellenistic Alexandria, where Dionysus was intensely cultivated by the ruling Ptolemies,[21] Callimachus embeds a quotation of the *Bacchae* into an epigram:

Εὐμαθίην ᾐτεῖτο διδοὺς ἐμὲ Σῖμος ὁ Μίκκου
  ταῖς Μούσαις· αἱ δὲ Γλαῦκος ὅκως ἔδοσαν
ἀντ' ὀλίγου μέγα δῶρον. ἐγὼ δ' ἀνὰ τῇδε κεχηνὼς
  κεῖμαι τοῦ Σαμίου διπλόον ὁ τραγικὸς
παιδαρίων Διόνυσος ἐπήκοος· οἱ δὲ λέγουσιν
  'ἱερὸς ὁ πλόκαμος', τοὐμὸν ὄνειαρ ἐμοί. (*ep.* 48 Pf. = *AP* 6.310, *Ba.* 494)

Simos son of Mikkos gave me to the Muses, asking for
  success in school, and they, like Glaukos, gave
a great gift in return for a little. So I'm set here,
  my mouth open twice as wide as the Samian's, I,
Tragic Dionysos, listening to schoolboys recite
  for the millionth time, 'The lock is sacred...' (tr. Nisetich)

---

16 Aeschylus' Pentheus as a soldier-king who dies in battle: Aesch. *Eum.* 24–26; March 1989; Sommerstein 2016, 33. Mythical innovation and cross-dressing in *Bacchae*: Buxton 2013, 219–40
17 *Glor. Ath.* 6. = *Mor.* 349A3.
18 Plut. *Alex.* 53.4, *Ba.* 266; see Sandys *ad loc.*
19 Lane Fox 1973, 44–48.
20 See Bosworth 1996, 120.
21 Rice 1983; Dunand 1986; Cusset 2001, 14–18.

The epigram purports to mark the votive dedication of a tragic Dionysus mask that hangs in a schoolroom, weary of listening to schoolchildren recite their lessons. The concluding quotation from *Bacchae* suggests that the play was well established as a school text in the third century – one of its most 'numinous' lines has become hackneyed.[22] Indeed, not only was *Bacchae* included in the ten-play 'selected' edition of Euripides, but a second-century (?) BCE papyrus from Egypt, P.Tebt III.901, contains the beginnings of the first verse of the play copied out multiple times in a schoolboy's hand.[23] From the point of view of Ptolemaic religious politics, it is significant that in order to assert continuity with earlier Greek literature and culture, Callimachus alludes under the sign of Dionysus to an episode of Homer which mentions Dionysus, and to Euripides' *Bacchae*.[24]

The early Roman dramatists wrote plays on Dionysian subjects, which may have thematised Roman responses to Dionysus and Greek culture in ways that are now difficult to recover.[25] Of these, the surviving fragments of Accius' *Bacchae* are in a separate category, since their closeness to Euripides' version suggests that Accius' play may have been a relatively close adaptation. Scholars have examined in depth the cultural resonances of Accius' lexical choices as a translator.[26] For example, the 'Cadmeian' (Theban) women are 'translated' into *matronae*, with a thick layering of vocabulary rich with Roman resonances (Eur. *Ba*. 35–36; Acc. *Ba*. 235–36 R²⁻³= 406-8 Dangel):

καὶ πᾶν τὸ θῆλυ σπέρμα Καδμείων, ὅσαι
γυναῖκες ἦσαν, ἐξέμηνα δωμάτων·

deinde omni stirpe cum incluta Cadmeide
vagant matronae percitatae insania

This brief example shows Euripides' classic text being freighted with cultural associations as it is translated into the Romans' poetic language.[27]

---

22 See Gow and Page 1975, II.183.
23 Cribiore 1996, #129 (p. 204) with plate XIV. For papyrus citations see Austin 2005.
24 Ll. 2–3 allude to *Il.* 6.234–36; Lycurgus' persecution of Dionysus and subsequent punishment has featured at 6.130–43.
25 See Mac Góráin, Introduction, pp. 8–9.
26 See Mariotti 1965; Zimmermann 2002; and Rosato 2005, 155–99.
27 For a re-use by Virgil see Mac Góráin 2013, 133.

Performances

Modern criticism identifies Dionysus as a god of performance. He presided over the dramatic festival at Athens, and there were performative dimensions to his worship, both within and beyond drama. One response to the ancient complaint that certain plays had 'nothing to do with Dionysus' has been to point to the 'change of identity' brought about by participation in both drama and mystery cult, a view which sees performance itself as inherently Dionysian.[28] We turn now to the ancient evidence for performances of the *Bacchae*, real or imagined, complete or partial, focussing on what they tell us about *Bacchae* and attitudes to Dionysus. Once again, the Latin sources, or those Greek ones that bear on Roman or Italian affairs, have distinct resonances that suggest a contrast between Greek and Roman attitudes to Dionysian worship.

An anecdote from Diogenes Laertius' biography of Aristippus places Plato and Aristippus together at the court of Dionysius II of Syracuse.[29]

> καί ποτε παρὰ πότον κελεύσαντος Διονυσίου ἕκαστον ἐν πορφυρᾷ ἐσθῆτι ὀρχήσασθαι, τὸν μὲν Πλάτωνα μὴ προσέσθαι, εἰπόντα·
> "οὐκ ἂν δυναίμην θῆλυν ἐνδῦναι στολήν." [Eur. Ba. 836, spoken by Pentheus]
> τὸν δ' Ἀρίστιππον λαβόντα καὶ μέλλοντα ὀρχήσασθαι εὐστόχως εἰπεῖν·
> "καὶ γὰρ ἐν βακχεύμασιν
> οὖσ' ἥ γε σώφρων οὐ διαφθαρήσεται." [Eur. Ba. 317-8, spoken by Tiresias] (Diog. Laert. 2.78)

> One day Dionysius over the wine commanded everybody to put on purple and dance. Plato declined, quoting the line:
> "I could not put on a women's robe."
> Aristippus, however, put on the dress and, as he was about to dance, was ready with the repartee:
> "Even amid the Bacchic revelry
> She who has self-control will not be corrupted." (tr. R. D. Hicks, adapted)

The quotations and capping suggest the play's cultural currency. They also characterize the two philosophers' positions: Plato's austere reluctance to play-act echoes Socrates' hostility to mimetic poetry in the *Republic*, while Aristippus responds with opportunistic pragmatism. The context of the quotations matters too: Plato makes himself the loser by quoting Pentheus from moments before his transvestite downfall, while Aristippus quotes Tiresias' response to Pentheus'

---

28 Seaford 2006, 102 and in general on Dionysus and theatre, 87–104.
29 For other versions, some of which place the story in Macedonia, see Swift Riginos 1976, 106–7.

suspicions about the corruption of women in Dionysian ritual. Clearly, then, the exchange replays the conflict in the *Bacchae* between philosophical and prurient or moralizing attitudes to the cult; and Aristippus' victory suggests that Dionysian ecstasy, even if it begins with pretence or performance, is a more successful path to philosophical enlightenment.[30]

As for dramatic performances proper, we know that the play could be performed in part as well as in its entirety. A second-century BCE inscription from Delphi records that a certain Satyros performed, in the stadium, 'a song with a chorus, "Dionysus", and a *kitharisma* from Euripides' *Bacchae*' – whatever that means (*SIG*³ 648B).[31] In greater and more arresting detail, Plutarch describes the performance of a scene from the *Bacchae* (we do not know whether it was a complete production), in which the head of Crassus, killed in the battle of Carrhae in 53 BCE, is used as a stage-prop for the head of Pentheus. The context is that Hyrodes II, the king of Parthia, is visiting the court of the Armenian king Artavasdes II. The two have recently been reconciled, and their reconciliation is cemented by the engagement of Hyrodes' son Pacorus to the sister of Artavasdes. According to Plutarch, both kings were well acquainted with Greek language and literature, and the performance is part of the engagement festivities.[32] The head of Crassus is brought in and greeted with jubilation by the Parthians. Jason of Tralles, the tragic actor, sets aside his Pentheus costume, takes hold of the head of Crassus, and in a state of Dionysian frenzy (ἀναβακχεύσας) sings these lines of Agave as if divinely inspired (μετ' ἐνθουσιασμοῦ):

[5] φέρομεν ἐξ ὄρεος
ἕλικα νεότομον ἐπὶ μέλαθρα,
μακάριον θήραμα.
[6]
καὶ ταῦτα μὲν πάντας ἔτερπεν· ᾀδομένων δὲ τῶν ἑξῆς ἀμοιβαίων πρὸς τὸν χορόν
{<A.>} τίς ἐφόνευσεν;
{<B.>} ἐμὸν τὸ γέρας,
ἀναπηδήσας ὁ Ἐξάθρης – ἐτύγχανε γὰρ δειπνῶν – ἀντελαμβάνετο τῆς κεφαλῆς, ὡς αὐτῷ λέγειν ταῦτα μᾶλλον ἢ ἐκείνῳ προσῆκον. [7] ἡσθεὶς δ' ὁ βασιλεὺς τὸν μὲν οἷς πάτριόν ἐστιν ἐδωρήσατο, τῷ δ' Ἰάσονι τάλαντον ἔδωκεν. εἰς τοιοῦτόν φασιν ἐξόδιον τὴν Κράσσου στρατηγίαν ὥσπερ τραγῳδίαν τελευτῆσαι. (Plut. *Crass*. 33)[33]

---

30 On philosophy and wisdom in *Bacchae* see Oranje 1984, 156–66; Navarro González 2016.
31 See Csapo and Slater 1995, 45 (I.108); Chandezon 1998, 55; Prauscello 2006, 109.
32 There is some basis to the claim of these rulers' Greek culture; see Bertinelli 1993, 421–22; Sauron 2007, 254; Stepanyan 2015.
33 On the accuracy of the quotation see Seaford 1996, 243.

> We bring from the mountain
> A tendril fresh-cut to the palace,
> A wonderful prey.
> This delighted everybody; but when the following dialogue with the chorus was chanted:
> (Chorus) 'Who slew him?'
> (Agave) 'Mine is the honour,'
>
> Pomaxathres [or 'Exathres', the man who had killed Crassus], who happened to be one of the banqueters, sprang up and laid hold of the head, feeling that it was more appropriate for him to say this than for Jason. The king was delighted, and bestowed on Pomaxathres (or Exathres; the text is uncertain) the customary gifts, while to Jason He gave a talent. With such a farce as this the expedition of Crassus is said to have closed, just like a tragedy. (tr. Perrin)

Whether the story is genuine or a fiction,[34] for Plutarch it shows life imitating tragedy. Indeed Plutarch often draws on tragic and Dionysian motifs to illustrate character.[35] In this case, as David Braund has shown, structures and motifs taken from *Bacchae* cast Crassus as a Pentheus-like figure who brings about his own tragic downfall.[36] The cultural layering of the story is especially noteworthy given this volume's focus on Roman attitudes to Dionysus: Plutarch with his Greek eye records 'Easterners' (Parthians and Armenians) putting on Greek drama, and this becoming the occasion to celebrate the Parthian defeat of Rome. Within this nexus of cultural interactions, the anecdote replays the 'Easterner' Dionysus' defeat of the 'Westerner' Pentheus, particularly if we cast Crassus as an embodiment of Roman hostility to the Bacchanalia, and suspicion of the 'Eastern' Dionysus.[37]

A couple of epigrams from the Greek Anthology comment on pantomimic renditions of *Bacchae*, pantomime being a performance art in which one actor wordlessly dances all the parts.[38] Pylades of Cilicia was a leading exponent of

---

34 Credulous: Kotlińska-Toma 2015, 156–158; skeptical: Easterling 1997, 221.
35 Pelling 1988; Pelling 1999; Mossman 1988.
36 Braund 1993; *Crassus* is paired with *Nicias*, which also ends with tragic catastrophe and quotation; see Braund 1993, 469 and Bertinelli 1993, 422; Zadorojniy 1997.
37 See also Sauron 2007, 254–55.
38 On the form see Garelli 2007; Hall and Wyles 2008; Manuwald 2011, 184–86. On these poems see Gow-Page 1968, II, 80–81, 209–10; Garelli 2007, 164–68; Hall 2008, 22; Hunt 2008, 175; Alonso Fernández 2013, 194–97.

tragic pantomime in Augustan Rome, and may have been a freedman of Augustus.[39] Antipater of Thessalonica eulogizes Pylades performing what looks like it may have been based on the *Bacchae* (*AP* 16.290):

> Αὐτὸν βακχευτὴν ἐνέδυ θεόν, ἡνίκα βάκχας
> ἐκ Θηβῶν Ἰταλὴν ἤγαγε πρὸς θυμέλην,
> ἀνθρώποις Πυλάδης τερπνὸν δέος, οἷα χορεύων
> δαίμονος ἀκρήτου πᾶσαν ἔπλησε πόλιν.
> Θῆβαι γιγνώσκουσι τὸν ἐκ πυρός· οὐράνιος δὲ
> οὗτος ὁ παμφώνοις χερσὶ λοχευόμενος.

When he brought the Bacchants from Thebes to the Italian stage, Pylades put on the form of the Bacchanal god himself, to all men's delight and terror, for by his dancing he filled the whole city with that deity's intemperate fury. Thebes knows the one born of fire; the heavenly god is this one here, brought to birth by these all-expressive hands. (tr. Gow-Page, ep. 78)

This epigram shuttles between the world of *Bacchae* and the pantomime's world, a slippage appropriate to the metatheatricality of the *Bacchae*. Pylades, himself an Eastern migrant to Rome, is credited with having brought the bacchants (or *Bacchae*, an allusion to the play by its title) from Thebes to the Italian stage, picking up from how Dionysus had brought the bacchants from the East to Thebes. The poem plays on several elements from *Bacchae*. There is emphasis on the god's birth (λοχευόμενος), recreated by Pylades with all-expressive hands rather than voice. The word ἐνέδυ picks up on the theme of acting and dressing in *Bacchae* (cf. Pentheus' ἐνδῦναι at 836, quoted by 'Plato', above). The oxymoronic phrase ἀνθρώποις Πυλάδης τερπνὸν δέος is reminiscent of Dionysus' self-description as most terrible but most gentle to mortals (*Ba.* 861 δεινότατος, ἀνθρώποισι δ' ἠπιώτατος).[40] Pylades' animation of the city (Rome) with untempered frenzy (δαίμονος ἀκρήτου πᾶσαν ἔπλησε πόλιν) evokes the filling of the wine-bowl, but also, by alluding to Thebes in the grip of a Dionysian frenzy (cf. Cadmus at 1295, πᾶσά τ' ἐξεβακχεύθη πόλις), implies the suggestibility of Rome to Dionysian infatuation.

The other epigram (*AP* 16.289) describes a dancer (according to the MSS the otherwise unknown Xenophon of Smyrna) miming a series of Dionysian parts in what could be a version of *Bacchae* (some scenes are omitted):

---

39 See also *AP* 9.248 on Pylades' playing the role of Dionysus, with possible allusion to *Bacchae*. On Pylades see Jory 2003 and 2004; Garelli 2007, esp. 147–208; Hunt 2008.
40 Cf. Hor. *Odes* 3.25.18 *dulce periculum*, on which Nisbet-Rudd 2004 cite τερπνὸν δέος.

> Αὐτὸν ὁρᾶν Ἰόβακχον ἐδόξαμεν, ἡνίκα Ληναις
> ὁ πρέσβυς νεαρῆς ἦρχε χοροιμανίης,
> καὶ Κάδμου τὰ πάρηβα χορεύματα καὶ τὸν ἀφ' ὕλης
> ἄγγελον, εὐιακῶν ἰχνελάτην θιάσων,
> καὶ τὴν εὐάζουσαν ἐν αἵματι παιδὸς Ἀγαυὴν
> λυσσάδα. φεῦ θείης ἀνδρὸς ὑποκρισίης.

> We thought we were looking at Bacchus himself when the old man lustily led the maenads in their furious dance, and played Cadmus tripping it in the fall of his years, and the messenger coming from the forest where he had spied on the rout of the Bacchants, and frenzied Agave exulting in the blood of her son. Heavens! how divine was the man's acting. (tr. Paton)

Apart from the structural correspondences with the *Bacchae* – the sequence of scenes from parodos through the first scene with Cadmus, the first messenger speech, the Agave scene – there are a number of matching details: from the emphasis on Cadmus' old-man dancing to the echo in ἰχνελάτην of the hunting imagery that pervades the *Bacchae* to Agave's exultation.[41] More generally, the viewer's impression that the actor had embodied Bacchus, down to the appreciation of the man's divine acting, θείης ἀνδρὸς ὑποκρισίης, resonates with the idea of acting a role (at least in a festival for Dionysos) as a form of worship offered to the god of drama himself. But more than that, the first line Αὐτὸν ὁρᾶν Ἰόβακχον ἐδόξαμεν echoes Pentheus' words to the disguised Dionysus as he experiences the hallucination (or clairvoyance) of infatuation (918–19):

> καὶ μὴν ὁρᾶν μοι δύο μὲν ἡλίους δοκῶ, > ὁρᾶν ... ἐδόξαμεν
> δισσὰς δὲ Θήβας καὶ πόλισμ' ἑπτάστομον·

Pentheus sees double, and in a sense the poet does too: he sees Bacchus while recognizing that it is the actor, but is nonetheless affected by the Dionysian performance. The focus on performance in both of these epigrams, and the troping of performance as ritual, seems to point to the way in which the *Bacchae* uses metatheatre and (per Seaford) allusions to mystery initiation to present ritual as performance.

Like Plutarch's Crassus story, these epigrams see their subject with Greek eyes, and it is not surprising that even in Augustan Rome, Dionysus should have been so warmly celebrated in the world of theatrical performance. Tacitus' perspective on a Dionysian masquerade is rather different, as we would expect from

---

[41] Cadmus' age: 185–89, 193, 252; hunting: *Ba.* 227–28, 231, 453, 730, 846–47; Agave's exultation: 1198.

a sober Roman historian. We conclude this section with Messalina's bacchanal (*Ann.* 11.31).

> at Messalina non alias solutior luxu, adulto autumno simulacrum vindemiae per domum celebrabat. urgeri prela, fluere lacus; et feminae pellibus accinctae adsultabant ut sacrificantes vel insanientes Bacchae; ipsa crine fluxo thyrsum quatiens, iuxtaque Silius hedera vinctus, gerere cothurnos, iacere caput, strepente circum procaci choro. ferunt Vettium Valentem lascivia in praealtam arborem conisum, interrogantibus quid aspiceret, respondisse tempestatem ab Ostia atrocem, sive coeperat ea species, seu forte lapsa vox in praesagium vertit.

> Meanwhile Messalina, never before more unrestrained in her debauchery, was celebrating a mock-vintage in the house at the height of autumn. The wine presses were being trodden, the vats were overflowing, and women girt in animal skins were leaping about like maenads sacrificing or out of their minds. Messalina herself was shaking the thyrsus with her hair flowing, Silius beside her wreathed in ivy, wearing tragic buskins, tossing his head about, a wanton chorus shrieking around them. The story goes that Vettius Valens climbed up a very tall tree as a joke. When asked what he could see, he replied "a frightful storm from Ostia." So either something resembling a storm was on the horizon, or maybe a chance word let fall turned into a prophecy.

The passage intervenes between Messalina's 'marriage' to her lover Silius and her downfall.[42] The excessive Dionysian scenario, a perversion of what might have been a benign vintage celebration, characterizes Messalina as depraved, licentious and transgressing the boundaries of her sex.[43] Tacitus introduced the sequence of the 'marriage' between Messalina and Silius as 'like a drama' (*fabulosum*, 11.27.1), and there is a cluster of theatrical motifs, notably Silius' buskins and the shrieking chorus. The first words of the paragraph, *At Messalina*, have a stagey quality to them, as if marking the empress' entry.[44] While the Julio-Claudian court was no stranger to performances formal or metaphorical,[45] there is specific recollection here of *Bacchae* as Vettius Valens climbs up the tree, re-enacting Pentheus' spying on the maenads.[46] He exclaims that there is a storm on the horizon, which may look to the onrush of the maenads from *Bacchae* 1088–95 as

---

[42] On the passage, see most recently Alonso Fernández 2013, 188–91.
[43] Santoro L'hoir 2006, 234–37; Stackelberg 2009, 615–19.
[44] See Quinn 1968, 135 on *At Regina*, which occurs three times in *Aeneid* 4 (1, 296, 504), like a stage direction marking the queen's entry.
[45] Bartsch 1994.
[46] La Penna 1975; Henrichs 1978, 159.

Agave and her sisters close in on Pentheus.⁴⁷ Allusion to the *Bacchae* is an enriching element in the story, whether or not Tacitus found it in his sources.⁴⁸ It contributes to the censorious Roman tone, which resonates with other instances of Roman antipathy to maenadism or Dionysian swagger as expressions of political evil – from Livy's critique of the Bacchanalia to hostile accounts of Mark Antony's theatrical Bacchism.⁴⁹ We may conclude that performances of various kinds have thematised cultural attitudes to Bacchus as well as the philosophical and metatheatrical dimensions of Euripides' *Bacchae*.

Narratives

Bacchae proved a fertile source of inspiration for authors writing in narrative modes, whether epic or epyllion, the mythical digression in didactic poetry, or prose chronicle. Narrative retellings focussed on some of the same aspects of *Bacchae* that were emphasized in accounts of the play's performance, including the conjuring of the god's presence and the phenomenology of Dionysian possession. All of the narratives which we consider here are to a greater or lesser extent exercised by the justice and morality of the killing of Pentheus, and may be seen as engaging in a debate about the most problematic aspect of the play. In each case there is some response to the *sparagmos* of Pentheus, a motif which also made its way into the Euripidean biographical tradition.⁵⁰

The earliest surviving retelling is Theocritus' twenty-sixth poem, titled 'Lenae, or Bacchae' in the MSS and the Antinoe papyrus. This brief epyllion narrates the commencement of Bacchic ritual by Ino, Autonoe and Agave, followed by

---

47 So, La Penna 1975, 122–23.
48 Malloch 2013, 432 suggests Tacitus may not have made it up.
49 See Jaccottet 2008, 204.
50 On sparagmos in Euripides' biography see Lefkowitz 2012, 93, and Billings 2018, 68–70 for Nietzsche's reception of this idea. The sparagmos in fragment 33v of Dionysius' *Bassarica* may allude to Euripides' *Bacchae*; see Benaissa 2018, 180–83. Lucian relates an anecdote about Demetrius the Cynic at *Adv. Ind.* 19, "Once in Corinth Demetrius the Cynic found some illiterate person reading aloud from a very handsome volume, the *Bacchae* of Euripides, I think it was. He had got to the place where the messenger is relating the destruction of Pentheus by Agave, when Demetrius snatched the book from him and tore it in two: 'Better,' he exclaimed, 'that Pentheus should suffer one rending at my hands than many at yours.'" (tr. Fowler and Fowler)

Pentheus' *sparagmos* at their hands, and concluding with a moralizing intervention in the poet's voice.[51] The poem's debt to *Bacchae* is clear, even though Theocritus omits a great deal, and scholarly expressions of the allusive relationship vary.[52] The poem re-uses Euripides' pun on the name Pentheus[53] as the women carry the dismembered man back to Thebes:

ἐς Θήβας δ' ἀφίκοντο πεφυρμέναι αἵματι πᾶσαι,
ἐξ ὄρεος πένθημα καὶ οὐ Πενθῆα φέροισαι. (25–26)

They all arrive in Thebes bepurpled with blood,
carrying pain and not Pentheus from the mountain.

The major apparent addition is the poet's moralizing (and textually uncertain)[54] reflection on the story before concluding with a hymnic farewell to Dionysos, Semele, and her sisters:

Οὐκ ἀλέγω· μηδ' ἄλλος ἀπεχθομένῳ Διονύσῳ
φροντίζοι, μηδ' εἰ χαλεπώτερα τῶνδε μογήσαι,
εἴη ἐννάετης ἢ καὶ δεκάτῳ ἐπιβαίνοι·
αὐτὸς δ' εὐαγέοιμι καὶ εὐαγέεσσιν ἅδοιμι.   30
ἐκ Διὸς αἰγιόχω τιμὰν ἔχει αἰετὸς οὕτως.
εὐσεβέων παίδεσσι τὰ λώια, δυσσεβέων δ' οὔ.
Χαίροι μὲν Διόνυσος, ὃν ἐν Δρακάνῳ νιφόεντι
Ζεὺς ὕπατος μεγάλαν ἐπιγουνίδα κάτθετο λύσας·
χαίροι δ' εὐειδὴς Σεμέλα καὶ ἀδελφεαὶ αὐτᾶς,   35
Καδμεῖαι πολλαῖς μεμελημέναι ἡρωίναις,
αἳ τόδε ἔργον ἔρεξαν ὀρίναντος Διονύσῳ
οὐκ ἐπιμωματόν. μηδεὶς τὰ θεῶν ὀνόσαιτο.

I care not. And let not another care for an enemy of Dionysus—not though he suffer a fate more grievous than this and be in his ninth year or entering on his tenth. But for myself may I be pure and pleasing in the eyes of the pure. So has the eagle honour of aegis-bearing Zeus. To the children of the righteous, not of the unrighteous, comes the better fate. Farewell to Dionysus, whom Lord Zeus set down on snowy Dracanus when he had opened his mighty

---

51 On this poem see Van Groningen 1963; Griffiths 1979, 98–104; Cairns 1992; Cusset 1997 and 2001; Sistakou 2016, 115–21. Cusset 2001 reads the sparagmos of Pentheus in metapoetic terms as the evil lot in store for a bad poet.
52 Gow 1952 II: 476, 'There are verbal reminiscences of the *Bacchae*, but the story is differently set … and the debt to Euripides is slight.' Contrast Dover 1971, 263–64; Cairns 1992, 5–8; Cusset 1997, 455; Friesen 2015, 76–81.
53 Eur. *Ba*. 367–8, 508, 1244.
54 See Gow 1952 II, xxx.

thigh. Farewell to comely Semela and her sisters, Cadmean dames honoured of many a heroine, who, at Dionysus' instigation, did this deed, wherein is no blame. At the acts of gods let no man cavil. (tr. Gow)

The poet's asseveration of loyalty to Dionysus in the face of a cruel kin killing at the god's bidding seems to respond to the end of *Bacchae*. Cadmus criticizes Dionysus, telling him that he goes too far, and that gods should not resemble mortals in their anger: ἀλλ' ἐπεξέρχηι λίαν ... ὀργὰς πρέπει θεοὺς οὐχ ὁμοιοῦσθαι βροτοῖς. (1346–8). Dionysus' response, that Zeus ordained these things long ago (1394), may inform Theocritus' appeal in 26.31 to Zeus as the overseer of piety. The poem, then, takes Dionysus' side against Pentheus and the Thebans, a stance which may be read in line with Ptolemaic religious politics and in the context of Ptolemaic patronage of Theocritus.[55] Nonetheless, we find Hunter's suggestion, that the end of Theocritus 26 reflects ongoing debate about the meaning of *Bacchae*, persuasive.[56]

Theocritus' partisan reading seems to have provoked a response in the *Cynegetica*, a poem attributed to Oppian, but in fact penned by a different poet in second-century CE Syria.[57] The story of Dionysus and Pentheus is rewritten within a digression at *Cynegetica* 4.230–353, the aetiology for the practice whereby hunters befuddle panthers by mixing wine with their water; within this digression, a substantial narrative runs from Dionysus' Theban homecoming to Pentheus' death (4.287–319). Pentheus ignores the advice of Cadmus and Agave (292) and orders the imprisonment of the god. In a wild mythological innovation, the maenads, but apparently not including Agave, pray that Dionysus will turn them into raw-meat-eating beasts, and Pentheus of ill-omened name (Πενθῆα δυσώνυμον, 4.305 – that pun again) into a bull, so that they can eat the young king. He does so, and they 'divide' Pentheus among themselves: δάσαντο, 4.315 – the word has echoes of feasting, as well as of divvying up spoils. There is, again as in Theocritus 26, a concluding moral from the narrator:

τοιάδ' ἀείδοιμεν, τοῖα φρεσὶ πιστεύοιμεν·
ὅσσα Κιθαιρῶνος δὲ κατὰ πτύχας ἔργα γυναικῶν,
ἢ μυσαρὰς κείνας, τὰς ἀλλοτρίας Διονύσου,
μητέρας οὐχ ὁσίως ψευδηγορέουσιν ἀοιδοί.

---

55 Cusset 2001, 15–18; Friesen 2015, 81–84.
56 Hunter 2006, 47.
57 Hopkinson 1994, 197–204; Englhofer 1995, 169–73; Bartley 2003, 129–49; Sestili 2010, 275–77. Hopkinson 1994, 198, pointing out similarities with epyllia like Theocritus 26, suggests the possibility of a lost Hellenistic original.

> This is the sort of thing we should sing about; this is the sort of thing we should believe in our hearts.
> Those deeds of women in the valleys of Mount Cithaeron,
> Or those loathsome mothers, alien to Dionysus –
> Those are impure lies told by poets. (4.316-9)

This is a marked intervention in the reception of *Bacchae*. The phrase Κιθαιρῶνος ... κατὰ πτύχας would seem to signal *Bacchae*, and Euripides and Theocritus are obvious candidates for the ἀοιδοί.[58] The poet has also extended the *sparagmos*, drawing on the Pentheus-as-if-animal theme in *Bacchae*, by means of a double metamorphosis – it is not quite the same thing for panthers to kill a bull as for maenads to kill Pentheus – and removed Agave from the killing, while still making Dionysus' transformative power supply the proximate means of sparagmos. In tragedy and especially in *Bacchae*, Dionysus is often represented, addressed, or imagined as a bull.[59] Pentheus himself does so in his first lines of the cross-dressing scene (920-2). Pentheus-as-an-actual-bull in the *Cynegetica* thus performs both a rewriting of myth and an interpretative rereading of Euripides' play *qua* Dionysiac text; ritual echoes are decoded back into mythical narrative, as Dionysus transforms Pentheus – literally, this time – into a sacrificial animal. And yet, in an ironic reversal of Dionysiac purity (ὅσιος and ὁσία are frequent in the *Bacchae*), the old, *Euripidean* story is an impure one for bards to tell (οὐχ ὁσίως). The poet of the *Cynegetica*, then, has capped Theocritus, implying that it is impious to reproduce the Euripidean version, let alone endorse its morality.[60] The *Cynegetica* poet performs what the narrator of Theocritus 26 only suggests: a pro-Dionysian rereading of *Bacchae* which sanitizes the myth without hobbling Dionysus. As such, the *Cynegetica* bears witness to the enduring pull of *sparagmos*, but also to the well-established notion that *Bacchae* is a locus for religious controversies.

Ovid's retelling of the *Bacchae* (*Met.* 3.511-733) during his Theban history works off multiple sources including the *Bacchae* itself, but also the Homeric

---

[58] *Ba*. 62 ἐς Κιθαιρῶνος πτυχὰς; 797 ἐν Κιθαιρῶνος πτυχαῖς; 945 τὰς Κιθαιρῶνος πτυχὰς; 1219 ἐν Κιθαιρῶνος πτυχαῖς.
[59] *Ba*. 100, 1017, 1159 (Chorus); Pentheus himself mistakes a bull for Dionysus (618) and vice versa (920-22); Agaue mistakes Pentheus' head for that of a bullock (μόσχος, 1185). Seaford 1996 *ad* 920-22 sees a ritual element in Pentheus' vision of Dionysus-as-bull.
[60] Bartley 2003 on *Cyn*. 316, these final lines 'could almost be read as a direct answer to Theocritus 26.27-32'.

Hymn (7) to Dionysus, prose mythography, Virgil's reworking of Euripides' *Bacchae*, and perhaps Pacuvius' *Pentheus* (if indeed this play existed).[61] It shares with *Bacchae* themes of vision and spectatorship, which in Ovid stretch from Tiresias' inner vision to the visual dynamics of the killing of Pentheus.[62] Ovid's main structural coup is to replace the dialogue scenes between Pentheus and the Stranger of the *Bacchae* with an interview between Pentheus and Acoetes, in which Acoetes relates the story of the Tyrrhenian pirates from the Homeric hymn as a cautionary tale. The pirates are metamorphosed into dolphins, in line with the binding principle of Ovid's epic. This splicing of *Bacchae* and the hymn points up similarities between them: they hinge mainly on theodicy, but after the pirates have been metamorphosed into dolphins, they gambol about as if forming a chorus (*inque chori ludunt speciem*, 3.685), perhaps a nod to the Bacchic chorus of Euripides' play. Acoetes is ostensibly a devotee of the god, but there is a hint that he is Dionysus in disguise when he quips that no god is more present than he (*nec enim praesentior illo | est deus*, 3.658–9); this in turn may point to the ultimate indeterminacy of the identity of the Stranger in *Bacchae*, who purports to be a devotee of the god, but whom we assume to be Dionysus in disguise.[63] Ovid's Pentheus echoes Euripides', most notably the charge that the rites of Dionysus are fake (*commentaque sacra*, 3.558 ~ πλασταῖσι βακχείαισιν, *Ba.* 218), but his anti-Dionysian rhetoric also has a distinctly Roman feel: he echoes the xenophobic taunts of Virgil's Latins,[64] and even some of the criticisms of the Bacchic cult found in Livy's Bacchanalian narrative, which are themselves indebted to Pentheus in Euripides' *Bacchae*.[65] When the inevitable sparagmos happens, it fulfils an expectation created by Tiresias' pun earlier in the episode: he warns Pentheus that unless he bows to the god: *mille lacer spargere locis* (3.522), 'you will be scattered about in a thousand places'. The sparagmos itself is predicated on a perceptual metamorphosis which Ovid found ready-made in Euripides: the god makes Agave mistake Pentheus for a wild beast. But while the killing of Pentheus is the devastating climax of the *Bacchae*, Ovid reduces it to a scene of almost comic bathos.

---

61 On the episode see Feldherr 1997, Keith 2002 (sources), Barchiesi 2007 and Godwin 2014 (commentaries), Janan 2009 (Lacanian study), Miller 2016 (mythographic source). For Virgil's use of *Bacchae* see Mac Góráin 2013. On Pacuvius' *Pentheus* see Schierl 2006, 418–22.
62 See Feldherr 1997, 28 and Hardie 2002, 166–72.
63 Much to the derision of Dodds 1960, xlviii–l, Norwood and Verrall believed that the stranger was in fact a devotee of the god.
64 At 3.531–63 he gives a cartoon version of an already cartoonish speech by Numanus at *Aen.* 9.598–620.
65 For correspondences between Ovid, *Met.* 3.511ff. and Livy 39.10–16, see Freyburger 2013, 99.

> saucius ille tamen 'fer opem, matertera' dixit
> 'Autonoe! moveant animos Actaeonis umbrae!' 720
> illa, quis Actaeon, nescit dextramque precanti
> abstulit, Inoo lacerata est altera raptu.
> non habet infelix quae matri bracchia tendat,
> trunca sed ostendens dereptis vulnera membris
> 'adspice, mater!' ait. visis ululavit Agaue 725
> collaque iactavit movitque per aera crinem
> avulsumque caput digitis conplexa cruentis
> clamat: 'io comites, opus hoc victoria nostra est!'

> Stricken, he still shouts 'Help me, aunt Autonoë! Let Actaeon's shade move your spirit! She, not remembering Actaeon, tears away the suppliant's right arm. Ino, in frenzy, rips off the other. Now the unhappy man has no limbs to hold out to his mother, but, showing his wounded trunk shorn of its members, he cries 'Mother, see!' Agave howls, and twists her neck about, and thrashes her hair in the air, and tearing off his head, holding it in her bloody hands, shouts 'Behold, sisters, this act marks our victory!' (tr. Kline)

The link with the killing of Actaeon is familiar from *Bacchae* – it may have been in Aeschylus' *Lycurgeia*[66] – and Nonnus will later re-use it, but the darkly comic touch comes in lines 723–25: Pentheus cannot perform a supplication since he has no arms and instead shows the wounds where his arms once were; Agave shrieks and rips off his head. Ovid's aesthetic choice may be a response to the grave tone of the tragic scenes involving Dionysian madness in Virgil's *Aeneid*.

Antiquity's last epic retelling of the story was by Nonnus, who devoted three books (44–46) of his forty-eight book *Dionysiaca* to the 'Pentheid.' The debt to *Bacchae* is clear, even though Nonnus makes the story entirely his own with significant additions and variations.[67] As in Ovid's version, the story of the Tyrrhenian pirates is told to warn Pentheus about the risks of impiety, this time by Tiresias (45.105–68). As to the justice of the dénouement, one major difference is that Nonnus' Pentheus is more evil and less balanced a character than Euripides'. Early on in the story, we learn that he seized the ancestral throne (κοιρανίην πατρώιον ἥρπασε, 44.50), which prompts Agave to have a disturbing dream about his *sparagmos*, though she does not recognize herself as the wild beast in it. In a confrontation with the disguised Dionysus, Pentheus himself insists that the story of Dionysus' parentage from Zeus is a lie, but says that he wishes it were true so that he could have the son of Zeus as his prey (44.49–51). Alongside the

---

66 See Sommerstein 2016.
67 *Bacchae* and the 'Pentheid': Tissoni 1998, 63–71; Shorrock 2001, 195; Simon 2004, 130–32; Perris 2015, 509–11; Friesen 2015, 238–50; see also Accorinti 2016, index s.v. 'Pentheus'.

accentuation of Pentheus' hybris, Nonnus' Dionysus feels pity for human suffering, in a marked departure from Euripides' Dionysus.[68] 'Dionysus felt respect (ἠδέσσατο) for old Kadmos in his grief. With a face/mask free of sadness (ἀπενθήτου[69] δὲ προσώπου), he mixed a tear with a smile and brought Agave back to her senses' (46.268–70). And then: 'So the women, downcast, mourned, while lord Bacchus, looking on, felt pity (ἐλέαιρε) for them' (46.357). This newfound mercy on the part of Dionysus is one of several elements in the *Dionysiaca* which have led scholars to a Christian(izing) reading of the poem and its protagonist.[70] If we accept these Christianizing readings, then we may see Nonnus' retelling pulling *Bacchae* into a Christian story, and thus into a Roman story, perhaps in response to the literary strategies of New Testament authors (see the next section).

One of the most fascinating ancient retellings of *Bacchae* is also one of the latest. Johannes Malalas' *Chronographia* (sixth century CE), a Greek prose chronicle, retells world history from the creation of Adam to the reign of Justinian; the fifteenth chapter of Book Two tells the story of Pentheus from the betrothal of Agave to the deaths of Pentheus and Dionysus.[71] Malalas' is a late-Roman, Antiochene-Constantinopolitan, Christian worldview, in which the Incarnation is the turning-point in world history, secular history is Romanized, mythical gods and heroes are rationalized as kings, and, most saliently, Olympian gods are dehellenized.[72] Malalas' mythographic *modus scribendi* can broadly be described as euhemeristic.[73] Polymedon, a man of the senatorial class descended from Picus Zeus, seduces Semele, and she gives birth prematurely to a mortal son: Dionysus, later to be deified for discovering grapevines. Jealous of Pentheus' position as de facto ruler of the Theban empire (βασιλεία), Dionysus returns from the East to Thebes with an army, works miracles, teaches mysteries (to his female relatives),

---

[68] Tissoni 1998, 335–36; Friesen 2015, 247–49. Simon 2004, 253 notes, but does not comment on, Dionysus' pity. Perris 2011 addresses pity and audience response in *Bacchae*.
[69] The Pentheus/penthos pun has been faithfully reproduced at 46.73–74.
[70] See Tissoni 1998, 71–79, prefigured to some extent by Bowersock 1994, 156–66, and followed by Friesen 2015, 238–50. See also Shorrock 2007; Hernández de la Fuente 2013; and some of the essays in Accorinti 2016.
[71] Edition: Thurn 2000. References are to book/chapter and page/line of Thurn's edition. English translation: Jeffreys *et al.* 1986 (pp. 20–22 for Pentheus and Dionysus). General discussion: Jeffreys 2003. Euripides in Malalas: D'Alfonso 2006, esp. pp. 14–16 on *Bacchae*. Dionysus in Malalas: Reinert 1985.
[72] Hörling 1980; Scott 1990; Jeffreys 1990a.
[73] Hörling 1980, 57–63; Garstad 2016. D'Alfonso 2006, 1 treats euhemerism as part and parcel of Malalas' *interpretatio christiana*. Reinert 1985, 1, 26 specifically addresses Malalas' rationalization of Dionysus.

and introduces sun-worship. He is captured in battle and imprisoned, but Agave persuades Pentheus to release him; the cousins eventually agree to reconcile and go to Cadmus, accompanied by Agave, for mediation. After the reconciliation, however, Dionysus ambushes Pentheus and has him beheaded, giving the head to Agave. Dionysus himself is then driven out of Thebes, at the citizens' and senators' behest, by Lycurgus, before dying in Delphi, where his tomb can still be seen (Malalas, *Chr.* 2.15; 29.56–32.39 Th). Malalas signals his source explicitly, with a garbled quotation:

> But Dionysus was angry with Pentheus for imprisoning and insulting him: Pentheus told everyone that Dionysus was illegitimate. This is the reason why Euripides, after he had discovered writing to this effect some years later, composed a play about the Bacchae in the poetic manner (ποιητικῶς) and gave Pentheus these words: 'Semele, pregnant to some mortal, placed the blame for the affair on Zeus' (Σεμέλη δὲ λοχευθεῖσα ἐκ βροτοῦ τινος εἰς Ζῆνα φέρουσα τὴν ἁμαρτίαν λέχους) (*Chr.* 31.7–12 Th).[74]

Above all, Malalas is interested in the mythic content of Euripides' plots.[75] Euripides is cited by name in the *Chronographia* more often than any other ancient poet, typically as an authoritative witness to the false, pagan, 'poetic' version of a given myth – often by way of the adverb ποιητικῶς ('poetically'), which for Malalas connotes a sort of poetic license. Malalas never mentions the Hellenistic Theocritus; cites Ovid only once, in a vague reference to the 'poetic' version of the Phaethon myth (*Chr.* 1.3; 5.42–44 Th); and never mentions Nonnus. On the other hand, he was most likely working from memory or at best from an intermediary rather than from a text of Euripides' play.[76] Malalas' Pentheus story thus reads as a wholesale reworking – Reinert calls it a 'historiographic exegesis' – of Euripides' *mythos* from a post-tragic angle.[77]

---

74 See D'Alfonso 2006, 14–16. ποιητικῶς is Thurn's supplement from the Slavic version. Compare *Bacch.* 28–29 and, especially, Σεμέλη λοχευθεῖσ' at *Bacch.* 2.
75 Jeffreys 1990a, 215; D'Alfonso 2006, 1.
76 D'Alfonso 2006, 14, 16 ('citazione a memoria'). Contrast Reinert 1985, 4. Indirect access to Euripides: Jeffreys 1990b, 179. Indirect access to Latin authors and, perhaps, limited knowledge of Latin: Jeffreys 1990a, 60, 1990a, 171–72. E. Patzig, in a 1901 review (of Bourier's *Über die Quellen der ersten vierzehn Bücher des Johannes Malalas*) cited in Jeffreys 1990b, 179, argues for direct use of Euripides. Carrara 1987, 23 n. 20 emphatically asserts that Malalas could have read, but did not in fact read, Euripides while writing the *Chronographia*. D'Alfonso 2006, 3–7 is cautiously optimistic about the prospect of direct use for *some* plays. See Reinert 1985, 31 n. 8 for further bibliography. On Malalas' immediate Greek sources, see Jeffreys 1990b, 196–97, 216. For a controversial dissenting view, see Treadgold 2007, 235–56, 311–29; and the response in Garstad 2016.
77 Reinert 1985, 4.

Malalas' narrative is animated by a series of tensions between euhemerized mortality and Dionysiac myth and cult, particularly in its theomachic, Orphic, epiphanic, and magical aspects. Malalas' Dionysus is a human being, and in this he is just like any other Olympian god in the *Chronographia*.[78] As an illegitimate pretender to the throne, however, he holds a secular position somewhat analogous to that of Euripides' Dionysus. Lycurgus, mentioned only in this episode and described merely as a 'knowledgeable man' (ἄνδρα σοφόν, 31.27 Th), effectively reprises his theomachic role from *Iliad* 6 to oust Dionysus on the bidding of the senate and citizens.[79] Malalas also strips away the epiphanic element which is so fundamental to *Bacchae*.[80] Dionysus is, however, a magician who teaches the Thebans 'Bacchic' rituals and prayers to the sun, and is ultimately deified (30.70–75 Th), all in keeping with Malalas' interests in gnosticism, Orphism, and theurgy.[81] At the same time, he is a rival claimant to empire returning west after a successful eastern campaign, 'an aristocratic youth with swashbuckling tendencies not dissimilar to those of Perseus'.[82] In this, Malalas' eminently capable Dionysus reflects a late-antique spin on the long-established tendency to present pagan heroes in the guise of generals, as indeed Nonnus and Lucian (*Bacchus*) had done with Dionysus himself.[83]

The main target for explicit exoneration is Agave, who caused her son's death (31.95–96 Th) but is not to blame for it, and who certainly did *not* behead him (31.21–3 Th).[84] (Remember that both Theocritus 26 and the *Cynegetica* focus squarely on the Theban women's part in Pentheus' *sparagmos*.) Like the *Theotokos* Mary in the *Christus Patiens* (see below) – and unlike Medea in Euripides' play, an important source for the *Chr. Pat.* – Agave is a grieving, sympathetic mother who did not kill her child. In effect, Malalas flips Euripides' plot on its head so that what was in *Bacchae* a scurrilous rumour of infidelity and secret childbirth is now the true story, and what was in *Bacchae* the true story is in fact a pagan, 'poetic' fiction retailed by the great man, Euripides.

---

78 See Hörling 1980, 55–57 and Reinert 1985 on Dionysus in the *Chronographia*. According to Hörling 1980, 58, ἀνήρ is a significant rubric in the *Chronographia* when it describes a pagan god; Dionysus furnishes one such example (*Chr.* 2.15; 30.73 Th.).
79 Reinert 1985, 20, 'the entire episode is obviously contrived to terminate Dionysus' career as a tyrannos in Boeotia—since no ancient source ever posited Dionysus as a king of Thebes.'
80 Epiphany in *Bacchae*: Bierl 1991, 181; Segal 1997, 231–38; Perris 2016, 21–26.
81 Jeffreys 1990a, 63–65.
82 Jeffreys 1990a, 62.
83 Reinert 1985, 9–10; Garstad 2014.
84 Reinert 1985, 19 compares Malalas' rehabilitation of Agave to that of Phaedra. See also D'Alfonso 2006, 15.

Christian discourse

This section overlaps with the previous one to the extent that with Nonnus and Malalas we have already entered the realm of Christianity, while some of the texts treated in this section are also narrative in form. Echoes of *Bacchae* in Christian texts may be seen in the context of the similarities between Jesus and Dionysus, and of the broader presence of Dionysian motifs in Christian discourse. As early as the second century CE, Justin the Martyr pointed out that Dionysus was the son of God (υἰὸν τοῦ Διός) and the inventor of wine, which he used in his mysteries (ἐν τοῖς μυστηρίοις), and that he was torn apart (διασπαραχθέντα) and ascended to heaven.[85] Stimulated, perhaps, by Hölderlin's 'Brod und Wein,' which was written around 1801, eighteenth- and nineteenth-century thinkers vigorously pursued analogies between Christ and Dionysus, in some cases with a view to establishing the genetic dependence of Christianity on pagan cult.[86] Some of the best recent work on Jesus-Dionysus correspondences focuses not on genetic relations, however, but on rhetorical expressions of comparison or contrast between the two figures.[87] Two recent monographs were produced independently of one another, but at times deal with the same material. Francesco Massa has thoroughly examined references to Dionysus in literary and figurative Christian discourse of the third and fourth centuries CE.[88] In relation to textual sources, Massa demonstrates how Christian apologists including Clement of Alexandria, Origen, Firmicus Maternus, and the author of the *Christus Patiens*, sometimes exploit and at other times seek to downplay similarities between Jesus and Dionysus, often appealing in sophisticated ways to Euripides' *Bacchae*, which becomes a central point of reference for Christians to talk about Dionysus. Another recent monograph, by Courtney Friesen, explores the 'cultural contestations' between Greeks, Jews, Romans and Christians by tracking the reception of Euripides' *Bacchae* from third-century Alexandria to the time of the *Christus Patiens*, which may be as late as the twelfth century CE.[89] Ambiguities and interpretative questions already present in the master-text are worked out in the cultural contestations of

---

[85] *Apol.* 1.54.
[86] See Massa 2012.
[87] See Wacht and Rickert 2010; Seaford 2012, 120–30; Hernández de la Fuente 2013.
[88] Massa 2014.
[89] Friesen 2015. He covers: Theocritus 26; Ezekiel, *Exagoge*; Philo, *Legatio ad Gaium*; Horace, *Epistles* 1.16; Clement of Alexandria; Artapanus, the 'Moses fragment'; Celsus, *Alethes Logos* and Origen, *Contra Celsum*; the Wisdom of Solomon; Dio Chrysostom, *Alexandrian Oration* (*Or.* 32); Philo, *De ebrietate*; the Acts of the Apostles; Nonnus, *Dionysiaca*; and *Christus Patiens*.

the book's subtitle. Form, meaning, abstraction, and reinterpretation combine in the ancient reception of the play. Ancient society replays the conflict staged in the tragedy through its reception.[90] At first glance, this view accords well with the play's reception elsewhere.[91] Both separately and between them, these two monographs attest to the importance of *Bacchae* in Christian and contiguous discourses, and we refer the reader to them for extensive coverage of the texts in this section.[92]

Contested territory in the debate on Jesus-Dionysus correspondences is the New Testament. It has been argued that *Bacchae*, specifically, resonates with the passion narrative and with the *Acts of the Apostles*, and that the echo of *Bacchae* in Luke-*Acts* was perceived by Origen (*Contra Celsum* 2.34). These resonances have proven crucial to the play's reception in modern times.[93] There appear to be both verbal and structural echoes. One verbal echo is found in Luke's use of the word θεομάχος at *Acts* 5:39. Another, more famous example is Luke's use of the 'don't kick against the pricks' proverb. Euripides' Dionysus says, 'I would rather sacrifice to him [i.e. Dionysus] than, human against god, angrily kick against the goad (πρὸς κέντρα λακτίζοιμι)' (*Ba.* 794–95). Paul, in his defence speech to the governor Festus, retells the story of his conversion, adding a detail not found in the other accounts in *Acts*: 'We all fell down on the ground and I heard a voice saying to me, in the Hebrew dialect [i.e. Aramaic], "Saul, Saul, why do you persecute me? It's hard for you to kick against the goad (πρὸς κέντρα λακτίζειν)"' (*Acts* 26.14; cf. 9:4, 22:7).

On the one hand, this proverb was widely used in Greek poetry before *Bacchae* (e.g. Pi. *Pyth.* 2.94–6, Aesch. *Ag.* 1624) and may also have been found in Jewish tradition. On the other hand, *Bacchae* is the closest extant Greek predecessor, and a well-known tragedy to boot; there are broader thematic parallels (e.g. *mania* vs. *sōphrosunē*; conversion and epiphany) at work; and the context within Paul's epiphany–conversion narrative resonates with Euripides' play. Seaford thus argues that extensive and striking parallels between *Bacchae*, Paul's conversion narrative, and Paul and Silas' prison escape are so egregious as to point

---

90 Friesen 2015, 265.
91 On abstraction (especially 'the Dionysiac') in the modern reception of *Bacchae*, see e.g. Perris 2016, 163–70.
92 See also Massa in this volume.
93 See e.g. Seaver 1912/1914; Seaford 1996 and 1997; Weaver 2004; Moles 2006; Friesen 2015, 207–35, with bibliography at 207 n. 3; Perris 2016, 59–78. Sceptical about Acts and *Bacchae*: Massa 2014, 72–77. On Origen and the comparison see Friesen 2015, 169; less committal is Massa 2014, 78.

to a shared ancestor: mystic initiation as a rite of passage.[94] What is more, we can see that Luke, through ironic inversion, uses Dionysian motifs such as drunkenness and madness to emphasize how unlike Dionysiac religion Christianity – even including glossolalia – really is.[95]

Among all these echoes, however, only the goads proverb and the word *theomachos* are explicit, and neither is unique to *Bacchae* in the first place. At most, these echoes allow the attentive reader of *Acts* to frame typological parallels as putative reminiscences of Euripides' play. So, ultimately, argues Friesen: 'My contention, rather, is that the *Bacchae* illuminates the literary context of Acts in ways that have not been sufficiently appreciated.'[96] Moles goes further, arguing passionately for Luke's deliberate use of *Bacchae*.[97]

Both *Bacchae* and Acts are incredibly influential master-texts; it is to be expected that ancient and modern readers would read one in light of the other and vice versa; *Bacchae* has been worked into the fabric of the reception of *Acts* just as *Acts* has been worked into the fabric of the reception of *Bacchae*.[98] Broadly speaking, *Acts* narrates the earliest engagement of Christianity, a Near Eastern mystery cult, with the Roman world. Luke's narrative activates Euripides' play as a telling intertext, and speaks to the capacity of Dionysus, and *Bacchae* more specifically, to address Roman anxieties about mystery religions as well as to address Christian anxieties about Roman political geography.

Friesen's 'receptions' vary in their degree of closeness to Euripides' play, and while all are very much πρὸς τὸν Διόνυσον, as perceived echoes of Euripides, some are in the eye of the beholder. There are two main sub-categories: sources that quote or reference *Bacchae* directly are incontrovertible receptions. For example, Celsus' *Alethes Logos*, the fragments of which are preserved and discussed in Origen's *Contra Celsum*, uses a sequence of *Bacchae* quotations as grounds for an argument about the plausibility of the incarnation (*Cels.* 2.33–5). For his part, Celsus uses Dionysus as a parallel for Christ, quoting (once) from and alluding

---

[94] Seaford 1997.
[95] Friesen 2015, 221–34. On Luke and the Classics in general see MacDonald 2015.
[96] Friesen 2015, 212. Also, at p. 219, there is a 'cumulative effect of suggesting that Paul's former madness and his epiphany and conversion in Acts 26 should be understood in relation to Euripides' narrative.'
[97] Moles 2006, 65, 'a maximalist case'. On Paul and *Bacchae* see also Cover 2018.
[98] See the works of Dormeyer and Ziegler cited by Friesen 212 n. 27 for accounts of how *Bacchae* frames ancient reader-reception of Acts.

(once) to Euripides' *Bacchae* within an argument that the incarnation was rationally impossible.[99] Origen, in his rebuttal, works through Celsus' points one by one, with the key point being that Jesus suffered willingly, that the passion was part of the divine plan, and that, accordingly, Celsus' argument is wrong because true virtue can embrace death.[100]

Clement of Alexandria, the subject of extensive discussion in both Massa's and Friesen's monographs, provides many examples of clever repurposing of lines from the *Bacchae* for a Christian apologetic agenda, and he quotes *Bacchae* in each of his three works, *Protrepticus*, *Paedogogus*, and *Stromateis*).[101] In his *Protrepticus*, or exhortation to the Greeks to convert to Christianity, Clement takes a dim view of Dionysian and other pagan cults. In the concluding chapter 12, however, he uses Dionysiac religion as an analogical foil for Christianity, and offers a Christianized *Bacchae*: he urges first Pentheus and then Tiresias to turn away from Dionysian religion; he associates Cithaeron with Zion; compares chaste Christian women to maenads; applies mystery cult terminology to Christianity, and radically reinterprets the Dionysiac experience to subordinate it to Christian experience. In *Stromateis* 4, he quotes five lines of *Bacchae* in a discussion of martyrdom and Christian mysticism.[102] According to Friesen, Clement's use of *Bacchae* – specifically Dionysus' comments on night-time ritual at *Ba.* 470–76 – in *Stromateis* 4 is a 'most remarkable literary move', by which he ironically and explicitly (κατὰ τὴν τραγῳδίαν, 'according to the tragedy') repurposes the words of the 'Greek god of sensuality' to adumbrate an account of Christian virtue: martyrdom, the ultimate expression of Christian gnosticism, entails the separation of the body; mystic initiation is a form of ritual death in which the soul is separated from the body; Christ channels the Euripidean Dionysus a kind of mystagogue.[103]

A second category of examples in Friesen's monograph encompasses prose works or passages which make sense more as receptions of Dionysus rather than as responses to *Bacchae* specifically. Philo, for example, twice uses Dionysiac tropes for corrective purposes. In the *Legatio ad Gaium*, the figure of Dionysus

---

[99] Friesen 2015, 161–64 claims that Celsus' engagement with *Bacchae* extends much further than this. But only fragments 2 and 3 (as numbered by Friesen) are clear quotations or references by name; other correspondences, from the themes of demonstration/epiphany and divine vengeance, to the idea of Pilate as Pentheus, and so on, are arguably typological.
[100] Friesen 2015, 164–72. See also Massa 2014, 106–13.
[101] See Massa 2010 and 2011, reworked at Massa 2014, esp. 161–89; Friesen 2015, 118–33; see esp. 118 n. 2 drawing on Stählin's index.
[102] See Massa 2014, 185–89.
[103] Massa 2014, 186; Friesen 2015, 128–33, quoted at 133.

exemplifies Gaius' pretensions and aspirations; in *De ebrietate*, the image of drunken maenadism, as put in the mouth of Eli's servant in 1 Samuel 1, exemplifies common misconceptions about Jewish mysticism and true union with the divine.[104] Each is more or less concerned with Dionysus, or at least the Dionysiac, but *Bacchae* is conspicuously absent from both. The so-called 'Moses fragment' of Artapanus' *Concerning the Jews* – preserved, along with fragments concerning Abraham and Joseph, in Eusebius and Clement – has been said to share with the story of Pentheus and Dionysus certain narrative tropes and other elements not in the LXX account, in particular magical doors and a well-timed earthquake.[105] The 'Wisdom of Solomon', finally, denounces Canaanite ritual in language reminiscent of Dionysiac cult, using words like *thiasos*, *teletē*, and *mustēs*; at the same time, there are shared motifs such as child-killing, indigeneity, and holiness.[106] But there is nothing to point unambiguously to *Bacchae*.[107]

This cannot be said of the *Christus Patiens*, our concluding example, a dramatic cento which recycles lines from Euripides' *Bacchae*, *Medea* and *Hippolytus* (and other sources) to retell, in three sections, the passion and crucifixion; the burial; and the resurrection of Christ.[108] Much scholarship on this work has been concerned with dating and authorship (it has been ascribed to Gregory of Naziansus).[109] More recent work has examined the Euripidean intertextuality from a literary point of view.[110] *Christus Patiens* may be read as a Christianization of *Bacchae*, one which interrogates the relations between Bacchic cult and Christianity.[111] By virtue of its very nature as a passion play made up of pagan verses, the *Christus Patiens* tests the notion of Christian tragedy.[112] And by virtue of specific parallels between the myth of Pentheus and the passion narrative, it echoes –

---

104 Friesen 2015, 86–93, 197–206.
105 Friesen 2015, 146–8. *Il.* 5.749 = 8.393, not cited by Friesen, is an important pre-Euripidean parallel for *automatos* being used to describe magically opening doors.
106 Friesen 2015, 176–86.
107 In this category one might also group 3 Maccabees, in which Cousland 2001 discerns echoes of *Bacchae*; López Salvá 2013 notes correspondences with *Bacchae* but does not insist on dependence. See Friesen 2015, 87 with n. 8.
108 Tuilier 1969, 19–26 outlines the contents.
109 Edition: Tuilier 1969. On the vexed questions of authenticity, authorship, and date, see Tuilier's edition but also e.g. Trisoglio 1996 (and the review in Tuilier 1997); Most 2008; Massa 2014, 263–67.
110 See most recently Bryant Davies 2017; Pollmann 2017, 140–57 = Pollmann 1997.
111 See Massa 2014, 263–77; Friesen 2015, 251–60.
112 Friesen 2015, 255; 'anti-tragedy', Pollmann 2017, 156.

quotes, ventriloquizes – *Bacchae* not only textually but also, in fact, conceptually; Christ is associated with both Pentheus and Dionysus.[113] Thus the controversy over theodicy in *Bacchae* (explicitly addressed at *Ba.* 1349) is here resolved in an all-encompassing Christology, whereby the resurrected god is both sacrificial victim and triumphant saviour, and both Dionysus and Pentheus are (arguably) Christianized. This ultimate Dionysian–Christian 'crossover', then, illustrates how a mimetic literary production could, in a Christian context, activate the unique status of Dionysus and of *Bacchae* in the pagan milieu.

The advent of Christianity constitutes a major watershed in the play's reception, as the way in which some Christian texts appeal to the *Bacchae* accords it an authoritative status, although one which falls short of the status of religious or liturgical text in its own right.[114] By a process of bi-directional influence, *Bacchae* was Christianized and Christianity, in its own way, mysticized such that, by the time of Nonnus and (pseudo-) Gregory, perhaps the most surprising thing of all is that a Christianized Dionysus could be relatively straightforward. Interestingly, Christianization of *Bacchae* was to be a highly significant dimension of the play's modern reception in the 'long sixties' (that is, 1958–1973).[115]

Conclusions

This chapter has traced the *Bacchae*'s complex reception history across performance, narrative retellings, and Christian discourse. We add some additional material in summary form in the appendix which follows, including some putative echoes and reworkings of *Bacchae* in literary texts, as well as some candidates for reception in visual media. Several points may be made by way of conclusion. The sheer number and diffusion of citations, echoes, and reworkings attest to the enduring popularity of the play and its appeal as a poetic artefact that inspired later poets. Examination of the play's reception often allows us to chart cultural relations, especially between Greece and Rome, paganism and Christianity, and (in line with this volume's orientation towards Rome and Italy) many of the cases studied point to or express specifically Roman attitudes. Beyond primarily 'literary' and 'cultural' receptions, engagements with *Bacchae* very often involved

---

113 Massa 2014, 267–76; Friesen 2015, 259–60. Of course, the shady presence of Medea (by way of lines from *Medea*), the archetypal child-killing mother, problematizes the Dionysus–Christ/Pentheus–Pilate/Agave–Mary complex; on Mary see Bryant Davies 2017.
114 On religious texts in Dionysian cult see Massa 2013.
115 On which see e.g. Perris 2016, 48–58.

participating in a debate on Dionysian cult, whether Theocritus' Ptolemaic endorsement or Clement's sophisticated Christian polemic. *Bacchae* becomes analogous to a religious text in its own right, and we conclude that receptions of the play do in fact tell us much about attitudes to Dionysus.

Appendix: Receptions of *Bacchae* until the twelfth century CE

What follows here is a conspectus of possible receptions of *Bacchae*. Where practical, we provide primary sources accompanied by a basic description and references to secondary literature. We do not catalogue the numerous direct quotations in, say, Athenaeus or Plutarch. (As Dodds 1960, xxix n. 1 observes, *Bacchae* 'was widely quoted and excerpted in the Roman period, as may be seen from the "testimonia" cited in Kirchhoff's [1885] *apparatus*'.) Where a source has been discussed above, we provide a cross-reference.

Background: Pentheus, Euripides, and *Bacchae*

Gantz 1993, 481–83 addresses the origins of the Dionysus-Pentheus myth.

Ancient biographies of Euripides: Suda, *s.v.* 'Euripides'; *Vita Euripidea*. See Lefkowitz 2012, 87–103; Scullion 2003; Revermann 2000; Easterling 1997, 211–27. In particular, the story of Euripides being torn apart clearly echoes *Bacchae*; see Lefkowitz 2012, 93.

Σ Ar. *Ran.* 67, 'The Didascaliae record that after Euripides' death his son, Euripides, produced *Iphigenia in Aulis*, *Alcmaeon*, and *Bacchae* in the city.'

Hall 2016 and Wyles 2016 address the first performance and early reception of *Bacchae*.

Aristophanes: *Frogs* (405 BCE)

Aristophanes' *Frogs* (Lenaea 405) is arguably the earliest and best-known example of the reception of *Bacchae*. Wyles 2016, 69 assumes that *Frogs* must predate *Bacchae*, with the likeliest date for *Bacchae* being the standard date of 405 (City Dionysia, *after* the Lenaea). Hall 2016, 17, while preferring 405, allows 406 'at a pinch'. Either way, *Frogs* is vital to the later reception of Dionysus/Bacchus. See

Lada-Richards 1999 on Dionysus in *Frogs*; Carpenter 1997 on the comic Dionysus versus the Dionysus of myth.

Wall painting, sanctuary of Dionysus in Athens (6th? to 4th? century BCE)

Pausanias 1.20.3 describes a painting of 'Pentheus and Lycurgus being punished for the violent things they did to Dionysus' in situ in the sanctuary of Dionysus. No painter is mentioned; the location of the paintings is merely 'there' (αὐτόθι, i.e. in the precinct). This gives us a *terminus post quem* of the mid-sixth century for the older temple; the heyday of Athenian wall-painting was the fourth century.

Iophon: *Pentheus*, ?*Bacchae*? (late 5th century BCE)

Only fragments survive of this play by Sophocles' son, which may be the same as the *Bacchae* attributed to him.

Dionysius of Syracuse, Plato and Aristippus (early 4th century BCE)

See pp. 45–46.

Chaeremon: *Dionysus*, *Oeneus* (mid-4th century BCE)

Bacchae may have influenced two plays by Chaeremon. See *Dionysus* F4 and *Oeneus* F14 *TrGF*; Collard 1970; Xanthakis-Karamanos 1980, 77–79.

Philodamus of Scarphaea: Paean to Dionysus (late 4th century BCE)

Furley and Bremer 2001, II.64 read intertextuality with the *Bacchae* in Philodamus' hymn; see especially line 1, 14–17, 56.

Apulian Phiale, in the style of the Thyrsus Painter (mid-4th century BCE)

BM F133, *RVAp* 10/190; Taplin 2004, 2007, 156–58 with fig. 51. Of extant vases, this is the only serious candidate for being a reception of *Bacchae*; the interpretation depends on identifying the central figure as Pentheus in disguise, and on attributing to Euripides the cross-dressing element. See also Philippart 1930 for images of the myth, eschewing (despite his title) a strict distinction between Euripidean and non-Euripidean versions. On visual representations of Dionysus generally, see Gasparri 1986a, 1986b; Carpenter 1986, 1997; Isler-Kerényi 2007, 2015. Pentheus: Tomasello 1958; March 1989; Bažant and Berger-Doer 1994; Weaver 2009, 17–29.

Alexander the Great (mid-4th century BCE)

See p. 43.

Lycophron: *Pentheus* (3rd century BCE)

Only the title of this play survives (F6 *TrGF*).

Theocritus: *Idyll* 26 (3rd century BCE)

See pp. 51–53.

Callimachus (3rd century BCE): *Hymn 5, Epigram 48*

Hunter 2006, 46 argues that the Actaeon paradigm from *Bacchae* underlies Callimachus' *Hymn 5*. See pp. 43–44 on *Ep.* 48 (Pfeiffer).

Plautus: *Amphitruo* (3rd–2nd centuries BCE)

Scholars have read this play as a reworking of *Bacchae*, with a focus on metatheatre. See Stewart 1958; Slater 1990; Schiesaro 2016, 30; contrast Christenson 2000, 54–55.

Greek Anthology 7.105, 9.248, 16.289, 16.290 (3rd–2nd centuries BCE)

AP 7.105.3–4 alludes to *Bacch.* 300:

> Διόνυσος ὅταν πολὺς ἐς δέμας ἔλθῃ,
> λῦσε μέλη·

> Whenever Dionysus enters someone's body in full force (πολύς), he loosens their limbs.

See pp. 48–49 on 16.289 (anon.), and 16.290 (Antipater of Thessalonica); see also *AP* 9.248 (Boëthus).

Ezekiel: *Exagoge* (3rd–2nd centuries BCE)

The *Exagoge*, a dramatization of Moses' life in Greek trimeters probably composed in Alexandria, contains one or two textual echoes of *Bacchae*. Compare *Ex.* 234–35/*Bacch.* 1077–83, *Ex.* 235–36/*Bacch.* 274. There are also typological parallels in the Red Sea narrative, the burning bush scene, and the overall theomachy plot. Text: *TrGF* I, 288–301. Text, translation, and commentary: Jacobson 1983; Lanfranchi 2006; Kotlińska-Toma 2015, 202–33. See also Xanthakis-Karamanos 2001; Whitmarsh 2013, 211–27, especially 218–19 on tragic hypotexts (including *Bacchae*).

*SIG*³ 648B, Delphi (early 2nd century BCE)

This inscription records that in 194 BCE, Satyrus of Samos won the pipe-playing competition without a contest and then, in the stadium, performed a lyre solo from Euripides' *Bacchae* and a choral song entitled 'Dionysus'.

See p. 46.

Pacuvius: *Pentheus* (2nd century BCE)

On Pacuvius' *Pentheus* see Schierl 2006, 418–22.

Accius: *Bacchae* (late 2nd century BCE)

See p. 44.

Alexander Comicus: *Dionysus* (2nd–1st centuries BCE)

Just one fragment (F1 K-A) survives of Alexander's comedy; the deictic mention of a mirror (κάτοπτρον) appears to refer to women-only Dionysiac rituals and thus to recall the cross-dressing scene in *Bacchae*; cf. Ar. *Thesm.* 140 for use of κάτοπτρον. On Dionysus in Greek comedy, see Lada-Richards 1999; Revermann 2014, 280.

Crassus and the Parthians (53 BCE)

See pp. 46–47.

Catullus 63, 64 (mid-1st century BCE)

Catullus 64.257 is almost a translation of *Bacchae* 739; the surrounding lines are also resonant. Harrison 2004 discerns the influence of *Bacchae* on Catullus 63, mostly as a source of conventional ritual details. For Catullus 63 as 'a kind of reversal of Euripides' *Bacchae*', see Hunter and Fantuzzi 2004, 479–80.

Propertius 3.17, 3.22 (1st century BCE)

Propertius 3.17 (*nunc, o Bacchae*) places Pentheus' death, including the three *thiasoi* led by his mother and aunts, in the god's aretalogy: *Pentheos in triplices funera grata greges* ('Pentheus' death, welcomed by three gangs', 3.17.24). In 3.17 (*frigida tam multos placuit*), while enumerating reasons why Tullus should return to Italy, the poet observes that *Penthea non saevae venantur in arbore Bacchae* ('[here] the savage Bacchants do not pursue Pentheus in his tree', 3.22.33); see *Bacch.* 1061–64 for the tree.

Horace (1st century BCE)

The Bacchus ode, 2.19 (*Bacchum in remotis*) contains many details present in the *Bacchae*, and the phrase *tectaque Penthei / disiecta non leni ruina* (14–15) in the god's aretalogy may refer to the palace miracle in the play, or to the myth more generally. At *Ep.* 1.16.73–79 Horace adapts *Bacchae* 492–98, casting the disguised Dionysus as *vir bonus et sapiens*; Mayer 1994 suggests that he may have been using Accius' *Bacchae*; see Friesen 2015, 96–117. Further allusions appear at *Sat.* 2.2.2 (Orestes and Agave) and 2.3.3.3–4 (Agave's madness). Hunter 2006, 48ff. reads allusions to the *Bacchae* in *Odes* 1.37; see Hardie 1977.

Virgil: *Aeneid* (1st century BCE)

For a structural reworking of *Bacchae* in the *Aeneid* see Mac Góráin 2013. See Giusti 2018, 91, 98, 133, 143–45 for Virgil's use of *Bacchae* in constructing Carthage.

Hyginus: *Fabulae* 184, 239 (1st century BCE)

Fabula 184, 'Pentheus and Agave', condenses the Euripidean plot: Agave, together with Ino, and Autonoe, maddened by Liber, tore Pentheus limb from limb (*membratim laniauit*). *Fabula* 239, a catalogue of 'Mothers who killed their sons', includes Agave.

Livy: *Ab Urbe Condita* 39 (1st century BCE–1st century CE)

Schiesaro 2016, 31 sees echoes of *Bacchae* in Livy's Bacchanalian narrative. See pp. 40–41, and Introduction, pp. 13–17.

Strabo: *Geography* (1st century BCE–1st century CE)

Strabo quotes *Bacchae* in discussions of Homer (1.2.20; *Bacch.* 13ff.), poetics (10.3.13; *Bacch.* 55ff., 72ff.), and India (15.1.7; *Bacch.* 13ff.).

Ovid: 'Pentheus and Bacchus' (1st century BCE–1st century CE)

See pp. 54–56 on *Met.* 3.511–733. Parallels with *Bacchae* have also been read in 'Tereus and Procne' (*Met.* 6.424–674) by Siegel 1994.

3 Maccabees (1st century BCE–1st century CE)

Cousland 2001 makes a case for reception of *Bacchae* in 3 Maccabees. There is no intertextuality, as such, but there are typological overlaps; allusions to common themes such as theomachy and divine retribution are strongly suggestive of literary echoes.

pseudo-Vergilian *Culex* (1st century CE)

An aside in the *Culex* mentions Agave hiding in a cave after killing Pentheus (*Cul.* 110–14).

Porta Maggiore relief (1st century CE)

A sculptural relief in the Porta Maggiore basilica (*LIMC* 'Pentheus' 7.61, first century CE) depicts a pantomime scene from some kind of Pentheus-related performance. Agave, flanked by two maenads, dances with a mask of Pentheus (i.e. his head) in one hand and a sword in the other. In its emphasis on histrionics and theatricality, on family dynamics, and on Agave herself, this image can be said to be working in a Euripidean mode. See Sauron 2007, 253–54, citing G. Bendinelli, 'Il monumento sotterraneo di Porta Maggiore in Roma', *Monumenti Antichi* 21 (1926): 729 with plate 39, 2.

Messalina (mid-1st century CE)

See pp. 50–51.

Nero (mid-1st century CE)

Nero is said by Dio to have 'performed some *Atthis* or *Bacchae* on the lyre' (61.20); see Suet. *Nero* 21–25 for his musical and theatrical performances.

Seneca the Younger (1st century CE)

Atreus as stage-director in *Thyestes* has been read as a response to Dionysus playing an equivalent role in the *Bacchae*; see Schiesaro 2003, 153–58.

Two passages in *Oedipus* seem to play on the sparagmos of Pentheus in Euripides; see 436–44 and 515–18. On Bacchus and *Bacchae* in this play, see Boyle 2012, esp. notes on the Ode to Bacchus at 110–201; and on 436–44 he notes that "Agave functions both as a paradigm of the 'impious' mother who 'unknowingly' destroys her son (a paradigm already fixed in the past of the Theban royal house and now realized as present by Jocasta ... and as family precedent for Oedipus. Her 'unknowing' filicide is clearly intended to prefigure Oedipus' 'unknowing' parricide."

Valerius Flaccus: *Argonautica* (1st century CE)

Two similes in the *Argonautica* recall moments from *Bacchae*. At 3.263–66, the Argonauts at Cyzicus, realizing what they have done, are compared to a maenad (*Thyias*, either Agave or a generalizing singular) who, deserted by Bacchus, finally recognizes Pentheus' head. At 7.300–6, Medea, tasked with following Venus out of the palace, is compared to Pentheus, left in the palace at Thebes by Bacchus, putting on his Bacchic costume: *pudibundaque tegmina matris / tympanaque et mollem subito miser accipit hastam* ('the poor boy suddenly takes his mother's shameful clothes, the drum, and the soft spear', 303–4).

Statius: *Achilleid*, *Agave* (1st century CE)

Juvenal mentions Statius' lost pantomime *Agave* (*Sat.* 7.82–87). The *Achilleid* is replete with references to *Bacchae* (compare, for instance, the cattle *sparagmos* at *Bacch.* 734–36 with the maenadic ritual described at *Ach.* 1.596). See Heslin 2005, 237–57, esp. 243–45.

Plutarch: *On the Glory of the Athenians* (1st–early-2nd–centuries CE)

See p. 43.

Dio Chrysostom, *Alexandrian Oration* (1st–early-2nd centuries CE)

In this oration (*Or.* 32) delivered in the theatre at Alexandria, Dio criticizes the Alexandrians for unruly public behaviour. In particular, he compares them to a chorus of maenads and quotes *Bacch.* 709, 'scratching the ground with their fingertips' (*Or.* 32.59.3–4). See Gangloff 2006, 276–77; Friesen 2015, 187–96.

Ps.-Apollodorus: *Bibliotheca* 3.36 (1st–2nd centuries CE)

The relevant section of the *Bibliotheca* retells the story of *Bacchae* from Dionysus' return to Thebes and the Theban women's revels to Pentheus' spying, Agave's madness, and the *sparagmos*.

The New Testament (1st–2nd centuries CE)

See pp. 61–62.

Aristides, *Apology* (2nd century CE)

In his invective against pagan gods, Aristides mentions Semele's birth (*Ap.* fr. 9.7) and the madness that Dionysus causes his followers to undergo (*Ap.* fr. 10.9). See Funke 1965–66, 255.

Lucian (2nd century CE)

In *Adversus Indoctum*, Demetrius the Cynic mocks a poorly educated Corinthian for his poor reading of 'the bit where the messenger narrates what happens to Pentheus and what Agave does' (19). In *Bacchus* (1–2), Dionysus' armies are described ripping up India's herds, while the Indian spies' report recalls the first messenger speech of *Bacchae*. And in *De morte Peregrini* (2.10–13), Lucian recalls what happened when he criticized Peregrinus' self-immolation right by the pyre: 'I was almost torn to shreds by the Cynics, like Actaeon torn apart by his dogs, or his cousin Pentheus torn apart by the Maenads' (2.10–13). See Funke 1965–66, 244 on *Salt.* 41.10 and Sauron 2009, 255–56 on *Cal.* 16 for less certain examples.

Aulus Gellius: *Attic Nights* (2nd century CE)

Favorinus quotes *Bacch.* 386–88 at *Attic Nights* 1.15.17.1.

Clement of Alexandria (2nd–3rd centuries CE)

See p. 63.

Celsus: *Alethes Logos* (late-2nd century CE)

See pp. 62–63.

Pseudo-Oppian: *Cynegetica* (early 3rd century CE)

See pp. 53–54.

Origen: *Contra Celsum* (mid-3rd century CE)

See pp. 62–63.

Pseudo-Callisthenes: *Alexander Romance* (4th century CE?)

The so-called *Alexander Romance* (i.e. the *Historia Alexandri Magni*, recension α, 1.46a.8.42–44) refers to the tree from which Pentheus fell.

Basil of Caesarea (4th century CE)

In an imploring letter to Martinianus, Basil compares Cappadocia's troubles to Pentheus' *sparagmos* (*Ep.* 74.1.19–21).

Julian: Seventh Oration (4th century CE)

Julian quotes *Bacchae* 370–71 while praising Ὁσία (Holiness) in his oration 'To the Cynic Heraclius, about how to be a Cynic and whether a Cynic should make up stories'.

Firmicus Maternus: *On the Errors of Pagan Religions* (4th century CE)

Firmicus' euhemerizing, critical description of Liber in Thebes alludes to Pentheus, and makes pointed reference to the history of Dionysiac tragedies: 'There was also another Liber, a tyrant in Thebes, famous for his magical powers. Such crimes (*scelera*) as he committed, the great sin (*facinus*) he ordered a mother to do to her son or sisters to their brother: every day these are passed down, on the stage, by the authors of tragic poetry' (*De errore* 6.6). On Firmicus see also Massa in this volume.

Synesius: *On Providence* (4th–5th centuries CE)

Synesius' *On Providence* (2.5) arguably alludes to *Bacchae* 485–86, where it is established that mysteries are best performed at night: ἀγνωσία σεμνότης ἐπὶ τελετῶν, καὶ νὺξ διὰ τοῦτο πιστεύεται τὰ μυστήρια ('ignorance means seriousness as far as initiation rituals go, and it is for this reason that the mysteries are entrusted to the night', *De prov.* 2.5.8–9). See Funke 1965–66, 273.

Theodoretus, *Cure of Greek Maladies* (5th century CE)

Theodoretus quotes *Bacchae* 472, '[the rituals are] forbidden for the uninitiated to know' (*Graec. aff. cur.* 1.86.3–4).

Nonnus, *Dionysiaca* (5th century CE)

See pp. 56–57.

Timotheus of Gaza, *On Animals* (5th–6th centuries CE)

In a section headed 'About the leopard' Timotheus retells the story from the *Cynegetica* in which Dionysus' followers (here τροφοί, nurses) willingly transform into leopards and kill Pentheus (*De animalibus* 11.5–8). Notably, the following section (11.9–11) describes the same wine-based leopard-trapping technique detailed in ps.-Oppian's *Cynegetica*.

Ioannes Malalas, *Chronographia* (6th century CE)

See pp. 57–59.

Ioannes Lydus, On the Offices of the Roman State (6th century CE)

John the Lydian quotes *Bacchae* 13 ('the gold-rich lands of Lydia') when recounting John the Cappadocian's greed in Lydia (*De magistratibus* 224.4–7 Bandy).

Ioannes Antiochenus, *Historia Chronica* (7th century CE)

In a brief fragment (F14 Roberto = F7 *FHG*), John of Antioch condenses Malalas' account from the *Chronographia* (see pp. 57–59).

George Cedrenus, *Compendium Historiarum* (11th century CE)

Cedrenus paraphrases Malalas' account (see pp. 57–59) at *Compendium Historiarum* 1.43.

Ioannes Tzetzes (12th century CE)

In *Histories* 61 (= *Chil.* 6. 556–86), John Tzetzes explicitly cites and paraphrases both Euripides' mythical (μυθικῶς) story from *Bacchae* as well as the allegorical (ἀλληγορῶν) account of 'John'. And in a letter addressed to 'Isaac Comnenus', while discussing famous figures who betrayed their family, Tzetzes mentions 'The Antiochean [and his account of] Agave betraying her son to death' (*Ep.* 6.14.1–2 Leone). *FHG* includes the Tzetzes passage as a testimonium to John of Antioch (*Hist. Chr.* F7, see above); Roberto's new edition does not. Tzetzes does use 'John the Antiochean' to refer to either John of Antioch *or* John Malalas. Based on narrative details, however, it seems more likely that Tzetzes refers here to John of Antioch's *Historia Chronica*, which in any case made much use of Malalas' *Chronographia*.

Christus Patiens = Χριστός Πάσχων, (4th? 12th? century CE)

See pp. 64–65.

Bibliography

Accorinti, D. ed. 2016. *Brill's Companion to Nonnus of Panopolis*. Leiden/Boston.
Alexopoulou, M. 2013. 'Christus Patiens and the reception of Euripides' *Bacchae* in Byzantium.' In *Dialogues with the Past 1, Classical Reception Theory and Practice*, edited by A. Bakogianni. London, 123–37.
Alonso Fernández, A. 2013. 'Maenadic ecstasy in Rome: fact or fiction?', In Bernabé *et al.*, 185–99.
Austin, C. 2005. 'Les papyrus des *Bacchantes* et le PSI 1192 de Sophocle.' In *Euripide e i papiri. Atti del convegno internazionale di studi (Firenze 10–11 giugno 2004)*, edited by G. Bastianini and A. Casanova. Florence, 157–68.
Barchiesi, A. 2007. *Ovidio* Metamorfosi *III–IV*. Rome.
Bartley, A.N. 2003. *Stories from the Mountains, Stories from the Sea: The Digressions and Similes of Oppian's* Halieutica *and the* Cynegetica. Göttingen.
Bartsch, S. 1994. *Actors in the Audience*. Cambridge, MA.
Bažant, J. and Berger-Doer, G. 1994. 'Pentheus.' In *LIMC* 7.1, 306–17.
Benaissa, A. ed. 2018. *Dionysius. The Epic Fragments*. Cambridge.
Bernabé, A., M. Herrero de Jáuregui, A.I. Jiménez San Cristóbal, R.M. Hernández, eds. 2013. *Redefining Dionysos*. Berlin/Boston.
Bertinelli, M.G.A., C. Carena, M. Manfredini, and L. Piccirilli, 1993. *Plutarco. Le vite di Nicia e di Crasso*. Milan.
Bierl, A. 1991. *Dionysos und die griechische Tragödie. Politische und 'metatheatralische' Aspekte im Text*. Tübingen.
Billings, J. 2018. '*Bacchae* as Palinode.' *IJCT* 25, 51–71.
Bosworth, B. 1996. *Alexander and the East: The Tragedy of Triumph*. Oxford.
Bowersock, G. 1994. 'Dionysus as an epic hero.' In *Studies in the Dionysiaca of Nonnus*, edited by N. Hopkinson. Cambridge, 156–66.
Boyd, B.W. ed. 2002. *Brill's Companion to Ovid*. Leiden/Boston.
Boyle, A.J. ed. 2012. *Seneca. Oedipus*. Oxford.
Braund, D. 1993. 'Dionysiac tragedy in Plutarch, *Crassus*.' *CQ* 43, 468–74.
Bremmer, J.N. 1984. 'Greek maenadism reconsidered.' *ZPE* 55, 267–86.
Bryant Davies, R. 2017. 'The Figure of Mary Mother of God in *Christus Patiens*: fragmenting tragic myth and passion narrative in a Byzantine appropriation of Euripidean tragedy.' *JHS* 137, 188–212.
Buxton, R. 2013. *Myths and Tragedies in their Ancient Greek Contexts*. Oxford.
Cairns, F. 1992. 'Theocritus, *Idyll* 26.' *PCPS* 38, 1–38.
Carpenter, T.H. 1986. *Dionysian Imagery in Archaic Greek Art*. Oxford.
Carpenter, T.H. 1997. *Dionysian Imagery in Fifth-Century Athens*. Oxford.
Carrara, P. 1987. 'A line from Euripides quoted in John Malalas' *Chronographia*.' *ZPE* 69, 20–24.

Chandezon, C. 1998. 'La base de Satyros à Delphes: le théâtre classique et son public à l'époque hellénistique.' In *La Tradition Créatrice du Théâtre Antique. I. En Grèce Ancienne.* Cahiers du GITA n. 11, 33–58.

Christenson, D.M. ed. 2000. *Plautus. Amphitruo.* Cambridge.

Colaclides, P. 1973. 'Acts 17:28a and *Bacchae* 506', *Vigiliae Christianae* 27.3, 161–64.

Collard, C. 1970. 'On the Tragedian Chaeremon', *JHS* 90, 22–34 [repr. and revised in *Tragedy, Euripides and Euripideans. Selected Papers.* Bristol 2007, 31–55].

Conte, G.B. 2017. *Stealing the Club from Hercules: On Imitation in Latin Poetry.* Berlin/New York.

Cousland, J.R.C. 2001. 'Dionysos *theomachos*? Echoes of the *Bacchae* in 3 Maccabees.' *Biblica* 82, 539–48.

Cover, M. 2018. 'The death of tragedy: The form of God in Euripides' *Bacchae* and Paul's *Carmen Christi*.' *Harvard Theological Review* 11, 66–89.

Cribiore, R. 1996. *Writing, Teachers, and Students in Graeco-Roman Egypt.* Atlanta.

Csapo, E. et al. eds. 2014. *Greek Theatre in the Fourth Century B.C.* Berlin.

Csapo, E. & Slater, W.J. 1995. *The Context of Ancient Drama.* Ann Arbor, MI.

Cusset, C. 1997. 'Théocrite, lecteur d'Euripide: l'exemple des *Bacchantes*.' *REG* 110, 454–68.

Cusset, C. ed. 2001. *Les Bacchantes de Théocrite: Texte, Corps et Morceaux.* Paris.

D'Alfonso, F. 2006. *Euripide in Giovanni Malala.* Alessandria.

Dodds, E.R. 1960². *Euripides Bacchae.* Oxford.

Dover, K.J. ed. 1971. *Theocritus: Select Poems.* London.

Dover, K.J. ed. 1993. *Aristophanes: Frogs.* Oxford.

Dunand, F. 1986. 'Les associations dionysiaques au service du pouvoir lagide (IIIe s. av. J.-C.)' In *L'association dionysiaque dans les sociétés anciennes.* Collection de l'École française de Rome – 89. Actes de la table ronde organisée par l'École française de Rome (Rome 24–25 mai 1984), 85–104.

Easterling, P.E. 1997. 'From repertoire to canon.' In *The Cambridge Companion to Greek Tragedy*, edited by P.E. Easterling. Cambridge, 211–27.

Edmunds, L. 2001. *Intertextuality and the Reading of Roman Poetry.* Baltimore, MD.

Englhofer, C.M. 1995. 'Götter und Mythen bei Oppianos von Apameia.' *Grazer Beiträge* 21, 157–73.

Feldherr, A. 1997. 'Metamorphosis and sacrifice in Ovid's Theban narrative.' *AW* 38, 25–55.

Fischer-Lichte, E. 2014. *Dionysus Resurrected: Performances of Euripides' The Bacchae in a Globalizing World.* Malden, MA.

Freyburger, G. 2013. 'Liber-Bacchus dans la poésie augustéenne: du passé de Rome au temps d'Auguste.' In *Poésie augustéenne et mémoires du passé de Rome: en hommage au professeur Lucienne Deschamps*, edited by O. Devillers and G. Flamerie de Lachapelle. Paris/Bordeaux, 93–99.

Friesen, C.J.P. 2015. *Reading Dionysus: Euripides'* Bacchae *and the Cultural Contestations of Greeks, Jews, Romans and Christians.* Tübingen.

Funke, H. 1965–66. 'Euripides.' *Jahrbuch für Antike und Christentum* 8/9, 233–79.

Furley, W.D. and J.M. Bremer eds. 2001. *Greek Hymns. I: The texts in translation; II: Greek Texts and Commentary.* Tübingen.

Gantz, T. 1993. *Early Greek Myth: A Guide to Literary and Artistic Sources.* Baltimore, MD.

Garelli, M.-H. 2007. *Danser le mythe: le pantomime et sa réception dans la culture antique.* Louvain.

Garstad, B. 2014. 'Hero into general: reading myth in Dionysius of Halicarnassus, Nonnus of Panopolis, and John Malalas.' *Preternature: Critical and Historical Studies on the Preternatural* 3.2, 227–60.

Garstad, B. 2016. 'Euhemerus and the *Chronicle* of John Malalas', *The International History Review* 38.5, 900–29.

Gasparri, C. 1986a. 'Dionysos.' In *LIMC* 3.1, 414–514.

Gasparri, C. 1986b. 'Dionysos/Bacchus.' In *LIMC* 3.1, 540–66.

Gildenhard, I. and M. Revermann, eds. 2010. *Beyond the Fifth Century: Interactions with Greek Tragedy from the Fourth Century BCE to the Middle Ages*. Berlin/New York.

Giusti, E. 2018. *Carthage in Virgil's* Aeneid. *Staging the Enemy under Augustus*. Cambridge.

Godwin, J. ed. 2014. *Ovid. Metamorphoses III, An Extract: 511–733*. London.

Gow, A.S.F. ed. and trans. 1952^2. *Theocritus*. 2 vols. Cambridge.

Gow, A.S.F. and D.L. Page, eds. 1968. *The Greek Anthology: The Garland of Philip and Some Contemporary Epigrams*. Cambridge.

Griffiths, F.T. 1979. *Theocritus at Court*. Leiden.

Groningen, B.A. van, 1963. 'Les Bacchantes de Théocrite.' In *Miscellanea di studi alessandrini in memoria di Augusto Rostagni*, edited by L. Ferrero *et al.* Turin, 338–49.

Hall, E. 2016. 'Perspectives on the impact of *Bacchae* at its original performance.' In Stuttard, 11–28.

Hall, E. and R. Wyles, eds. 2008. *New Directions in Ancient Pantomime*. Oxford.

Hardie, A. 1977. 'Horace *Odes* 1.37 and Pindar *Dithyramb* 2.' *PLLS* 1, 113–40

Hardie, P. 2002. *Ovid's Poetics of Illusion*. Cambridge.

Harrison, S.J. 2004. 'Altering Attis: ethnicity, gender and genre in Catullus 63.' *Mnemosyne* 57, 520–33.

Henrichs, A. 1978. 'Greek maenadism from Olympias to Messalina.' *HSCP* 82, 121–60.

Hernández de la Fuente, D. 2013. 'Parallels between Dionysos and Christ in late antiquity: miraculous healings in Nonnus' *Dionysiaca*.' In Bernabé *et al.*, 464–87.

Heslin, P.J. 2005. *The Transvestite Achilles. Gender and Genre in Statius'* Achilleid. Cambridge.

Hinds, S. 1998. *Allusion and Intertext: Dynamics of Appropriation in Roman Poetry*. Cambridge.

Hopkinson, N. ed. 1994. *Greek Poetry of the Imperial Period*. Cambridge.

Hörling, E. 1980. *Mythos und Pistis. Zur Deutung heidnischer Mythen in der christlichen Weltchronik des Johannes Malalas*. Lund.

Hunt, Y. 2008. 'Roman pantomime libretti and their Greek themes: the role of Augustus in the Romanization of the Greek classics.' In Hall and Wyles, 169–84.

Hunter, R. 2006. *The Shadow of Callimachus*. Cambridge.

Hunter, R. and M. Fantuzzi, 2004. *Tradition and Innovation in Hellenistic Poetry*. Cambridge.

Hutcheon, L. 2006. *A Theory of Adaptation*. New York.

Irwin, W. 2001. 'What is an allusion?' *The Journal of Aesthetics and Art Criticism* 59.3, 287–97.

Irwin, W. 2004. 'Against intertextuality.' *Philosophy and Literature* 28.2, 227–42.

Isler-Kerényi, C. 2007. *Dionysos in Archaic Greece: An Understanding through Images*. Trans. W.G.E. Watson. Leiden/Boston.

Isler-Kerényi, C. 2015. *Dionysos in Classical Athens. An Understanding through Images*. Trans. A. Beerens. Leiden/Boston.

Jaccottet, A.-F. 2003. *Choisir Dionysos. Les associations dionysiaques ou la face cachée du dionysisme*. 2 vols. Zurich.

Jaccottet, A.-F. 2008. 'Das bakchische Fest und seine Verbreitung durch Kult, Literatur und Theater.' In *Festrituale in der römischen Kaiserzeit*, edited by J. Rüpke, 201–213. Tübingen.

Jacobson, H. ed. and trans. 1983. *The Exagoge of Ezekiel*. Cambridge.
Jeffreys, E. 1990a. 'Malalas' world view.' In *Studies in John Malalas*, edited by E. Jeffreys, B. Croke, and R. Scott. Sydney, 55–66.
Jeffreys, E. 1990b. 'Malalas' sources.' In *Studies in John Malalas*, edited by E. Jeffreys, B. Croke, and R. Scott. Sydney, 167–216.
Jeffreys, E. 2003. 'The beginning of Byzantine chronography: John Malalas.' In *Greek and Roman Historiography in Late Antiquity, Fourth to Sixth Century A.D*, edited by G. Marasco. Leiden/Boston, 497–527.
Jeffreys, E. et al. (trans.) 1986. *The Chronicle of John Malalas: A Translation*. Melbourne.
Jory, J. 2003. 'The achievement of Pylades and Bathyllus.' In *Theatres of Action: Papers for Chris Dearden*, edited by J. Davidson and A. Pomeroy. Auckland, 187–93.
Jory, J. 2004. 'Pylades, pantomime, and the preservation of tragedy.' In *Mediterranean Archaeology* 17 [Special Issue, Festschrift in Honour of J. Richard Green]. Sydney, 147–56.
Jouan, F. 1992. 'Dionysos chez Eschyle.' *Kernos* 5, 71–86.
Keith, A. 2002. 'Sources and genres in Ovid's *Metamorphoses* 1–5.' In Boyd, 235–69.
Kirchhoff, J.W.A. ed. 1855. *Euripidis Tragoediae*. Berlin.
Kotlińska-Toma, A. 2015. *Hellenistic Tragedy: Texts, Translations, and a Critical Survey*. London.
Kuch, H. 1993. 'Continuity and change in Greek tragedy under post-classical conditions.' In *Tragedy, Comedy and the Polis*, edited by A.H. Sommerstein et al. Bari, 545–57.
Lada-Richards, I. 1999. *Initiating Dionysus: Ritual and Theatre in Aristophanes' Frogs*. Oxford.
Lane Fox, R. 1973. *Alexander the Great*. London.
Lanfranchi, P. ed. and trans. 2006. *L'exagoge d'Ezéchiel le tragique*. Leiden.
La Penna, A. 1975. 'I Baccanali di Messalina e le Baccanti di Euripide (nota a Tacito *Ann*. XI 31, 4–6.' *Maia* 27, 121–23.
Lefkowitz, M. 2012² [1981]. *The Lives of the Greek Poets*. Baltimore/London.
López Salvá, M. 2013. 'Dionysos and Dionysism in the third book of Maccabees.' In Bernabé et al., 452–63.
MacDonald, D.R. 2015. *Luke and Vergil: Imitations of Classical Greek Literature*. Lanham, MD.
Mac Góráin, F. 2013. 'Virgil's Bacchus and the Roman Republic.' In *Augustan Poetry and the Roman Republic*, edited by J. Farrell and D. Nelis. Oxford, 124–145.
Malloch, S.J.V. ed. 2013. *The Annals of Tacitus. Book 11*. Cambridge.
Manuwald, G. 2011. *Roman Republican Theatre*. Cambridge.
March, J.R. 1989. 'Euripides' *Bakchai*: a reconsideration in the light of vase-paintings.' *BICS* 36, 33–65.
Mariotti, I. 1965. 'Tragédie romaine et tragédie grecque. Accius et Euripide.' *MH* 22, 206–16.
Martindale, C. 1993. *Redeeming the Text: Latin Poetry and the Hermeneutics of Reception*. Cambridge.
Massa, F. 2010. 'La promotion des *Bacchantes* d'Euripide chez les Pères de l'Église.' *Cahiers Glotz* 21, 419–34.
Massa, F. 2011. 'Tra adesione dionisiaca e conversione cristiana: Clemente di Alessandria e il Tiresia delle *Baccanti* di Euripides.' *QUCC* 97, 147–66.
Massa, F. 2012. 'The meeting between Dionysus and the Christians in the historiographical debate of the XIX and XX centuries.' *Historia Religionum* 4, 159–82.
Massa, F. 2013. 'Écrire pour Dionysos: la présence de textes écrits dans les rituels dionysiaques.' *Revue de l'histoire des religions*, 2, 209–32.

Massa, F. 2014. *Tra la vigna e la croce: Dioniso nei discorsi letterari e figurativi cristiani (II–IV secolo)*. Stuttgart.

Mayer, R. ed. 1994. *Horace*. Epistles. Book I (Cambridge)

Miller, J.F. 2016. 'Ovid's Bacchic helmsman *and* Homeric Hymn 7.' In *The Reception of the Homeric Hymns*, edited by A. Faulkner, A. Vergados, and A. Schwab. Oxford, 95–108.

Moles, J.L. 2006. 'Jesus and Dionysus in the *Acts of the Apostles* and early Christianity.' *Hermathena* 180, 65–104.

Montes Cala, J.G., M. Sánchez Ortiz de Landaluce, and R.J. Gallé Cejudo, eds. 1999. *Plutarco, Dioniso y el vino: Actas del VI simposio Español sobre Plutarco*. Madrid.

Mossman, J.M. 1988. 'Tragedy and epic in Plutarch's *Alexander*.' *JHS* 108, 83–93.

Most, G. 2008. 'On the authorship of the *Christus Patiens*.' In *Quaerite faciem eius semper: Studien zu den geistesgeschichtlichen Beziehungen zwischen Antike und Christentum*, edited by A. Jördens et al. Hamburg, 229–40.

Navarro González, Á. 2016. 'The Dionisism in the *Bacchae: Megála kaì Phanerá*.' In *Greek Philosophy and Mystery Cults*, edited by M.J. Martín-Velasco and M.J. García Blanco. Newcastle, 187–204.

Nisbet, R.G.M. and N. Rudd, eds. 2004. *A Commentary on Horace: Odes Book III*. Oxford.

Oranje, H. 1984. *Euripides' Bacchae: The Play and its Audience*, translated by W.A. Weir. Leiden.

Pelling, C.B.R. 1988. *Plutarch. Life of Antony*. Cambridge.

Pelling, C.B.R. 1999. 'Dionysiac diagnostics: some hints of Dionysus in Plutarch's *Lives*.' In Montes Cala et al., 359–68 = *Plutarch and History*, 2011. Swansea, 449–71.

Perris, S. 2011. 'Perspectives on violence in Euripides' *Bacchae*.' *Mnemosyne* 64, 37–57.

Perris, S. 2015. 'Bacchant Women.' In *Brill's Companion to the Reception of Euripides*, edited by R. Lauriola and K.N. Demetriou. Leiden/Boston, 507–548.

Perris, S. 2016. *The Gentle, Jealous God. Reading Euripides'* Bacchae *in English*. London.

Perris, S. (forthcoming) 'Drama and its discontents: violence in adaptations of Greek tragedy.' In *Adapting Greek Tragedy: Contemporary Contexts for Ancient Texts*, edited by. V. Liapis and A. Sidiropoulou. Cambridge.

Philippart, H. 1930. 'Iconographie des 'Bacchantes' d'Euripide.' *Revue belge de philologie et d'histoire* 9, 1–72.

Pollmann, K. 1997. 'Jesus Christos und Dionysos: Überlegungen zu dem Euripides-Cento *Christus Patiens*', *Jahrbuch der Österreichischen Byzantinistik* 47, 87–106 = K. Pollmann, K. 2017. *The Baptized Muse. Early Christian Poetry as Cultural Authority*. Oxford, 140–57.

Prauscello, L. 2006. *Singing Alexandria. Music between Practice and Textual Transmission*. Leiden/Boston.

Quinn, K. 1968. *Virgil's* Aeneid. *A Critical Description*. London.

Radke, G. 2003. *Tragik und Metatragik. Euripides' Bakchen und die moderne Literaturwissenschaft*. Berlin/New York.

Reinert, S.W. 1985. 'The image of Dionysus in Malalas' Chronicle.' In *Byzantine Studies in Honor of Milton V. Anastos*, edited by S. Vryonis, Jr. Malibu, 1–41.

Revermann, M. 2000. 'Euripides, tragedy and Macedon: some conditions of reception.' *ICS* 24–25 (1999–2000), 451–67.

Revermann, M. 2014. 'Divinity and religious practice.' In *The Cambridge Companion to Greek Comedy*, edited by M. Revermann. Cambridge, 275–88.

Ribbeck, O. 1875. *Die römische Tragödie im Zeitalter der Republik*. Leipzig.

Rice, E. ed. 1983. *The Grand Procession of Ptolemy Philadelphus*. Oxford.

Roux, J. ed. 1970–72. *Euripide: Les Bacchantes*. 2 vols. Paris.

Rosato, C. 2005. *Euripide sulla scena latina arcaica. La "Medea" di Ennio e le "Baccanti" di Accio*. Lecce.
Sanders, J. 2006. *Adaptation and Appropriation*. London.
Sandys, J.E. 1900⁴. *The* Bacchae *of Euripides*. Cambridge.
Santoro L'hoir, F. 2006. *Tragedy, Rhetoric, and the Historiography of Tacitus' Annales*. Ann Arbor, MI.
Sauron, G. 2007. 'L'actualité des *Bacchantes* d'Euripide dans les conflits idéologiques de la fin de l'époque hellénistique', In *Images et modernité hellénistiques. Appropriation et représentation du monde d'Alexandre à César*, edited by F.-H. Massa-Pairault and G. Sauron. Rome, 247–59.
Schierl, P. 2006. *Die Tragödien des Pacuvius. Ein Kommentar zu den Fragmenten mit Einleitung, Text und Übersetzung*. Berlin/New York.
Schiesaro, A. 2003. *The Passions in Play. Thyestes and the Dynamics of Senecan Drama*. Cambridge.
Schiesaro, A. 2016. 'Bacchus in Roman drama.' In *Roman Drama and its Contexts*, edited by S. Frangoulidis, S.J. Harrison, and G. Manuwald. Berlin/New York, 25–41.
Scott, R. 1990. 'Malalas' view of the classical past.' In *Reading the Past in Late Antiquity*, edited by G. Clarke. Sydney, 147–61.
Scullion, S. 2003. 'Euripides and Macedon, or the silence of the *Frogs*.' *CQ* 53.2, 389–400.
Seaford, R. ed. 1996. *Euripides* Bacchae. Warminster.
Seaford, R. 1997. 'Thunder, lightning and earthquake in the *Bacchae* and the *Acts of the Apostles*.' In *What is a God? Studies in the Nature of Greek Divinity*, edited by A.B. Lloyd. London, 139–51.
Seaver, G. 1912/1914. *The Dionysus-Cult in its Relation to Christianity, as seen in the Bacchae of Euripides*. London.
Segal, C. 1997 [1982]. *Dionysiac Poetics and Euripides' Bacchae. Expanded Edition with a New Afterword by the Author*, Princeton, NJ.
Sestili, A. ed. 2010. *Oppiano. Il Cinegetico. Trattato sulla caccia. Introduzione, traduzione e note*. Rome.
Shorrock, R. 2001. *The Challenge of Epic: Allusive Engagement in the* Dionysiaca *of Nonnus*. Leiden.
Shorrock, R. 2007. *The Myth of Paganism: Nonnus, Dionysus and the World of Late Antiquity*. London.
Siegel, J.F. 1994. *Child-Feast and Revenge: Ovid and the Myth of Procne, Philomela and Tereus*. Unpublished PhD dissertation, New Brunswick, NJ.
Silk, M.S. and J.P. Stern, 1981. *Nietzsche on Tragedy*. Cambridge.
Simon, B. ed. and trans. 2004. *Nonnos de Panopolis: Les Dionysiaques, Tome XVI, Chantes XLIV–XLVI*. Collection des Universités de France. Paris.
Sistakou, E. 2016. *Tragic Failures: Alexandrian Responses to Tragedy and the Tragic*. Berlin.
Slater, N.W. 1990. '*Amphitruo, Bacchae* and metatheatre.' *Lexis* 6, 101–25
Sommerstein, A.H. ed. and trans. 2008. *Aeschylus: Fragments*. Cambridge, MA.
Sommerstein, A.H. 2013. 'Aeschylus' *Semele* and its companion plays.' In *I papiri di Eschilo e di Sofocle*, edited by G. Bastianini and A. Casanova. Florence, 81–94.
Sommerstein, A.H. 2016. '*Bacchae* and earlier tragedy.' In Stuttard, 29–41.
Stepanyan, A.A. 2015. 'Relations between tragedy and historical experience in Plutarch (*Crassus* 33).' *Journal of the Society for Armenian Studies* 24, 112–23.
Stewart, Z. 1958. 'The *Amphitruo* of Plautus and Euripides' *Bacchae*.' *TAPA* 89, 348–73.

Stuttard, D. ed. 2016. *Looking at* Bacchae. London.
Swift Riginos, A. 1976. *Platonica: The Anecdotes Concerning the Life and Writings of Plato.* Leiden.
Taplin, O. 2004. 'A disguised Pentheus hiding in the British Museum?' *Letras Clássicas* 8, 27–35.
Taplin, O. 2007. *Pots & Plays: Interactions between Tragedy and Greek Vase-Painting of the Fourth Century BCE.* Los Angeles, CA.
Thomas, R.F. 1986. 'Virgil's *Georgics* and the art of reference.' *HSCP* 90, 171–98.
Thurn, I. ed. 2000. *Ioannis Malalae Chronographia.* Berlin/New York.
Tissoni, F. 1998. *Nonno di Panopoli: I canti di Penteo (Dionisiache 44–46). Commento.* Florence.
Tomasello, E. 1958. 'Rappresentazione figurate del mito di Penteo', *Sicolorum Gymnasium* 11.2, 219–50.
Treadgold, W. 2007. *The Early Byzantine Historians.* New York.
Trisoglio, F. 1996. *San Gregorio Nazianzeno e il* Christus Patiens: *Il problema dell' autenticità gregoriana del dramma.* Florence.
Tuilier, A. ed. 1969. *Grégoire de Nazianze: La passion du Christ. Tragédie.* Paris.
Tuilier, A. 1997. 'Grégoire de Nazianze et le *Christus Patiens*: À propos d'un ouvrage recent.' *REG* 110, 632–47.
Versnel, H. 1990. *Inconsistencies in Greek and Roman Religion I. Ter Unus. Isis, Dionysos, Hermes. Three Studies in Henotheism.* Leiden/New York.
von Stackelberg, K.T. 2009. 'Performative space and garden transgressions in Tacitus' death of Messalina.' *AJP* 130, 595–624.
Wacht, M. and F. Rickert, 2010. 'Liber (Dionysos).' In *Reallexikon für Antike und Christentum*, vol. 23, coll. 67–99.
Weaver, B. 2009. 'Euripides' *Bacchae* and classical typologies of Pentheus' "sparagmos."' *BICS* 52, 15–43.
Weaver, J.B. 2004. *Plots of Epiphany: Prison-Escape in Acts of the Apostles.* Berlin/New York.
Whitmarsh, T. 2013. *Beyond the Second Sophistic: Adventures in Greek Postclassicism.* Berkeley, CA.
Wiseman, T.P. 2006. 'Documentation, visualisation, imagination: the case of Anna Perenna's cult site.' In *Imaging Ancient Rome: Documentation – Visualisation – Imagination*, edited by L. Haselberger and J. Humphrey. Portsmouth, RI, 51–61.
Wyler, S. 2011. 'L'acculturation dionysiaque à Rome: l'invention d'une alterité.' In *Identités romaines. Conscience de soi, et représentation de l'autre dans le Rome antique*, edited by M. Simon. Paris, 191–201.
Wyles, R. 2016. 'Staging in *Bacchae*.' In Stuttgard, 59–70.
Xanthakis-Karamanos, G. 1980. *Studies in Fourth-Century Tragedy.* Athens.
Xanthakis-Karamanos, G. 2001. 'The *Exagoge* of Ezekiel and fifth-century tragedy. Similarities of theme and concept.' In *Rezeption des antiken Dramas auf der Bühne und in der Literatur*, edited by B. Zimmermann. Stuttgart, 223–39.
Zadorojniy, A.V. 1997. 'Tragedy and epic in Plutarch's 'Crassus.'' *Hermes* 125, 169–82.
Zimmermann, B. 2002. 'Accius' und Euripides' *Bakchen*.' In *Accius und seine Zeit*, edited by S. Faller and G. Manuwald. Würzburg, 337–43.

Stéphanie Wyler
Images of Dionysus in Rome: the archaic and Augustan periods

Abstract: This chapter examines Italian images of Dionysus with a view to exploring the dynamics of acculturation of a Greek figure. The aim is to show that images provide major evidence not only for studying art history, but also religious and cultural history; and that far from being representations of cultic ritual, or being mere adaptations of imported iconographic schemes, Roman and Italian images of Dionysus furnish a figurative and reflexive discourse on the very processes of appropriation and domestication. In the case of each representation, the chapter specifies the ways in which Greek forms acquire local inflections, and identify the ways in which these respond and correspond to Roman or Italian rituals as well as to social and political realities. Where possible, the images are put in the context of Roman literary treatments of related phenomena. Two sets of images are subjected to scrutiny: a miscellaneous cluster from the archaic period, and a more homogeneous body of sacro-idyllic landscapes from the Augustan era. The early images are particularly sensitive to cultural analysis. The Augustan images show landscape being marked as ritual space through Dionysian and other motifs; and the taming of nature which they evince coheres with the new Augustan view of Dionysus, which is a response to Mark Antony's cultivation of an exuberant Dionysian persona. The main pieces of evidence on which this chapter draws are: a set of fragments of statuary believed to come from the sixth-century sanctuary of Sant'Omobono in the Forum Boarium; some descriptions of the decorative programme of the late-fifth-century temple of Ceres, Liber and Libera; an image of Liber on an inscribed third-century Praenestine *cista* (*CIL* I², 563. Berlin, Charlottenburg, inv. Misc. 6239); Liber on the fourth-century Cista Ficoroni; a Dionysian fresco from Lanuvium; and frescoes and stucco panels from the Villa della Farnesina, all dating to the early Augustan period.

Let us begin with a simple question: are there images of the Roman Dionysus? If we consider 'Dionysus' as a generic name for the Roman god Liber and the huge range of theonyms he is called through Roman literature (Bacchus, Bassareus, Eleleus, Euan, Euius, Iacchus, Lenaeus, Lyaeus, Nocturnus, Nycteleius, Nyseus, Semeleius, Thyoneus and so on),[1] we certainly have plenty of images, commissioned by Roman

---

1 E.g. Ovid, *Met.* 4.11–17. Wyler 2011a, 192–96.

https://doi.org/10.1515/9783110672237-003

patrons from artists working in Rome. The relevant article of the *Lexicon Iconographicum Mythologiae Classicae* counts no fewer than 300 items,[2] and this is obviously not exhaustive. But at the same time, most of them are designated as a 'Roman copy of a (lost) Greek original'[3] or, at least, derived from Greek models. Whatever his iconographic type – be he a baby, young or bearded, whether he appears in a mythical or ritual context –, he is always described as 'Greek-ish' – probably like most appearances of the god in literary texts that do not explicitly mention the Roman Liber in the specific context of the *Liberalia*. Indeed, in relation to images of Dionysus in Rome, one of the major issues at stake is the relationship between the Greek and the Roman god(s), the process of acculturation and the dynamic construction of his (or their) 'Romanness.'

Considering the images, there are at least two directions we can explore to interrogate the specificity of Roman iconography representing the god and his realm. I shall begin by looking at the archaic Roman images, at a time when literature cannot yet be helpful, in order to see if the god had a fixed visual identity before the massive invasion of Hellenistic art throughout the Mediterranean.[4] They are not numerous, but they are worth presenting since they are not well known and they pose interesting questions that broaden our perspective on the evidence for Dionysus. A second approach to question the later flow of Dionysian images in Roman art consists in considering Dionysian fashions at Rome in one particular period, in order to understand why they flourished in a specific context, and whether the form was inspired by Greek templates. For this purpose we might select one or more *corpora*, such as the Oriental triumphs on imperial *sarcophagi* and mosaics.[5] I have chosen to explore in this paper a very specific group of images from the Augustan period that represent Dionysian rituals performed in so-called 'sacro-idyllic landscapes.' This choice has been guided by the fact that we have no trace of such compositions in Greek visual arts (which does not mean that they did not exist, insofar as we have echoes in Hellenistic literature).[6] Moreover, these images are sharply delimited in time between the mid-first century BCE and mid-first century CE, just like the overall corpus of the 'sacro-idyllic landscapes':[7] it might be

---

[2] 268 items in *LIMC* III s.v. 'Dionysos/Bacchus' (Gasparri 1986b), plus 42 in the *Supplementum* (Wyler 2009).
[3] Huet and Wyler 2005.
[4] E.g. Zanker 1998.
[5] E.g., on this topic, and particularly how the motif of the cart in the Dionysian triumph has been received throughout the ages, see Boardman 2014. See also Buccino 2013.
[6] E.g. Prioux 2017.
[7] With some echoes later on in the Imperial era; see Croisille 2010, 132–36. On these paintings see Peters 1963, with a catalogue in Silberberg 1980, and more recently Hinterhöller-Klein 2015,

no accident if this context were to reveal a new trend in the iconography of Dionysus, at a time when the god is supposed to have been defeated by Augustus in the form of the god's famous follower Mark Antony *neos Dionysos*.

This paper intends thus to appraise the way Roman art figures the evolving image of the god by focusing, like a two-faced herm, on two iconographic clusters that appear to be turning points in the connexion between Greek and Roman cultures.[8] The first part deals with the earliest available images of the god that allow us to assess some of his structural features, whereas the second part considers the imaginative world in which he and his realm are represented. The temporal gap between both bodies of evidence is deliberate, in order to emphasize a long period of Roman history where Dionysian material is not so extensive in Rome, and often shaded by highlights such as the Bacchanalian affair of 186 BCE or the megalography at the Villa of Mysteries in Pompeii. In both parts, my aim is to show that images provide major evidence not only for studying art history, but also religious and cultural history, if we acknowledge that they are neither illustrations of the cult, nor imported pictures, but a figurative and reflexive discourse on the Roman Dionysus.

Archaic images of Dionysus/Liber in Rome

The oldest evidence in Rome is a tiny, but exciting archaeological clue. A set of terracotta fragments have recently been gathered together by Anna Mura Sommella.[9] She argues that the head of a woman with a *tutulus* (i.e., her hair plaited into a bun on top of her head), now kept in the Ny Carlsberg Glyptotek in Copenhagen,[10] belongs together with some remains kept in the Capitoline Museum,[11] which come from the sanctuary of Sant'Omobono in the Forum Boarium, and date back to the second phase of the temple (530–520 BCE).[12] In her

---

with previous bibliography. On the echoes between Augustan texts and paintings, see Leach 1988, 197–260.
8 On the 'two Hellenizations of Rome', see Fraenkel 1964, 16; Veyne 1979; Wallace-Hadrill 1998.
9 Mura Sommella 2011.
10 Copenhagen, Ny Carlsberg Glyptotek, inv. HIN 26. H. 26 cm. Cristofani 1990, 142, fig. 6.1.2.
11 Roma, Musei Capitolini, Antiquarium Comunale. Mura Sommella 2011, fig. 2, 10 and 11.
12 For an overview of the sanctuary and the history of excavations, see Terrenato 2012; Diffendale 2016; and Brocato et al. 2017; Brocato and Terrenato 2017.

view, this group was an *acroterion* representing the divine couple Liber and Ariadne (or should we call her Libera?),[13] standing with a panther.[14]

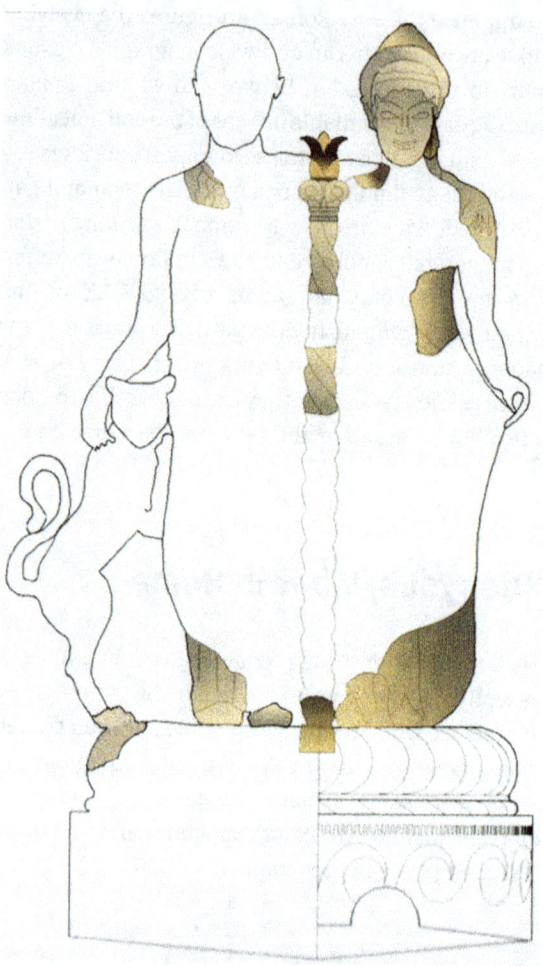

Fig. 1: Graphic reconstruction of the terracotta group with Liber and Libera on the roof of the Sant'Omobono temple. 530–520 BCE. Design P. Lulof and G. Pala. After Mura Sommella 2011: fig. 16.

---

13 On the problematic identification of Liber's consort in images, see Wyler 2013.
14 After Mura Sommella 2011, fig. 16.

This identification would suit the overall iconography of the temple particularly well: like the well-known couple of Hercules and Minerva, both couples would represent a god introducing a human or a hero into the divine sphere.[15]

These two examples of divinisation are linked to Fortuna and Mater Matuta, who were worshipped in this temple on the Sant'Omobono site, and they appear to be paradigmatic for the myth of Ino, the aunt and nurse of Dionysus: according to Ovid (in the sixth book of the *Fasti*),[16] once arrived in Rome, she was turned into Mater Matuta (Leucothea) and her son Melicertes into Portunus (Palaemon), with the help of Hercules and Carmenta.[17] The iconography of the temple and the topography of this area might have significantly inspired the poet's treatment of the aetiological myth.[18]

A hand, half a foot, fragments of a cloth, the paw of a panther and a twisted sceptre: it is hard to reconstitute the whole iconography of the god, but its structural configuration with Ariadne is common to the archaic Greek *koine* (in fact, the closest parallels found by Mura Sommella are maenads painted on ceramics from Athens and Laconia).[19] The fact that this decor was commissioned by Etruscan rulers, who were kings of Rome at that time, partly explains the circulation of these motifs, insofar as Dionysian images, either imported or locally made, are well attested in Etruscan territory as early as the second half of the sixth century BCE;[20] but the circulation also proves that the decor made sense for Romans in the culture

---

15 The myth of the apotheosis of Ariadne is at least as old as Hesiod, *Theog.* 947–49 and is probably represented on vases as early as the mid-sixth century BCE, e.g. on a black-figure Athenian cup by the Little Master Band (New York, Metropolitan Museum 17.230.5); see Vatin 2004, 19–20. Carpenter 1986, 21–25 is sceptical about the identification of the woman depicted with Dionysos before the beginning of the fifth century and suggests that it might be Semele. The catasterism of Ariadne into the constellation Corona is treated by Ovid, *Fast.* 3.459–516. On the interpretation of these two groups as models for the apotheosis for kings and triumphators, see Coarelli 2011, 72.

16 Ovid, *Fast.* 6.473–568, included in the aetiology of the *Matralia* (11 June). On this passage, see Littlewood 2006, 145–69, who mentions the 'terracotta decoration at all these sanctuaries (dedicated to Mater Matuta in Etruria and Latium) which features Dionysiac figures and motifs' (147).

17 On the other hand, the identification of the Dionysian couple would confirm the analysis of Mario Torelli on the triumphal aspect of the temple, in association with the reliefs on the pediment representing procession of carts with maybe Dionysus and Ariadne (Roma, Musei Capitolini, Antiquarium Comunale); see Mura Sommella 2011, 184, fig. 18 and Mura Sommella 2007, 182–84. On the interpretation of the reliefs with Heracles, see Torelli 1997.

18 Prescendi 2011.

19 Mura Sommella 2011, 179.

20 Cristofani 1986, 538 (first vases around 530 BCE: e.g. n° 16 with (probably) Ariadne 81). See also Colonna 1991, 117–18.

of that time. Even if the god's formal pattern was imported (presumably from a Greek model via Etruria), this was a plausible and effective image of the Roman Liber, whose *interpretatio* with Dionysus was already well underway.[21] Moreover, he is included in a royal and public sanctuary which was connected with the triumph to the extent that the *pompa triumphalis* actually passed by the temple. This is probably the most ancient visual evidence of the god in Rome, and we realise how complex he already is as soon as we try to identity the cultural influences in play, Greek, Etruscan, and Roman.

Soon after that, the sanctuary of the triad Ceres, Liber, and Libera on the Aventine Hill was erected at the beginning of the fifth century BCE.[22] We have no basis for reconstructing the iconography of the cult statues. But we know from Pliny the Elder that the temple itself was supposed to have been decorated by two sculptors and painters, who were the two first Greek artists officially called to work in Rome, Damophilos and Gorgasos, who probably came from around the Straits of Messina, and who signed their work with Greek verses.[23] Besides, the very first bronze statue in Rome consecrated to a divinity was, according to the same Pliny, dedicated to Ceres in the Aventine sanctuary, with the money seized from the *adfectator regni* Spurius Cassius in 485 BCE;[24] made by a Greek artist (according to Filippo Coarelli),[25] it may have been used as the cult statue of the goddess. However, as far as I know, there are no images of the Aventine triad (as there are for the Capitoline one) that could inform us about the way Liber was configured here, where he was worshipped as the god of the *Liberalia*. We might assume that it was as Greek-featured as the god at Sant'Omobono, which may be the normal Roman way to figure him (and Libera might have been very close to Ariadne). This tradition reporting that the temple of the Aventine was the place of these artistic innovations of the time and of the overseas importation may have been forged afterwards – just like the parallel with the Eleusinian triad.[26]

---

21 On the actual multiplicity of versions of the god in Italy, see Miano in this volume.
22 In 496 or 499 BCE, Dion. Hal. *Ant. Rom.* 6.17.2–3 and 6.94.3; see also Livy, 2.20.10–13 and Dion. Hal. *Ant. Rom.* 6.13.2. On its location: De Cazanove 1983 (in the present park of San Vincenzo de Paoli all'Aventino), followed e.g. by Coarelli 1993; Mignone 2016 argues for a probable location in the Forum Boarium.
23 Pliny, *Nat.* 35.154 (45), quoting Varro. On the origins of Damophilos and Gorgasos see Colonna 1982.
24 Pliny, *Nat.* 34.15; Livy, 2.41; Dion. Hal. *Ant. Rom.* 7.79.
25 Coarelli 1997, 34.
26 If indeed the triad on the Aventine does actually date from the beginning of the fifth century BCE, Dionysos/Iakchos had not yet been introduced at Eleusis (Metzger 1995). By the end of the Republic, the *interpretatio* between both triads was commonly accepted (e.g. Cicero, *Nat. D.* 3.21).

However, on the basis of Pliny's testimony, we might conclude that the image of the archaic Liber was already Greek-fashioned from a formal point of view, even if the architecture of the temple retained Tuscan features all through the Republic.[27]

If we imagine that the cult statue of Liber dated from the beginning of the fifth century BCE, we might expect him to have been bearded, just like the different types of archaic Dionysos throughout the Greek and Italic *koine*.[28] At this point, it is worth questioning whether this status-mark signifying age and respectability comes from a Greek visual pattern or already belonged to a 'genuine' archaic Roman Liber, pre-existing the importation of the 490s, as the Latin theonym Liber would seem to suggest. In the early third century BCE, the earliest inscription which certainly mentions the Roman name of the god (in its archaic form), '*Leiber*', is written above his image, in a narrative scene engraved on a bronze *cista* from Praeneste.[29]

The god is bearded, bare-chested, one shoulder and his lower body draped in cloth, wearing shoes and holding a soft vine stock in his left hand. He raises his other hand to the shoulder of Apollo, who walks in his direction but turns his head backwards, looking towards Hercules behind him. Mercury, Jupiter and Juno are represented on the left. The central figure, a winged Victoria is about to award a garland, probably to Mars jumping up from a *dolium* or large earthenware vessel with the help of Minerva, in front of Diana and Fortuna.[30]

---

27 The fact that the architecture of the temple itself, before it burnt in 31 BCE, was defined by Vitruvius (3.3.5) as typically archaic ('araeostyle buildings' with wooden beams, implying a 'straddling-to-heavy, low, broad design'), with a pediment in the Tuscan style (adorned with 'statues of terracotta or gilt bronze') may appear in tension with the Greek decoration. On this basis, Coarelli 1993, 260 thinks it was a Greek temple ('probabilmente di un periptero'). We cannot rule out a combination of traditional Etruscan architecture with the new Greek decorative technique of *crustae* (understood here as plates with painted reliefs: Rouveret 1981, 171, n. 1). See Mac Góráin, Introduction, in this volume.

28 Carpenter 1986 and Gasparri 1986a, 508 (beardless Dionysos seems to appear in the mid-fifth century in Greek art).

29 *CIL* I², 563. Berlin, Charlottenburg, inv. Misc. 6239. Bordenache Battaglia 1979, 50–54, nr. 5, pl. 60–63.

30 See Miano in this volume. For the interpretation of this unknown myth, see Simon 1978; Massa-Pairault 1987; Menichetti 1995, 80–95.

Fig. 2: Bearded Liber on a bronze *cista* from Praeneste. Third century BCE. Design after *MonInst* 9. Pl. 58–9.

This mythological scene is complex and may refer to a local myth which is difficult to understand without the help of textual evidence. A striking point is that the Latin theonym is used, whereas other Dionysian names, *Fuflunus* (a Latinized form of the Etruscan *Fufluns*) and *Hiacos* (a Latin rendering of Greek *Iakchos*),[31] appear on other bronze mirrors and *cistae* from Praeneste between the fifth and the third centuries BCE. Daniele Miano convincingly suggests that the fragmentation of Dionysian local interpretations and translations might be explained by the lack of a cult of Liber at Praeneste. This would allow artists and patrons, at a crossroads between Latin and Etruscan cultures, to draw freely on a variety of features of Dionysus and to adapt them. It transpires that the iconography of the god varies just as much as his name.

My point here is to enquire whether this bearded Liber from the Praenestine bronze *cista* might have recalled a more 'genuine' aspect of the Roman god, compared to the contemporary Etruscan Fufluns and the Greek Iacchos at Praeneste, but also to the archaic Greek form of the god that may probably have adorned the temple at Sant'Omobono and possibly been worshipped on the Aventine Hill, even if both these images (the god at Sant'Omobono and Liber on the *cista*) must have been felt as Roman by most of people in the middle Republic. Indeed one might argue that Dionysus' beard is consistent with the appellation *Liber Pater*. In the passage of the *Fasti* on the *Liberalia*, Ovid suggests, amongst

---

31 Bibliographical references in Miano.

several reasons, that the god protects the youth 'because [he is] Father' (*quia tu pater es*):[32] his beard seems to cohere well with this patriarchal aspect of the god.

But several arguments weaken this hypothesis. First, the antiquity of the double name *Liber Pater* is not as certain as it may seem. Admittedly, in the second century BCE, Lucilius ranks Liber among the gods qualified as *Patres*, with Neptune, Saturn, Mars, Janus and Quirinus.[33] It is not easy to restore the whole context of this fragment in which Apollo is complaining about his (new?) epiclesis *pulcher*, elsewhere applied to male prostitutes (*exoletus*).[34] This satiric verse could be understood either as evidence for the antiquity of the double name *Liber Pater* or, on the contrary, for the criticism against the increasing tendency to add this honorific title to a crowd of gods, specifically in poetry: '*ut nemo sit nostrum quin aut pater optimus diuum …*' According to the euhemerist tradition, rather fashionable in Rome at that time,[35] Dionysos/Liber is considered as one of the more recently deified benefactors of humanity, with Romulus, Hercules, Aesculapius and the Dioscuri: Lucilius' verse might then be understood as a criticism against the recent addition of *Pater* to *Liber*, or even his divinisation.[36]

As a matter of fact, the normal way to name him is to use the single name Liber, at least in Republican prose and in the few inscriptions mentioning him in

---

[32] Ovid, *Fast.* 3.771–78: *restat ut inueniam quare toga libera detur | Lucifero pueris, candide Bacche, tuo: | Siue quod ipse puer semper iuuenisque uideris | et media est aetas inter utrumque tibi ; | Seu quia tu pater es, patres sua pignora, natos, | commendant curae numinibusque tuis ; | Siue quod es Liber, uestis quoque libera per te | sumitur et uitae liberioris iter.* ('It remains for me to discover why the gown of liberty is given to boys, fair Bacchus, on your day, whether it be because you seem ever to be a boy and a youth, and your age is midway between the two; or it may be that, because you are a father, fathers commend to your care and divine keeping the pledges that they love, their sons; or it may be that because you are Liber, the gown of liberty is assumed and freer life is entered upon under your auspices.' Translation Frazer 1989, updated).
[33] Lucilius, 24–27 Warmington: *ut | nemo sit nostrum quin aut pater optimus diuum, | aut Neptunus pater, Liber Saturnus pater, Mars | Ianus Quirinus pater siet ac dicatur ad unum.* ('So that there is not one of us who is not called "father"; "father" the best of the gods is called; Neptune also is "father", Liber and Saturn are "father", Mars, Janus, Quirinus are "father"; one and all are called so.' Translation Warmington 1961b).
[34] Serv. *Aen.* 3.19.
[35] We know that Ennius wrote a *Euhermus siue sacra historia*, see Vahlen 1928, which was the Latin translation of the *Hiera anagraphe* by Euhemerus: Cicero, *Nat. D.* 1. 119, Lactantius, *Div. Inst.* 1.11. Borgeaud 2017.
[36] E.g. Cicero, *Nat. D.* 3.45.

a cultic context.³⁷ Cicero or Livy, for instance, never use the double name.³⁸ The first attestation in prose appears in Varro's *Res rusticae*,³⁹ where he starts by invoking him simply as Liber among the twelve rustic *Dii Consentes*.⁴⁰ After that, the double name progressively becomes the rule, used notably by Vitruvius, Hyginus, Pliny the Elder,⁴¹ up until Servius who feels the need to explain that Bacchus is the same as Liber Pater.⁴² In poetry, by contrast, *Pater* is associated with the Greek version of the theonym, as early as the beginning of Latin literature. Pseudo-Ennius⁴³ uses the name *Bacchus Pater* in *Athamas*; and Accius in his *Bacchae* uses *Dionysus Pater*.⁴⁴ Each time, a Greek theonym is used instead of *Liber*. I suggest here that the Republican theonym might have been simply *Liber* and become *Liber Pater* at the beginning of the Augustan era. From then on, the double names becomes widespread, and the 'Augustan turn' might have emphasized this way to honour the god, a reversal of and respectable response to Mark Antony's defeated *neos Dionysos*: the 'actual' and reinstated god is, then, the παλαιός, that is to say *Pater*.⁴⁵ If this hypothesis makes sense, the ancient Liber was not necessarily *Pater*, nor bearded.

A second argument suggesting that the beard of Liber was not necessarily felt to be typically Roman can be observed in Ovid's text itself. Amid his multiple explanations of the protection by Liber of the *liberi*, he associates the 'fatherhood' of the god with his youth: *et media est aetas inter utrumque tibi* (*Fast.* 3.774). This alternative or dual aspect certainly evokes an iconography like this hermaic pillar from the Palatine Hill.⁴⁶

---

37 On the epigraphic evidence: Wyler forthcoming b.
38 Except in Cicero, *Flac.* 60, where Mithridates VI of Pontus is proclaimed by the people of Tralles with the honorific titles of *deus, pater, conseruator Asiae*, and after that with four variations on the name of the god: *Euhius, Nysius, Bacchus, Liber*. Liber must here be understood as the normal Latin translation of Dionysos. See Manuwald in this volume.
39 Varro, *Rust.* 1.2.19: *sic factum ut Libero patri, repertori uitis, hirci immolarentur, proinde ut capite darent poenas*. ('So it was that he-goats were offered to father Liber, the discoverer of the vine, so that they might pay with their lives for the injuries they do him.' Translation after Hooper and Ash 1934).
40 Varro, *Rust.* 1.1.5: in this rural pantheon, Jupiter and Tellus are called *Pater* and *Mater*.
41 6 times in Vitruvius, 7 in Hyginus Astronomicus and 9 in Hyginus Mythographus, 25 in Pliny the Elder, 40 in Servius.
42 Servius, *Buc.* 5.30.
43 On the authenticity of this text attributed to Ennius, see Manuwald 2012.
44 Ps.-Ennius, *Scen.* 128–32 Warmington; Accius, *Trag.* 204–5 Warmington.
45 Jaccottet and Wyler forthcoming.
46 Rome, Museo Palatino, inv. 601 and 614. Tomei 1997, 132, nr. 111–12.

Fig. 3: Bifrontic Herm of Liber from the Palatine. Rome, Museo Palatino, inv. 614 and 601. With permission of the Ministero dei beni e delle attività culturali e del turismo, Soprintendenza Speciale per il Colosseo, il Museo Nazionale Romano e l'area archeologica di Roma. Augustan. Photo S. Wyler.

It represents the god as *bifrons*, young on one side, bearded on the opposite, in a 'neo-attic' archaizing style typical of the Roman taste of the Augustan period.[47] In the case of the herm, the beard must be understood as part of the fake archaism with its Attic connotation: it is part of the reconstructed image of the god. In that 'neo-attic' trend, both faces of the god have coexisted in Rome from the second century BCE onwards. It is not impossible that the *cista* with *Leiber* might have already been inspired by this Hellenizing tendency, if not yet by the 'neo-attic' style. In Ovid's time, the double face of the god indicated a wide range of its iconographic possibilities and not a chronological evolution of its form.

A similar argument can be used to challenge the hypothesis that the bearded Liber of the *cista* (who is not called *Pater*) reflects the iconography of an archaic Liber. On other *cistae*, he is represented as a beardless young god following the iconography common to the Etruscan and Greek worlds,[48] as on the well-known

---

47 Wyler 2006a.
48 Gasparri 1986a, 509–12 (e.g. n° 264–80, young Dionysos, drunk, supported by satyrs and sileni); Cristofani 1986, n° 20, 21 (with the *bulla*), 27 etc.

Cista Ficoroni, which dates back to the fourth century and is signed by a Roman artist, *Nouios Pautios Romai*.[49]

Fig. 4: Handle of the cista Ficoroni, Rome, Museo Nazionale Etrusco di Villa Giulia, inv. 24787. 350–30 BCE. Licence CC-BY-SA 4.0, (Creative Commons Attribution-Share Alike 4.0 International). Photo Sailko.

The god appears on the handle of the lid, between two satyrs, wearing a *bulla*, the protective locket of Etruscan and Roman free-born boys: he is represented as a *puer* himself and, at the same time, as the divine domestic figurine to which boys dedicate their *bulla* once grown up, when they assume the *toga libera*.[50] The body of the box, portraying scenes with Argonauts, can be interpreted as representing the values of the educated aristocratic youth, as suggested by Agnès

---

49 Rome, Museo Nazionale Etrusco di Villa Giulia, inv. 24787, 350-330 BCE (inscription: *CIL* 1.561, *ILLRP* 1197, *ILS* 8562). Dohrn 1972; Coarelli 2011, 207–18.
50 De Cazanove 2011, 14–15. The birth of Dionysus is depicted on actual golden *bullae*: Cristofani 1986, n° 12.

Rouveret.⁵¹ This iconographic programme echoes the function of the box, a gift given by a mother (*Dindia Macolmia*) to her daughter, presumably for her wedding, the women's part in the social order which contains the rite of passage.⁵² The entire decoration of the *cista* elaborates on the function of the Roman Liber as celebrated at the feast of the *Liberalia*, mainly the protection of teenagers as they become adults (Libera playing a similar role for the girls): and this is expressed by means of Greek myth and iconography. The *cista* reveals the adaptation and the synthesis between both cultures – and this juvenile Dionysus may in fact be much more Roman than the bearded Leiber.

Just like the variety of theonyms used on these *cistae* that Daniele Miano examines in his chapter in this volume, the contrast between the young god on the Cista Ficoroni and the bearded Leiber proves that several iconographic types co-existed as early as the middle Republic, and probably even earlier. But it is impossible to identify a specific archaic Roman image of this god: his Romanness comes from the interpretation of the image, its function and performance context, its adaptation thanks to peculiar attributes (such as the *bulla*), and not from a specific iconographic feature of the god – and this is true in every part of the Hellenized world.⁵³

Such a cultural and aesthetic synthesis might have resulted in harmonious homogenization. But Greek and Roman cultures continued to interact with one another, and Dionysian images continued to represent a point of balance between both Greek and Italian iconographic languages (at least in Rome). This is particularly true if we consider the rising tide of images that flow from the Hellenistic kingdoms thoughout Republican Italy in the second and first centuries BCE: the famous megalography at the Villa of the Mysteries in Pompeii is a suggestive example of that trend.⁵⁴ In Rome, amongst several strands developed during the first century BCE, a particular twist was taken with the 'war

---

51 Rouveret 1994: Heracles and Pollux (punishing Amycus) must be understood as the idealised image of athletic warriors, whereas Orpheus figured with a Papposilenus at a fountain would represent a form of a mystic (probably Pythagorean) wisdom. This engraved frieze echoes thus the adoption in Rome of the Greek *kalokagathoia* emphasized notably by the epitaph of Scipio Barbatus (who died in 280 BCE) on his sarcophagus (qualified as *fortis uir sapiensque*, *CIL* 6.1285) and on the Roman *comitium*, where the statues of Alcibiades and Pythagoras were erected at the end of the fourth century, 'during the Samnite war' (Pliny, *HN* 34.26 and Plutarch, *Num.* 8.20).
52 Prieto-Luley 2018, 295.
53 On the theoretical background to that approach and an application to a Pompeian Dionysian image from the Samnite and Roman eras, see Wyler forthcoming b.
54 From the vast bibliography, see Gazda 2000 for a synopsis and orientation on the context and concept of these frescoes.

of images' used in the propaganda between the different rulers during the first century BCE, from Marius to Caesar and obviously Mark Antony,[55] when Dionysian images definitely tipped over to the Oriental side. But, paradoxically enough, it is after Octavian's victory that the image of the god and his realm starts to invade and proliferate in the private sphere of the Romans: it keeps a strong Greek connotation, but is yet again reinterpreted to the new aesthetic and ideology of the Principate. The *Neos Dionysos* is dead, long live *Liber Pater*!

Augustan Dionysian landscapes

Turning now to the Augustan age, let us consider a fresco fragment from a house at Lanuvium which was painted in the years 20-10 BCE,[56] we can see a Dionysian sanctuary and a ceremony being performed in front of the temple.

The cult statue, in bronze, has been brought out: the god is represented sitting, with beard and crown, a thyrsus in his left hand and a *kantharos* in the other. His identity is very clear thanks to his attributes and the iconographical type of the image, which might be based on an archaizing type inspired by Alkamenes' statue of the god in the sanctuary of Dionysos Eleuthereus in Athens, which gained currency during the Roman period.[57] But it is emphasized by an inscription under his feet, calling him ΔΙΟΝΥΣΟΣ, painted in gilt Greek capital letters. Under a temporary canopy, he officiates at various moments of mystery ritual represented here in a unique scene: the placing of the *liknon* on the veiled head of the initiate while two priestesses hold up a couple of torches; the sacrifice of a goat led by a young satyr in front of a large tree decorated with a thyrsus and a *tympanon*; and a young boy standing with a woman under a vegetal pergola adorned with a stretched awning. A more detailed analysis of this very rich image is beyond the scope of the present paper: here I would like to emphasize two points. The first is that a second smaller inscription probably mentions ΕΙΝΩ behind one of the torch-bearers. It may be the end of an incomplete word (the

---

[55] The sources are covered well by Caneva 2016, even if some of his conclusions merit further discussion. On the mudslinging between Octavian and Mark Antony, see Borgies 2016.
[56] Lanuvium, Museo Civico. See Attenni 2002; Wyler 2006c.
[57] The statue by Alkamenes, in gold and ivory, is mentioned by Pausanias, 1.20.3. Coins and statuettes coming from Athens during the Roman period attest its diffusion: e.g. Gasparri 1986a, nr. 131, 133–6, notably 133 (a tetradrachm from Athens, 90/89 BCE, *BMC* Athens 376) and 136 (an archaizing statuette from the Roman period, now in the Hermitage Museum, Saint Petersburg, inv. 18.832).

fresco is fragmented just here), or might refer to Ino,[58] the aunt of Dionysos, who was worshipped in Rome precisely in the temple of Sant'Omobono, assimilated to Mater Matuta-Leucothea, celebrated during the *Matralia* and counted amongst the divinized mortals, just like Liber, in the euhemerist tradition.[59] This identification of Ino must remain hypothetical, but the echo between this fresco and the shrine in the Forum Boarium, where she is associated with Liber, is suggestive with respect to a Roman interpretation of the image: in both cases the Greek element cohabits with local tradition.

Fig. 5: Fresco fragment from Lanuvium, Museo civico di Lanuvio. With permission of the Soprintendenza del Lazio e dell'Etruria Meridionale. Photo S. Wyler.

The second point concerns the ritual scene's environment, which looks like an outdoor shrine, maybe a *lucus* or a suburban sanctuary, expressed by the blue sky (which is relatively rare in Roman painting), the tree, the pergola and the

---

58 Attenni 2002, 69, n. 77.
59 Prescendi 2011. Cicero, Tusc. 1.28: *Ino Cadmi filia nonne Leucothea nominata a Graecis Matuta habetur a nostris?*

rocky ground. It is worth comparing this scene with a more ancient one, on the *emblema* of a round mosaic that adorns the floor of the House of the Centaur in Pompeii (VI.9.3-5),[60] which dates back to the Samnite period (at the end of the second century BCE).

Fig. 6: Mosaic from the House of the Centaur, Pompeii VI, 9, 12, Naples, Museo Archeologico Nazionale, inv. 100019, late-second century BCE. With permission of the Soprintendenza per i beni archeologici di Napoli. Photo S. Wyler.

---

60 Now in Naples, Museo Archeologico Nazionale, inv. 100019. Bragantini 1993, 855, 857, nr. 69.

There is the same kind of outdoor temple; the statue of the juvenile god is standing on a pedestal, holding a thyrsus and pouring wine from a vase to his panther at his feet, in front a red *tympanon*. A tree is visible on the right, and probably an enclosed *lucus* in the background. But the rocky environment is much wilder than in the fresco from Lanuvium and, above all, the scene represented in the centre is very different: it takes place in a mythical world where three *Erotes* are present (two in front with torches and a third on the back of the huge lion, enchaining the lion with garlands), whereas two maenads, one with a thyrsus and the other with a *kantharos*, attend to this taming of the Oriental wildness.

The comparison between both images suggests that the normal milieu of Dionysian rituals is an outdoor sanctuary, that is to say in more-or-less wild nature – which suits most of the myths, if we think, for example, of the *oreibasia* on Cithaeron or Parnassus or on the shore of Naxos. But contrary to those mythical places, there is always a temple, a shrine, a human construction revealing that this nature belongs also to ritual culture. These images obviously do not depict actual rites, but illustrate the way in which they were thought about, and the imaginative worlds which they were intended to access. We shall return to this crucial distinction in our conclusion.

Turning to our landscapes, the most significant difference between the Lanuvian fresco and the Pompeian mosaic appears to be that in the Lanuvian example the Dionysian mysteries are depicted in a much more civilized way, where all the wildness is under control. Even the natural elements have been domesticated: for example, the pergola on the right may well represent the Dionysian ἀειθαλὲς ἄντρον or 'evergreen cave,' known from texts and inscriptions as a site of mysteries.[61] Instead of painting a proper grotto as the site of the rite, as Greek artists had done, the Roman painter chose to allude to it by showing this pergola. Why? In order to be realistic? Probably not: the way images of this kind function, time and space are a synthesis of the entire ritual process.[62] A much more interesting answer is that, at the very beginning of the Augustan age, when this fresco was painted, the way in which nature was perceived and represented underwent a noticeable change. It is no accident that one of the few Roman painters mentioned by Pliny the Elder is the famous Studius (or Ludius), who reportedly 'invented' landscape painting in the age of Augustus, as a proper

---

[61] Jaccottet 2003, vol. 2, n° 31 and vol. 1, 155–60. On the cave as cult-site see Jaccottet and Wyler 2018.
[62] On the symbolic language of Roman visual culture see, e.g., Hölscher 2004.

novelty.⁶³ Now, since images of Dionysian ritual had traditionally been placed in natural surroundings and outdoor sanctuaries, they were adapted to the new art of landscape. This aesthetic adjustment coheres with a new perception of Dionysus in Augustan Rome.

This claim can be confirmed by the success of Dionysian scenes in the Augustan 'sacro-idyllic' landscapes. If we consider the decorative program of the Villa della Farnesina in Rome, on the banks of the Tiber, completed in the twenties BCE and that may have belonged to Agrippa and Julia, or probably earlier,⁶⁴ both landscapes and Dionysian scenes appear to be in the majority – at least in the surviving part of the villa.⁶⁵ The reliefs on the ceilings of *cubicula* B and D show eight stucco panels that allude to the initiation of a woman and a child. For instance, on one panel from *cubiculum* B,⁶⁶ a Silenus is just about to unveil the *liknon* to a young *mystes*, whose head is covered by a hood that a priestess, behind him, holds down with her hand. A second maenad, who holds a *tympanon*, seems to be talking to her. The environment is typified by a column decorated with a ribbon on the right and a pillar on the left, which hides the trunk of a tree, so that we only see the branches and leaves, adorned with ribbons too. With this visual choice, both pillar and tree appear to be unified, to express synthetically a landscape that is as much cultured as it is natural.⁶⁷ In the same way, the rocky ground merges with artificial bases on which cultic elements and figures are represented, like the mystic basket here. The same is true of the naked satyr on the following panel on the same ceiling.⁶⁸ Seated on a rough-hewn rock covered by the skin of an animal, he reaches out for a branch behind him, directly above the head of the young boy who is being initiated by a priestess in front of him. Two pillars flank the group whereas, on the right-hand side a satyr is pouring wine from a goatskin into a crater, in front of a massive rough-hewn rock, into which a thyrsus has been inserted.

This last detail is interesting. This thyrsus is not just a cultic instrument that a worshipper will casually have left to one side (here the argument for 'realism' would be wholly unconvincing). Rather, it serves as an attribute to define the environment and ambiance. In visual language it designates the rock and landscape as a Dionysian sanctuary. We have the same process with the other

---

63 Pliny, *HN* 35.116–17. On these paintings and the genre of 'landscape', see Croisille 2010.
64 La Rocca 2008.
65 The surviving décor is now housed in the Museo Nazionale Romano (Palazzo Massimo); see Bragantini and De Vos 1982; Mols and Moormann 2008. On the Dionysian décor see Wyler 2006b.
66 Museo Nazionale Romano, inv. 1072. Bragantini and De Vos 1982, 138, fig. 78.
67 Wyler forthcoming a.
68 Bragantini and De Vos 1982, 138–39, fig. 79.

stuccos on the ceiling of the next-door bedroom, the *cubiculum* D.[69] Three women are preparing a rustic shrine. Once again there is a tree, visible in the surviving top-left corner. On the right, standing on a pedestal or a pillar (or possibly the wall of a *temenos*), stands a hermaic statue, characterized by a phallus dangling downwards, qualifying him at least as a male divinity. Just like the landscape, this generic cult statue is waiting to be dressed as the god he is supposed to incarnate for the ceremony.[70] That is precisely what the women are doing: they are Dionysian priestesses, typified by the thyrsus put on the rock onto which the woman on the right has climbed, the dress she wears, with this characterizing squared bow on her waist, and the offerings she brings, which include a cone-shaped cake.[71] Without the ceremony, the performance of the women, and the décor, this environment could be a generic crossroads sanctuary, dedicated to Priapus or any other god of the countryside.

The construction of the image reveals how flexible such an 'artificialized' environment may be, combining nature and culture. In another stucco from the Villa della Farnesina, the centre of the ceiling of the first *cubiculum* B depicts a proper 'sacro-idyllic landscape', though one which is not Dionysian.[72] We still have trees and buildings, small figures (mostly women) in the act of adorning statues and performing ritual gestures. But without any attribute, this landscape must remain generically ritual, along with the entire corpus of such contemporary scenes.

An example, for comparison, of generic ritual landscape is provided by a fresco from a columbarium in the Villa Doria Pamphili.[73]

---

69 Museo Nazionale Romano, inv. 1037. Bragantini and De Vos 1982, 193, fig. 112.
70 Wyler forthcoming c.
71 Wyler 2011b, 173–78.
72 Museo Nazionale Romano, inv. 1071. Bragantini and De Vos 1982, 138, fig. 72.
73 From the wall F, XX, 20-10 BCE, now in the Museo Nazionale Romano. Bendinelli 1941, 26–28, fig. 12; Ling 1993.

Fig. 7: Fresco from a columbarium in the Villa Doria Pamphili, 20–10 BCE. Rome, Museo Nazionale Romano (Palazzo Massimo). With permission of the Ministero per i beni e le attività culturali – Museo Nazionale Romano. Photo S. Wyler.

We have here the visual 'invention' of a fantasized space that seems the opposite of the city and of public life, but nor does it pretend to represent real countryside. It is an idealized scene of rustic life in the centre of which shines the *pietas* of ordinary people from the land (they do not seem particularly rustic, and are mainly women, travellers, anglers, and shepherds). In a word, the dream of rustic *pietas* sung of by Virgil, Horace and Tibullus, at a time when the land of Italy had been pacified and become more accessible for travelling through the empire. In the Augustan context, the Hellenistic world of the *Bucolics* takes on a new resonance after the civil war and the propaganda of Augustus.[74]

And yet, the Dionysian atmosphere of the ritual scenes which we have considered merges with the generic imaginative 'no-cities-world': they share many common features, and the Dionysian version is a particular development of the genre, one which shows nature full of diffuse sacredness but that needs

---

[74] Leach 1988; Cucchiarelli 2012, 20–21.

human beings to actualize it. On a last stucco from the Farnesina,[75] a panther being caressed by a very quiet maenad in front of a benevolent Silenus has been domesticated by the new aesthetic of the Principate. The sense is not new: it is very close to the mosaic of the House of the Centaur in Pompeii, where a wild lion is being tamed by erotes and maenads. But the atmosphere is very different, much quieter and more intimate. This is precisely the opposite of the excessively exuberant manifestations of Mark Antony in Ephesus, Tarsus and Alexandria, dressed as the god together with Cleopatra as a new Isis-Aphrodite,[76] which typifies the 'Oriental Hellenistic decadence', according to the Augustan propaganda. Just as Augustan art had invented a new style that reinterpreted Attic classicism,[77] it adapted a new image of 'dionysism', acceptable to the new Rome.

The same phenomenon can be detected, I think, in contemporary literature.[78] Suffice it to consider how the portrait of the god has evolved from Catullus to Ovid: the Republican poet's disturbing Iacchus at first appears to frighten Ariadne, with his disquieting followers dancing with snakes and playing cacophonous music, and Catullus stops the description just before the god rescues her.[79] Half a century later, Ovid explicitly rewrites some of Catullus' verses and transforms the god into an amorous husband, one who apologizes to his wife for having been tempted by an Indian beauty.[80] Horace too represents the god in interesting ways: at a symposium he enjoins moderation and control of drunkenness in order to gain access to the blessed initiates' world.[81] We could cite examples from other poets: R. A. Smith has discussed the taming of Bacchus in the *Georgics*.[82] At the end of the Augustan integration, when Dionysian violence is the subject of song, the god is no longer its actual source: it is a fake, a madness inspired by another god who dresses up his vengeance as a *Bacchicus*

---

75 Museo Nazionale Romano, inv. 1071. Bragantini and De Vos 1982, 138, fig. 74.
76 Ephesus (spring 41 BCE): Plutarch, *Ant.* 24.4–5. Tarsus (summer 41 BCE): Plutarch, *Ant.* 26.5. Athens (without Cleopatra, in 39-38 BCE): Cassius Dio, 48.39.2 and Seneca the Elder, *Suas.* 1.6. Alexandria (35-30 BCE): Velleius Paterculus, 2.82 and Cassius Dio, 50.4–5.3. For Antony's proto-Dionysian drunkenness already in 49 BCE in Italy see Plutarch, *Ant.* 9.5–8 with Śnieżewski 1998.
77 Zanker 1987.
78 See also Mac Góráin, Introduction, p. 21; and Miller in this volume.
79 Catullus, 64.251–62.
80 Catullus, 64.144, *nunc iam nullo uiro iuranti femina credat*, is transposed by Ovid into *Fast.* 3.475, *nunc quoque nulla uiro, clamabo, femina credit*; for the whole episode, see *Fast.* 3.460–516.
81 Horace, *Carm.* 1.27.
82 Smith 2007; but for emphasis on the persistence of danger in the figure of Bacchus, see Mac Góráin 2014.

furor (such as Amata in the *Aeneid* or the Thracian women in the *Georgics* and the *Metamorphoses* who tear Orpheus limb from limb out of heartache).[83] Even if this frightening aspect has to remain as part of the mythical and literary background, the acceptance of the god turns him into a beneficent and benevolent Augustan divinity of viticulture, symposium and mystery, patronizing young people and poets. It was probably not by chance that images of Dionysus proliferated from the 20s BCE onwards, after the defeat of the *neos Dionysos*,[84] as the new princeps strengthened his grip on power. It is notable that the proliferation began in the domestic rather than the public sphere, before Augustus became *pontifex maximus* upon Lepidus' death in 12 BCE, which allowed him to intensify his programme of religious restoration.[85]

The new aesthetic features of the god that can be observed in the calm wildness of Dionysian landscapes reflect a profound change in the perception of the god and his realm. The images still express a sense of strangeness. They aim to recreate a vision of another world, a better world beyond the present one, to which Romans could have access through mysteries, the symposium and art – a world close to the Golden Age now finally accessible. This 'somewhere else' may appear Greek in form – that is indeed peculiar, but also a structural feature of Dionysian images in Rome. This was probably already the case in the archaic period, to provide a paradigm that hinted at the divine associations of the triumphing king. But from the sanctuary of Sant'Omobono up to the painted Augustan landscapes and beyond, Dionysus is definitely Roman.

Bibliography

Attenni, L. 2002. *Frammenti di affresco con scene d'iniziazione dionisiaca*. Quaderni del museo civico di Lanuvio 1. Velletri.
Bendinelli, G. 1941. *Le pitture del colombario di Villa Pamphili*. Rome.
Boardman, J. 2014. *The Triumph of Dionysos: Convivial Processions, from Antiquity to the Present Day*. Oxford.
Bordenache Battaglia, G. and A. Emiliozzo, 1979. *Le ciste prenestine. Corpus* (vol. 1.1). Florence.
Borgeaud, P. 2017. 'Variations évhéméristes.' *Revue de l'histoire des religions* 4, 593–612.
Borgies, L. 2016. *Le conflit propagandiste entre Octavien et Marc Antoine. De l'usage politique de la 'vituperatio' entre 44 et 30 a. C.* Brussels.

---

[83] Virgil, *Aen.* 7.374–405 with Mac Góráin 2013; Ovid, *Met.* 9.1–72.
[84] Mac Góráin 2013, 124–25.
[85] Scheid 2002, 788–94.

Bragantini, I. and M. De Vos, 1982. *Museo Nazionale Romano. Le pitture*, vol. II.1. *Le decorazioni della villa romana della Farnesina*. Rome.
Bragantini, I. 1993. 'La Casa del Centauro.' In *Pompei. Pitture e mosaici* vol. 4, Rome, 819–59.
Brentchaloff, D. and A. Hermary, 2000. 'L'Hermès double de Fréjus.' *MMAI* 78, 53–83.
Brocato, P., M. Ceci, and N. Terrenato, eds. 2017. *Ricerche nell'area dei templi di Fortuna e Mater Matuta*, vol. 1. Rome.
Brocato, P. and N. Terrenato, 2017. 'The archaic temple of S. Omobono: new discoveries and old problems.' In *The Age of Tarquinius Superbus: Central Italy in the Late 6th Century*, edited by P.S. Lulof and C. Smith. Louvain, 97–106.
Buccino, L. 2013. *Dioniso trionfatore. Percorsi e interpretazione del mito del trionfo indiano nelle fonti e nell'iconografia antiche*. Rome.
Caneva, S. 2016. 'Configurations publiques de Dionysos dans le cadre de l'hellénisation de Rome.' In *Dieux des Grecs, Dieux des Romains. Panthéons en dialogue à travers l'histoire et l'historiographie*, edited by C. Bonnet, V. Pirenne-Delforge, and G. Pironti. Rome, 99–116.
Carpenter, T.H. 1986. *Dionysian imagery in Archaic Greek art. Its Development in Black-Figure Vase Painting*. Oxford.
Coarelli, F. 1993. 'Ceres, Liber, Liberaque, aedes; aedes Cereris." *LTUR*, edited by E.M. Steinby, vol. 1. Rome, 260–61.
Coarelli, F. 1997. 'La cultura artistica a Roma in età repubblicana. In *Revixit ars. Arte e ideologia a Roma, dai modelli ellenistici alla tradizione repubblicana*. Rome, 15–84.
Coarelli, F. 2011. *L'art romain des origines au IIIe siècle av. J.-C.* Paris.
Colonna, G. 1982. 'La Sicilia e il Tirreno nel V e IV secolo.' In *Kokalos* 26–27, Atti del V Congresso Internazionale di studi sulla Sicilia antica (1980-1981). Palermo, 157–91.
Colonna, G. 1991. 'Riflessioni sul dionisismo in Etruria.' In *Dionysos. Mito e mistero*, edited by F. Berti and C. Gasparri. Ferrara, 117–55.
Cristofani, M. 1986. 'Dionysos/Fufluns.' *LIMC* 3, 531–40 (1) and 419–27 (2).
Cristofani, M. 1990. 'Antefissa da Caere. Antefissa a testa femminile.' In *La grande Roma dei Tarquini* (exhibition catalogue, Rome 1990), edited by M. Cristofani. Rome, 142.
Croisille, J.-M. 2010. *Paysages dans la peinture romaine. Aux origines d'un genre pictural*. Paris.
Cucchiarelli, A. ed. 2012. *Publio Virgilio Marone. Le Bucoliche*. Rome.
De Cazanove, O. 1983. '*Lucus Stimulae*: les aiguillons des Bacchanales.' *MEFRA* 95.1, 55–113.
De Cazanove, O. 2011. 'Naissance et petite enfance dans le monde romain.' In *Thesaurus Cultus et Rituum Antiquorum* vol. 7. Los Angeles, 11–16.
Diffendale, D.P. et al. 2016. 'Sant'Omobono: an interim *status quaestionis*.' *JRA* 29, 7–42.
Dohrn, T. 1972. *Die Ficoronische Ciste*. Berlin.
Fraenkel, E. 1964. *Kleine Beiträge zur klassischen Philologie*. Vol. 2: *Zur römischen Literatur. Zu juristischen Texten. Verschiedenes*. Rome.
Frazer, J.G. tr. 1989. *Ovid. Fasti*. Cambridge, MA.
Gasparri, C. 1986a. 'Dionysos.' In *LIMC* 3.1, 414–514.
Gasparri, C. 1986b. 'Dionysos/Bacchus.' In *LIMC* 3.1, 540–66.
Gazda, E. 2000. *The Villa of the Mysteries in Pompeii: Ancient Ritual, Modern Muse*. Ann Arbor, MI.
Hinterhöller-Klein, M. 2015. *Varietates topiorum. Perspektive und Raumerfassung in Landschafts- und Panoramabildern der römischen Wandmalerei vom 1. Jh. V. Chr. bis zum Ende der pompejanischen Stile*. Vienna.

Hölscher, T. 2004. *The Language of Images in Roman Art*. New York.
Hooper, W.D. and H.B. Ash, trs. 1934. *Cato and Varro. On Agriculture*. Cambridge, MA.
Huet, V. and S. Wyler, 2005. '"Copie romaine d'un original grec", ou les arts grecs revisités par les Romains.' *Mètis* (n. s.) 3, 151–77.
Jaccottet, A.-F. 2003. *Choisir Dionysos. Les associations dionysiaques ou la face cachée du dionysisme*. 2 vols. Zürich.
Jaccottet, A.-F. and S. Wyler, 2018. '"Le bel antre toujours vert": une architecture éphémère, entre texte et imaginaire.' In *Espaces et architectures fictives dans l'Antiquité romaine*, edited by G. Viard and R. Robert. Bordeaux, 141–60.
Jaccottet, A.-F. and S. Wyler, eds. Forthcoming. *Neoi. Des hommes nouveaux dieux: de la titulature hellénistique à l'imitatio romaine*.
La Rocca, E. 2008. 'Gli affreschi della casa di Augusto e della villa della Farnesina: una revisione cronologica. In *Le due patrie acquisite. Studi di archeologia dedicati a Walter Trillmich*, edited by E. La Rocca, P. Léon and C.P. Presicce. Rome, 223–42.
Leach, E.W. 1988. *The Rhetoric of Space. Literary and Artistic Representations of Landscape in Republican and Augustan Rome*. Princeton, NJ.
Ling, R. 1993. 'The paintings of the columbarium of Villa Doria Pamphili in Rome.' In *Functional and Spatial Analysis of Wall Painting*, edited by E.M. Moormann. Amsterdam, 127–35.
Littlewood, R J. 2006. *A commentary on Ovid's Fasti, Book 6*. Oxford.
Maggiani, A. 2002. 'Nel mondo degli specchi etruschi.' In *Incisori di specchi e ciste tra Lazio ed Etruria*, edited by A. Emiliozzi and A. Maggiani. Rome, 7–22.
Mac Góráin, F. 2013. 'Virgil's Bacchus and the Roman republic.' In *Augustan Poetry and the Roman Republic*, edited by J. Farrell and D. Nelis. Oxford, 124–45.
Mac Góráin, F. 2014. 'The mixed blessings of Bacchus in Virgil's *Georgics*.' *Dictynna* 11.
Manuwald, G. ed. 2012. *Tragicorum Romanorum Fragmenta*, vol. 2, *Ennius*. Göttingen.
Menichetti, M. 1995. *Quoius forma virtutei parisuma fuit. Ciste prenestine e cultura di Roma medio-repubblicana*. Rome.
Metzger, Henri .1995. 'Le Dionysos des images éleusiniennes du IVème siècle.' *RA* (n.s.) 1, 3–22.
Massa-Pairault, F.-H. 1987. 'De Préneste à Volsinii: Minerve, le *fatum* et la constitution de la société.' *La parola del passato* 42, 200–35.
Mignone, L.M. 2016. *The Republican Aventine and Rome's Social Order*. Ann Arbor, MI.
Mols, S.T. and E.M. Moormann, 2008. *La villa della Farnesina. Le pitture*. Milan.
Mura Sommella, A. ed. 2007. *Príncipes etruscos: entre Oriente e Occidente*. Barcelona.
Mura Sommella, A. 2011. 'La dea col tutulo dal tempio arcaico del Foro Boario.' In *Deliciae fictiles IV: Architectural terracottas in Ancient Italy. Images of Gods, Monsters and Heroes*, edited by P. Lulof and C. Rescigno. Oakville, CT, 177–87.
Peters, W. J. T. 1963. *Landscapes in Romano-Campanian Mural Painting*. Groningen.
Prescendi, F. 2011. 'La déesse grecque Ino-Leucothée est devenue la déesse romaine Mater Matuta: réflexions sur les échanges entre cultures "voisines."' In *L'oiseau et le poisson. Cohabitations religieuses dans les mondes grec et romain*, edited by N. Belayche and J.-D. Dubois. Paris, 187–202.
Prieto-Luley, L. 2018. *Recherches sur les cistes prénestines. Approche pluridisciplinaire de petits et moyens conteneurs cylindriques et de leurs représentations en Italie centrale (470-270 avant J.-C)*, PhD. Tours.
Prioux, E. 2017. 'Le paysage des offrandes votives chez Léonidas de Tarente.' *Cahiers Mondes Anciens* 9.

Rouveret, A. 1981. *Pline l'Ancien. Histoire naturelle. Livre 36.* Paris.
Rouveret, A. 1994. 'La ciste Ficoroni et la culture romaine du IVe s. av. J.-C.' *BSAF*, 225–42.
Scheid, J. 2002. 'Religion et politique au début de l'Empire.' *ACF* 102, 787–803.
Silberberg, S.R. 1980. *A Corpus of the Sacral-Idyllic Landscape Painting in Roman Art.* Ann Arbor, MI.
Simon, E. 1978. 'Il dio Marte nell'arte dell'Italia centrale.' *SE* 46, 135–47.
Smith, R.A. 2007. '*In vino civitas*: the rehabilitation of Bacchus in Vergil's *Georgics*.' *Vergilius* 53, 58–87.
Śnieżewski, S. 1998. 'Divine connections of Marcus Antonius in the years 43–30 BC.' *GB* 22, 129–44.
Terrenato, N. et al. 2012. 'The S. Omobono Sanctuary in Rome: assessing eighty years of fieldwork and exploring perspectives for the future.' *Internet Archaeology* 31.
Tomei, M. A. 1997. *Museo Palatino.* Milan.
Torelli, M. 1997. 'I fregi figurati delle "regiae" latine ed etrusche.' In *Il rango, il rito e l'immagine. Alle origini della rappresentazione storica romana.* Milan, 87–121.
Vahlen, J. ed. 1928. *Q. Ennius Varia, Ennianae Poesis Reliquiae.* Leipzig.
Veyne, P. 1979. 'L'hellénistation de Rome et la problématique des acculturations.' *Diogène* 106, 3–29.
Vatin, C. 2004. *Ariane et Dionysos. Un mythe de l'amour conjugal.* Paris.
Wallace-Hadrill, A. 1998. 'To be Roman, go Greek. Thoughts on Hellenization at Rome.' In *Modus Operandi, Essays in Honour of Geoffrey Rickman*, edited by M. Austin, J. Harries, and C. Smith. London, 79–91.
Warmington, E. H. 1961a. *Remains of Old Latin 1. Ennius and Caecilius.* Cambridge, MA.
Warmington, E. H. 1961b. *Remains of Old Latin 3. Lucilius. The Twelve Tables.* Cambridge, MA.
Warmington, E. H. 1967. *Remains of Old Latin 2. Livius Andronicus, Naevius, Pacuvius, and Accius.* Cambridge, MA.
Wyler, S. 2006a. 'À la barbe de Dionysos: les valeurs d'une image "archaïsante" à Rome.' *Ktema* 31, 189–201.
Wyler, S. 2006b. 'Roman replication of Greek art at the Villa della Farnesina.' *Art History* 29.2, 215–234.
Wyler, S. 2006c. 'Images dionysiaques à Rome: à propos d'une fresque méconnue de Lanuvium.' In *Religions orientales, culti misterici. Neue Perspektiven, nouvelles perspectives, prospettive nuove*, edited by C. Bonnet, P. Scarpi and J. Rüpke. Stuttgart, 135–45.
Wyler, S. 2009. 'Dionysos/Bacchus.' *LIMC Supplementum.* 1, 183–89; 2, 90–94.
Wyler, S. 2011a. 'L'acculturation dionysiaque à Rome: l'invention d'une altérité.' In *Identités romaines. Conscience de soi, et représentation de l'autre dans le Rome antique*, edited by M. Simon. Paris, 191–201.
Wyler, S. 2011b. 'Le phallus sous le péplos: vêtements et travestissements dionysiaques sur les images romaines.' In *Parure et artifice: le corps exposé*, edited by L. Bodiou, F. Gherchanoc, V. Huet, and V. Mehl. Paris, 171–87.
Wyler, S. 2013. 'Dionysos/*Loufir*/*Liber* et sa parèdre. Le fronton du temple et le culte de S. Abbondio.' *MEFR* 125.1 (online).
Wyler, S. Forthcoming a. 'Sacra per topia. Images de rituels dans les paysages "sacro-idylliques" romains.' In *Rituels en image, images de rituel. Grèce, Rome, Egypte, Mésopotamie* (proceedings of the international colloquium in Geneva, 12-14 March 2015), edited by A.-F. Jaccottet.

Wyler, S. Forthcoming b. '*Loufir*/Liber at the crossroads of religious cultures in Pompeii (third-second centuries BCE).' In *Gods and Goddesses in Ancient Italy*, edited by E.H. Bispham and D. Miano. London.

Wyler, S. Forthcoming c. 'L'habit fait-il le dieu? Gestes et parures autour des hermes rustiques dans l'art romain.' In *Performances corporelles et vestimentaires en Grèce et à Rome: le rituel en question*, edited by F. Gherchanoc and V. Huet.

Zanker, P. 1987. *Augustus und die Macht der Bilder*. Munich. = id. 1988. *The Power of Images in the Age of Augustus*, tr. A. Shapiro, Ann Arbor, MI.

Zanker, P. 1998. *Eine Kunst für die Sinne. Zur Bilderwelt des Dionysos und der Aphrodite*. Berlin.

Daniele Miano
Liber, Fufluns, and the others: rethinking Dionysus in Italy between the fifth and the third centuries BCE

Abstract: In response to a dossier of different theonyms and iconographic profiles for a set of gods in central Italy from the 5th–3rd centuries that correspond to Dionysus, this chapter considers the relationship between Fufluns, Liber, Hiaco (and other by-forms) with reference to two main concepts. (a) Translation: based on the work of Jan Assman, Homi Bhabha and others, we may investigate to what extent these divine forms were 'translations' or 'interpretations' of a Greek archetype. (b) Multiplicity: following the work of Versnel, Henrichs and others, we may consider the cluster of gods under the rubric of religious polymorphism: was Dionysus one god or many? The chapter argues for the fragmentation of Dionysus in Italy in the 5th–3rd centuries, and for the significance of local myths and forms of worship of the god as against a generalized 'Roman' standard. The discussion focusses on two case studies, Vulci in Etruria and Praeneste in Latium, with particular reference to local colour. The Etruscan evidence surveyed comprises epigraphic and iconographic attestations of Fufluns Paχie on fifth-century ceramics and a fourth-century mirror respectively. Praenestine evidence analysed includes bronze mirrors and *cistae* which depict Fufluns, L(e)iber and Hiaco. In conclusion it addresses the significance of the fragmentation of Dionysus in Italy for the interpretation of the Bacchanalian affair of 186 BCE.

Introduction

If one wishes to discuss the way in which Dionysus was worshipped by the non-Hellenic populations of Italy, one must necessarily deal with two distinct but overlapping questions: the first is that of multiplicity, the second of translation.

I am much grateful to the editor for his invitation to contribute to the original conference and to this volume and for our subsequent warm and intellectually stimulating exchanges and conversations, and to Stéphanie Wyler, Francesco Massa and Laura Puritani for sending to me some of their unpublished and published works. I wrote the original paper during a Postdoctoral Research Fellowship awarded by the Irish Research Council, and I revised it during a Research Fellowship awarded by the Alexander von Humboldt Foundation.

https://doi.org/10.1515/9783110672237-004

Multiplicity is an essential characteristic of Dionysus, as of any other god. In a passage of *De natura deorum* (3.58), also discussed in this volume by Gesine Manuwald, Cicero has the character Q. Aurelius Cotta comment on the multiplicity of gods, listing at least five different *Dionysoi*, and John the Lydian reproduces a similar catalogue (*Mens.* 4.51).[1] Different mythical genealogies and cults mark different 'aspects' or personae of Dionysus – terms that I use with awareness of their vagueness, but that point at the difficulty of defining with precision this tension between one and many. Cotta rejects this overabundance of *Dionysoi* as absurd (3.60). There is a palpable tension in this passage between unity and multiplicity: mythology shows that there are many gods, whereas Cotta's philosophy argues that there must be one. So, at different discursive levels, Dionysus can be one and many. Recent scholarship on Greek polytheism has greatly focused on this aspect of ancient deities.[2] With regard to Dionysus in particular, Henk Versnel and Albert Henrichs have underlined that the great number of divine personae identified with Dionysus and their concurring unity in different contexts and at different levels is a defining characteristic of the god.[3] As Henrichs has provocatively stated, one could turn 'the monotheistic creed of oneness in trinity, or of unity in multiplicity, into a pagan declaration of faith in a Dionysos who is simultaneously one and many: "Dionysos is a god, Iakchos is a god, Sabazios is a god. And yet they are not three gods, but one god."'[4]

It is worth noting that Cicero uses a form directly transliterated from Greek, Dionysus, rather than the common Latin translation Liber, as he frequently does elsewhere.[5] Translatability is a further essential characteristic of polytheism: two or more gods from different linguistic areas could be considered mutual translations. In Classical scholarship having gods in different languages considered the equivalent of each other has rarely been studied in terms of translation, but rather of interpretation or using hierarchical categories such as Hellenization or Romanisation.[6] The idea of gods in translation was formulated by Jan Assmann in the nineties and expanded by other scholars working on the Near East, such as

---

1 With a notable difference: Cicero writes that the Dionysus of the Orphic rites is son of Jupiter and Luna – whereas John the Lydian has Semele. This detail makes it probable that Cicero and John the Lydian are using (directly or indirectly) a common Greek source, and Cicero confuses Semele and Selene, incorrectly translating the name as Luna. See Henrichs 2013, 560.
2 Versnel 2011a; Parker 2011.
3 Versnel 2011b; Henrichs 2013.
4 Henrichs 2013, 555.
5 See Manuwald in this volume.
6 On *interpretatio* see Ando 2005; Bettini 2016; Parker 2017, 33–76.

Mark Smith.[7] According to Assmann, translation is one of the ways in which different gods are united. The most ancient documents attesting this practice are Babylonian: it was common that, especially in legal documents, the names of Babylonian gods would be translated from Sumerian, and from the late second millennium BCE onwards, lists of names of gods with translations in different languages were produced in Mesopotamia. Although Greeks and Romans did not produce such lists, translating gods was a common practice, attested by countless documents, and discussed already by Herodotus in book 2 with a profound awareness of the nuances and the complexity of the process.[8] Assmann argued that the translatability of gods must be based on one or more elements that the divinities in question shared.[9]

This problem can be connected with the broader concept of cultural translation, theorised by Homi Bhabha.[10] Playing on the etymological ambiguity of the term 'translation' as transportation and interpretation, Bhabha argues that the translator moves in a liminal space between different languages or semantic systems, and that the work of translation creates something entirely new. Temporally, translation happens in the present; it tends to be always an unfinished and temporary business, but can project itself towards the past and the future. This aspect of Bhabha's theory is particularly useful because it focuses on translation as a continuous process, in which the status of the source or the resulting item is relatively unimportant in essentialist terms. Potentially, focusing on cultural translation also allows us to appreciate the agency of the translators, as it is these individuals and groups between semantic systems than engage in the process. If the metaphor of cultural translation has been criticised by some for being too vague, there have in turn been vigorous defences against these critiques.[11] Recently, Peter Burke has brilliantly used cultural translation to describe a variety of historical phenomena of the Renaissance, thus showing that the concept can be useful beyond contemporary, postcolonial contexts.[12] Burke distinguishes cultural translation from the closely related concept of hybridization precisely for the question of agency: he believes that if a process of hybridization can be done unconsciously, a process of cultural translation always implies a conscious

---

7 Assmann 1996; Assmann 2008, esp. 54–58; Smith 2008.
8 See Burkert 1985; Calame 2011.
9 Assmann 2008, 54.
10 Bhabha 1994, 303–37.
11 Maitland 2017, 18–27.
12 Burke 2016, 11–41.

choice. It seems to me that in the present case of Dionysus the metaphor of cultural translation is particularly cogent and powerful to characterise what was happening in ancient Italy between Etruscan, Greek, and Latin gods and goddesses.

The question of translation involves a discussion of what names Dionysus was called in languages other than Greek, such as Liber in Latin and Fufluns in Etruscan. On the basis of which common elements were these translations formulated? The question of multiple divine personae is intimately interconnected with that of translation. Which Dionysus was translated? Who performed the act of translation? And how many different translations were possible? Is it fair to say that Liber is Dionysus in Latium, or Fufluns Dionysus in Etruria? Was there a Dionysus in Italy, or multiple divine figures, identified with a different set of multiple divine figures for a number of different reasons? To what extent may one consider Dionysus in Italy as a unitary rather than a fragmented phenomenon?

An argument for a unity of Dionysus in Italy is strongly based on the perspective provided by Roman sources. When Livy narrates the Bacchanalian affair in book 39, he describes the story of the corruption of the Bacchanalian rituals as an Italian phenomenon, which had started with a *Graecus ignobilis* who imported a new form of rites to Etruria (39, 8, 3), and a dubious Campanian priestess called Paculla Annia (39, 13, 9). The *SC* decree from Tiriolo (*ILLRP* 511) also confirms the Roman understanding of the Bacchanalia as an Italian issue.[13] Another argument for unity is based on the uniform character of phenomena pertaining to visual culture. Across the languages and cultures of ancient Italy there is a broad acceptance and local elaboration of Greek iconographies, including Dionysian elements such as satyrs, maenads and the god Dionysus himself.[14] But how should we interpret these images without the aid of written sources, strong contextual evidence or inscriptions? Versnel has underlined the methodological frailty of a unifying interpretation of iconographic evidence, even when it pertains to a single linguistic area: identical representations may be used to signify radically different personae or aspects of the deity.[15] When we consider iconographies across different languages and cultures, a unifying interpretation inevitably becomes even frailer. Distinct cultures might give different meanings to the same images, and without contextual information or written signs such as inscriptions, we

---

13 A comprehensive recent discussion is Briscoe 2008, 230–90, but see also Bispham 2007, 116–23; Cazanove 2000; Pailler 1988; and Steinhauer in this volume.
14 For an approach based on iconography see Cerchiai 2011; Cerchiai 2014; Puritani 2016; and Puritani 2018.
15 Versnel 2011a, 521–22.

moderns are hardly in the position to appreciate this. The risk, therefore, is of giving a unifying interpretation of ancient evidence based on the faulty assumption that iconography must have a universal meaning.

In this chapter I argue against a unifying interpretation of Dionysus in Italy. On the one hand, I do not think that a Roman perspective should be adopted, and on the other I argue that the uniformity of Dionysian imagery in Italy might conceal a variety of disparate meanings hidden from the eye of the beholder, which are revealed only when inscriptions and other contextual evidence help us appreciate them. In a forthcoming paper, Stéphanie Wyler argues that the evidence on Loufir in Pompeii shows, on the one hand, a strongly local adaptation of Hellenistic models, and on the other the sanctuary seemingly unaffected by the Bacchanalian affair.[16] I shall also argue that a careful consideration of local evidence yields a much better understanding of Dionysus in Italy than has been achieved hitherto, and I shall put more emphasis than has previously been done on the process of translation of a Greek god from a cultural point of view, looking at multiple translations. I shall consider how Dionysus was translated in two Italian cities, Vulci in Etruria and Praeneste in Latium, between the fifth and the third centuries BCE.

Vulci

Vulci is a remarkable place to look at Dionysus in Italy. In the second half of the sixth century BCE local potters produced a number of artefacts known as the Ivy Leaf Group, because ivy leaves are often used as decorative patterns.[17] The workshop was active in the decades after 550 BCE and some of the known vases represent Dionysus. What to make of this Dionysus? Was he already identified with an Etruscan god? This is a question that cannot be answered, but the Ivy Leaf Group shows that the iconography of Dionysus was not only known from imported Greek pottery, but that it was so familiar that it was reproduced in the local production.

It is in the following century that we have four epigraphic documents from Vulci that testify to the translation of Dionysus as Fufluns. The most ancient of these objects in an Attic red-figure *kylix* cup attributed to the Penthesileia painter

---

16 Wyler forthcoming.
17 Werner 2005.

(460–455 BCE). Inside the cup one can see Apollo fighting Tityos with Leto witnessing the struggle. Outside, groups of young men and women are represented. The inscription is on the bottom of the cup, after glazing, and it reads *fuflunsl paχ[---]*.[18] The object was found at Pian della Badia during excavations promoted by Lucien Bonaparte, Napoleon's brother, to whom the Pope awarded lands and the title of Prince of Canino.[19] A further inscription is on an Attic red-figure *kylix* cup attributed to the Marley group (425–400 BCE). Inside the cup is represented an old Silenos riding a fawn. Outside there are three female figures in movement, one with a baby. The object also comes from the Bonaparte excavations. The inscription, with a rather uncertain hand, is on the bottom on the cup, and it reads *fuflunsul paχies velclθi*.[20] A third inscription was found on a fragment of a handle of black-painted Attic pottery (probably fifth century BCE), which was discovered in the 1980s near the western gate of the city.[21] The final inscription that I discuss is on an Attic red-figure *rhyton* cup in the shape of a donkey with a representation of Eros (end of the fifth, beginning of the fourth century BCE), discovered during the Bonaparte excavations. The inscription, on the handle, reads *fuflun(s)l paχies velclθi*.[22]

The inscription: *fuflunsl paχies velclθi* can be translated as 'of Fufluns Paχie (genitive), at Vulci (locative)'. The divine name Fufluns is followed by the epithet Paχie; this is the Etruscan rendering of a Greek word, either Βάκχος or Βάκχιος.[23] In a recent paper, Marco Antonio Santamaría has argued that Βάκχος originally referred to the worshipper of Dionysus, whereas Βάκχιος subsequently came to be an epithet of the god, which would mean 'god of the Bacchants'.[24] This would suggest that perhaps Paχie comes directly from Βάκχιος. The name and the epithet of the god is in the genitive, which clearly here must express divine ownership of the object. The locative *velclθi*, 'at Vulci', is equally interesting. In his monograph on Etruscan votive inscriptions, Daniele Maras has underlined how in such a context the name of a city in locative cannot be merely a specification of place, which would be redundant: it must be rather interpreted as a way to

---

[18] Maras 2009, Vc.co 3 = *CIE* 11101.
[19] For the little we know of the history of the excavations, see Cristofani and Martelli 1978, 119–23; Della Fina 2004. The excavations started in 1828 and were first promoted by Princess Alexandrine, Lucien's wife.
[20] Maras 2009, Vc.co 5 = *CIE* 11073.
[21] Maras 2009, Vc.co 4 = *CIE* 10985: *[---]aχies v[---]*.
[22] Maras 2009, Vc.co 6 = *CIE* 11110. The missing sigma is likely to be a mistake of the engraver rather than a variant of the divine name.
[23] Maras 2009, 396; Cristofani and Martelli 1978, 127, with previous bibliography.
[24] Santamaría 2013.

clarify the local character of the god, in the way in which local epithets work in Greek and Latin.[25] One can think of Athena Lindia, or of Venus Erycina: they are not just Athena at Lindos or Venus at Eryx but they are specific and distinct goddesses, with individualised characteristics, with the local specification often hiding a process of translation from a different language (such as in the case of Eryx).[26] So the Fufluns Paχie inscriptions at Vulci put together an Etruscan divine name, an epithet of Greek derivation and a local specification which makes clear that this is an individual god, residing at Vulci and there only. The number of documents and their distribution over half a century make clear that we are dealing with a custom repeated over time (a ritual?). In spite of the presence of local production, all the inscriptions above are on imported Attic pottery, but it is unclear what the significance of this might be: I would be inclined to think that expensive imported pottery was considered better suited to an offering than cheaper local productions.

What kind of god was Fufluns Paχie? Marina Martelli has argued that he was a god strictly connected with wine, mostly because in local pottery from Vulci and other places in Etruria Fufluns-Dionysus is often represented with a *kantharos* cup, but this is hardly surprising, given that Fufluns already took over the iconography of Dionysus in the second quarter of the fifth century BCE.[27] Giovanni Colonna has given these texts a mystical interpretation. His argument goes as follows: these inscriptions probably come from graves, but if they were regular gifts to a divinity one would expect to find them in a sanctuary. Therefore, they should be considered evidence of rites of initiation, objects that the Bacchants would take to their graves as a proof of their different status in the netherworld.[28] This is difficult to support: to formulate his argument, Colonna assumes that there is a substantial uniformity between Greek and Etruscan practices. Moreover, Colonna assumes that these objects come from graves, but there can be no absolute certainly about it as we are ignorant of precise contexts, due to the antiquarian character of the Bonaparte excavations. Even if they came from graves, does this necessarily imply the presence of initiation rituals? One might invoke as a parallel the objects with Latin inscriptions called *pocola deorum*. Most of them were produced at the beginning of the third century BCE: they were pieces of pottery of various shapes with the painted inscription *pocolom* followed by the

---

25 Maras 2009, 94.
26 On this point, see Parker 2003 and, in transcultural contexts, Parker 2017, 77–110.
27 Cristofani and Martelli 1978, 132. The earliest evidence for the attribution of the iconography of Dionysus to Fufluns is the archaic mirror I shall discuss in the following section.
28 Colonna 2005, 2018–19.

name of a deity in the genitive.[29] Many of these objects were found in Etruscan *necropoleis*, and three were found in Vulci, dedicated to Vulcanus, Ceres and Aequitas.[30] Of course these *pocola* are completely different from the Fufluns Paχie inscriptions: they are much later, and the formula is painted on the pottery by the workshop during the production of the piece, rather than engraved after glazing at the moment of the offering. But both kinds of objects testify to the practice of having a formula of divine ownership inscribed on pottery found in graves, in this case clearly without any implication of initiation.

One can focus on the epithet Paχie and give a Dionysian interpretation of the god Fufluns at Vulci, but the locative *velclθi* is no less significant to the interpretation of the inscriptions and the related practices: with whatever ritual he was honoured, the god was one of Vulci, a divinity who had some kind of connection with Dionysus through the common epithet Paχie /Bakchios, but must have had a profoundly local character.

This strong local character is confirmed by the final document regarding Fufluns at Vulci. It is a mirror kept in Berlin, which was produced in the first half of the fourth century BCE (fig. 8).[31] One can see a young Fufluns embracing his mother Semla (Semele), next to a standing Apulu (Apollo). In this case we have a scene in which the mother of Fufluns is labelled with an Etruscan rendering of her Greek name. However, the scene does not recall any obvious Greek myth, and it is not clear to what extent it makes sense to look for one. Erika Simon has argued that the scene represents the resurrection of Semele by Dionysus during the Delphic festival of Herois, but such a specifically Delphic myth on an Etruscan mirror would be quite astonishing.[32] Bonfante has argued that the scene represents Fufluns/Dionysus after a descent to Hades to bring Semla back to the living.[33] I do not believe that the scene must necessarily be inspired by a mythological narrative. A mirror recently excavated from the environs of Orvieto shows exactly the same composition with some minor variations, but, other than Apulu, the other characters have different names: there is a young Turnu (Eros), and the embracing characters are the lovers Atunis (Adonis), and Turan (Aphrodite).[34] The identical composition of the two mirrors implies that the scenes are meant to show relationships between different gods and characters in a stereotypical way.

---

29 Cifarelli, Ambrosini and Nonnis 2002–2003.
30 *CIL* I² 439, 445, 453.
31 *ES* 83 = *CSE DDR* 1, 5.
32 Simon 2013, 505–6.
33 Bonfante 1993, 231–32.
34 Feruglio 1998.

Liber, Fufluns, and the others — 119

This may also be true for the mirror from Vulci, which would not be the representation of a specific myth, but a way of conveying a relationship between Fufluns, Semla and Apulu.

Fig. 8: Mirror with Fufluns embracing Semla, Vulci (from *ES* 83)

Wyler has shown that a terracotta relief from Vulci, produced around 250 BCE, which represents a Dionysian character (Fufluns?), with Ariadne/Ariatha, is indeed a local variant of a broader Hellenistic iconography widespread in Italy and Sicily, which features Dionysus and a female goddess frequently identified with Venus/Aphrodite.[35] At Vulci this iconography has details which suggest an astrological interpretation. The relief also shows that at Vulci Fufluns was not associated with a female goddess but rather with mortal women (Semla, Ariatha).

Praeneste

The Latin town of Praeneste is deservedly famous for its high-quality bronze workshops, which produced a large number of engraved mirrors and *cistae*, mostly found in graves during eighteenth- and nineteenth-century excavations. Several of these mirrors and *cistae* also have inscriptions meant to identify the represented figures. Whereas engraved *cistae* are a typical product of Praeneste, and are only inscribed in Latin, several mirrors were inscribed in Etruscan up until the fourth century BCE. The question of the extent to which these objects must be considered Etruscan or local is debated.[36] From the fourth century BCE onwards, locally produced mirrors have a different shape than those imported from Etruria (pear-shaped rather than circular), are occasionally inscribed in Latin, and show the characters of a strong local tradition. For the earlier period the situation is less clear. Marisa Bonamici is inclined to think that the Praenestine mirrors inscribed in Etruscan were imports realised by workshops operating in Perugia and Tarquinia.[37] In any case it is generally admitted that there must have been some kind of interchange between Etruscan and Latin craftsmen, and for the later production it has been argued that this is a possible explanation for some eccentric characteristics of the Latin language used to inscribe these objects.[38] One could imagine Etruscan craftsmen living in Praeneste and working with Latin craftsmen to satisfy the needs of wealthy clients.

---

35 Wyler forthcoming; Cristofani 1986, no. 62.
36 A good summary of the debate in van der Meer 2016; also Franchi De Bellis 2005, 13–15.
37 See Bonamici 2002.
38 Mancini 1997.

Fig. 9: Mirror with Fufluns, Menerva, Artamis and Esia, Praeneste (from *ES* 87)

An archaic circular mirror, dated around 475–450 BCE on stylistic grounds, was found near Praeneste in 1794, and is now in the Bologna Museum (fig. 9).[39] The mirror shows four characters with their names inscribed: on the left we have *Menarva* and *Fuflunus* holding a *kantharos* cup, looking towards *Artamis*, who is holding in her arms a female figure called *Esia*. As in the previous instance, no obvious Greek myth is identifiable. It has been proposed that Esia must be identified with Ariadne, although in Etruscan she is normally called Ariatha, and the scene represents a little-known mythical story.[40] The *Odyssey* alludes to Ariadne killed by Artemis (11.321–25), but the full story is in a fragment of Pherecydes of Athens.[41] According to Pherecydes, Athena appeared to Theseus and ordered him to abandon Ariadne and go back to Athens, which he did. After being consoled by Aphrodite, Ariadne is taken by Dionysus, who gave her a golden crown after mating with her. Subsequently, Artemis killed Ariadne for throwing away her virginity.

According to this interpretation, Esia in the mirror would be Ariadne, killed by Artemis as a punishment because she had lost her virginity to Dionysus. However, the scene remains puzzling to me: although in the fragment of Pherecydes Athena warns Theseus that he must leave Ariadne, I see no good reason why she should be present in the engraving. Secondly, Robert Fowler has shown that the sentence about Artemis killing Ariadne in the fragment is probably a later addition which is likely not to belong to the narrative of Pherecydes and, if this is the case, there would be no reason to associate the scene with the fragment.[42] Moreover, on the mirror Artamis seems to be kidnapping Esia rather than killing her. To emphasise how the interpretation of this scene is uncertain, I can refer to a recent paper of Marjatta Nielsen and Anette Rathje, where exactly the opposite interpretation of the scene is given: they claim that Artamis is rescuing Esia, and that the scene testifies to the powers of salvation of the goddess.[43] I think that one has to accept that no simple explanation from known myths can make sense of this scene, which might represent a local myth of which we have no written record.

The form *Fuflunus* in the nominative is very peculiar. Gerhard Radke used it to argue that the name Fufluns had a Latin or Italic etymology, and it came from

---

39 *CSE* Italia 1, I, 10. For the date, most recently Maggiani 2002, 19 has 'pieno quinto secolo.'
40 Lambrechts 1978, 72–73. Also Bonfante 1993, 232, who refers only to the *Odyssey*; and Colonna 2005, 2021, where the name *esia* is explained as coming from Greek αἰσία, 'auspicious', because she is consecrated to the goddess.
41 BNJ 3 F 148a.
42 Fowler 2000–2013, II, 472.
43 Nielsen and Rathje 2009.

an unattested *Foflunos*.⁴⁴ I do not think it is very productive to think of etymologies, but it is certainly striking to see this form attested in a mirror from Praeneste, and I wonder whether the workshop producing the mirror may have been open to Latin influences. As it has a round shape, this object is usually considered an import from south Etruria, but there is no reason to rule out local production, perhaps by an itinerant Etruscan craftsman or a mixed workshop.⁴⁵ As the interaction between Etruscan and Latin has been used to explain some peculiarities of the Latin language used on Praenestine bronzes from the fourth century BCE, the same might hold true for the form Fuflunus one century earlier. What is certain is that exactly the same scene, and the same inscriptions in Etruscan, are also present on a pear-shaped mirror, certainly produced at Praeneste, probably around 350 BCE, now in Brussels.⁴⁶ This later copy shows the continuous significance of Fuflunus in Praeneste. The mixture of linguistic and cultural influences one can see on these two mirrors also has a bearing on the general interpretation of their meaning. Who was Fuflunus to the Praenestines? A fancy foreign god, who was nice to decorate mirrors with? To what extent was he Etruscan or Praenestine? What is certain is that the Latinised form of the name suggests a degree of local adaptation.

---

44 Radke 1965, 136.
45 Van der Meer 2016, 72 envisages the possibility of itinerant craftsmen and admits that mirrors from Praeneste inscribed in Etruscan show linguistic peculiarities which seem to suggest an interaction with Latin, although he is sceptical as to the permanent presence of workshops with Etruscan workers because of the lack of epigraphic evidence other than the mirrors. I think, however, that the mirrors themselves represent good enough epigraphic evidence.
46 Lambrechts 1978, 67–73. For a fourth-century BCE date see CSE Italia 1, 1, 30.

Fig. 10: Mirror with Hiaco, Menerva and Fortuna, Praeneste (from Matthies 1912)

An even greater local character is to be found in a mirror of the later series, inscribed in Latin. This mirror was found in Praeneste and it is in the Museo Nazionale di Palestrina (fig. 10).⁴⁷ It is dated around 350 BCE, and it is therefore contemporary to the Fufluns/Semla mirror from Vulci and to the copy of the Fuflunus mirror from Praeneste. In the foreground, we see Minerva and Fortuna embracing each other. On the background, we have a character labelled Hiaco riding a chariot led by monsters, surrounded by wild beasts, while Victoria crowns him. This scene in the background is unanimously interpreted as the celebration of the triumph of Hiaco. Franchi De Bellis has demonstrated that this Hiaco must be a Latin rendering of Ἴακχος. The initial H represents a problem to this interpretation, although there have been several attempts to explain it.⁴⁸ Other than the name, Hiaco has very little resemblance to the Ἴακχος of Eleusis. The march on a chariot crowned by Victoria seems hard to explain other than as the divine representation of a triumphal ceremony in the presence of the goddesses Fortuna and Minerva. Dionysus is also represented riding a chariot led by monsters on an early fourth-century BCE Attic *pelike*, although on this object he is not crowned by Nike, and he seems to be riding faster.⁴⁹ I wonder if the same character, Hiaco, should not also be identified with the one represented on another, uninscribed mirror from Praeneste, which shows a Dionysus-inspired character holding a thyrsus, and riding a chariot led by panthers, crowned by Victoria.⁵⁰ One can see the difference between the iconography on the Attic *pelike* and the Praenestine mirrors, where the triumphal character of Hiaco is highlighted by the presence of Victoria crowning him. I believe that the triumphal iconography of the scene makes it likely that the explanation of the engraving rest, at least partially, in Praenestine ceremonies and rituals.

The final piece of evidence I should like to discuss is a Praenestine *cista*, which gives yet another translation of Dionysus, and which is also discussed by Stéphanie Wyler in this volume (fig. 11). The object is normally dated to around the late fourth or early third centuries BCE, although there is great uncertainty in the dating of Praenestine *cistae*.⁵¹ The scene represents a meeting of gods: Juno, Jupiter, Mercury, Hercules, Apollo, Liber, Victoria, Minerva, Mars, Diana and Fortuna. Liber holds a vine branch, which identifies him as a translation of Dionysus.

---

47 CSE Italia 6, 83 = CIL 1² 2498.
48 Franchi De Bellis 2005, 113.
49 Gasparri 1986, no. 461.
50 *CSE* Italia 6, 83.
51 Bordenache Battaglia 1979, no. 5.

This is also the earliest appearance of the name Liber (inscribed *leiber*). The central element of the scene is Minerva doing something to Mars, under whom is located an amphora. Erika Simon has recalled the myth of Otus and Ephialtes imprisoning Ares in a bronze vase for 13 months, and surmised that Liber might be supervising the liberation (*Il.* 5.385–98).[52] Menichetti thought in terms of a mythological representation of local *rites de passage* of young men into adulthood.[53] Many other theories have been formulated.[54] In any case what matters to us is the representation of Liber with the iconographic characteristics of Dionysus.[55]

Fig. 11: Cista with a meeting of gods, Praeneste (from *Mon. Inst.* 1873)

There are other characters who might be identified with Dionysus, appearing on three other uninscribed Praenestine *cistae*. On the first, he appears with other characters next to an altar.[56] On a second *cista* he appears in what would seem to be a Dionysian procession.[57] On the third, he is represented with a satyr walking towards young women bathing, with a parallel female figure walking in the same direction.[58] Satyrs are often represented on *cistae* and mirrors. This has led Wiseman to believe that at Praeneste there was a cult of Liber, and that the scenes

---

52 Simon 1978.
53 Menichetti 1996, 80–95.
54 Bordenache Battaglia 1979, 52–54.
55 On this Praenestine *cista*, see also Wyler in this volume.
56 Bordenache Battaglia 1979, no. 4.
57 Bordenache Battaglia 1979, no. 14.
58 Bordenache Battaglia 1979, no. 22.

on mirrors and *cistae* must refer to dramatic performances and mime-plays in his honour, influenced by similar performances in Magna Graecia.[59] Without any direct Praenestine evidence of a cult of the god, such as votive gifts or similar items, however, it is of course very hard to say if it is the case, and we should beware of applying what we know of the Roman Liberalia to explain the complex iconographies appearing on Praenestine bronzes. Moreover, as these *cistae* are not inscribed, the identification of the characters must remain uncertain. Were the characters meant to represent Liber, Hiaco, or some other possible translation of Dionysus not transmitted to us?

So, who was Dionysus at Praeneste? The obvious thing one immediately notices is that the translation seems to be erratic: he is known by several names, from the Latinised Etruscan name Fuflunus to Hiaco and Liber, and even the iconography changes quite significantly from one image to another. I have already discussed Wiseman's theory of Liber as the god of drama, which I personally do not find very compelling, in the case of Praeneste. The triumphal iconography with Hiaco crowned by Victoria which appears on some of the mirrors, on the other hand, is striking, and I wonder if 'Dionysus' at Praeneste might have been associated with triumph. One must also notice that, while Liber or Hiaco is occasionally shown with a thyrsus and with vine branches, he does not seem to appear with drinking vessels. In the archaic Fuflunus mirror, the god is shown holding a *kantharos* cup, but it would appear that the translated Dionsysus at Praeneste does not have strong associations with wine. Liber, Fuflunus and Hiaco at Praeneste are all represented together with the goddess Minerva, although the other characters in the scenes vary.[60] This is in stark contrast with Vulci, where Fufluns is rather associated with mortal women such as Semla and Ariatha.

Conclusions

To make some concluding remarks, in this paper I have discussed the presence of Dionysus in Italy as a question of translation between Greek, Latin, and Etruscan. This discussion has shown all the complexity and the difficulty of considering an ancient god with such a multiple and complex identity as Dionysus in translation. Dionysos, Bakchios, Iakchos were freely translated into Etruscan and

---

59 Wiseman 2008, 119–24.
60 This is a suggestion for which I am grateful to Jackie Elliott.

Latin. As translations must be based on one or more common elements, it is reasonable to assume that such must have been the case. However, it is at times very different to determine which common elements one must work with. In Vulci wine and mysteries have been proposed, and although I find the wine theory more convincing in its simplicity, the common basis might be altogether different, and unknowable to us. Most importantly we have seen in Vulci a god, Fufluns, to whom was attributed an epithet of Dionysus and his iconography, but also a local specification (*velclθi*). He was connected with Semla, the mythical mother of Dionysus, but on the mirror the two also share a connection with Apulu, which must probably be explained locally. This allows us to make a strong case that Fufluns Paχie at Vulci was a god with a strong local identity. Thinking in terms of cultural translation, one must underline the absolute newness of this mixture of different elements. The extent to which Fufluns is identifiable with Dionysus in abstract and essentialist terms is not so important; nor is it important to determine the original basis of this identification – it seems to me that the people of Vulci found themselves in a liminal space between different semantic systems, and were able to produce something powerfully new, a response to the ubiquity and the pervasiveness of Greek iconography and culture in Etruria and the persistence of the indigenous traditions led to the creation of an entirely new deity, as Vulcian and Etruscan as he was Greek.

The case of Praeneste seems to show the exact opposite, because the local evidence seems to be much more erratic in the translation of Dionysus. The mirror in Etruscan shows Fuflunus with Minerva and Artemis in what would seem to be an eccentric myth, and, although it is uncertain whether the item was produced by a local workshop, the name Fuflunus might show some Italic and Latin influence – moreover, we have a later copy of the mirror certainly produced by a local workshop. The Hiaco mirror is equally eccentric and, although Hiaco appears to be a transliteration of Ἴακχος, the scene would appear to be influenced by local triumphal ceremonies. When Liber appears, he does so in a context which is difficult to interpret, a meeting of gods whose central element is an obscure scene involving Mars and Minerva. So the translation of Dionysus at Praeneste seems significantly more fragmented than Dionysus at Vulci, and would seem to consist of a number of divine figures with different names. A possible reason might be that, without the constraint of a local cult of Liber, Fuflunus or Hiaco, the evidence we have seen must be interpreted as an expression of individual choices of the artists, who had more freedom to create images which seemed fit to them (or to their clients) although, regrettably, the evidence does not allow to reconstruct the identity of the individuals involved, and understand the extent of their agency. One should also take into account the increased level of complexity created by the interaction of Greek, Etruscan, and Latin elements that probably helped destabilise the translations of Dionysus. In the evidence under consideration, these different translations of Dionysus at Praeneste are associated with Minerva, which implies that, in spite of the erratic translation of the name, there seem to be certain recurring characteristics, beyond the mere iconography. In view of these circumstances, even though we cannot be sure whether there was Dionysian cult at Praeneste, one cannot really speak in terms of a mere transposition of the Greek god, as the representations always have local inflections, from the Latinized name Fuflunus to the reference to the Latin ceremony of the triumph. If the translations of Dionysus at Praeneste are more ephemeral than at Vulci, precisely for this reason they show how the temporality of cultural translation is primarily in the present: it is an ever-unfinished business that individuals and groups renew and engage with all the time. At the same time, the present act of translation uses and reinterprets the timeless symbolic repertoire of myths and rituals. The cultural translation of Dionysus in Italy, therefore, occupies not only a linguistic liminal space between Greek, Etruscan, and Italic, but also a temporal liminal space between historical acts of translation and the timelessness of myth.

One must observe that, in spite of the fragmentation and the diversity, these characters are still recognizable as translations of Dionysus, and this is mostly through iconography, the use of names and epithets deriving from those attributed to Dionysus, like Paχie and Hiaco, and the association with characters associated with Dionysus in myths, like Semele and Ariadne, especially at Vulci. The obscure scenes on mirrors and *cistae*, bearing no obvious connection with any known myth, are best explained as references to unknown variants of myths, perhaps elaborated locally, or as references to local ceremonies. The mixture of local specificity and fragmentation is evident: one is still able to recognize a 'Dionysian' pattern in the evidence from Vulci and Praeneste, but must, at the same time, admit significant local differences. These differences mostly depend on which meaning would have been given to Dionysus in a specific act of translation. These acts of translation are not necessarily, nor obviously related to the relationship between Dionysus and a Fufluns or Liber that would predate Greek influence. The case of Praeneste in particular shows that these varying translations could have been related to individual choices and interpretations, and that a continuous flow of new translations was possible.

This chapter has shown that the multiplicity of Dionysus in translation produces radically different phenomena in different places. Dionysus, Fufluns, Paχie, Bakchios, Hiaco, Iakchos and Liber in Italian towns must be investigated in their specificity, and we must resist the impulse to look for a lowest common denominator, and to explain the obscure aspects of the evidence by assuming a general uniformity with material from other places. The fragmentation of 'Dionysus' in Italy also raises important issues as regards the interpretation of the later Bacchanalia as an Italian phenomenon. Moving away from the reassuring coherence of Roman sources, I have shown that the Roman perspective on the Bacchanalia as an Italian phenomenon is, from many points of view, illusory, at least for the period under consideration.

Bibliography

Ando, C. 2005. 'Interpretatio romana.' *CPh* 100, 41–51 = *The Matter of the Gods. Religion and the Roman Empire*. Berkeley and Los Angeles, 43–58.

Assmann, J. 1996. 'Translating gods: religion as a factor of cultural (un)translatability.' In *The Translatability of Cultures: Figurations of the Space Between*, edited by S. Budick and W. Iser. Stanford, 25–36.

Assmann, J. 2008. *Of God and Gods: Egypt, Israel, and the Rise of Monotheism*. Madison, WI.

Bernabé, A., M. Herrero de Jáuregui, A.I. Jiménez San Cristóbal, R.M. Hernández, eds. 2013. *Redefining Dionysos*. Berlin and Boston.

Berti, F. ed., 1991. *Dionysos. Mito e mistero. Atti del convegno internazionale. Comacchio 3–5 novembre 1989*. Comacchio.

Bettini, M. 2016. 'Interpretatio romana: category or conjecture?' In Bonnet, Pirenne-Delforge and Pironti, 17–36.

Bhabha, H.K. 1994. *The Location of Culture*. London and New York.

Bispham, E. and C.S. Smith, eds, 2000. *Religion in Archaic and Republican Rome: Evidence and Experience*. Edinburgh.

Bispham E.H. 2007. *From Asculum to Actium*, Oxford.

Bonamici, M. 2002. 'Diaspora prenestina.' In Emiliozzi and Maggiani, 83–94.

Bonfante, L. 1993. 'Fufluns Pacha: the Etruscan Dionysus.' In Carpenter and Faraone, 221–35.

Bonnet, C., V. Pirenne-Delforge and G. Pironti, eds. 2016. *Dieux des Grecs, dieux des Romains. Panthéons en dialogue à travers l'histoire et l'historiographie*. Rome.

Bordenache Battaglia, G. 1979. *Le ciste prenestine*, I. Rome.

Briscoe, J. 2008. *A Commentary on Livy, books 38–40*. Oxford.

Bruhl, A. 1953. Liber Pater. *Origine et expansion du culte dionysiaque à Rome et dans le monde romain*. Paris.

Burke, P. 2016. *Hybrid Renaissance: Culture, Language, Architecture*. Budapest.

Burkert, W. 1985. 'Herodot über die Namen der Götter: Polytheismus als historisches Problem.' *Museum Helveticum* 42, 121–32.

Calame, C. 2011. 'I nomi degli dei greci. I poteri della denominazione nella riconfigurazione di un pantheon.' *Mythos* 5, 9–20.

Carpenter, T.H. and C.A. Faraone, eds., 1993. *Masks of Dionysus*. Cornell, NY.

Cazanove, O. de 2000a. 'I destinatari dell'iscrizione di Tiriolo e la questione del campo di applicazione del Senatoconsulto De Bacchanalibus.' *Athenaeum* 88, 59–69.

Cerchiai, L. 2011. 'Culti dionisiaci e rituali funerari tra *poleis* magnogreche e comunità anelleniche.' In *La vigna di Dioniso: vino, vite e culti in Magna Grecia*. Taranto, 483–514.

Cerchiai, L. 2014. 'Una festa etrusca per Dioniso?' In *Sacrum facere. Atti del II seminario di archeologia del sacro. Contaminazioni: forme di contatto, traduzione e mediazione nei sacra del mondo greco e romano*, edited by F. Fontana and E. Murgia. Trieste, 95–105.

Cifarelli, F.M., L. Ambrosini, and D. Nonnis, 2002–2003. 'Nuovi dati su segni medio-repubblicana: a proposito di un nuovo *pocolom* dall'acropoli.' *Rendiconti della pontificia accademia romana di archeologia* 75, 245–325.

Colonna, G. 2005. 'Riflessioni sul dionisismo in Etruria.' In *Italia ante Romanum Imperium*, ed. G. Colonna. Rome, 2015–41 = Berti 1991, 117–55.

Cristofani M., and M. Martelli, 1978. 'Fufluns Paxies: sugli aspetti del culto di Bacco in Etruria.' *Studi etruschi* 46, 119–73.

Cristofani, M. 1986. 'Fufluns.' In *LIMC* 3, 531–40.

Della Fina, G.M., ed. 2004. *Citazioni archeologiche. Luciano Bonaparte archeologo*. Rome.

Emiliozzi, A. and A. Maggiani, eds. 2002. *Caelatores. Incisori di specchi e ciste tra Lazio ed Etruria*. Rome, 83–94.

Feruglio, A.E. 1998. 'Uno specchio della necropoli di Castel Viscardo, presso Orvieto, con Apollo, Turan e Atunis.' In *Etrusca et Italica: Scritti in ricordo di Massimo Pallottino*. Pisa, 299–314.

Fowler, R.L. 2000–2013. *Early Greek Mythography*. 2 vols. Oxford.

Franchi De Bellis, A. 2005. *Iscrizioni prenestine su specchi e ciste*. Alessandria.

Gasparri, C. 1986. 'Dionysos.' In *LIMC* 3, 414–514.

Henrichs, A. 2013. 'Dionysos: one or many?' In Schlesier, 554–82.

Lambrechts, R. 1978. *Les miroirs étrusques et prénestins des Musées Royaux d'Art et d'Histoire à Bruxelles*. Brussels.

Maggiani, A. 2002. 'Nel mondo degli specchi etruschi.' In Emiliozzi and Maggiani, 7–22.

Maitland, S. 2017. *What is Cultural Translation?* London and New York.

Mancini, M. 1997. 'Tracce di interferenza tra etrusco e latino a Praeneste.' *Studi etruschi* 63, 315–45.

Maras, D.F. 2009. *Il dono votivo: Gli dei e il sacro nelle iscrizioni etrusche di culto*. Pisa.

Matthies, G. 1912. *Die praenestinischen Spiegel*. Strasbourg.

Menichetti, M. 1995. *Quoius forma virtutei parisuma fuit: Ciste prenestine e cultura di Roma medio-repubblicana*. Rome.

Nielsen, M., and A. Rathje, 2009. 'Artumes in Etruria – the borrowed goddess.' In *From Artemis to Diana. The Goddess of Man and Beast*, edited by T. Fischer-Hansen and B. Poulsen. Copenhagen, 261–302.

Pailler, J.-M. 1988. *Bacchanalia. La répression de 186 av. J.-C. à Rome et en Italie: vestiges, images, tradition*. Rome.

Palethodoros, D. 2007. 'Dionysiac imagery in archaic Etruria.' *Etruscan Studies* 10, 187–201.

Parker, R. 2003. 'The problem of the Greek cult epithet.' *OAth* 28, 173–83.

Parker, R. 2011. *On Greek Religion*. Ithaca, NY.

Parker, R. 2017. *Greek Gods Abroad. Names, Natures, and Transformations*. Berkeley, CA.

Puritani, L. 2015. 'Fufluns und seine Pflanzen in der archaischen Vasenmalerei des 6. Jahrhunderts v. Chr.' In ΦΥΤΑ ΚΑΙ ΖΩΙΑ. *Pflanzen und Tiere auf griechischen Vasen*, edited by L.C. Lang-Auinger and E. Trinkl. Vienna, 139–46.

Puritani, L. 2018. 'Mythos, Kult, Theater? Überlegungen zu den Satyren in Etrurien.' In *Festschrift für Heide Froning. Studies in Honour of Heide Froning*, edited by T. Korkut and B. Özen-Kleine. Istanbul, 411–25.

Radke, G. 1965. *Die Götter Altitaliens*. Münster.

Santamaría, M.A. 2013. 'The term βάκχος and Dionysos Βάκχιος.' In Bernabé *et al.*, 38–57.

Schlesier, R., ed. 2011. *Dionysos: A Different God? Dionysos and Ancient Polytheism*. Berlin and New York.

Simon, E. 1978. 'Der Gott Mars in der Kunst Mittelitaliens.' *Studi etruschi* 46, 135–47.

Simon, E. 2013. 'Greek myth in Etruscan culture.' In *The Etruscan World*, edited by J. MacIntosh Turfa. London, 495–512.

Smith, M.S. 2008. *God in Translation: Deities in Cross-Cultural Discourse in the Biblical World*. Grand Rapids, MI.

van der Meer, L.B. 2016. 'Reevaluating Etruscan influences on the engravings of Praenestine pear-shaped mirrors and cistae.' *Etruscan Studies* 19, 68–86.

Versnel, H.S. 2011a. *Coping with the Gods*. Leiden and Boston.

Versnel, H.S. 2011b. '*Heis Dionysos!* One Dionysos? A polytheistic perspective.' In Schlesier, 23–46.

Werner, I. 2005. *Dionysos in Etruria: The Ivy Leaf Group*. Stockholm.

Wiseman, T.P. 2008. 'Liber: myth, drama and ideology in Republican Rome.' In *Unwritten Rome*, Exeter, 84–139 = *The Roman Middle Republic: Politics, Religion, and Historiography c. 400–133 B.C.*, edited by C. Bruun. Rome, 2000, 265–99.

Wyler, S. (forthcoming) '*Loufir / Liber* at the crossroads of religious cultures in Pompeii (third-second centuries BCE).' In *Gods and Goddesses in Ancient Italy*, edited by E.H. Bispham and D. Miano. London.

Julietta Steinhauer
Dionysian associations and the Bacchanalian affair

Abstract: This chapter explores the social dynamics of Bacchic worship in mid-Republican Rome and the extent to which Livy's narrative of the events, when compared to the *senatus consultum de bacchanalibus*, enables us to reconstruct a coherent picture of Bacchic worship in this period. The article argues two main points. (a) Bacchic worship as targeted in the *senatus consultum* was wide ranging and diverse, as reflected by the decree. A brief sketch of the classical evidence for Bacchic worship from Italy confirms the multifaceted forms of worship that we should anticipate for mid-Republican groups, rather than apply retrospective considerations of highly structured associations as suggested for Imperial *collegia*, based to a certain degree on legal sources. (b) When comparing the evidence supplied by Livy in book 39 to the regulations enacted by the senate in 186 BCE, important discrepancies can be observed with regard to the gender constellations of the worshipping groups: while Livy identifies female worshippers and a priestess (who allowed for male participation in the cult) as main culprits for the debauchery, the *senatus consultum* is formulated in favour of female participants and priestesses as well as mixed-gender groups. This discrepancy can perhaps be explained by Livy's own moralising agenda and Augustan ideas of gender-specific behaviour. It should not be seen, however, as an actual reflection of the social dynamics of Bacchic groups in mid-Republican Rome.

Introduction

The Bacchanalian affair of 186 and Livy's account of these events have provoked many scholars to offer explanations, some arguing for a political, others for a religious motivation behind the senate's decision to react so strongly to religious matters. Extracts of the senate's decree which mandated the abolition of Bacchic shrines in Rome and Italy and put in place strict rules for Bacchic worshippers, all under the threat of capital punishment, has come down to us in the form of an inscribed bronze tablet.[1] Livy in book 39 offers an extended version of the events. Here he describes in detail the circumstances which led to the senate's decision

---

1 *CIL* I² 2, 581 = *ILS* 18 = *ILLRP* 511; English translation in Beard-North-Price 1998: II, 290–91.

https://doi.org/10.1515/9783110672237-005

against bacchanals: the cult of Bacchus, initially brought to Italy by a Greek priest and open to women only, was completely changed by a Campanian priestess who, by introducing men to the cult and reforming the mysteries to more frequent and nocturnal events, paved the way for debauchery, sexual misconduct and even homicide among the worshippers.

In this chapter, I will not further explore the particular question of identifying the senate's reasoning behind the decree as others have provided some excellent work on the matter.[2] I am interested in the social dynamics of the worshipping groups that celebrated the Bacchanals, their organisation and motivation and the part they played in the religious landscape of mid-republican Rome before and after the scandal in 186. Both the *senatus consultum* and the Livian story must be seen as strong evidence for the existence of Bacchic worship of Dionysus in Italy from at least the third century BCE. With this in mind, I argue that the groups that supported Bacchic *sacra* were to some extent comparable to Greek Hellenistic *thiasoi*. They should, however, not be equated with the *collegia*[3] of the Imperial period as has often been done in scholarship.[4] While there were clear similarities between the Imperial *collegia* and the early groups, the groups targeted by the senate were rather diverse in their organisational structure. Indeed, the phrasing of the *senatus consultum* suggests that there were plenty of possibilities for worshipping groups to gather, possibly no two of which were the same. The senate, however, targeted the structure(s) of the worship, rather than the worship itself, or indeed a putative, specific kind of association that might exactly fit the provisions/prescriptions of the decree.

Second, when comparing the *senatus consultum* and the evidence Livy provides, there are some discrepancies between the narrative and the inscription that need to be considered: (a) the senate seems to allow for mixed groups whereas Livy sees the introduction of men to the cult together with women as the original problem; (b) women fare better from the decree in that they can stay priestesses and can participate in higher numbers. In Livy, it is precisely a priestess who starts the lawlessness. This can best be explained as being reflective of Livy's agenda and the morals of his own time.

---

2 For example, North 1979; Pailler 1988; Gruen 1996.
3 A *collegium* is commonly defined as a group of people that come together for various purposes, be they religious, professional or social, to an extent comparable to modern associations. According to Gaius, the legal basis for *collegia* was already mentioned in the Law of Twelve Tables (8,27 = Gaius Dig. 47,22,4). North 2003 gives a useful overview of the current debate on a definition of religious associations.
4 For a brief history of scholarship aligning the Bacchanalian associations with *collegia*, see below, p. 139.

The evidence

A major problem for all scholars working on the pre-Imperial worship of Bacchus in Italy is the scarcity of evidence, particularly epigraphic. This stands in stark contrast to Greece where, in the Hellenistic period, Dionysian worship in individual groups is well-established and therefore offers material for comparison. To use the Greek evidence to understand better what happens in Rome is, I believe, valid for several reasons, but mostly because the direct links between the Italian and Greek worshippers are too obvious to be ignored: as we shall see throughout the chapter, Bacchic worship in Italy is closely linked to Greek settlers and Greek culture, be it in burial culture or on vases. Dionysian art of the late Republic and Augustan era is equally inspired by Greek ideas of the deity and its worship.[5] Greek influence is still visible in the epigraphic evidence from the Imperial period, whether direct or indirect. With the exception of the fourth century CE, one third of all inscriptions attesting to the activities of Dionysian worshippers from the first to the third centuries CE from Italy and Rome are written in Greek.[6] Furthermore, in the Latin inscriptions, the naming practices for the groups themselves (*sp(e)ira, thiasus*),[7] the members (bacchants, *boukoloi*),[8] the various cultic offices as well as ritualistic aspects, are directly based on Greek terminology. In Greece and Asia Minor, Dionysian associations flourish when Roman supremacy takes hold and many Romans are to be found among the members of these associations. Similarly, Greeks were involved in the worship in Italy and Rome, leaving no doubt about the cult's cross-cultural character.[9] Finally, whereas literary sources and Roman art give us a basis to believe that Dionysus was worshipped at least from the early republican period, if not earlier (as demonstrated by the contributions of Mac Góráin and Wyler in this volume) no such evidence exists for Dionysian associations in the epigraphy before the Imperial period, making the Greek evidence an even more valuable point of comparison.[10]

---

5 Wyler 2006, 224–28.
6 See fig. 1.
7 Σπεῖρα; θίασος.
8 Βάκχαι/βάκχοι; βουκόλοι.
9 Some Greeks even established their own Dionysian groups, see for example *IGUR* I 160 and Scheid 1986.
10 This is due to the fact that the epigraphic habit in Italy takes hold so much later than in Greece, at least to a certain extent, see n. 50.

Dionysian worship in the Classical period

Dionysian worship in Italy dates back as far as the fifth century BCE. Giovanni Casadio has argued that southern Italy and the Greek colony Cumae in particular had a very lively and publicly visible Bacchic scene in the classical period.[11] In fact, in Casadio's maximally optimistic reading of the evidence,[12] Dionysian worship in this city was not only supported by the local tyrant, Aristodemus, but he even arranged that young aristocrats actively participate in Dionysian rituals and worship.[13] There is another piece of evidence for Bacchic worship from this city, a large tufa slab covering the grave of a Bacchic worshipper inscribed with the words: 'Lying buried in this place is illicit unless one has become bacchos.'[14] The meaning of this inscription and specifically the meaning of the perfect participle middle/passive βεβαχχευμένον (Attic: βεβακχευμένον) have been much discussed.[15] And whereas the content is highly debated, the fact that this is related to Bacchic worship is undisputed. For the purposes of this chapter it suffices to say that whatever the true meaning of the word, it clearly refers to an individual Bacchant or perhaps a family[16] or even group of Bacchants buried here under the condition of having undergone either an initiation into Dionysian mysteries or a certain lifestyle of Bacchic devotion. The owner(s) of the grave had consciously set up this slab of stone to prevent anyone else from burying here the body of a person not devoted to Bacchus.[17]

---

11 Casadio 2009.
12 This evidence mostly consists of Dionysius of Halicarnassus' *Ant. Rom.* 7.2.4–12.2, an account of the tyrant Aristodemus of Cumae's career and the worship of Dionysus under his reign.
13 However, Casadio is very certain that the ritual banquet held by Aristodemus was a bacchanal despite the fact that his source, Dionysius, never specifies any deity at all, rather speaks of 'the gods'. The same applies to the fact that Aristodemus applied rules of cross-dressing to the male elite, arguing that such reversal of the traditional roles was clearly Dionysian, whereas cults dedicated to other deities equally had elements of role-reversal within their cultic tradition as for example Demeter and Kore, whose cult was significant in this part of Italy too.
14 Transl. Casadio οὐ θέμις ἐν/ τοῦθα κεῖσθ/ αι ἰ μὲ τὸν βε/ βαχχευμέ /νον.
15 For the most recent overview of the discussion see Casadio 2009, 36 and n. 14.
16 Dionysus was among many other things, a 'dieu familiale' as Jaccottet convincingly argued (2003, I, 81).
17 The evidence for Dionysian worshippers involved in burial care is known especially from Greece and Asia Minor in the Roman period. One of the most prominent examples is the famous second-century CE inscription of the Iobacchoi from Athens: "If, however, an Iobacchos dies, he shall receive a crown worth up to five drachmas and those who join the funeral shall receive a jar of wine but those who do not attend the funeral will be excluded from the wine." *IG* II² 1368,

The more obvious evidence for the worship of Dionysus in southern Italy from an early age onwards is visual-material.[18] It is especially represented by the red-figure pottery from Apulia.[19] These vessels were often found in graves but many of them, being designed for banquets, may indicate an initial use in ritual banquets, held by individual groups of worshippers. Dionysian scenes and *thiasoi* were a popular theme on these vases and they may have been used at symposia held by Dionysian associations.[20]

Evidence for Dionysian worship and burial rites in southern Italy is equally represented by a gold lamella from the Greek colony Hipponion in southern Italy. The ritual context of such gold lamellae which were found in Magna Graecia and Greece dating over a large period of time from the late fifth century BCE through to the second century CE is unclear.[21] Often, they are (unhelpfully) categorised either as Bacchic, Orphic, or both.[22] However, they seem to represent a variety of gods, cults and rituals, each highlighting different aspects and foci of worship, perhaps representing local or individualised forms of worship and thought. Some of these lamellae are clearly connected to Bacchic worship. In the lamella from Hipponion that I point to here, the deceased is advised to behave in a certain way once s/he arrives in Hades. It reads:

> ll. 15–16: And you, too, having drunk, will go along the sacred road on which other Glorious initiates (mystai) and Bacchants (Bacchoi) travel.[23]

The 'road that other *mystai* and *Bacchoi* travel' presumably led to a good place in the afterlife that is yet to be found by the deceased. Both terms are commonly used by Dionysian associations to specify their members.[24] The gold tablets hold

---

ll. 159–63. What we see more often in this period is the devotion to Dionysus expressed in grave stelae, be it by text or ornamental decorations.
18 For a general survey of evidence for Dionysus in the visual material evidence from fifth-century BCE southern Italy, see Cole 1980 esp. 234–36.
19 Carpenter 2011.
20 Cole 1980, 137.
21 The tablet from Hipponion is the earliest of the 'gold lamellae' dating to the end of the fifth century BCE. The other pieces were found scattered throughout the Greek and Roman worlds. A helpful collection of transcriptions and the texts in original and edited form can be found in Graf and Johnston 2013.
22 For an overview see Parker 1995.
23 Transl. Graf and Johnston 2013, 5.
24 Συνβάκχοι and Βάκχοι appear in over thirty inscriptions in the corpus of inscriptions of Dionysian groups published by Jaccottet. In her corpus, Jaccottet 2003 collected the epigraphic, literary and archaeological evidence for Dionysian associations in Greece and Rome in two volumes, one with the sources themselves among which are over 200 inscriptions, and one with the

no further information as to how these groups were organised, let alone concerning their activities.²⁵

What we can gather from these examples, is that the *Bacchoi* buried in Cuma and the 'Orphic-Bacchic' worship in southern Italy (as seen from the example of the Hipponion tablet) indicate worship of Dionysus in exclusive groups at a relatively early stage. To what extent they had anything in common with each other, let alone with the groups banned in 186 BCE, remains unclear. The only connection thus far seems to be that all were called Bacchants, and were participating in Bacchic cult and ritual on a personal level. This requires a conscious decision by an individual to be part of a defined group. Being a member of such a group involved participation in certain rituals or the maintenance of a certain lifestyle that allowed the worshipper at the end to be buried in a clearly defined place or respectively to walk 'along the path that other initiates and *Bacchoi* have walked' once they are dead. What is more, the individuals or their families had to invest financially in the inscribing of the texts which were found in southern Italy.²⁶

The *senatus consultum de Bacchanalibus*

The decree of the senate against Bacchanals has come down to us in the form of a bronze tablet that contained an abbreviated copy of the senate's decree to be displayed in the Ager Teuranus in Calabria, southern Italy.²⁷ The document gives evidence of the senate's reaction to cultic practices which were, it seems, unacceptable for the Roman government.

If one looks at the precise orders given by the *senatus consultum* it becomes clear that what the authorities were actually targeting was not so much a specific deity or worship in itself but rather the various organisational structures that the worship had taken. Indeed, the legal phrasing of the decree gives the impression

---

explanatory notes. Similarly συνμύσται appear eleven times and μύσται over eighty times. With this in mind, I will argue that these *mystai* and more importantly *Bacchoi* saw themselves as exclusive, defined groups of worshippers, that one could choose to be part of or not.

25 Another possibility of interpretation that I cannot explore here further but that is important to mention in this context is that the term *mystai* may have referred to initiates of the cult of Demeter and Persephone which is often linked with Dionysus. The two goddesses and Dionysus were introduced to Rome in the early fifth century as Ceres, Liber, and Libera (Dion. Hal. *Ant.* 6.17.3–4; Tac. *Ann.* 2.49) and later became the 'Eleusinian Triad'.
26 Other interpretations of the lamellae are possible too. In addition to Graf and Johnston 2013 see Bernabé and Jiménez San Cristóbal 2008; Tzifopoulos 2010; and Edmonds 2008.
27 I² 2, 581.

that one of the main objectives – apart from the founding of new sanctuaries/bacchanals – seems to have been the financially and administratively independent groups of Bacchists that are mentioned in the second part of the decree. At first glance, these groups look similar to those that were later defined as *collegia*. Understandably, this is the way in which most modern scholars tend to interpret the decree.

The interpretation of the worshipping communities holding bacchanals that are mentioned in the senatorial decree as *collegia* (as defined by modern scholarship) was suggested as early as 1932 by Eduard Fraenkel, although with caution, as Fraenkel allows for other forms of communities to be targeted here: 'jede Form eines freieren Zusammenschlusses.'[28] A similar interpretation was put forward by John North in 1979: 'The implication seems to be that the Italian cult, banned by the senate in 186 B.C., had developed its own characteristics, distinct from those of the Greek cults from which it must ultimately derive. The institution which will have mediated the change must be the *collegium*, the standard form of association in republican Italy.'[29] Over the course of time, and in particular in German scholarship, this interpretation was developed, especially by Hildegard Cancik-Lindemaier[30] and even finds its way into the relevant translations, which now merely translate *bacchanalia* as 'Vereine'.[31] Gradually, this interpretation has become the *communis opinio*, with Arnaoutoglou claiming that: 'The first ban on associations, SC de Bacchanalibus (*ILS* 18 = *FIRA* I2 30), was issued in 186 BCE.'[32] Lastly, the Bacchanalian affair is given by Herz and Schmidt as an example par excellence for the legal reaction against *collegia*.[33]

A more fruitful way to make sense of these early groups is perhaps to look closer at the decree of 186 and Livy rather than to import perspectives from a later period. And while I can see that the phrasing of the decree may suggest that what

---

[28] Fraenkel 1932, 37.
[29] North 1979, 9.
[30] Cancik-Lindemaier 1996.
[31] See e.g. Kupfer 2004, 169: 'Vorsteher (sc. eines Bacchusvereins)' and 181 § 2.1 b) 'Weder ein Mann noch eine Frau darf Vorsteher eines (damit institutionalisierten) Bacchusvereins sein'; Cancik-Lindemaier 1996, 82: 'Die bacchischen Kultgemeinden waren also – wie zu erwarten – als collegia organisiert und werden nun als collegia verboten'.
[32] Arnaoutoglou 2003, 30.
[33] Herz and Schmidt 2015: 'The Senate kept a watch on the *collegia*, particularly in respect of any undesirable political activity, which could lead to the disbanding of a *collegium* (Senatus consultum de Bacchanalibus).' On the legal situation of collegia in Rome see Cancik-Lindemaier 1996, 82 and n. 12: 'Die Freiheit der Vereinsbildung sodalitas oder collegium ist bereits in den XII-Tafel-Gesetzen (8,27) garantiert'. See also Kippenberg 2005, 41.

the authorities were dealing with were a particular kind of individually organised groups of worshippers with specific hierarchies, cultic and financial independence, it points at the same time to the multifaceted nature of the groups as I explore in the following section.

The decree seems to be predominantly concerned with the prevention of legal loopholes and therefore restricting the options of Bacchic worship to a specific, controllable form. For example, we learn that the decree now permits only a limited number of people to participate in the ritual (*sacra*), namely five people. It also specifies the gender of those able to participate as exactly two men and three women.[34] The specific number and the clear indication of the composition of these groups in terms of gender is particularly striking even though it says nothing about the way in which the groups had been structured before the decree. Yet, the fact that now fewer men than women could participate stands out and may indicate that before the decree, a worshipping group could constitute any number of people, that it could be mixed, male-only or female-only, and that the social status of the participants may have played no role.

Moreover, male worshippers are stripped of all administrative and religious offices which suggests that there had been a range of administrative offices available to them in the past or speculated to be held in the future.[35] Women, by exclusion, were still able to become priestesses, possibly as a nod to the cult's roots: Dionysus in most Greek cities in the Hellenistic period required a priestesshood, as well as a priesthood. It is also possible that priesthood within the cult had been taken up as frequently by men as by women before the decree. In many cults with

---

34 *CIL* I² 581, ll. 19–21: *Homines plous V oinvorsei virei atque mulieres sacra ne quisquam/fecise velet, neve inter ibei virei plous duobus, mulieribus plous tribus /arfuise velent.*
35 Ll. 10–18: *Sacerdos ne quis vir esset. magister neque vir neque mulier quisquam esset. Neve pecuniam/ quisquam eorum communem habuisse vellet. Neve magistratum/ neve pro magistratu neque virum neque mulierem quisquam fecisse vellet./ Neve posthac inter se coniurasse neve convovisse neve conspondisse /15 Sacra in occulto ne quisquam fecisse vellet. Neve in publico neve in/ privato neve extra urbem sacra quisquam fecisse vellet, nisi/ praetorem urbanum adisset isque de senatus sententia, dum ne minus/ senatoribus centum adessent, cum ea res consuleretur, iussissent.* (No man can be a priest, no man or woman shall be a magistrate, no one shall wish to have a common fund, no man or woman shall be a pro-magistrate and that no one should have rituals (*sacra*) in secret, neither on private ground nor outside of the city).

mixed-gender priesthoods, men outnumbered women, especially within the hierarchy and administrative power.[36] Finally, men specified as Roman citizens, allies or *foederati*, were not allowed to join the (female) Bacchants, leaving this option to slaves, foreigners and women alone.

The senate's 'positive' behaviour towards women requires attention. It is commonly explained either on the basis of political motivations, diminishing any possible concentration of political (male) power within each worshipping group and/or the alleged 'traditional' popularity of the cult among women. The interpretation of a close connection between Bacchic cult and women derives from a comparison with the groups described in Euripides' *Bacchae*, where the tragedian describes what may be understood as *thiasoi* of women only. Can we take the myth as some kind of representation of the ritual practice, an allusion to such practices, a later interpretation of such practices or was it simply a story? Scholars have been discussing the relationship of myth and ritual for many centuries and within the scope of this chapter I shall not discuss this in any depth, but simply point out some gender aspects that are important for my argument.[37] Jaccottet in her discussion of the Dionysian material found that within the epigraphic corpus the terms directly taken from the myths, are often linked to female positions.[38] When thinking about the 'recreation' of the Dionysiac myths, one needs to consider that there are scarcely any female-only groups in the epigraphic evidence from Greece and Rome. Jaccottet describes it as 'absence presque totale des associations féminines'.[39] In fact, civic Dionysiac festivals known to us from Greece were either mixed gender or male only, as were some Hellenistic associations too, although the majority were open to men only.[40] Livy's version, especially as regards the transformation of the cult and the introduction of 'bad' rites

---

36 Equally among Dionysian associations, which were 'sous l'autorité incontestée et incontestable des hommes' Jaccottet 2003, I, 91.
37 See the discussion in Jaccottet 2003, I, 112–14 who demonstrates just how difficult it is to make any decisions on the matter retrospectively.
38 Jaccottet 2003, I, 114 and Jaccottet 2003, I, 118: 'La place particulière des femmes dans le monde bachique est une autre donnée qui nous permettra de saisir le réseau complexe des liens existant entre le dieu et le monde humain.'
39 Jaccottet 2003, I, 80. Yet, it seems to be the *communis opinio* that 'The cult of Bacchus, as the Greek god Dionysus was known in Italy, was very popular in Republican Rome, especially with women'; thus Holland 2012, 208. Already Fraenkel 1932, 372 underlined that women were particularly representative of the cult of Dionysos and therefore experienced better treatment in the decree: 'die Frauen werden gemaess dem Charakter des Kultes etwas bevorzugt.' I am sceptical here, as the sources do not seem to indicate such a preference, at least not to my knowledge. The Greek evidence clearly indicates various scenarios: Female-only, male-only and mixed *thiasoi*.
40 See Jaccottet 2003, I, 88–94 on mixed *thiasoi*.

by a priestess, also contributed substantially to the common understanding that it was particularly the female worshippers that needed restriction. Some scholars have even argued that it was the disproportionate participation of women which sparked the Senate's interest.[41] In view of the decree, this makes little sense. If the women were the problem, why not completely ban their participation, as is done for male priests? Also, the question remains which women took part? The senate seems to be supportive of female bacchants of any description.[42]

It is impossible to reconstruct the most common gender composition of the worshipping groups before 186 BCE. What can be said, however, is that the *senatus consultum* is concerned with status when it comes to male participation, clearly indicating that the rules were set for a certain part of the population but not for all. To me it seems noteworthy that the mixed-gender aspect of the cult is the one *preserved* by the senate, rather than, say, a total restriction on women only. By permitting only groups consisting of both genders, female-only groups were *de facto* excluded.[43]

The administrative and religious positions described in the decree, that is, priests, magistrates and pro-magistrates, the common fund, and perhaps even the common vows and oaths, have been seen as elementary parts of what is commonly understood as a *collegium*. This is partly due to the fact that the terminology used here to describe the offices and the fund is, put simply, common terminology used by Imperial associations (with a religious or any other focus) to describe internal hierarchies, using the same 'public' language as the state.[44]

This is not to say that all Imperial *collegia* were one and the same. Rather, the *collegia* used common terminology and phrases to describe their internal organisation and hierarchy, at least superficially, in the epigraphic records. For all we know, there is no reason to think that just because later associations used the same common terminology, we should necessarily interpret the roles as being

---

[41] Most prominently Balsdon 1962, 37–43.
[42] Schultz 2006, 92 argues that 'Ostensibly this prohibition applied only to men, but in practice it must have extended to all the members of politically prominent families.'
[43] However, there seems to be an acknowledgement that such female-only groups existed: Briscoe 2008, 249: 'Bacas obviously means Bacchic women'.
[44] There is also the common argument that *collegia*, 'In terms of their internal organization [...] followed the model of the civic municipalities with magistrates, a council and plebs. The financial assets of the *collegium* included the income generated by members' contributions and also real estate and money donated as *fideicommissum*'; see Herz and Schmidt 2015. North 1979, 92 also points out that it is impossible to know to what extent the distinction between *pro-magistratus* and *magistratus* were effectively reflecting the reality of the associations' practices or were an attempt to avoid legal loopholes.

completely identical: surely the magistrate of a Dionysian association in Rome interpreted his role according to the local needs and given cultic structures, whereas the man with the same title, leading the Bacchic worshippers, in say, Cumae, would have shaped the office differently. To sum up, the phrasing of the decree, covering all eventualities, indicates that not each and every association was well organised, or organised in the same way. Indeed, the organisation of each Bacchic community very likely differed from place to place, just as the worship of the god itself was so diverse and, as seen in the examples of Cumae and Hipponion, subject to an individual's 'religious' interpretation.[45]

The fact that violation of the decree was a capital offence and the geographical extent to which the *senatus consultum* was enacted beyond the city, as well as its very detailed character, gives the impression that we are dealing with a widespread phenomenon indeed, and one that was not easily controllable. The senate's decree is phrased in such a way as to encompass diverse groups of worshippers that hold Bacchanalia, without defining the form of cultic worship. Moreover, the decree applied to the whole of Italy and to Romans, Latins and *socii*.[46] The prohibitions are also clearly directed at the private sphere. For example, the phrasing of l. 16, that nobody shall practise *sacra* in secret (*ocquoltod*), neither in public nor in private, nor outside the city, indicates that Bacchic worship was in fact held in private, or that the senate was afraid it might be. The reference to rituals outside the city further underlines the aspect of diversity of the cultic practices of each group. It may also refer to a specific part of Dionysian worship, the celebrations in the wilderness, *eis oros* (nature, mountains)[47] – a very Dionysian habit indeed. All of these are only permitted under the conditions laid out in the decree. In fact, despite the detailed prohibitions, it was still possible to gather in small groups if one adhered to the new regulation. Even 'running' a Bacchic sanctuary was still a possibility. But the hurdles that had to be overcome were high: worshippers now had to plead before the *praetor urbanus* who would then take the case to the senate for a decision, with no fewer than a hundred members present (ll. 4–6). The senate likely decided on a case-by-case basis.

Overall, the impression given by the *senatus consultum* is that of popular Bacchic groups that had been well established before the enactment of the decree

---

45 See for example Versnel 2011.
46 *CIL* I² 2, 581, 7; see Cazanove 2000 for the argument that the Senate's target is more limited.
47 See for example *SEG* 17, 503; *IMilet* 457, 3rd–2nd c. BCE.

and were by no means a sudden phenomenon.[48] What is more, the harsh reaction may indicate that the senate opposed a possible involvement of men of a certain status, likely due to their potential political influence.[49] Women, on the other hand, were still permitted to lead the Bacchic groups as priestesses.

What is lacking are epigraphic attestations for cultic activities for these Bacchic groups in the Republican period, before and after 186 BCE. The huge gap in evidence from the senatorial decree up until the second century CE cannot be explained exclusively by the fact that the epigraphic habit took hold only in the second half of the first century CE but it is likely the best explanation for the dearth of material.[50] In addition, evidence for associations peaks slightly later, in the second century CE. In fact, only two inscriptions may date to the first or second century CE, the rest is later.

Tab. 1: Epigraphic evidence for Dionysiac associations in Rome and Italy

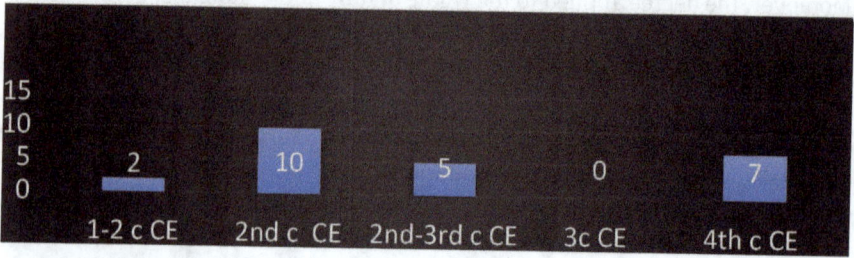

It seems that 'going public' with one's ritual activities was not common before or after 186 BCE as a general rule, not only for the Bacchic communities. It was mainly practised in the Imperial period and here it is particularly in the second century that we can gather more information about the worshipping communities of 'Bacchists' as the table below shows although the overall evidence is sparse.

---

[48] This is supported by Livy's report too (39.15.6–7). Briscoe 2008, 234 argues that Bacchic rites as for example described by Plautus around the time of the decree, show that they were well known to the audience.

[49] Similarly Schultz 2006, 89 on the involvement of the male aristocratic elite.

[50] Religious associations in Greece for example are almost exclusively known through inscriptions only. For the Latin West, however, less than two per cent (fewer than 4,200 of approximately 220,000 surviving Latin inscriptions on stone) are datable to the time before 44 CE; see Solin 1999, 91. More is known about the artists of Dionysus, the *technitai* that appear in both literature and epigraphy; see e.g. Le Guen 2001.

Tab. 2: List of all inscriptions referring to Dionysian association in Rome and Italy

Date (all CE)	Place	Description	Language	Reference
1. 1st–2nd	Rome	Epigram of young initiate	Greek	*IGUR* 1228
2. 1st–2nd	Cora (Latium)	Spira of Liber Pater	Latin	*CIL* X 6510
3. 2nd	Rome	Funerary stele of Nartecofore	Latin	*CIL* VI 2255
4. 2nd	Rome	Priests and priestesses of a sacred speira	Greek	*IGUR* 156
5. 2nd	Rome	Sarcophagus with Bacchist	Greek	*IGUR* 1324
6. 160–165	Torre Nova (Latium)	Inscription honouring Agrippinilla	Greek	*IGUR* 160
7. 2nd?	Rome	Funerary stele of a young cymbal player	Latin	*CIL* VI 261
8. 2nd?	Rome (Tusculum)	Funerary epigram of young myst of Dionysus	Greek	Jaccottet 180
9. 2nd?	Rome (Portus)	'Trajanesian' Speira	Greek	*IG* XIV 925
10. 2nd?	Rome	Dedication by a spirarches (restoration of stibadium)	Latin	*CIL* VI 2251
11. 2nd?	Rome	Dedication by a spirarches (restoration of stibadium)	Latin	*CIL* VI 2252
12. 2nd?	Rome	Funerary Stele for a wife by husband and spira	Latin	*CIL* VI 2253
13. Severan dynasty	Rome	Dedication of a statue of Hecate by a spira	Latin	*CIL* VI 261
14. Septimius Severus	Puteoli	Thiasus Placidianus	Latin	*CIL* X 1583
15. Septimius Severus	Puteoli	Thiasus Placidianus	Latin	*CIL* X 1584
16. 198–211	Puteoli	Thiasus Placidianus	Latin	*CIL* X 1585
17. 209–211	Rome	Dedication of a sanctuary by a spira	Latin	*CIL* VI 461
18. 313	Rome	Hierophant of Liber	Latin	*CIL* VI 507
19. 376	Rome	Archibuculus of Liber	Latin	*CIL* VI 510
20. 376	Rome	Archibuculus of Liber	Latin	*CIL* VI 504
21. 374–385 (A–D)	Rome	4 related monuments mentioning an archibuculus of Liber	Latin	A=Jaccottet 194

Date (all CE)	Place	Description	Language	Reference
				B=*CIL* VI 31940
				C=*CIL* VI 1675
				D=*ILS* 1264
22. ?	Rome	Epitaph of a boukolos	Greek	*IGUR* 981
23. ?	Rome	Dedication by a hierophant of Dionysos	Greek	*IGUR* 159

If it were not for the copy of the *senatus consultum* and the survival of Livy 39, we would be completely ignorant even of the existence of these Bacchic communities.

Livy and the Bacchanalian affair

For the Augustan era we have Livy's account of the Bacchanalian affair, a semi-fictional report of the actual events in 186 BCE and equally a reflection of his own time.[51] Livy tries to explain the senate's measures by naming the horrendous practices involved in the worship: initiation, secrecy, illegal actions, outrageous sexual behaviour and crimes were part of the problem which led to the processes of the Bacchanalia.[52] The tipping point was reached for the senate, when the number of adherents soared and, more importantly, when not only citizens, but equally members of the aristocracy became involved in this 'reformed cult of Dionysus' that was allegedly brought to Rome by a foreigner, 39.13.14:

> 'They formed an immense multitude, almost equal to the population of Rome; amongst them were members of noble families both men and women.' (transl. C. Roberts 1905)

A comparison of the *senatus consultum* and Livy's version of the events reveals that Livy was certainly well acquainted with the content of the decree.[53] Yet, if one focuses on one aspect only, namely the gender aspect (the fact that in the

---

[51] For a connection between a contemporary interpretation of past events in Livy, see Wendt 2016, 49, n. 27 with bibliography.
[52] 39.13.
[53] Briscoe 2008, 233: 'With certain (not unimportant) differences in detail, the decisions recorded in the inscription correspond to those reported by Livy at 18.7–9.' For a thorough analysis of the likeness of Livy's account and the decree see Fraenkel 1932.

senate's decree women are disproportionately represented in a ratio of 3:2 and could take up priesthoods), his interpretation may be a reflection of his time rather than of the situation in 186 BCE. In the current political climate of Augustus' reforms, certain gender roles had just been enforced under the Augustan laws (*lex Julia et Papia*).[54] The bar for 'moral' expectations was set high within marriage, banning adultery and promoting chastity,[55] exemplified by Augustus' banishment of his own daughter for disobeying the rules. This sentiment becomes particularly clear in the consul's speech where he first blames the women (39.15.9: 'primum igitur mulierum magna pars est, et is fons mali huiusce fuit') and at the end addresses the men to protect their wives' and children's chastity, threatened by involvement in bacchanals.[56] The behaviour of the Bacchists that Livy describes goes against all of the moral rules supposedly re-established by Augustus (39.8.3–8). If we look at the decree, however, women seem less of a concern to the senate as argued above. On the contrary, they have been given the only powerful positions still available and they outnumber men in the 'newly-tailored' groups.[57]

It is in particular the permission of female priests which, when aligned with Livy's account makes little sense: in Livy's narrative, according to the freedwoman Hispala, who is herself sympathetically portrayed, it was indeed a Dionysian priestess, Paculla Annia, supposedly a Campanian woman, who had 'reformed' the cult and had undertaken initiations.[58] She was the culprit who started what got out of hand in a matter of a few years. If this woman (or any other female priestess for that matter) had truly been guilty or perceived as a serious danger, surely the senate would have banned this in the future and prohibited female officials too.

---

54 The connection between Livy's report of the Bacchanalian affair and the Julian Law on marriage has also been made by Scafuro 2009, 349–50, albeit with a focus on the relationship between the two protagonists, Hispala and Aebutius.
55 Suet. *Aug.* 34.
56 39.15.12–15.
57 One may draw a comparison with Livy's description of the events surrounding the sanctioning of the *Lex Oppia* a few decades earlier (34, 1–8). The law was decreed to prevent women from wearing expensive clothes and possessing wealth during the second Punic war. Here too, as in the case of Livy's description of the Bacchanals, the female participation in the debate and the women's actions are described as unreasonable. I agree with Culham's interpretation (1982, 792) that 'Women were actually useful to men in this way. Men could compete with each other indirectly, without themselves behaving in an untraditional fashion or acquiring the reputation of being themselves devoted to luxury.' It looks as if here too it was the women who were blamed by Livy for being inconsiderate and selfish, and above all not willing to obey.
58 She began by initiating her sons, therefore mixing men with women Livy 39.13.8–10.

When Livy first introduces the events of 186 BCE he reports that an unskilled and undistinguished Greek (*Graecus ignobilis*)[59] brought the cult to Etruria. He then defines this particular cult as a mixed-gender affair, in compliance with the *senatus consultum*. He adds that as part of the ritual, the worshippers drank wine in order to attract more worshippers. As a result, the worshippers (39.8.6) committed all sorts of alcohol-induced crimes. The cult is characterised as Bacchic by the consumption of wine and the cymbals that were played to drown the cries of those murdered.[60]

In Hispala's report, the cult was initially open to women only until Paculla Annia's so-called reforms. Priesthood alternated between *matronae*, and on only three days annually women could be initiated into the Bacchic cult which is here for the first time named explicitly (yet never in the *senatus consultum*).[61] It all started to go wrong at the exact moment when this priestess introduced men, and rites were performed in common.[62] Here too, Livy seems to add information that is not contained in the decree. On the contrary, the only thing that the decree permits are those groups that consist of both men and women.

More generally, Livy seems to focus specifically on the dangers of female agency in the Bacchanalian scandal, making women not only responsible for the corruption of the cult but addressing ancient gender stereotypes of female Bacchants too.[63] Blaming the Bacchanalian affair on women was not invented by Livy. Already earlier, Varro had remarked that the cult of Liber was taken to a new stage by women who celebrated the Bacchanalia, referring to the events of 186.[64] Various fragments of Plautus point in a similar direction, describing women's active involvement and strong connection to the cult that was clearly familiar to his audience.[65] Scheid points out that Livy, in his emphasis on female

---

59 For a discussion of the possible origins of this Greek and connections to Etruscan religion, see Takács 2000, 305–6.
60 It is perhaps no coincidence that other cults with an overproportionate participation of women are described as 'foreign' or 'Greek' and involve the consumption of wine. Rebecca Flemming has discussed similar phenomena in Roman sources treating the cult of Ceres with a particular focus on Cicero: Flemming 2007, 92–98. She describes 'foreignness' or 'Greekness' as well as the possession of 'outsider knowledge' as key factors used to describe female agency in the cult of Ceres in Rome: Flemming 2007, 103.
61 39.13.8.
62 39.13.10: 'From the time that the rites were performed in common, men mingling with women and the freedom of darkness added, no form of crime, no sort of wrongdoing, was left untried.'
63 39.15.9.
64 Rüpke 2016, 18, citing Varro, *ARD* fr. 93 Cardauns.
65 Walsh 1996, 191–92.

participation, brings to light social as much as religious dynamics, which are related to the role of matrons in Roman society.⁶⁶ However, it needs to be emphasized that there is a clear dichotomy in Livy's representation of the female characters. While the priestess Paculla Annia is blamed for the corruption of the cult, the messenger, Hispala, the freedwoman and courtesan who has the crucial role as a witness, is described in rather positive terms. When introducing her, Livy emphasises that she was in many ways a good person and deserving better than the life allotted to her.⁶⁷ Later, Hispala is praised by the consul for coming forward with the details of the conspiracy and it seems to be the case that she was in effect a mere victim of the conspiracy as she was initiated with her mistress while still a slave but stayed clear of any involvement in the rites after her manumission (39.12.6–7).⁶⁸ Aebutia, Hispala's lover's aunt, is also presented favourably: she informed the consul about the bacchanalia in the first place and her laudable character is confirmed by yet another female character, the consul's mother-in-law Sulpicia, equally described as a woman of 'respectable character'.⁶⁹ All three women, each representing a stratum of society – a freedwoman, a woman of equestrian rank, as well as a senatorial woman – are acting clearly in line with Roman moral expectations. These expectations are, however, not met by Paculla Annia, who is already early on identified as a 'Campanian' woman and with that fitting into Livy's narrative bias against Campanians after the revolt of Capua in 216.⁷⁰ Livy contrasts the strong virtue of the Roman women, even those of lower ranks, with the loose morals of the Campanian woman, who, in many ways is in a threateningly powerful position as the conductress of the conspiracy.

That the original cult had been introduced by a man, the unknown Greek who came to Rome from Etruria, who reminds the reader of the wandering *manteis* described in Greek sources,⁷¹ was important to show the 'otherness' of the cult;

---

66 On social and gender dynamics in mid-Republican Rome see Scheid 1992, 393; see also n. 57 above.
67 Liv. 39.9.5: 'There was a freedwoman called Hispala Fecenia, a noted courtesan, but deserving of a better lot than the mode of life to which she had been accustomed when very young, and a slave, and by which she had maintained herself since her manumission' (translation Sage 1936). Livy also emphasizes the good character of Hispala by pointing to her devotion to her lover whom she financially supported and who would be her heir (39.9.6–7).
68 For a reading of the episode as a 'conspiracy narrative' see Pagán 2004, 50–67.
69 39.11.3–5.
70 Farney 2007, 194, n. 58.
71 The Derveni Papyrus describes these 'priests' as: 'those who make a craft of holy rites' m col. XX, transl after Laks and Most 1997. Similarly Plato at *Republic* 2.364b: 'begging priests and soothsayers go to rich men's doors and make them believe that they by means of sacrifices and incantations have accumulated a treasure of power from the gods that can expiate and cure with

but it was equally important to emphasize that it was only when women became involved and, to make matters worse, that a Campanian woman had agency, that it turned out to be a problem.[72] The practice of initiation through a priestess as described by Hispala is reminiscent of a particular cult practice described in a famous inscription from Miletus. In this third-century BCE inscription a priestess of Dionysus offers religious services to women in exchange for a biennial (*trieteris*) payment.[73] One of these services, which can perhaps best be described as a kind of 'franchise' of cultic practice, enabled women to hold initiations themselves in their own communities, yet giving a fee to the main priestess.[74] This sounds very much like Paculla Annia's business, who, even though Hispala does not mention it, may have equally charged customers for initiations. To what extent Paculla Annia changed the rules as claimed in Livy – if there were any in the first place – is a matter of speculation. Surely, if she did, this applied to her own group during her term of service as priestess but was hardly a general rule that applied to all other Bacchic groups. Here, Livy clearly creates a scapegoat and at the same time emphasizes his argument, perhaps also reflecting the senate's political stance on or rather fear of the power of women on an individual level, with a Campanian woman as conductress of a ceremony that included senators and slaves alike.[75] As mentioned before, the overall epigraphic evidence, shows that with a few exceptions, Dionysian groups were open to men and women and even families from Hellenistic times onwards.[76] With that in mind, Livy's claim that Paculla Annia initiated her sons into the cult should not have come as a surprise to an ancient audience. The sentiment of outrage felt by Livy when describing the

---

pleasurable festivals' and [365a]: 'and that there are also special rites for the defunct, which they call functions, that deliver us from evils in that other world, while terrible things await those who have neglected to sacrifice.' Takács 2000: 305 suggests a wandering Dionysian priest: 'the "Greek of humble origin" (*Graecus ignobilis*, in Livy, 39.8.3) may be understood as an ethnically Greek, itinerant priest of Dionysus'. Most recently, Heidi Wendt discussed this specific Greek as problematic in Livy's view as he did not disclose either his teachings or his occupation; Wendt 2016, 49.

72 There is a striking parallel with the description of the cult of Ceres that was supposedly comprised of women from Magna Graeca too; see Flemming 2017, 102.
73 Jaccottet 2003, II, 148–50 no. 150, 277–76 BCE.
74 Ll. 18–20: καὶ ἐάν τις γυνὴ βούληται τελεῖν τῶι Διονύσωι | τῶι Βακχίωι ἐν τῆι πόλει ἢ ἐν τῆι χώραι ἢ ἐν ταῖς νήσοις, [ἀπο] | διδότω τῆι ἱερείαι στατῆρα κατ' ἑκάστην τριετηρίδα. ('And if any woman wishes to perform initiations for Dionysus Bakkhios in the polis or in the chora or in the islands, let her give to the priestess a stater (gold coin) every *trieteris*.' Transl. after Cole 2007). On this inscription see also Henrichs 1969 and Henrichs 1978.
75 Eidinow 2017, 268–69.
76 Jaccottet 2003, I, 79–80 and 88–91.

extension of the cult to men and the focus on underage initiation seems to arise from moral expectations, values and practices either due to the agenda of his narrative or set in his own 'Augustan' age.⁷⁷ Or, if one follows Gruen's approach of *Realpolitik*, who claims that Livy's version is a 'Romanticised and embellished tale' characterised by 'exaggeration, distortion and calumny'⁷⁸ one may say that Livy was trying vehemently to make sense of the senate's behaviour and at the same time to justify it.⁷⁹ And too true, a certain fascination with the cult of Dionysus by the upper classes of the Augustan era can be detected in the wealth of Dionysian imagery that was found in houses located in the Vesuvius area, as well as in Rome, all contemporary with Livy.⁸⁰ It is impossible to say whether these images reflected actual initiations as they were performed during this period, whether they were images of completely different rites, or whether they were illustrations of merely decorative value. The status of Dionysian images is taken up by Stéphanie Wyler and Daniele Miano in this volume. In any case, it is clear that the topic was popular enough to be reproduced in wall decorations in the first century BCE as shown by, for example, the initiation scenes into Dionysian mysteries from cubicula B and D in the villa unearthed beneath the Villa Farnesina in Rome (19 BCE).⁸¹

Outlook: The Imperial evidence

When in the second half of the first century CE the epigraphic habit flourishes in Italy and Rome, we can finally identify individual associations. Now, some three centuries after the *senatus consultum*, the Dionysian associations were as diverse

---

77 Vasaly 2015, 1–4 offers a useful historiographic overview of the discussion of the extent to which Livy was influenced by Augustan politics and the Augustan age.
78 Gruen 1990, 61 and 64.
79 There has been an attempt to explain the dramatic soap-opera-like character of the narrative by appealing to the influence of drama: see Walsh 1996 and Wiseman 1998.
80 This is illustrated for example by the images of the Villa of Mysteries in Pompeii which date to the middle of the first century BCE.
81 See Wyler 2006, 224, and Wyler in this volume. In both cases we can connect the cult of Dionysus to the aristocracy, or at least to the wealthier classes of the Roman population as these houses were inhabited by people who could afford such splendid paintings. And again, the images appear in private houses. Equally, *triclinia* and in particular outdoor *stibadia* that created the impression of nature, were found in aristocratic houses in Pompeii may well have served for the festivities of such communities. For a description of a *stibadium*: Pliny, *Ep.* 5.6. On the pre-Imperial outdoor *stibadia* see Dunbabin 1996.

as in 186 BCE, a creative form of worship, serving religious and social needs alike, shunning all standardisation inflicted on them. Of more than 200 inscriptions collected by Anne-Françoise Jaccottet in her two volumes on Dionysian associations, twenty-three are from Rome and Italy, all dating from the time of the Principate (Tab. 1 and Tab. 2). Most inscriptions, were found in Rome, two in Latium and three in Puteoli.[82] Many inscriptions were written in Greek and the associations had other Greek elements, such as the naming practice of their officials. The most common term by which members of the Roman *collegia* of Dionysus described themselves was *speira*, itself a Greek word.

However, the associations were also very Roman in many ways and named Liber Pater as their main deity, especially in the late antique evidence. Most striking are the diversity and uniqueness of each group, though they all communicate in a shared technical terminology. As seen throughout this essay, Dionysus or Bacchus is hardly ever mentioned – and yet, there is a strong 'recognisability' in the use of a particular Bacchic language.[83]

Conclusions

In this chapter I have shown that Bacchic worship in one form or another was part of Italy and Rome from as early as the fifth century BCE, acknowledged and supported by all strata of society. The scarcity of evidence, particularly of inscriptions, forces us to focus on the *senatus consultum* and Livy, as well as the Greek Hellenistic evidence. I have argued against a 'retrospective' interpretation of Dionysian associations as *collegia* in the sense of Roman Imperial (often legal) sources, as (a) the evidence does not permit such a conclusion and (b) the Imperial *collegia* were in themselves so diverse and manifold that a comparison could only be valid on a case-by-case basis.

A closer look at the gender constellations outlined in the senatorial decree showed that the kind of Bacchic groups that the senate favoured after 186 were of mixed gender and in favour of women, which neatly fits with what we know

---

[82] The three inscriptions from Puteoli were all erected by the same association (Thiasus Placidianus).

[83] This language was used to name their association and fellow members which were called for example Bacchants and *boukoloi* and their sacred staff such as the *thyrsophoroi* and *phallophoroi*. This is perhaps best exemplified by the inscription to Agrippinilla from Torre Nova (*IGUR* I 160).

about Bacchic worship more generally, but which fits less well with Livy's narrative. In Livy's narrative we are told that it was the introduction of mixed-gender groups of Bacchic worshippers which marked the tipping point. Livy's moral agenda in this 'tale' is projected through the characters of various women, each representing a certain stratum of Roman society and one outsider. The Roman women are throughout described positively while the outsider, the Campanian priestess brought nothing but misfortune to Rome.

To what extent Livy's description of the *bacchanalia* reflects even a kernel of the historical reality of the cultic activity in the early second century BCE is debateable. What we can say for sure, however, and what the Imperial inscriptions clearly demonstrate is that what one understood as Bacchic, was always a matter of an individual's or a small group's interpretation.

Bibliography

Ando, C. ed. 2003. *Roman Religion*. Edinburgh.
Arnaoutoglou, I. 2002. 'Roman Law and *collegia* in Asia Minor.' *Revue internationale des droits de l'antiquité* 49, 27–44.
Avramidou, A. 2006. 'Attic vases in Etruria: another view on the divine banquet cup by the Codrus Painter.' *AJA* 110, 565–79.
Balsdon, J.P.V.D. 1962. *Roman Women: Their History and Habits*. London.
Bauman, R.A. 1990. 'The suppression of the Bacchanals: five questions.' *Historia* 39, 334–48.
Beard, M., J.A. North, and S.F. Price, 1998. *Religions of Rome*, 2 vols. Cambridge.
Bendlin, A. 2005. '"Eine Zusammenkunft um der religio willen ist erlaubt…?" Zu den politischen und rechtlichen Konstruktionen von religiösen Vergemeinschaftungen in der römischen Kaiserzeit.' In Kippenberg and Schuppert, 65–107.
Bernabé, A., and A.I. Jiménez San Cristóbal. 2008. *Instructions for the Netherworld. The Orphic Gold Tablets*. Leiden/Boston.
Briscoe, J. 2008. *A Commentary on Livy Books 38–40*. Oxford.
Cancik-Lindemaier, H. 1996. 'Der Diskurs Religion im Senatsbeschluß über die Bacchanalia von 186 v. Chr. und bei Livius (B. XXXIX).' In *Geschichte – Tradition – Reflexion. Festschrift für Martin Hengel zum 70. Geburtstag, Vol. II Griechische und römische Religion*, edited by H. Cancik, H. Lichtenberger, and P. Schäfer. Tübingen, 77–96.
Cardauns, B. ed. 1976. *M. Terentius Varro. Antiquitates Rerum Divinarum. Teil I: Die Fragmente*. Wiesbaden.
Carpenter, T.H. 2011. 'Dionysos and the blessed on Apulian red-figured vases.' In Schlesier, 253–61.
Casadio, G. 2009. 'Dionysus in Campania: Cumae.' In Casadio and Johnston, 33–45.
Casadio, G. and Johnston, P. eds., 2009. *Mystic Cults in Magna Graecia*. Austin, TX.
Cazanove, O. de, ed. 1986. *L'association dionysiaque dans les sociétés anciennes*. Collection de l'École française de Rome – 89. Actes de la table ronde organisée par l'École française de Rome (Rome 24–25 mai 1984). Rome.

Cazanove, O. de 2000. 'I destinatari dell'iscrizione di Tiriolo e la questione del campo di applicazione del Senatoconsulto *De Bacchanalibus*.' *Athenaeum* 88, 59–69.

Cole, S.G. 1980. 'New Evidence for the mysteries of Dionysos.' *GRBS* 21, 223–83.

Cole, S.G. 2007. 'Finding Dionysus.' In *A Companion to Greek Religion*, edited by D. Ogden. Oxford, 327–41.

Culham, P. 1982. 'The "Lex Oppia".' *Latomus* 41, 786–93.

Dumézil, G. 1970 [1966]. *Archaic Roman Religion. With an Appendix on the Religion of the Etruscans*. Trans. P. Krapp. Foreword by M. Eliade. Chicago/London.

Dunbabin, K.M.D. 1996. 'Convivial spaces: dining and entertainment in the Roman villa.' *JRA* 9, 66–80.

Edmonds, R.G. ed. 2011. *The "Orphic" Gold Tablets and Greek Religion: Further along the Path*. Cambridge.

Eidinow, E. 2017. 'In search of the "beggar-priest"'. In *Beyond Priesthood: Religious Entrepreneurs and Innovators in the Roman Empire*, edited by R. Gordon, G. Petridou, and J. Rüpke. Berlin/Boston, 255–76.

Farney, G. 2007. *Ethnic Identity and Aristocratic Competition in Republican Rome*. Cambridge.

Flemming, R. 2007. 'Festus and the role of women in Roman religion.' *In Verrius, Festus, & Paul: Lexicography, Scholarship, & Society*, Bulletin of the Institute of Classical Studies Supplement 93, 87–108.

Fraenkel, E. 1932. 'Senatus consultum de Bacchanalibus.' *Hermes* 67, 369–96.

Fuhrer, T. 2011. 'Inszenierungen von Göttlichkeit: die politische Rolle von Dionysos/Bacchus in der römischen Literatur.' In Schlesier, 373–89.

Gounardopoulou, L. and M.B. Hatzopoulos, eds. 1998. *Inscriptiones Macedoniae Inferioris I; Inscriptiones Beroiae*. Athens.

Graf, F. and S.I. Johnston, 2013². *Ritual Texts for the Afterlife: Orpheus and the Bacchic Gold Tablets*. London/New York.

Gruen, E.S. 1996 [1990]. 'The Bacchanalian affair.' *Studies in Greek Culture and Roman Policy*. California, 48–54.

Henrichs, A. 1969. 'Die Maenaden von Milet.' *ZPE* 4, 223–41.

Henrichs, A. 1978. 'Greek maenadism from Olympias to Messalina.' *HSCPh* 82, 121–60.

Herz, P. and P.L. Schmidt, 2015. 'Collegium.' In *Brill's New Pauly. Antiquity volumes*, edited by H. Cancik and H. Schneider H., English edition by C.F. Salazar. (online).

Holland, L. 2012. 'Women and Roman religion.' In *A Companion to Women in the Ancient World*, edited by S.L. James and S. Dillon. Oxford, 204–14.

Jaccottet, A.-F. 2003. *Choisir Dionysos. Les associations dionysiaques ou la face cachée du dionysisme*. 2 vols. Zurich.

Jaccottet, A.-F. 2011. 'Integrierte Andersartigkeit: die Rolle der dionysischen Vereine.' In Schlesier, 413–31.

Kippenberg, H. 2005. 'Diskurse römischer Juristen über private römische Vereine.' In Kippenberg and Schuppert, 37–63.

Kippenberg, H. and G.F. Schuppert, eds. 2005. *Die Verrechtlichte Religion. Der Öffentlichkeitsstatus von Religionsgemeinschaften*. Tübingen.

Kupfer, K. 2004. 'Anmerkungen zu Sprache und Textgattung des *Senatus consultum de Bacchanalibus (CIL I² 581)*.' *Glotta* 80, 158–92.

Laks, A. and G. Most, eds. 1996. *Studies on the Derveni Papyrus*. Oxford.

Le Guen, B. 2001. *Les associations de Technites dionysiaques à l'époque hellénistique*. 2 vols. Nancy.

MacMullen, R. 1982. 'The epigraphic habit in the Roman Empire.' *AJP* 103, 233–46.
Mitterlechner, T. 2016. 'The banquet in Etruscan funerary art and its underlying meaning.' In *Dining and Death: Interdisciplinary Perspectives on the 'Funerary Banquet' in Ancient Art, Burial and Belief*, edited by C.M. Draycott and M. Stamatopoulou. Louvain, 523–52.
Nippel, W. 1997. 'Orgien, Ritualmorde und Verschwörung? Die Bacchanalien-Prozesse des Jahres 186 v. Chr.' In *Große Prozesse der römischen Antike*, edited by U. Manthe and J. von Ungern-Sternberg. Munich, 65–73.
North, J. 2003. 'Réflexions autour des communautés religieuses du monde gréco-romain.' In *Les communautes religieuses dans le monde gréco-romain. Essais de definition*, edited by N. Belayche and S.C. Mimouni. Turnhout, 337–47.
North, J.A. 1979. 'Religious toleration in Republican Rome.' *PCPS* 25, 85–103, reprinted in Ando 2003, 199–219.
Nousek, D. 2010. 'Echoes of Cicero in Livy's Bacchanalian narrative.' *CQ* 60, 156–66.
Pagán, V.E. 2004. *Conspiracy Narratives in Roman History*. Austin, TX.
Pailler, J.-M. 1986. 'Lieu sacré et lien associatif dans le dionysisme romain de la République.' In Cazanove, 261–73.
Pailler, J.-M. 1988. *Bacchanalia. La répression de 186 av. J.-C. à Rome et en Italie: vestiges, images, tradition*. Rome.
Parker, R. 1995. 'Early Orphism.' In *The Greek World*, edited by A. Powell. London, 483–510.
Parker, R. 2005. *Polytheism and Society at Athens*. Oxford.
Pairault-Massa, F.-H. 1987. 'En quel sens parler de la romanisation du culte de Dionysos en Étrurie?' *MEFRA* 99, 573–94.
Edmonds, R.G. ed. 2010. *The 'Orphic' Gold Tablets and Greek Religion. Further along the Path*. Cambridge.
Rousselle, R. 1987. 'Liber-Dionysus in early Roman drama.' *CJ* 82, 193–98.
Rüpke, J. 2016. *Religious Deviance in the Roman World. Superstition or Individuality?* Cambridge.
Schlesier, R., ed. 2011. *Dionysos: A Different God? Dionysos and Ancient Polytheism*. Berlin/New York.
Scafuro, A.C. 2009. 'Livy's comic narrative of the Bacchanalia.' In *Oxford Readings in Livy*, edited by J.D. Chaplin and C.S. Kraus, 321–52, reprinted from *Helios* 16 (1989), 119–42.
Scheid, J. 1986. 'Le thiase du Metropolitan Museum (*IGUR* I 160).' In Cazanove, 275–90.
Scheid, J. 1992. 'The religious roles of Roman women.' In *A History of Women from Ancient Goddesses to Christian Saints*, edited by P. Schmitt Pantel, tr. A. Goldhammer. Cambridge, MA, 377–408.
Schultz, C.E. 2006. *Women's Religious Activity in the Roman Republic*. Chapel Hill, NC.
Solin, H. 1999. 'Epigrafia repubblicana. Bilancio, novità, prospettive.' In *Atti del XI Congresso Internazionale di Epigrafia Greca e Latina (Roma, 18–24 settembre 1997)*. Rome, 379–404.
Takács, S.A. 2000. 'Politics and religion in the Bacchanalian Affair of 186 B.C.' *HSCP* 100, 301–10.
Tzifopoulos, Y. 2010. *'Paradise' Earned: The Bacchic-Orphic Gold Lamellae of Crete*. Washington DC. *Hellenic Studies Series 23*, Washington DC: Center for Hellenic Studies. http://nrs.harvard.edu/urn3:hul.ebook:CHS_TzifopoulosY.Paradise_Earned_The_Bacchic-Orphic_Gold_Lamellae.2010
Vasaly, A. 2015. *Livy's Political Philosophy: Power and Personality in Early Rome*. Cambridge.
Versnel, H.S. 2011 *'Heis Dionysos!* One Dionysos? A polytheistic perspective.' In Schlesier, 23–46.

Walsh, P.G. 1996. 'Making a drama out of a crisis: Livy on the Bacchanalia. *Greece & Rome* 43, 188–203.

Wendt, H. 2016. *At the Temple Gates: The Religion of Freelance Experts in the Roman Empire.* Oxford.

Wiseman, T.P. 1998. 'Two plays for the Liberalia.' In *Roman Drama and Roman History.* Exeter, 35–51.

Wyler, S. 2006. 'Roman replications of Greek art at the Villa della Farnesina.' *Art History* 29, 213–32.

Gesine Manuwald
Dionysus/Bacchus/Liber in Cicero

Abstract: This chapter examines the occurrence of the god's different appellations Dionysus, Bacchus and Liber in the works of Cicero as well as their various functions and connotations. A range of perspectives on the god emerges across the surviving corpus of Cicero's works: philosophical, oratorical, rhetorical and epistolographic. The view taken of the god generally corresponds to the immediate rhetorical aim of Cicero or whichever of his characters is speaking. Significant examples are discussed under several headings: cultural theologies, metonymical value of *Bacchus/Liber*, Bacchic raving and *Liberalia* – a festival of freedom? From a linguistic point of view, Cicero employs all three names depending on the context: he refers to Liber when pointing out positive aspects of the Roman god and the associated festival and cult, chooses the name Bacchus metonymically for wine and its derivatives to illustrate raving, and speaks of Dionysus in discussions of the Greek god and his genealogy. The term Bacchus and related words tend to appear in passages with more negative connotations than the designation Liber; similarly, Cicero regarded the erection of statues of Bacchants in his house as inappropriate for his image.

Introduction

When in 496 BCE the Romans were hard pressed because of famine and opposition from the Latins, A. Postumius Albus Regillensis vowed the building of a temple for the divine triad of Ceres, Liber and Libera, prompted by the Sibylline books (Dion. Hal. *Ant. Rom.* 6.17.2–4). This temple, located close to the Aventine, was dedicated in 493 BCE (Dion. Hal. *Ant. Rom.* 6.94.3) and developed into an important centre for the plebeians during the Republican period.[1] While the three gods are often referred to by the modern term 'Aventine Triad', in contrast to the (more patrician) 'Capitoline Triad' (Jupiter, Juno, Minerva), distinctions between the three fertility deities constituting the former 'Triad' seem to have existed from the start. The (old-Italic) god Liber (along with his female equivalent Libera) was a god of fecundity with regard to agriculture, viticulture, cattle breeding as well

---

[1] See e.g. Bernstein 1998, 80–82 (with further references to sources and secondary literature).

as human fertility,² and he may also have been regarded as a divine personification of liberty. The god was celebrated at the festival of *Liberalia*, held annually on 17 March, when young males coming of age put on the virile toga for the first time.³

In the course of Rome's engagement with Greek culture, the 'Aventine Triad' was linked to the Greek equivalents Demeter, Dionysus and Kore / Persephone, including their characteristics, myths and cults.⁴ Moreover, imported Dionysian cults were apparently practised in Rome in such a way that the Senate felt obliged to issue the well-known *Senatus consultum de Bacchanalibus* of 186 BCE and to forbid at least extreme forms and escalating ecstasy, since it was believed that this might threaten public morals and order.⁵ By Cicero's time both the traditional Roman version of the god as well as his Greek form had been accepted in Rome (and fused to some extent); in addition to the old Italic appellation of the god as Liber, out of the god's Greek names, Bacchus in particular was used.⁶

While Cicero's works do not include extended discussions of the god Dionysus / Bacchus / Liber and his cult, which would reveal his own attitude in detail as well as give hints on contemporary thinking, Cicero mentions the god a number of times by different appellations and in different contexts, which provides enough material to enable some conclusions. This evidence is worth examining since Cicero is known to have engaged with philosophical and theological matters and thus may have had considered opinions on the role and perception of

---

2 In Augustine's polemical discussion (taking up Varro, *ARD*, F 93 C.) Jupiter, as Liber, is described as a god of 'the seeds of men' and, as Libera, as a goddess of 'the seeds of women'; thus, Liber is mainly seen as representing sexuality (*De civ. D.* 4.11).
3 On the *Liberalia* see Musiał 2013. – On Ovid's views on the rituals for that day and their possible origin see Ov. *Fast.* 3.713–90. – The famous fragment from a *fabula palliata* by Naevius *libera lingua loquemur ludis Liberalibus* (Naev. *Pall.* 113 R.²⁻³ = *Inc.* 27 W.), which is consistent with the standard boastful language of slaves in comedy, may have a specific meaning in its context on the basis of a pun on *liber*. The line has been understood in a metadramatic sense or been seen as evidence for the *Liberalia* (on 'Liber and his *ludi*' see Wiseman 2000, who assumes their early existence).
4 On the character and historical development of Dionysus / Bacchus / Liber in Rome and the relationship between the traditional Roman and the Greek elements of the god see e.g. Radke 1965, 175–83; Wacht / Rickert 2010; on the god's role in Rome in the first century BCE see Bruhl 1953, 117–59, esp. 119–32.
5 On this issue see also Steinhauer in this volume. – On the Greek and Roman aspects of the god as demonstrated in works of art see Wyler in this volume.
6 For the variety of names of the god see e.g. Ov. *Met.* 4.11–17 and already Enn. *Trag.* 107–11 R.²⁻³ = 123–27 V.² = 120–24 Joc. = 42 *TrRF.* – For an overview of the epithets applied to Dionysus see Bruchmann 1893, 78–94.

particular gods. In addition, because of the appearance of statements in public-facing genres and texts written for his peers, the totality of Cicero's comments, when viewed against their respective contexts, allows inferences on views current among the educated elite in the late Republic during a crucial period of transition.

Cicero makes a number of references to the god with his various names, employing all three common names. Among Roman authors of the archaic and classical periods, the god's Greek name Dionysus only appears in Cicero (*Nat. D.* 3.53; 3.58), apart from one occurrence each in the works of the Republican dramatists Plautus (Plaut. *Stich.* 661) and Accius (Acc. *Trag.* 240–2 R.$^{2-3}$ = 204–5 W.), for which there are local reasons: in Plautus the word is used metonymically, and in Accius the phrase occurs in the play *Bacchae*.[7] The following discussion will explore whether in Cicero's uses of the different names in different contexts specific nuances of meaning can be discerned, enabling conclusions on attitudes to the god and to what he represents held by Cicero and his contemporaries.

Cultural theologies

By the time Cicero composed the treatise *De natura deorum* (45 BCE), presenting the views on the gods promoted by different philosophical schools, he had familiarized himself with various Greek and Roman traditions, starting from his early education.

The treatise's section on Stoic doctrine includes a discussion of the different manifestations and genealogies of gods. This is part of the argument of the interlocutor C. Aurelius Cotta (who criticizes Stoic theology) to disprove that the gods currently honoured have been turned from humans into gods (Cic. *Nat. D.* 3.53); he gives a list of a range of narratives for different gods and ends by voicing the view that such stories must be rejected (Cic. *Nat. D.* 3.60). Early on Cotta mentions

---

[7] The term *Dionysia* (with reference to a festival) frequently occurs in Roman Republican comedy, albeit in the Greek setting of the *palliata* and with no specific Roman colouring in the contexts (Plaut. *Cist.* 89–90; 156; *Curc.* 644; *Pseud.* 58–59; Ter. *Haut.* 162; 733). – When Wyler (2011, 193) notes that *Dionysus* only occurs in Cicero's *De natura deorum*, this is not fully accurate. – Appellations specifically connected with the god's role as a god of wine, such as *vindemitor* (e.g. Ov. *Fast.* 3.407) or *vitisator* (e.g. Ov. *Fast.* 3.725), are not found in Cicero.

the Dioscuri and reports that according to one version Dionysus belongs a group of three Dioscuri:[8]

> Cic. *Nat. D.* 3.53: Dioscoroe etiam apud Graios multis modis nominantur: primi tres, qui appellantur Anactes Athenis, ex rege Iove antiquissimo et Proserpina nati, Tritopatreus, Eubuleus, Dionysus; secundi …

> 'The Dioscuri as well lend their names to numerous manifestations among the Greeks. The first three, who are called 'kings' at Athens, are Tritopatreus, Eubouleus, and Dionysus, sons of the oldest Jupiter (called 'King') and of Proserpina. The second Dioscuri …' [trans. P.G. Walsh]

In line with the argumentative structure of this sequence, Cicero does not have the interlocutor comment on the alternatives. Still, the name Dionysus appears in a learned context and provides a rather unusual perspective. Slightly later Cotta reports a distinction between five different Dionysi with different genealogies:[9]

> Cic. *Nat. D.* 3.58: Dionysos multos habemus, primum Iove et Proserpina natum, secundum Nilo, qui Nysam dicitur interemisse, tertium Cabiro patre, eumque regem Asiae praefuisse dicunt, cui Sabazia sunt instituta, quartum Iove et Luna, cui sacra Orphica putantur confici, quintum Nyso natum et Thyone, a quo trieterides constitutae putantur.

> 'We have a host of gods called Dionysus. The first is the son of Jupiter and Proserpina, the second the son of the Nile and allegedly the assassin of Nysa; the third, the son of Cabirus, was said to have been king of Asia, and to have had the Sabazian festival inaugurated in his honour. The fourth was the son of Jupiter and Luna; the Orphic rites are believed to be an offering to him. The fifth, the son of Nysus and Thyone, is thought to have established the triennial festival.' [trans. P.G. Walsh]

The descent of Dionysus as a son of Jupiter and Semele, well known since Homer and Hesiod (Hom. *Il.* 14.325; Hes. *Theog.* 940–42; see also e.g. Ov. *Met.* 3.253–315; *Fast.* 3.715–18), does not appear in this list (but see Cic. *Nat. D.* 2.62; *Tusc.* 1.28 [see below]). According to the context of the passage, these other, more obscure versions seem to have been adopted from traditions that had emerged in Greece

---

[8] Since Eubuleus is also an epithet of Dionysus (Macr. *Sat.* 1.18.12 = *PEGr* F Orph. 540.3–4), the distinction between Eubuleus and Dionysus is not entirely clear, but the sequence here is certainly meant to be a list of three (see also Pease 1958, ad loc.).
[9] On this passage see Walsh 1997, 205–6; Wyler 2011: 193–94. – For the realization that one god with the same name can appear differently in different contexts see Cic. *Nat. D.* 1.82.

(though presented partly in Latin terminology):[10] Cotta reports the state of affairs one is currently faced with; although he is made not to subscribe to these theories, the long list of different manifestations of several gods provides the opportunity to present them without any obvious position being taken.

In the previous book Cicero has the Stoic interlocutor Q. Lucilius Balbus talk about great men who were later deified (including Liber).[11] There he distinguishes between Liber as the son of Semele (i.e. the Greek Dionysus) and the Roman god Liber, for whose name he provides an etymological explanation:[12]

> Cic. *Nat. D.* 2.62: suscepit autem vita hominum consuetudoque communis ut beneficiis excellentis viros in caelum fama ac voluntate tollerent. hinc Hercules, hinc Castor et Pollux, hinc Aesculapius, hinc Liber etiam (hunc dico Liberum Semela natum, non eum quem nostri maiores auguste sancteque Liberum cum Cerere et Libera consecraverunt, quod quale sit ex mysteriis intellegi potest; sed quod ex nobis natos liberos appellamus, idcirco Cerere nati nominati sunt Liber et Libera, quod in Libera servant, in Libero non item) – hinc etiam Romulum, quem quidam eundem esse Quirinum putant. quorum cum remanerent animi atque aeternitate fruerentur, rite di sunt habiti, cum et optimi essent et aeterni.

'Our human experience and the common practice have ensured that men who conferred outstanding benefits were translated to heaven through their fame and our gratitude. Examples are Hercules, Castor and Pollux, Aesculapius, and Liber as well (by Liber I mean the son of Semele, not the Liber whom our ancestors solemnly and piously deified with Ceres and Libera, the nature of whose worship can be gathered from the mysteries. Because we call our children *liberi*, the offspring of Ceres were named Liber and Libera; the sense of 'offspring' has been retained in the case of Libera, but not in that of Liber). Romulus is a further example; people identify him with Quirinus. These men were duly regarded as gods because their souls survived to enjoy eternal life, for they were both outstandingly good and immortal.' [trans. P.G. Walsh]

The need to separate the 'Greek Liber', whose descent is given in its canonical form (son of Semele), from the 'Roman Liber' arises from the fact that the Greek god is referred to by his Latin name, rather than as Dionysus (or Bacchus). Apparently Cicero thereby has the speaker indicate that, despite the (now) identical name there is a factual difference; at the same time he makes him not only establish an etymological connection with *liberi*, who are the intended result of human fertility, but also create a connection to the 'Aventine Triad'. That Libera kept her

---

10 For a story of Liber / Dionysus as son of Jupiter and Proserpina, also mentioning Semele and Nysus, see Hyg. *Fab.* 167.
11 See also Hor. *Epist.* 2.1.4–10.
12 On this passage see Wyler 2011, 193.

name while Liber has also adopted others is alluded to, but the name Liber is central to the argument.

The distinction between a 'Greek Liber' and a 'Roman Liber' does not apply to all works by Cicero. In *Tusculan Disputations* (45 BCE) Liber recurs as an example of semi-divine beings deified after death. Because of the identification by descent the Greek god is presumably meant:

> Cic. *Tusc.* 1.28: ex hoc et nostrorum opinione 'Romulus in caelo cum diis agit aevum', ut famae adsentiens dixit Ennius, et apud Graecos indeque perlapsus ad nos et usque ad Oceanum Hercules tantus et tam praesens habetur deus; hinc Liber Semela natus eademque famae celebritate Tyndaridae fratres, qui non modo adiutores in proeliis victoriae populi Romani, sed etiam nuntii fuisse perhibentur.

> 'It is because of this that we Romans believe that 'Romulus passes his days in heaven with the gods', as Ennius said in conformity with tradition; and amongst the Greeks, from where he passed to us as far as Ocean, Hercules is considered so great and so helpful a god. Because of this, Liber, Semele's son, is so regarded, and the brothers, sons of Tyndareus, traditionally enjoy the same distinction: it is said of them that they not merely helped the Romans to victory in battle but carried the news of it as well.' [trans. A.E. Douglas]

An equally positive assessment of Liber is found in *De finibus* (45 BCE):

> Cic. *Fin.* 3.66: atque ut tauris natura datum est ut pro vitulis contra leones summa vi impetuque contendant, sic ii qui valent opibus atque id facere possunt, ut de Hercule et de Libero accepimus, ad servandum genus hominum natura incitantur.

> 'Nature has given bulls the instinct to defend their calves against lions with immense passion and force. In the same way, those with great talent and the capacity for achievement, as is said of Hercules and Liber, have a natural inclination to help the human race.' [trans. R. Woolf]

The discussions in the philosophical works suggest that the name Liber, if the god is at issue, provokes a positive portrait, either by a link to Italic traditions or by a reference to the deification of the demi-god.

Cicero also chooses the name Liber in one of his speeches against Verres, when he puts forward the charge that on Verres' orders a statue of Aristaeus was stolen from the Temple of Liber in Syracuse. Cicero adds about Aristaeus that he was regarded as the inventor of oil and was honoured together with Liber in this temple:

> Cic. *Verr.* 2.4.128: quid? ex aede Liberi simulacrum Aristaei non tuo imperio palam ablatum est? quid? ex aede Iovis religiosissimum simulacrum Iovis Imperatoris, quem Graeci Urion nominant, pulcherrime factum nonne abstulisti? quid? ex aede Liberae agninum [*Peterson*

: parinum *codd.* : porcinum *Georges* : aprinum *Schlenger* : porinum *Fröhner* : puerinum *Richter* : Paninum *Halm*] caput illud pulcherrimum, quod visere solebamus, num dubitasti tollere? atque ille Paean sacrificiis anniversariis simul cum Aesculapio apud illos colebatur; Aristaeus, qui {ut Graeci ferunt, Liberi filius} [*del. Ernesti*] inventor olei esse dicitur, una cum Libero Patre apud illos eodem erat in templo consecratus.

'Was not an image of Aristaeus, moreover, openly removed by your orders from the temple of Liber? And did you not carry away from the temple of Jupiter the most beautiful and deeply reverenced image of Jupiter Imperator, whom the Greeks call Urios? And did you hesitate to remove from the temple of Libera that really lovely head of …, which we used to go there to see? And that Paean was worshipped among those [i.e. the Syracusans] with annual sacrifices, together with Aesculapius; Aristaeus {as the Greeks transmit, Liber's son}, who is said to have discovered the olive, was honoured like a god along with Father Liber in the same temple by them.' [trans. L.H.G. Greenwood, adapted]

The constitution of the text is difficult, but the phrase describing Aristaeus as Liber's son according to a Greek view should most likely be deleted (as Ernesti suggested): it would be awkward to have two unconnected descriptions of Aristaeus next to each other, each referred to unconfirmed traditions (*ut Graeci ferunt* and *dicitur*); and if a familial relationship was in Cicero's mind, he would probably have stressed that the statue of Aristaeus was taken from the temple of the god's father. This means that Cicero uses the Roman cult title Liber Pater in the context of cult activity set in a Greek environment, though not for the official identification of the temple (see also Cic. *Verr.* 2.4.108): the emphasis on Liber (and Libera) may contribute to making Verres' deed appear more outrageous and as ignoring both Greek and Roman traditions and values.

Elsewhere in the speech Cicero illustrates by parallels how painful the loss of cult statues is for those who are victims of Verres' thefts:

Cic. *Verr.* 2.4.135: quid arbitramini Reginos, qui iam cives Romani sunt, merere velle ut ab iis marmorea Venus illa auferatur? …, quid Athenienses ut ex marmore Iacchum aut Paralum pictum aut ex aere Myronis buculam? longum est et non necessarium commemorare quae apud quosque visenda sint tota Asia et Graecia; verum illud est quam ob rem haec commemorem, quod existimare hoc vos volo, mirum quendam dolorem accipere eos ex quorum urbibus haec auferantur.

'What sum of money do you imagine the people of Regium, now Roman citizens, would demand before parting with their famous marble Venus? … or the Athenians for their marble Iacchus, their picture of Paralus, or their bronze heifer by Myron? It would be tedious, and needless, to mention all the noteworthy sights to be found in the several towns of Greece and Asia: my purpose in mentioning these few is to convince you that an extraordinary degree of pain has been caused to those whose towns have been robbed of such treasures.' [trans. L.H.G. Greenwood]

These examples include a marble statue of Iacchus from Athens: Cicero chooses a form of the god's name probably common in Athens with reference to this statue. This appellation is developed from the Greek cult, where Iacchus became identified with Dionysus / Bacchus; his name was then used interchangeably by Greek and Roman poets (e.g. Soph. *Ant.* 1152; Catull. 64.251; Virg. *E.* 6.15 [metonymically]).[13]

Cicero speaks of Iacchus again, in a different context in *De legibus* (c. 50s BCE), when 'Marcus' and 'Atticus' discuss regulating nocturnal rites. 'Marcus' asks the ('Athenian') 'Atticus' (Cic. *Leg.* 2.35 [trans. C.W. Keyes]): *quid ergo aget Iacchus Eumolpidaeque nostri et augusta illa mysteria, siquidem sacra nocturna tollimus?* – 'Then what will become of our Iacchus and Eumolpidae and their impressive mysteries, if we abolish nocturnal rites?' In Cicero the use of this name seems to be restricted to contexts of cult matters, while it remains uncertain whether he intends an association between Bacchus and the Eleusinian mysteries.[14]

The appellation of Dionysus as Euhius, equally derived from a ritual cry in the cult,[15] and the name Nysius, referring to Nysa, the mythical birthplace of Dionysus, are employed by Cicero elsewhere. In the speech *Pro Flacco* (59 BCE) he tries to defend the accused by undermining the trustworthiness of the 'Asian' witnesses when he argues that they had honoured Mithridates, Rome's enemy, as a god and called him by Dionysiac names. Owing to the thrust of the argument, Cicero does not make a direct comment on Mithridates (who is known to have adopted the name Dionysus [App. *Mithr.* 2.10; Plut. *Quaest. conv.* 1.6.2]) and rather criticizes the conduct of the people around him:

> Cic. *Flacc.* 60: quae quidem a me si, ut dicenda sunt, dicerentur, gravius agerem, iudices, quam adhuc egi, quantam Asiaticis testibus fidem habere vos conveniret; revocarem animos vestros ad Mithridatici belli memoriam, ad illam universorum civium Romanorum per

---

13 On 'Iacchus' and the relationship to Dionysus / Bacchus see Kern 1914.
14 In contrast to the translation by C.W. Keyes in the *Loeb* series (see above), J.E.G. Zetzel (in the *Cambridge Texts in the History of Political Thought* series) translates 'what will become of Iacchus and our Eumolpids, and those revered mysteries'. In the context, referring *nostri* only to *Eumolpidae* seems preferable, since this prepares the distinction between the Bacchanalia and the mysteries in what follows: 'Cicero' makes an exception for the Eleusinian mysteries, which he praises, speaking to the 'Athenian Atticus', and in which many Romans, including the interlocutors, were initiated (*Leg.* 2.36) while he goes on to approve of the ancestors' sternness towards the Bacchanalia (*Leg.* 2.37), which implies some reservation and makes claiming that god as 'ours' less likely.
15 This term is already attested for Ennius, even though the text is corrupt (Enn. *Trag.* 107–11 R.$^{2-3}$ = 123–27 V.^{2} = 120–24 Joc. = 42 *TrRF*).

tot urbis uno puncto temporis miseram crudelemque caedem, praetores nostros deditos, legatos in vincla coniectos, nominis prope Romani memoriam cum vestigio <omni> [*suppl. Oetling*] imperi non modo ex sedibus Graecorum verum etiam ex litteris esse deletam. Mithridatem dominum [*Lambinus* : deum *vel* dm̃ *vel* demum *vel* deinde *codd*.], illum patrem, illum conservatorem Asiae, illum Euhium, Nysium, Bacchum, Liberum nominabant.

'If, gentlemen, I were saying what the facts require me to say, I should be dealing more harshly than I have hitherto with the degree of trust that you should place in Asiatic witnesses; I should be taking your minds back to recall the Mithridatic War, to the horror of that barbarous massacre inflicted simultaneously upon all Roman citizens in every city, to the surrender of our praetors, the imprisonment of their officers and the almost total obliteration of all memory of the name of Rome and of every trace of our rule from the Greek settlements and from their very records. They called Mithridates Lord, Father, Saviour of Asia, Euhius, Nysius, Bacchus, Liber.' [trans. C. MacDonald]

The appellation of a man like Mithridates as described by Cicero with sacred names is meant to appear as a particular sacrilege. Moreover, Cicero does not seem to be attempting to record what the 'Asians' said, but to illustrate their assimilation of Mithridates with Dionysus by giving a list of cult titles to make their behaviour appear more outrageous. Cicero has the series end climactically with Liber, a name that the 'Asians' will hardly have used, but that, as a result of its range of meanings, may trigger associations of 'freedom', which contrasts with the Roman view of their enemy Mithridates.

Metonymical value of Bacchus / Liber

Cicero is aware that the name Liber does not always refer to the god, but may have a metonymical function with reference to the product he is mainly associated with in his role as a rural fertility deity. In *De natura deorum* Cicero has Balbus consider the metonymical force of divine names, such as 'Liber' for 'wine', and explain it by the recognition of their benefits:

Cic. *Nat. D.* 2.60: multae autem aliae naturae deorum ex magnis beneficiis eorum non sine causa et a Graeciae sapientissimis et a maioribus nostris constitutae nominataeque sunt. quicquid enim magnam utilitatem generi adferret humano, id non sine divina bonitate erga homines fieri arbitrabantur. itaque tum illud quod erat a deo natum nomine ipsius dei nuncupabant, ut cum fruges Cererem appellamus, vinum autem Liberum, ex quo illud Terenti [Eun. 732] 'sine Cerere et Libero friget Venus'.[16]

'With some justification, however, both the wisest men of Greece and our own ancestors have set up and lent names to many other divine natures because of the great benefits which they have conferred. They did this because they believed that anything which bestows some great service on the human race did not originate without divine beneficence. So they then applied the name of the deity itself to what that deity had brought forth. This is why we call corn Ceres, and wine Liber, as in that tag of Terence: 'Ceres and Liber, if not there, / The heat of Venus do impair.' ' [trans. P.G. Walsh]

These examples of metonymical use of names of gods are taken up elsewhere in Cicero's works:

Cic. *Nat. D.* 3.41: cum fruges Cererem, vinum Liberum dicimus, genere nos quidem sermonis utimur usitato, sed ecquem tam amentem esse putas qui illud quo vescatur deum credat esse?

'When we label the harvest as Ceres, and our wine as Liber, we are of course using a familiar turn of speech, but do you imagine that anyone is so mindless as to think that what he eats is a deity?' [trans. P.G. Walsh]

Cic. *De or.* 3.167: gravis est modus in ornatu orationis et saepe sumendus; ex quo genere haec sunt, 'Martem belli' esse 'communem', 'Cererem' pro frugibus, 'Liberum' appellare pro vino, 'Neptunum' pro mari, 'curiam' pro senatu, 'campum' pro comitiis, 'togam' pro pace, 'arma' ac 'tela' pro bello.

'The method is effective in ornamenting the style, and should often be adopted; and to the same class belong the phrase 'the impartiality of the War-god' and the use of the terms 'Ceres' for corn, 'Liber' for wine, 'Neptune' for the sea, 'the House' for parliament, 'the polling booth' for elections, 'civilian dress' for peace, 'arms' or 'guns' for war; ...' [trans. H. Rackham]

In these passages Cicero discusses or explains the metonymical designation of *vinum*, using the name Liber (cf. Lucr. 2.655–57). In other contexts, Liber appears instead of wine without any further comment. In one of the speeches against Verres Cicero alleges that the accused first used a bedroom to make political and legal decisions on the basis of bribery and then to indulge in love and wine:

---

[16] This line of Terence is quoted frequently by grammarians as an example of metonymy (for a list of passages see Pease 1958, *ad loc.*). – Donatus (*ad loc.*) notes the three-fold metonymy and tries to explain the proverb.

Cic. *Verr.* 2.5.27: sic confecto itinere cum ad aliquod oppidum venerat, eadem lectica usque in cubiculum deferebatur. eo veniebant Siculorum magistratus, veniebant equites Romani, id quod ex multis iuratis audistis; controversiae secreto deferebantur, paulo post palam decreta auferebantur. deinde, ubi pauilsper in cubiculo pretio, non aequitate iura discripserat, Veneri iam et Libero reliquum tempus deberi arbitrabatur.

'Whenever, his journey thus effected, he reached a town, he would be carried, in this same litter, direct to his bed-chamber. To this apartment Sicilian magistrates, to this apartment Roman knights betook themselves – you have heard many witnesses swear to the truth of this. Legal controversies were there brought before him privately, and shortly afterwards his decisions were brought away from him openly. Having thus briefly administered the law in his bedroom for an hour or two on principles more profitable than equitable, he felt it his duty to devote the rest of the day to the service of Venus and Bacchus.' [trans. L.H.G. Greenwood]

Because of the context, indulging in wine can only have negative connotations, particularly since Cicero goes on to describe Verres' excessive feasts in greater detail, while he ironically remarks on his enjoyment of wine: *qui populi Romani legibus numquam paruisset, illis legibus quae in poculis ponebantur diligenter obtemperabat* – 'who never in his life obeyed the laws of Rome, was none the less most careful to observe all the laws prescribed for the drinking of wine' (Cic. *Verr.* 2.5.28 [trans. L.H.G. Greenwood]). In metonymical usage, the term Liber does not necessarily indicate something positive to Cicero and his audience.[17]

Bacchic raving

In the discussion with 'Atticus' about nocturnal rites in *De legibus* (Cic. *Leg.* 2.35) 'Marcus' refers to the famous issue of the Bacchanalia and the resulting Senate decree of 186 BCE (*CIL* I² 581; Liv. 39.8–18) as a precedent for the envisaged restrictive arrangements for nocturnal rites according to the laws for Rome presented in this treatise (Cic. *Leg.* 2.37).[18] A little earlier 'Marcus' notes that the comic poets indicated what he dislikes about nocturnal rites (Cic. *Leg.* 2.36):[19] this

---

[17] Apart from the god's genealogy, Cicero does not engage with mythical stories connected with the god as an anthropomorphic being, such as Bacchus and Ariadne (e.g. Ov. *Fast.* 3.460–516).
[18] Gelzer (1936, 283–84) suggests that this passage and comments in Varro (Varro, *ARD*, F 93 C.) go back to the same early annalist.
[19] For an overview of references to the Bacchic cult in Roman drama and potential interrelationships with the historical situation see Flower 2000.

reference to the treatment of nocturnal mysteries and their consequences in comedies (e.g. Men. *Epit.* 451–52; Plaut. *Aul.* 35–36; Gell. *NA* 2.23.15–18) is given as proof of the negative consequences of the potential licentiousness during nocturnal rites, including those for Bacchus, and thus saves the speaker from explaining it in his own words. In terms of the repercussions for morally appropriate behaviour the cult of Dionysus therefore is disapproved of.

In the treatise *De divinatione* (45/44 BCE), where Cicero lists factors able to move the soul to such an extent that it enters an exceptional state, there is a reference to another literary text to illustrate the ecstasy of the soul created by strong grief: Cicero has the speaker, 'Cicero's brother Quintus', mention a woman who grieves for Teucer, presumably his mother Hesione, and quotes two lines, probably from Pacuvius' *Teucer*.[20] These verses illustrate the woman's status of being out of her mind by likening it to someone moved by Bacchic rites, i.e. with reference to Bacchants (Pac. *Trag.* 422–23 R.$^{2-3}$ = 373–74 W. = 251 S.):[21]

> Cic. *Div.* 1.80: fit etiam saepe specie quadam, saepe vocum gravitate et cantibus, ut pellantur animi vehementius, saepe etiam cura et timore, qualis est illa 'flexanima tamquam lymphata aut Bacchi sacris / commota, in tumulis Teucrum commemorans suum'.
>
> 'Also it often happens that by a certain image or depth of voice or by singing the soul is violently moved; the same thing happens often through worry or fear, just like her who: "with her mind changed as though mad or moved by the rites of Bacchus, was calling for her Teucer among the hills".' [trans. D. Wardle]

While in *De divinatione* Bacchic raving is employed as a metaphor for a specific state of the soul, without any negative evaluation, in controversies with political opponents the verb *bacchor* serves to characterize their unacceptable unrestrained behaviour negatively, which will have to do with the genre and the assumed views of the intended audience. The first metaphorical use of the verb *bacchor* in this sense occurs in the *Catilinarian Speeches*, delivered at the end of Cicero's consular year 63 BCE: Cicero alleges that both Catiline, once he has gone from Rome to C. Manlius in Etruria, and the conspirator C. Cornelius Cethegus,

---

[20] This is suggested by its partial quotation in Varro with attribution to this poet (Varro, *Ling.* 7.87).

[21] For *lymphata* in connection with Bacchic rites see Catull. 64.254–55. – *sacris* is generally understood as a noun describing the rites of Bacchus and dependent on *commota*. Pease (1920, *ad loc.*), however, suggests taking *sacris* with *tumulis*; this would make construction and word order rather complex.

once the senators have been assassinated,[22] would be in a state of ecstasy because of joy:

> Cic. *Cat.* 1.26: hic tu qua laetitia perfruere, quibus gaudiis exsultabis, quanta in voluptate bacchabere, cum in tanto numero tuorum neque audies virum bonum quemquam neque videbis!

> 'What delight you will take in their company, what joy you will experience, what pleasure you will revel in, seeing that from so sizeable a gathering you will be able neither to hear nor to see a single decent man!' [trans. D.H. Berry]

> Cic. *Cat.* 4.11: ..., versatur mihi ante oculos aspectus Cethegi et furor in vestra caede bacchantis.

> 'There appears before my eyes a vision of Cethegus, crazily revelling over your corpses.' [trans. D.H. Berry]

Later, Cicero ascribes a state identified by *bacchari* to his long-standing enemy P. Clodius Pulcher in the speech *De haruspicum responsis* (56 BCE). After Cicero had gone into exile and his house had been burnt down, Clodius acquired the site by auction. In this oration *bacchari* is meant to illustrate the mind-set determining Clodius' criminal and amoral activities (including an alleged incestuous relationship with his sister). This ecstatic state is not seen as being joyfully out of one's mind, but rather, as Cicero's explanation shows, a state of frenzy:

> Cic. *Har. resp.* 39: tu, cum furiales in contionibus voces mittis, cum domos civium evertis, cum lapidibus optimos viros foro pellis, cum ardentes faces in vicinorum tecta iactas, cum aedes sacras inflammas, cum servos concitas, cum sacra ludosque conturbas, cum uxorem sororemque non discernis, cum quod ineas cubile non sentis, tum baccharis, tum furis, tum das eas poenas, quae solae sunt hominum sceleri a dis immortalibus constitutae.

> 'When you utter your frenzied phrases at mob-meetings, when you overturn the houses of citizens, when you drive honest men with stones from the forum, when you hurl blazing torches on your neighbours' roofs, when you set fire to sacred buildings, when you stir up slaves, when you throw sacrifices and games into turmoil, when you know no distinction between wife and sister, when you bethink you not what bed-chamber you enter, then, then it is that *you* rave in delirium, and undergo the only punishments determined by the immortal gods to requite the wickedness of men.' [trans. N.H. Watts]

Closer to the original relationship with the wine god Bacchus is a passage in one of the *Philippics* composed against Mark Antony (44 BCE). Here the compound

---

22 On Cic. *Cat.* 1.26 see Dyck 2008, *ad loc.*

perbacchor is employed; the word occurs only in this passage in Cicero, and this seems to be its first attestation in Latin literature. Cicero thus characterizes the continuing state of ecstatic frenzy as a result of drinking, prostitution and vomiting, which Mark Antony indulged in when residing in Varro's villa, which he had brought into his possession and where he thus introduced a completely different lifestyle, as Cicero alleges. Perhaps because this speech was never delivered, Cicero is particularly outspoken:

> Cic. *Phil.* 2.104: at quam multos dies in ea villa turpissime es perbacchatus! ab hora tertia bibebatur, ludebatur, vomebatur.
>
> 'But how many days did you spend disgracefully carousing in that villa! From eight o'clock in the morning there was drinking, gambling, vomiting.' [trans. D.R. Shackleton Bailey / J.T. Ramsey / G. Manuwald]

Cicero's negative concept of an ecstatic state described by *bacchari* is also noticeable in his theoretical works on oratory, *Brutus* and *Orator* (46 BCE). Both pieces deal with the ability of an orator to move the audience emotionally. In *Brutus* Cicero considers that M. Calidius (praet. 57 BCE), an outstanding orator in his time, might have regarded too elevated and fiery a style of speaking as bacchic raving. In *Orator* Cicero says in his own person that an orator only speaking in an elevated and copious style appeared like a drunk Bacchant among the sober:[23]

> Cic. *Brut.* 276: ...; aberat tertia illa laus, qua permoveret atque incitaret animos, quam plurumum pollere diximus; nec erat ulla vis atque contentio, sive consilio, quod eos quorum altior oratio actioque esset ardentior furere atque bacchari arbitraretur, sive quod natura non esset ita factus, sive quod non consuesset, sive quod non posset. hoc unum illi, si nihil utilitatis habebat, afuit, si opus erat, defuit.
>
> '... The third merit, which consists in moving the listener and in arousing his emotions, – the orator's chief source of power, as I have said – he [i.e. Calidius] lacked, and he was in fact quite without force and intensity. This may have been due to deliberate choice, as of one holding that a more elevated style and a more vehement delivery was frenzy and delirium, or to a natural indisposition to that sort of thing, or to established habit, or to actual inability. This one quality was lacking to him; if useless, call it a lack, if essential, a defect.' [trans. G.L. Hendrickson]
>
> Cic. *Orat.* 99: ille enim summissus, quod acute et veteratorie dicit, sapiens iam, medius suavis, hic autem copiosissimus, si nihil est aliud, vix satis sanus videri solet. qui enim nihil

---

[23] The idea of a raving speech recurs elsewhere in *Brutus* without the bacchic illustration (Cic. *Brut.* 233). – The metaphor reappears in Quintilian, yet without Cicero's term *bacchari* (Quint. *Inst.* 12.10.73).

potest tranquille, nihil leniter, nihil partite, definite, distincte, facete dicere, praesertim cum causae partim totae sint eo modo partim aliqua ex parte tractandae, si is non praeparatis auribus inflammare rem coepit, furere apud sanos et quasi inter sobrios bacchari vinulentus videtur.

'For the plain orator is esteemed wise because he speaks clearly and adroitly; the one who employs the middle style is charming; but the copious speaker, if he has nothing else, seems to be scarcely sane. For a man who can say nothing calmly and mildly, who pays no attention to arrangement, precision, clarity or pleasantry – especially when some cases have to be handled entirely in this latter style, and others largely so, – if without first preparing the ears of his audience he begins trying to work them up to a fiery passion, he seems to be a raving madman among the sane, like a drunken reveller in the midst of sober men.' [trans. H.M. Hubbell]

The various metaphorical uses of *bacchari* show that Cicero does not approve of the situation of a human being described thereby, as it implies a loss of control. The original relationship to a cultic procedure is virtually ignored in this usage; it is only the ecstatic frenzied state that is at issue. The rejection of this state, which Cicero regards as sufficiently despicable so as to ascribe it to opponents, is matched, in positive terms, by a high appreciation of Roman virtues such as restraint and self-moderation (e.g. Cic. *Q. Fr.* 1.1.18).

Cicero's 'own' attitude to the god Dionysus / Bacchus / Liber cannot be ascertained, as his personal religiosity is not easy to establish.[24] That Cicero disapproves of Bacchic raving, however, is implied by his opposition to statues of Bacchants, Bacchus' ecstatic followers, which a friend had organized as decoration for Cicero's house: he regards them as inappropriate for the image of himself to be displayed:

Cic. *Fam.* 7.23.2 (to M. Fabius Gallus, Dec. 46 BCE): Bacchas istas cum Musis Metelli comparas. quid simile? primum ipsas ego Musas numquam tanti putassem atque id fecissem Musis omnibus approbantibus, sed tamen erat aptum bibliothecae studiisque nostris congruens; Bacchis vero ubi est apud me locus? at pulchellae sunt. novi optime et saepe vidi. nominatim tibi signa mihi nota mandassem si probassem. ea enim signa ego emere soleo quae ad similitudinem gymnasiorum exornent mihi in palaestra locum.

'You compare these Bacchantes with Metellus' Muses. Where's the likeness? To begin with, I should never have reckoned the Muses themselves worth such a sum – and all Nine would have approved my judgement! Still, that would have made a suitable acquisition for a library, and one appropriate to my interests. But where am I going to put Bacchantes? Pretty little things, you may say. I know them well, I've seen them often. I should have given you a specific commission about statues which I know, if I had cared for them. My habit is to

---

[24] See Manuwald 2018.

buy pieces which I can use to decorate a place in my palaestra, in imitation of lecture halls.' [trans. D.R. Shackleton Bailey]

Liberalia – a festival of freedom?

Cicero not only uses the word *bacchari* derived from the divine name Bacchus in a metaphorical sense, but he also argues with the name of the festival of *Liberalia*, which he interprets as a festival of liberty and thus connects indirectly with the god Liber.[25] In the months after Caesar's assassination on the Ides of March 44 BCE Cicero sometimes refers to the Senate meeting two days later, on 17 March (e.g. Cic. *Phil.* 1.1; 2.89; cf. App. *B Civ.* 2.126.525–26), the day of the *Liberalia*. By playing with the name of the festival, in two letters to Atticus Cicero laments that Caesar's death has not led to liberty because Mark Antony was given the opportunity to take charge by calling a Senate meeting on that day:

Cic. *Att.* 14.10.1 (19 April 44 BCE): meministine <me> clamare illo ipso primo Capitolino die senatum in Capitolium a praetoribus vocan<dum>? di immortales, quae tum opera effici potuerunt laetantibus omnibus bonis, etiam sat bonis, fractis latronibus! Liberalia tu accusas. quid fieri tum potuit? iam pridem perieramus.

'Do you remember how that first day on the Capitol I cried out that the Senate ought to be summoned to the spot by the Praetors? Great heavens, what might not have been accomplished then amid the rejoicing of all honest men, even the moderately honest, and the discomfiture of the bandits! You blame Bacchus' Day. What could we have done then? By that time we were long sunk.' [trans. D.R. Shackleton Bailey]

Cic. *Att.* 14.14.2–5 (28 or 29 April 44 BCE): nam Liberalibus quis potuit in senatum non venire? fac id potuisse aliquo modo; num etiam, cum venissemus, libere potuimus sententiam dicere? nonne omni ratione veterani qui armati aderant, cum praesidi nos nihil haberemus, defendendi fuerunt? ... [3] ...; istos omni cura praesidioque tueamur, et, quem ad modum tu praecipis, contenti Idibus Martiis simus; quae quidem nostris amicis divinis viris, aditum ad caelum dederunt, libertatem populo Romano non dederunt. ... [5] ... ne nos et liberati ab egregiis viris nec liberi sumus. ita laus illorum est, culpa nostra.

'As for Bacchus' Day, who could help coming to the Senate? Suppose that was somehow possible: when we *had* come, could we have spoken freely? Was it not essential at any cost to fend off the veterans who were standing by with arms in their hands while we were defenceless? ... Let us protect these men by every means our solicitude can devise, and be

---

25 For Liber's association with *liber* and *libertas* see e.g. Serv. ad Virg. *Aen.* 3.20; 4.58. – See also n. 3 above.

satisfied, as you recommend, with the Ides of March. That day opened the door of immortality to our heroic friends, but not the door of freedom to the Roman people. ... Truly we have been freed by heroes, but we are not free. Theirs then the glory, ours the blame.' [trans. D.R. Shackleton Bailey]

To what extent for this interpretation of the *Liberalia* a link to the god Liber is relevant cannot be ascertained. Cicero stresses the contrast between the expectations raised by this particular festival and the true situation in the *res publica* demonstrated by Mark Antony's actions; he therefore implicitly stresses the perceived lack of freedom via an etymological pun on *liber*.

Conclusions

The results of the analysis of Cicero's references to the god Dionysus / Bacchus / Liber and his use of terms connected with this god are diverse and wide-ranging. There are no indications that Cicero entertained any kind of 'personal' relationship to this god. Instead, he commented on him in 'theological' discussions and used words that had entered ordinary language, derived from this god's cult and special function as a god of wine. Looking at the various aspects, one might be able to say that Cicero seems to refer to Liber when pointing out the positive aspects of this Roman god and of the festival and the cult associated with him, to use the name Bacchus metonymically for wine and its derivatives to illustrate raving and to speak of Dionysus when talking of the Greek god and his genealogy. The term Bacchus and related words tend to appear in contexts with more negative connotations than the designation Liber. This agrees with the fact that Cicero regarded the erection of the apparently popular statues of Bacchants in his house as inappropriate for his image.

To what extent Cicero's attitude towards Dionysiac divinity is representative of contemporary Romans is hard to tell: on the one hand his beliefs may be indicative of the views of the Roman elite at the time.[26] On the other hand Servius transmits the view that Caesar was the first to transplant the *sacra Liberi patris* to

---

26 See generally Beard / North / Price 1998, I 115: 'Cicero's speech *On his House* is not an isolated survival, a lucky 'one-off' for the historian of late republican religion. A leading political figure of his day, the most famous Roman orator ever, and prolific author – Cicero's writing takes the reader time and again into the immediacy of religious debate and the day-to-day operations of religious business.', and for the context see I 114–66.

Rome (Serv. ad Verg. E. 5.29).[27] The trustworthiness and interpretation of this remark are controversial; it might indicate a revitalisation of the cult or mark the introduction of a new mystery cult, or it may be a reflection of Caesar's intentions to make the cult of Dionysus official and use it in his political propaganda. At any rate support for the strong action of the Senate against the extremes of the cult of Bacchus may no longer have been as widely shared, so that such actions by powerful men became possible.[28] Mark Antony had himself celebrated as Dionysus when he entered Ephesus in 41 BCE, continuing the tradition of Hellenistic kings and alluding to the positive qualities of the god (Plut. Ant. 24.3–4), though Plutarch comments that Antony's activity was harmful to most, and his posing as Dionysus is described critically by Cassius Dio (Cass. Dio 50.5.3).[29] If there was a renewed interest in the Greek aspects of the god Dionysus in the first century BCE,[30] Cicero's engagement with the different manifestations of the god, as he explains them in *De natura deorum*, may be even more telling and have been prompted by the contemporary atmosphere. At least it can be assumed that Cicero regarded the views underlying statements in speeches as acceptable to and shared by the respective audience.

Bibliography

Beard, M., J. North, and S. Price, 1998. *Religions of Rome. Volume 1: A History.* Cambridge.

Bernstein, F. 1998. *Ludi publici. Untersuchungen zur Entstehung und Entwicklung der öffentlichen Spiele im republikanischen Rom.* Stuttgart.

Borgies, L. 2016. *Le conflit propagandiste entre Octavien et Marc Antoine. De l'usage politique de la uituperatio entre 44 et 30 a. C. n.* Brussels.

Bruchmann, C.F.H. 1893. *Epitheta Deorum quae apud poetas Graecos leguntur, collegit, disposuit, edidit.* Leipzig.

Bruhl, A. 1953. *Liber pater. Origine et expansion du culte dionysiaque à Rome et dans le monde romain.* Paris.

Dyck, A.R. (ed.) 2008. *Cicero. Catilinarians,* Cambridge.

Flower, H.I. 2000. '*Fabula de Bacchanalibus*: the Bacchanalian Cult of the Second Century BC and Roman Drama.' In *Identität und Alterität in der frührömischen Tragödie,* edited by G. Manuwald. Würzburg, 23–36.

---

[27] On the interpretation of this notice see e.g. Turcan 1977; Pailler 1988, 728–43.
[28] See Wardle 2009, 105.
[29] See Borgies 2016, 297–300. – On the functionalization of Dionysus by Mark Antony and the god's role in Augustan literature see Fuhrer 2011. – For the presentation of humans as divine, also in comparison with Ceres and Liber, see Lucr. 5.1–21.
[30] Thus Bruhl 1953, 122.

Fuhrer, T. 2011. 'Inszenierungen von Göttlichkeit. Die politische Rolle von Dionysus / Bacchus in der römischen Literatur.' In Schlesier, 373–89.

Gelzer, M. 1936. 'Die Unterdrückung der Bacchanalien bei Livius.' *Hermes* 71, 275–87; repr. in *Kleine Schriften. Band III*. Hg. v. H. Strasburger und C. Meier. Wiesbaden 1964, 256–69.

Kern, O. 1914. 'Iakchos (1)', *RE* IX 1, 613–22.

Manuwald, G. 2018. 'Die ‚religiöse Stimme‘ Ciceros.' In *Autoren in religiösen literarischen Texten der späthellenistischen und frühkaiserzeitlichen Welt. Zwölf Fallstudien*, edited by E.-M. Becker and J. Rüpke. Tübingen, 39–55.

Musiał, D. 2013. 'Divinities of the Roman Liberalia.' *Przegląd Humanistyczny* 2, 95–100.

Pailler, J.-M. 1988. *Bacchanalia. La répression de 186 av. J.-C. à Rome et en Italie: Vestiges, images, tradition*. Rome.

Pease, A.S. (ed.) 1920 /1923. *M. Tulli Ciceronis de divinatione. Liber primus / Liber secundus*. Urbana, IL.

Pease, A.S. (ed.) 1955/1958. *M. Tulli Ciceronis de natura deorum. Liber primus / Libri secundus et tertius*. Cambridge, MA.

Radke, G. 1965. *Die Götter Altitaliens*. Münster.

Schlesier, R., ed. 2011. *Dionysos: A Different God? Dionysos and Ancient Polytheism*. Berlin/New York.

Turcan, R. 1977. 'César et Dionysos.' In *Hommage à la mémoire de Jérôme Carcopino*. Paris, 317–25.

Wacht, M. and F. Rickert, 2010. 'Liber (Dionysos)', *RAC* 23, 67–99.

Walsh, P.G. 1997. *Cicero. The Nature of the Gods. Translated with Introduction and Explanatory Notes*. Oxford.

Wardle, D. 2009. 'Caesar and religion.' In *A Companion to Julius Caesar*, edited by M. Griffin. Chichester/Malden, MA, 100–11.

Wiseman, T.P. 2000. 'Liber. Myth, Drama and Ideology in Republican Rome.' In *The Roman Middle Republic: Politics, Religion, and Historiography, c. 400–133 B.C.* (Papers from a Conference at the Institutum Romanum Finlandiae, September 11–12, 1998), edited by C. Bruun. Rome, 265–99, repr. in *Unwritten Rome*. Exeter, 84–139.

Wyler, S. 2011. 'L'acculturation dionysiaque à Rome. L'invention d'une alterité.' In *Identités romaines. Conscience de soi, et représentation de l'autre dans le Rome antique (IVe siècle av. J.-C. – VIIIe siècle apr. J.-C.)*, edited by M. Simon. Paris, 191–201.

John F. Miller

Bacchus and the exiled Ovid (*Tristia* 5.3)

Abstract: In the case of Ovid, consideration of Dionysus in Rome yields a rich amalgam of myth, cult, history, and prior literary imaginings. Particularly striking are cases where Greek and Roman elements intersect, such as the presentation in *Fasti* 3 of the main Roman feast of Liber/Bacchus, the Liberalia, and the remarkable hymnic movement near the start of *Metamorphoses* 4. The present paper focuses on *Tristia* 5.3, an appeal that the exiled Ovid makes to Bacchus from the wilds of Tomis during the annual celebration of the Liberalia back in Rome, where evidently poets gathered to celebrate a divine patron of poetry. The elegy anchors itself to the Liberalia through allusions to the *Fasti*'s presentation at the start. Bacchus emerges as by turns a comparative and a contrastive figure for the exiled poet – on the one hand, himself having left his native land and travelled among the Getae, on the other having been rewarded for his struggles with a place on Olympus. Ovid's request for Bacchus' intervention with Augustus as fellow deity is matched by the appeal to his fellow poets to the same effect. A closing reference to the blessing of Apollo in the context of what is permitted to Roman poets seems to evoke that divinity as a distinctly imperial figure as much as it suddenly adds a new god of poetic inspiration for the sake of variation.

Ovid in his exile poetry not infrequently conjures up sights or occasions back in Rome, from which he has been painfully banished – springtime activities in the Campus Martius, his last night in the City, an imperial triumph, a friend's consular installation, dining in a great man's company.[1] These imaginings are partly self-consolatory reveries; in part they aim to heighten the poet's appeals to friends or would-be patrons. All pointedly express what Philip Hardie aptly calls 'the opposition between past presence and present absence that defines the exile poetry as a whole.'[2] *Tristia* 5.3 offers a particularly rich example, a letter reflecting on the celebration of the annual festival of the Liberalia on March 17 by his fellow

---

This paper benefited greatly from discussion at the UCL Dionysus in Rome conference, especially with T.P. Wiseman, Alessandro Schiesaro, Stephen Heyworth, and Bobby Xinyue. Many thanks, too, for valuable comments on the written version by Ivana Petrovic, Anke Walter, Sara Myers, and especially Fiachra Mac Góráin.

[1] *Tr.* 3.12.17–26; *Tr.* 1.3; *Tr.* 4.2, *EP* 2.1, 3.4; *EP* 4.4, 4.9; *EP* 1.2.129–30.
[2] Hardie 2002, 287.

poets in Rome, whether formally as a *collegium poetarum*[3] or more loosely associated with the state celebration. The feast's Roman locus is in this case not specified, and in fact the traditional home of Liber in the Aventine temple (that he shared with Ceres and Libera) had been damaged by fire in 31 BCE and stood in ruins for much of the Augustan age. Even if the renovation at last begun by Augustus had commenced by the elegy's dramatic date of 11 or 12 CE – most likely is that the impulse to rebuild was the famines of 5–8 CE – the Aventine shrine was not rededicated until 17 by Tiberius.[4] Alternatively, Ovid may picture poets celebrating the Liberalia at another shrine in the City – apparently Bacchus had a *sacellum* on the Palatine[5] – or in a grove as with the symposium of poets at the close of Propertius 4.6. In any case, the exiled Ovid remembering these annual Roman festivities turns in the first instance to Bacchus/Liber himself. This Ovidian appeal from Tomis is a hymnic prayer to a god. At the same time, behind the triangulation of poet, poetic confrères, and divinity of poets looms, as throughout the collection, the ultimate authority of Augustus, who is himself divine in the world of the *Tristia*.[6]

A brief look at two other addresses to Bacchus in Ovid's later poetry will help to contextualize the plea from Tomis.[7] In his poetic calendar, the *Fasti*, Ovid offers a dense meditation on the Liberalia. The opening movement of that lively and sprawling panel illustrates well how Ovid can create a pointed dynamic between Greek myth and Roman cultic reality (3.713–26):[8]

> Tertia post Idus lux est celeberrima Baccho:
> Bacche, fave vati, dum tua festa cano.

---

[3] *Collegium poetarum*: Horsfall 1976.
[4] Fire: Dio 50.10.3, Tac. *Ann.* 2.49; poem's dramatic date: *Tr.* 5.10.1–2 mentions the third year of his exile; famines: Dio 55.22.3, 26.1–3, 27.1, 31.3–4, 33.4 with Wiseman 2000, 295–97; rebuilding and rededication: Tac. *Ann.* 2.49 *Isdem temporibus deum aedis vetustate aut igni abolitas coeptasque ab Augusto dedicavit, Libero Liberaeque et Cereri iuxta circum maximum, quam A. Postumius dictator voverat*...
[5] See E. Rodríguez Almeida in *LTUR* 1 (1993) 153–54 s.v. 'Bacchus (Palatium),' who offers evidence for such a shrine within the Augustan complex on the Palatine and near the Temple of Magna Mater.
[6] A conspicuous example is the elegy paired with the exilic appeal to Bacchus, *Tr.* 5.2, where Ovid prays to Augustus in the context of a letter to his wife. See Hardie 2002, 300–306.
[7] On Bacchus in Ovid, see Miller 2002; Barchiesi and Rosati 2007; Janan 2009; Hardie 2002, 166–72; and Miller 2016; on *Tr.* 5.3, Nagle 1980, 82; Hardie 2002, 303–306; Amann 2006, 224–25; and McGowan 2009, 143–46. On Liber and his history at Rome, see Bruhl 1953; Radke 1965, 175–83; Simon 1990, 126–34; Mac Góráin 2009; C. Gaspari in *LIMC* 3.540–66 s.v. 'Dionysos/Bacchus', and the Introduction to this volume.
[8] See further Miller 2002.

> nec referam Semelen, ad quam nisi fulmina secum 715
>   Iuppiter adferret, †parvus inermis eras†;
> nec, puer ut posses maturo tempore nasci,
>   expletum patrio corpore matris opus.
> Sithonas et Scythicos longum narrare triumphos
>   et domitas gentes, turifer Inde, tuas. 720
> tu quoque, Thebanae mala praeda, tacebere, matris,
>   inque tuum furiis acte Lycurge genus.
> ecce libet subitos pisces Tyrrhenaque monstra
>   dicere; sed non est carminis huius opus.
> carminis huius opus causas exponere quare 725
>   vitisator populos ad sua liba vocet.

On the third day after the Ides Bacchus is honoured with great festivity. O Bacchus, be propitious to me, your poet, while I sing of your festival. I will not tell of Semele, without whose visit from Jupiter's thunderbolts you would have been born defenceless (?), nor of the mother's work performed by your father's body, so that you could be born a boy at the proper time. It would take a long time to narrate your triumphs over the Sithonians and Scythians, and how your peoples, too, incense-bearing India, were subdued. You who were the sorry prey of your Theban mother will also receive no mention, and you too, Lycurgus, driven by madness against your own son. Look, I would like to speak of the Tyrrhenian monsters, men suddenly turned into fish, but that is not the task of this song. The task of this song is to explain the reason(s) why the Vine Planter calls the population to his cakes.

The quasi-hymnic (or anti-hymnic) *praeteritio* of Bacchic *aretai* well known from the Hellenic tradition concludes with the distinctly Roman sacral offering of cakes on this day.[9] After the grand sequence of important chapters in Bacchus' biography, the punchline may seem bathetic. Indeed, Ovid notes, punning on Liber's name, that he would like (723 *libet*) to talk about the Tyrrhenian pirates, but instead is stuck with the god's *liba* (726). The movement thus returns to where the poet began, with the divinity's very festive worship on the seventeenth of March, in Rome.

The penultimate couplet (723–24), noting that the men suddenly transformed into fish are not the business of the present calendar-poem, is a cross-reference to his *Metamorphoses*, on which he was working at the same time as the *Fasti*, and where he narrates at length the episode of Bacchus and the pirates (3.572–700).[10] Not long after that tale, as a sequence of Greek Bacchic tales continues at the start of Book 4 with the Minyades refusing the summons to worship Bacchus,

---

9 Varro, *LL* 6.14 with Miller 2002, 201 n. 10.
10 See recently Miller 2016, 95–108 with further bibliography.

we find another mini-hymn to the deity that is pointedly punctuated by reference to the god's cultic identity in Rome (4.11–30):

> turaque dant Bacchumque vocant Bromiumque Lyaeumque
> ignigenamque satumque iterum solumque bimatrem;
> additur his Nyseus indetonsusque Thyoneus
> et cum Lenaeo genialis consitor uvae
> Nycteliusque Eleleusque parens et Iacchus et Euhan,
> et quae praeterea per Graias plurima gentes
> nomina, Liber, habes. tibi enim inconsumpta iuventa est,
> tu puer aeternus, tu formosissimus alto
> conspiceris caelo; tibi, cum sine cornibus adstas,
> virgineum caput est; Oriens tibi victus, adusque
> decolor extremo qua tinguitur India Gange;
> Penthea tu, venerande, bipenniferumque Lycurgum
> sacrilegos mactas Tyrrhenaque mittis in aequor
> corpora; tu biiugum pictis insignia frenis
> colla premis lyncum; Bacchae Satyrique sequuntur,
> quique senex ferula titubantis ebrius artus
> sustinet et pando non fortiter haeret asello.
> quacumque ingrederis, clamor iuvenalis et una
> femineae voces inpulsaque tympana palmis
> concavaque aera sonant longoque foramine buxus.

> They offer incense, and call on Bacchus, Bromius, Lyaeus, the one born of lightning, twice born, the only one with two mothers; to these titles they add Nysan, unshorn son of Thyone, Lenaeus, planter of the festive vine, Nocturnal one, father Eleleus, Iacchus, Euhan, and the many names besides which you have throughout the Greek peoples, o Liber. For your youth is never destroyed, you are eternally a boy, you are most beautiful as seen in the heavens; your face resembles a virgin's when you stand without your horns; you have conquered the East, as far as the remote Ganges washes dark India. You, revered one, slew the impious Pentheus and Lycurgus wielding his axe, you hurled the Tyrrhenian sailors into the sea; you drive two yoked lynxes with their colourful reins. Bacchants and satyrs follow you, and the drunken old man who supports his tottering legs with a staff, and clings weakly to his sway-backed ass. Wherever you proceed, the shouts of youths resound and together with them the cries of women, and also the drums being played, and the hollow bronze cymbals, and the boxwood pipe.

Those who *do* honour Bacchus shout his various titles, itemized for several verses, and concluding with the usual blanket phrase to cover all possible names (16–17 *et quae . . . nomina . . . habes*).[11] Although the blanket phrase specifies Bacchus' titles all over Greece (*per Graias . . . gentes*), it gains climactic force not only

---

11 Norden 1913, 144–47; Appel 1909, 75–80.

via an apostrophe to the divinity but also by addressing him as Liber, the Roman Bacchus. Then, in a remarkable move for epic,[12] the narrator continues (17–30) with a Bacchic aretalogy structured much like the quasi-hymn of *Fasti* 3 – again, the sequence *puer*, Eastern conquest, punishment of Pentheus, and Lycurgus, and the Tyrrhenian pirates. So the address to Liber is not an apostrophe after all, but inaugurates a modulation from narration to outright hymn, as the narrator metamorphoses into Bacchic celebrant. And at the moment of that transformation the address to Bacchus by his old Latin name Liber identifies both the enthusiastic speaker and the divine honorand as Roman.

The appeal that Ovid makes to Bacchus from the wilds of Tomis aligns even more directly with the *Fasti*'s Liberalia. Here is revealed another dimension of the festivities in Rome on March 17 besides the honey-cakes and conferral of the *toga virilis* on Roman youths – namely, the celebration of Bacchus by Roman poets. As Stephen Hinds first pointed out,[13] this elegy's opening verses (1–6) are shot through with allusions to the start of Ovid's presentation of the Liberalia (quoted above):

> Illa dies haec est, qua te celebrare poetae,
>   si modo non fallunt tempora, Bacche, solent,
> festaque odoratis innectunt tempora sertis,
>   et dicunt laudes ad tua vina tuas.
> inter quos, memini, dum me mea fata sinebant,
>   non invisa tibi pars ego saepe fui,

> This is that day, Bacchus, on which poets are accustomed to honour you, if only I do not mistake the time, and when they bind their temples for the feast with fragrant garlands, and proclaim your praises while drinking your wine. Among them, I remember, I was often a participant not unwelcome to you, while my fate was allowing me.

Certainty eludes us on the relative chronology of composition between the *Fasti* and the exilic poetry and compelling cases can be made for allusions running in both directions.[14] Indeed, Ovid's approach to the god in his calendar-poem could evoke his appeal for Bacchus' favour from exile, when he was absent from the annual *sacra* in Rome (cf. *F.* 3.714 *Bacche, fave vati, dum tua festa cano*). The *Fasti*

---

12 Only elsewhere at A.R. 2.708–10 and Virg. *Aen.* 8.293–302. See Danielewicz 1990, 73–84; La Bua 1999, 156–57; Miller 2014, 447–50.
13 Hinds 1987, 20–21.
14 See, for instance, Fantham 1985; Myers 2014, 725–34 with further bibliography.

invites us to read its six books as having been issued from exile.[15] But the intertextual arc from *Tristia* 5.3 towards the *Fasti* is perhaps more direct: *dies* and *celebrare* match *lux ... celeberrima* (F. 3.713); again Bacchus is addressed by name (*F.* 3.714 *Bacche*); the single *vates* (*F.* 3.714 *fave vati*) is now in the company of other *poetae*. As often, *memini* points to literary memory. Clinching the reference, the play on the word *tempora* ('times' and 'temples') recalls the thematic first word of the whole *Fasti*, and, in the first pentameter, makes a joke: 'if only I, the poet of *tempora cum causis*, who celebrated the Liberalia, do not forget the day of that celebration.' On another level, that clause suggests yet another possible diminution to his powers since exile – lapsing memory along with faulty versifying, the general enervation, and the rest.[16] All in all, the allusion underscores the occasion of Liber's yearly Roman festival, here broadened beyond the *liba* and *toga libera* to include the community of poets.

The beginning of *Tristia* 5.3 at the same time brings to mind another imagined sacral event, the aforementioned festal symposium of poets that concludes Propertius 4.6, where that elegist invites his colleagues to sing of Augustus' conquests after he himself has commemorated the Palatine Temple of Apollo as a memorial of the victory at Actium (4.6.71–84). *Tristia* 5.3 stages another rare instance in Latin poetry of a ritual celebration only by poets.[17] That striking parallel is underscored by similar sympotic motifs[18] and in particular by a cluster of verbal echoes in Ovid's opening distich that fully activates the allusion:

> Illa dies haec est, qua *te* celebrare *poetae*,
>   si modo non fallunt tempora, *Bacche, solent*
>
> ingenium potis irritet Musa *poetis*:
>   *Bacche, soles* Phoebo fertilis esse *tuo*. (Prop. 4.6.75–76)
>
> Let the Muse awaken the genius of drunken poets. Bacchus, you are accustomed to stimulate your brother Phoebus.

---

15 For a strong case for such a reading see Heyworth 2018, 116–20; 2019, 11–12.
16 On the (ironic) pose of decline throughout the exilic works, see Williams 1994, 50–99; also Nagle 1980, 109–40.
17 Besides the address to Bacchus, ritual elements include the white garments of the symposiasts (71 *candida ... convivia*, on which see Rothstein *ad loc.*) and Propertius' *patera* (85); the whole movement also resumes the ritual scenario of the elegy's opening (1 *sacra facit vates*, etc.). Similar, too, is the symposium at Hor. *Od.* 4.15.25–32, where Roman poets, accompanied by their wives and children, and amidst the gifts of Liber, will sing of legendary heroes after duly praying to the gods.
18 Garlands: *Tr.* 5.3.3 *sertis*; Prop. 4.6.72 *rosae, vina: Tr.* 5.3.4; Prop. 4.6.73.

The wine-god who for Propertius would inspire verse in honour of Augustus now becomes the focal point of his own festal ceremonies, but in Ovid's poem Augustus, the one responsible for his exile and so for his absence from the Liberalia in Rome, is subtextually present through allusion from the start. And so, it would seem, is the great Augustan god Apollo, into whose Actian ceremonies Bacchus is intruded as the inspirational force near the end of Propertius' panegyrical elegy.[19]

Ovid's wistful opening recollection of past celebration (5–6 *sinebant*; *fuit*) is then set sharply against Ovid's present condition (7–8): *quem nunc suppositum stellis Cynosuridos Ursae | iuncta tenet crudis Sarmatis ora Getis*. Where formerly at Rome he enjoyed a symposium marked by sweet-smelling garlands, wine, and singing Bacchus' praises among fellow poets, now he has been relocated to a view of the northern sky, in the grip of the wild Sarmatian shore bordering the savage Getae. The syntactic shift, too, accentuates his radically transformed circumstances – from the free subject proud to share in Bacchus' worship – 6 *pars ego saepe fui* – he has now become object – *quem nunc suppositum* – a victim possessed by (*tenet*) the barbarian land. The participle accented at caesura (*suppositum*) also expresses his abject state (*OLD* 4b). Then (9–12), with the same sort of syntactic move from active voice to passive (*egi . . . circumsonor . . . passus*), he restates the wretched relocation, explicitly noting the distance from homeland – 11 *nunc procul a patria* – and figuring the displacement in generic terms – from the past 'soft life' in association with the Muses, the *mollem vitam* evocative of his love-elegy (9–10), to quasi-epic suffering on land and sea (12) and enduring the din of barbarian martial arms (11).[20] To have been in the chorus of the Pierides, *Pieridumque choro* (10), betokens a worshipful devotion to the Muses, which accords with his festive celebration of Bacchus as patron of poets.

The deformations wrought by Ovid's relegation from his beloved Rome to the miserable Tomis are of course one of the central themes of the *Tristia*. And this is not the first time that they have been expressed in Bacchic terms. In *Tristia* 1.7, the famous elegy which creates the legend of Ovid attempting to burn the *Metamorphoses*, he starts by enjoining anyone in possession of his portrait bust to remove the ivy crown from his hair, the *Bacchica serta* (1–2): *Si quis habes nostri similes in imagine vultus, | deme meis hederas, Bacchica serta, comis*. For at present the *corona* that should signify success – *felicia signa* – and that befits rejoicing poets, is not suitable to adorn the temples of an exile (3–4): *ista decent laetos*

---

19 See Heyworth 1994, 62–67.
20 Elegiac *mollitia*: e.g. Prop. 2.1.2, Ov. *Tr*. 2.307 and 349; *Pont*. 3.4.85–86. Pretensions to epic suffering in the exilic elegies: Williams 1994, 66–67 and 108–13.

felicia signa poetas: | temporibus non est apta corona meis. Temporibus . . . meis may have a double meaning such as was worked out at the start of *Tristia* 5.3; the symbol of happiness also does not suit his 'times,' that is his present 'circumstances' as an exile (for which see *OLD* 10). In either case, Ovid here would undo the properly Bacchic representation of himself that he and his poetic confrères embodied at the Liberalia by stripping away the god's sacred ivy, there expressive of celebration – *festa . . . tempora* (5.3.3) – here of a gladness and good fortune that no longer exist.

Ovid next, starting at verse 13, enumerates the possible causes of his plight – chance, divine wrath (an idea associated with Augustus throughout the *Tristia*),[21] or a gloomy fate attaching to his birth. Regardless of which reason obtains, he boldly tells Bacchus that he ought to have supported him, one of his votaries (15–16): *tu tamen e sacris hederae cultoribus unum | numine debueras sustinuisse tuo*. The assonance in repeated –*u* sounds affirms the closeness of the worshipper to his god, which the latter should repay. This would be, in particular, Ovid's pre-exilic participation in the poets' *laudes* of the god at the Liberalia – verse 6 *pars ego saepe fui* is in essence restated in 15 *e sacris hederae cultoribus unum*. Georg Luck suggests that the word *cultoribus* may have an official ring to it to judge by an inscriptional reference to innkeepers as *cultores Liberi patris*,[22] and, in fact, members of guilds were regularly called *cultores*.[23] Here by metonymy the ivy stands for the divine honorand, surely the same plant out of which the poetic celebrants' *serta odorata* (3) were made.[24]

No sooner has Ovid asserted Bacchus' obligation to reciprocate help for devotion than he questions the extent to which divine power anyway can change what the fates have ordained (17–18) – an abiding question for the ancients, here uttered with a view towards Bacchus, who would in that case be (for the moment) excused from his obligation (16 *debueras*) to the devotee cast into exile. When Ovid then notes that Bacchus himself earned a place in the heavens through his considerable efforts (19–20), it is unclear if this is in answer to the question of fate and divine efficacy or is headed in a new direction: *ipse quoque aetherias meritis invectus es arces, | quo non exiguo facta labore via est*. In either case, the sense of *quoque* is also unclear. 'You yourself were *even* brought to the starry citadel

---

[21] Particularly the anger of Jupiter: *Tr.* 1.1.72, 81–82; 1.3.11–12; 1.9.21; 3.5.7; 4.3.63–70; 4.5.5–6; 4.8.46; 4.9.14; 5.2.53; 5.14.27.
[22] Luck 1977, 290, citing *CIL* 8.9409. With the inscription fellows in the guild commemorate a fellow *cultor*.
[23] For examples, see Waltzing 1895–1900, 1.266, 2.816, 4.431–32. In inscriptions the term *cultores* is often, but not always, followed by the name of one or more divinities.
[24] Luck on *Tr.* 5.3.3. See Varro *LL* 6.14 for crowns of ivy at the Liberalia.

through your merits,' a rendering which might imply that in Bacchus' case fate was not totally determinative. Or the hexameter may rather mean 'You *too* were yourself brought to the starry citadel through your merits,' with *quoque* contextualizing Bacchus' ascent to Olympus among the usual roster of divinized heroes. Horace, for instance (*Odes* 3.3.9–16), in language similar to Ovid's, numbers Bacchus (*Bacche pater* = Liber) among Pollux, Hercules, and Quirinus – the deified Romulus – as one of those who won heavenly status for meritorious actions on earth.[25] Horace predicts that Augustus will someday join these gods, and the Princeps may be called to mind by Ovid's verse too, in view of his Bacchic figuration elsewhere in the era.[26] The pentameter (20) alludes to a Propertian verse about a less momentous achievement of Hercules,[27] who will thus be particularly evoked as a fellow newcomer in the heavens and who was himself a common comparand for Augustus.[28]

As more of Bacchus' biography unfolds (21–24), it does so not, as we expect, to bring Augustus as Bacchus to the surface of the text, but rather to draw a parallel between the god's life and Ovid's current situation. Bacchus did not dwell in his *patria* (21 *nec patria est habitata tibi*), just as the poet is *nunc procul a patria* (11). Likewise, the divinity's usual triumphal progress through India and the East here pointedly includes the warlike Getae (22 *Marticolamque Geten*), the northern people twice noted above as the barbarians who now make the poet's life so unbearable (8 *crudis ... Getis*; 11 *Geticis ... armis*). So Bacchus, too, was a kind of exile. All this is then applied after all to the question of fate's determinacy (cf. 14 and 17) with Ovid's concluding surmise that the Parcae spun a double fate for the doubly born Bacchus (25–26 *scilicet hanc legem nentes fatalia Parcae | stamina bis genito bis cecinere tibi*); the 'law' of his dual destiny refers on the one hand to the ordeal of his worldwide travels, and on the other to his glorious endpoint on the heavenly citadel.

In verses 27–28 Ovid shifts the focus back squarely onto himself, inviting a *direct* comparison with the divinity, but that move actually points up the gulf between the two situations: *me quoque, si fas est exemplis ire deorum, | ferrea sors vitae difficilisque premit*. We will sense that gulf immediately in the initial phrase

---

[25] *Hac arte Pollux et vagus Hercules | enisus arces attigit igneas, | quos inter Augustus recumbens | purpureo bibet ore nectar; | hac te merentem, Bacche pater, tuae | vexere tigres indocili iugum | collo trahentes; hac Quirinus | Martis equis Acheronta fugit . . .*
[26] See Castriota 1995, 87–123; most recently Mac Góráin 2013.
[27] Prop. 3.18.4 *et sonat Herculeo structa labore via* (with reference to the causeway connecting Baiae and Puteoli).
[28] See Nisbet and Rudd on Horace, *Odes* 3.14.1; Miller 2014, 457.

me quoque echoing the start of line 19 *ipse quoque*, of Bacchus ascending to Olympus. The principal basis of comparison in this distich must be that this god and this poet each have a fated destiny, but alongside the double fate of Bacchus stands the single lot of a cruel, hard life that Ovid now endures at Tomis. Yes, Bacchus too laboured mightily on his way to celestial status but Ovid here has no compensating endgame to match. At the end of the *Metamorphoses* he famously predicts that he will live on through his work (15.871–79), something that neither the wrath of Jupiter (*Iovis ira*) nor iron (*ferrum*) can destroy, and that he will be transported as immortal beyond the stars – metaphorically to join Bacchus, Hercules, and the rest. But now, at Tomis, *to* Bacchus, he laments being victim of an iron lot in life, *ferrea sors vitae*, with the adjective suggesting harshness as well as inexorability.[29]

In an elegy full of surprising turns, the next is to realize that the *exemplum deorum* he had in mind was not so much the life of Bacchus – in spite of the latter's separation from home and visit to the martial Getae. Ovid was rather looking *ahead* to a parallel punishment by Jupiter, of the arrogant Capaneus (29–30): *illo nec levius cecidi, quem magna locutum* / *reppulit a Thebis Iuppiter igne suo*. No more lightly than he fell from his assault ladder at Thebes, Ovid himself came crashing down. No offence is acknowledged here on the poet's part; what matters is the felling of both by lightning, literally in the Greek hero's case, figuratively in Ovid's, we see acknowledged in the following verse (31), *percussum fulmine*, a familiar image in the exile elegies for the sudden devastating punishment of exile levelled by the Princeps.[30] So – to return to the list of alternatives in 13–14 – the *ira deorum* was in fact operative as well as a *nubila Parca* (31–34): *ut tamen audisti percussum fulmine vatem,* / *admonitu matris condoluisse potes,* / *et potes aspiciens circum tua sacra poetas* / '*nescioquis nostri*' *dicere* '*cultor abest.*' The variable causality of his catastrophe did not there prevent Ovid from insisting on Bacchus' responsibility to an erstwhile worshipper. Just so here Bacchus 'nevertheless' (31 *tamen*, echoing verse 15) – could have reacted. Earlier the god is told what he *should* have done (16 *debueras*), here that he *could* have pitied the thunderstruck *vates* when he heard of what had happened; and that he could have sympathized not only because the victim of the earthly Jupiter was a poet, one of Bacchus' own poets, but because his mother Semele suffered the same fiery end at the hands of Jove (32 *admonitu matris condoluisse potes*). The unfairness of her incineration

---

29 For these two senses, see *OLD* 4 b and d respectively.
30 See the references in n. 21 above.

opens up another basis of comparison besides the *fulmen*.[31] And just as the report of my fate (31 *audisti*) could have prompted your sympathy, Bacchus, *sight* (33 *aspiciens*) of what is happening today can elicit a benevolent reaction (note the switch to present infinitive with *dicere*). As you behold the poets gathered in honour of your feast day around your altar – this is the most natural meaning of *sacra* here[32] – you can say, 'Some worshipper of mine is missing.' The singularity of the unnamed Ovid (34 *nescioquis . . . cultor*) underscores recall of Bacchus' past failure to provide for 'one of the sacred worshipers of his ivy' (15 *e sacris hederae cultoribus unum*). The fellow poets too come back into view, with a flashback to the scenario at the start. There the assembled worshippers spoke the god's praises (4 *dicunt laudes . . . tuas*); now Bacchus is invited to respond (*potes . . . dicere*), with Ovid – again, quite remarkably – going so far as to put words into the deity's mouth.

Those words – 'Some worshipper of mine is missing' – obliquely appeal to yet another aspect of the mythical world of Bacchus, after Ovid has invited the god's sympathy as a fellow exile (21–22) and on the basis of his mother Semele's suffering (32). The poet's (enforced) absence from the rites in the god's honour situates him among those prevented from worshipping Bacchus, an abominable situation always punished by the god. By exiling Ovid, then, and keeping him away from the community of poets at Liber's annual festival, Augustus has among much else impeded the proper worship of Bacchus, and so emerges as a kind of Pentheus figure. Ovid's own version of the Pentheus story in *Metamorphoses* 3 opens with Tiresias vainly warning the impious Theban king to honour Bacchus with temples (3.521 *quem nisi templorum fueris dignatus honore*). Augustus, we recall, for a long time neglected to restore Liber's temple in Rome. Pentheus' crimes feature imprisonment and attempted torture of one of the deity's devotees – another *cultor* – who turns out to be the helmsman who championed the god against the pirates.[33] There the acolyte, an alter ego of Bacchus, is miraculously freed from jail so that he can return to the company of the other Bacchic

---

31 At *Tr.* 4.63–70 Ovid again juxtaposes himself and Semele as victims of Jupiter's thunderbolt, again with Capaneus and also Phaethon.
32 Thus translate A.L. Wheeler and A.D. Melville. Luck *ad loc.* says '*sacra* = μυστήρια,' that is the religious proceedings (he compares *Met.* 3.518). However, *circum* seems strongly to suggest a place (cf. *OLD* 2 'gathered round or near') and *sacrum* can refer to an altar, as in the proverb *inter sacrum saxumque* (see *OLD* 1c). Luck's translation, in fact, agrees that the phrase refers to place ('Stätte'), even if less specifically.
33 Helmsman as Bacchic devotee: 3.574–76 *comitem famulumque sacrorum . . . sacra dei quondam . . . secutum*; cf. 3.691.

celebrants. But Ovid, hitherto a member of Bacchus' celebration in Rome, remains in exile awaiting rescue.[34]

By this point Ovid's argument has built up to his most direct appeal to Bacchus for assistance (35): *fer, bone Liber, opem*, 'kind Liber, bring me help.'[35] The shift to imperative coincides with a change to purely Roman nomenclature, *bone Liber*.[36] In proper prayer style Ovid wishes for the continued flourishing of the Bacchic world in an itemized list of the god's *aretai* – some of these found in the hymnic movements in the *Metamorphoses* and the *Fasti* quoted above.[37] The god is summoned to relieve the poet's misfortunes (43 *huc ades et casus releves, pulcherrime, nostros*). The common hymnic prayer for a god to come (*ades*) is especially relevant when addressed to Bacchus, the epiphanic god par excellence.[38] Ovid's urgent plea for the divinity's presence in Tomis (*huc*) also underlines his own absence from the Liberalia back in Rome. Entreating the god yet again (cf. 15 and 34) to remember (44 *memor*) his service draws attention to the same absence. He is *unum de numero ... tuo* (44), only not in person among those in Rome honouring Liber on his feast day.

Then comes a perhaps surprising addendum – he specifies *precisely how* Bacchus can help him. Since 'gods have dealings with one another, try to bend the power of Caesar with your own' (*sunt dis inter se commercia. flectere tempta / Caesareum numen numine, Bacche, tuo*). Augustus, twice evoked earlier with divine coloration – in Bacchus' ascent to heaven (19) and in the thunderbolt that crashed down on Ovid's head (31) – here emerges into full view as the one to be swayed. The previous Jovian figuration and that Bacchus is to 'try' to change Caesar's mind may make us wonder about the divine hierarchy in view, but the earthly and heavenly divinities are seemingly equals – a status that the pentameter's chiasmus would underscore – *Caesareum numen numine ... tuo*. Ovid finally cuts to the chase with Bacchus, asking him, like many other addressees in the exilic elegies, to intercede with the Emperor on his behalf. These are the poet's

---

[34] Later in this book of *Tristia* the exiled Ovid figures his Muse as bound and shut in by Caesar's law: 5.9.31 *sic mea lege data vincta atque inclusa Thalia*. At *EP* 1.6.37 he compares his hope of a lesser punishment to that of confined prisoners.
[35] The petition *fer opem* to divinities is common in the *Metamorphoses*, likewise usually at moments of intensity or crisis: 1.380, 546; 5.618; 9.775; 11.399; 13.669; 15.40. Earlier as a prayer in Ter. *Ad.* 487, *Andr.* 473; Turpil. *CRF* 118.
[36] For *bone* in Latin prayers, see Appel 1909, 99.
[37] 35–42 vines and wine, Bacchants and satyrs, Lycurgus, Pentheus, Ariadne's crown. Compare *Met.* 4.22–25 for the sequence Pentheus, Lycurgus, Bacchants and satyrs; *F.* 3.721–22 for another pairing of Pentheus and Lycurgus.
[38] See Henrichs 1993, 17–41 with further bibliography. On hymnic *ades*, Appel 1909, 115–16.

final words to Bacchus at this Liberalia, marked by a ring compositional recurrence of addressing Bacchus by name from verse 2.

But the poem does not end here. For the final twelve verses (47–58) Ovid's petition broadens by bringing back into view the poets who today assemble in Rome to celebrate Bacchus at his festival. On the one hand these are devotees of the god like himself, *pia turba* (47); on the other, he affiliates them with himself in terms of vocation – they share in his literary studies, *consortes studii* (47). In verse 48 he asks each of his fellow poets to make the same request, that is to join him in petitioning Bacchus to intercede with his fellow divinity, Augustus (48): *haec eadem sumpto quisquis rogate mero*. The elegy thus at last becomes yet another letter from exile to friends in Rome seeking their assistance. At the same time Ovid turns the public feast for Bacchus into an occasion for private petitions by each of the poets (28 *quisque*). The wine cup they raise in Bacchus' honour (29 *sumpto . . . mero*) will be matched by the toast to Ovid that one of the group is enjoined to deliver in the following two distichs (49–52). And that gesture, along with another on the absent Ovid's behalf, will mirror the actions, thoughts, and words imagined for Bacchus himself in the same festal scenario at verses 31 and following. There, remembering his mother being shattered by Jovian thunderbolts (32 *admonitu matris*), Bacchus could have sympathized (32 *condoluisse*) with the similarly treated Ovid; and the god, looking around at the poets celebrating him (33 *adspiciens circum tua sacra poetas*), could utter 'some one of my worshippers is missing' (34). Just so, one of those worshipful poets (49 *aliquis vestrum*), remembering me (51 *admonituque mei*), and looking around at all his fellows (51 *cum circumspexerit omnes*), should say 'where is Naso, who was but recently part of our chorus?' (52 *'ubi est nostri pars modo Naso chori?'*). The language of the latter quoted speech also picks up Ovid's own words of himself in verses 6 *pars* and 10 *choro*.[39] Where, however, Bacchus is imagined noticing that *some one* of his acolytes is missing at the celebration (34 *nescioquis*), the poets themselves repeatedly name him – 49 *Nasonis nomine dicto* and again in the quotation of verse 52. And so, at the very end, after Ovid predicates their help upon his own proper behaviour in the fellowship of poets (53–56), he seals the thought by asking that they preserve his name among them, *nomen . . . meum* (58).[40] That,

---

39 On the isolated exile's intensely felt need 'to be a part' that recurs throughout Ovid's exilic poetry, see Labate 1987, 104–5; Hardie 2002, 304.
40 Ovid's *nomen* (both 'name' and 'glory') is a frequent topic in the exilic poetry: e.g. *Tr.* 2.350, 3.10.2, 4.10.85, 5.9.32; *EP* 1.1.30, 1.2.7, 1.7.3, 2.2.44, 3.4.5, 3.6.50, 4.3.10. His name *Naso* (cf. *Tr.* 3.5.49 and 52) occurs 13 times in the *Tristia* and 28 times in the *Epistulae ex Ponto*, compared with 11 times in all his other poetry (*Amores* 4x, *Ars* 2x, *Remedia* 3x, *Fasti* 1x, *Ibis* 1x). On *nomina* in the *Tristia* see Oliensis 1997.

at least, is permitted (58 *quod licet*) in a city where, he tells us elsewhere,[41] Ovid's poems have been banned from the public libraries.

In uttering that final request, Ovid wishes that they, his fellow poets, may compose poetry under favourable circumstances (57): *sic igitur dextro faciatis Apolline carmen*. The way that he expresses that favour I find striking: *dextro ... Apolline*, 'with Apollo's blessing.'[42] Apollo is of course a common supporter of poets, as is the primary addressee of this poem, Bacchus. The phrase *dextro ... Apolline* evidently alludes to a verse of Propertius where the two deities are named in this connection (3.2.9 *nobis et Baccho et Apolline dextro*). Yet in a poem that throughout features poets celebrating Bacchus, it seems strange that Apollo is suddenly interposed, almost in place of Bacchus.[43] The manoeuvre reverses Bacchus' intrusion into the poets' celebration of Actian Apollo at the end of Propertius 4.6, to which Ovid alluded at the start of this elegy. Given the political atmosphere of the final couplet, as of the whole poem – *quod licet* (58) conjures up the oppressive atmosphere under Augustus[44] – the favour of Apollo may signify the favour of Augustus himself, one of whose main symbolic divinities was Apollo, while, to judge from the long-unrestored temple of Ceres, Liber, and Libera, he paid little attention to Bacchus.[45] May you, who remain in Rome, be able to continue writing poetry with the permission of Apollo, whereas I who write these verses to you from a barbarian land can only hope to have my name remembered as one of your fellows when you gather together, without me, to honour our Bacchus on his feast day.

---

[41] *Tr.* 3.1.65–74. While the extent of the ban of Ovidian books is debated (see Luck *ad loc.*), these verses make it seem extensive: Ovid's new book cannot find his 'brothers,' quite apart from the notorious *Ars amatoria*, and is itself excluded from the three libraries in Rome that it visits. See Houston 2014, 233.

[42] See, too, Amann 2006, 225.

[43] For Apollo preempting Bacchus in a Roman context see Prop. 4.1.133–34; Miller 2009, 323. T.P. Wiseman has suggested to me that the sudden mention of Apollo here may signal that, with the main Aventine home of Liber still not restored, the Liberalia at this time took place in the precinct of Palatine Apollo, the Emperor's great new cultic node in Rome. See further n. 5 above, on the possibility of a Bacchic shrine in or adjacent to the imperial compound on the Palatine.

[44] See Feeney 1992. On the 'aura of paranoia, secrecy, and dissimulation' in the *Tristia* that suggests 'the atmosphere of Augustus' Rome,' see Oliensis 1997, 179.

[45] See Mac Góráin, Introduction p. 21, and Wyler, pp. 99–106 in this volume, for the vogue for Dionysus in painting and poetry during the Augustan period.

Bibliography

Amann, M. 2006. *Komik in den Tristien Ovids*. Basel.
Appel, G. 1909. *De Romanorum precationibus*. Giessen.
Barchiesi, A. and G. Rosati, eds. 2007. *Ovidio, Metamorfosi Vol. II (Libri III–IV)*. Milan.
Bruhl, A. 1953. *Liber pater*. Paris.
Castriota, D. 1995. *The Ara Pacis Augustae and the Imagery of Abundance in Later Greek and Early Roman Imperial Art*. Princeton.
Danielewicz, J. 1990. 'Ovid's hymn to Bacchus (*Met*. 4.11 ff.): tradition and originality.' *Euphrosyne* 18, 73–84.
Fantham, R.E. 1985. 'Ovid, Germanicus and the composition of the *Fasti*.' *PLLS* 5, 243–81.
Feeney, D. 1992. '*Si licet et fas est*: Ovid's *Fasti* and the problem of free speech under the Principate.' In *Roman Poetry and Propaganda in the Age of Augustus*, edited by A. Powell. London, 1–25.
Hardie, P. 2002. *Ovid's Poetics of Illusion*. Cambridge.
Henrichs, A. 1993. '"He has a god in him": human and divine in the modern perception of Dionysus.' In *Masks of Dionysus*, edited by T.H. Carpenter and C.A. Faraone. Ithaca/London, 13–43.
Heyworth, S.J. 1994. 'Some allusions to Callimachus in Latin poetry.' *MD* 33, 51–79.
Heyworth, S.J. 2018. 'Editing and interpreting Ovid's *Fasti*: text, date, form.' In *Vivam! Estudios sobre la obra de Ovidio – Studies on Ovid's poetry*, edited by L. Rivero, M.C. Álvarez, R.M. Iglesias, and J.A. Estévez. Huelva-Murcia, 105–20.
Heyworth, S.J. 2019. *Ovid Fasti Book 3*. Cambridge.
Hinds, S.E. 1987. 'Generalising about Ovid.' *Ramus* 16, 4–31.
Horsfall, N. 1976. 'The *collegium poetarum*.' *BICS* 23, 79–95.
Houston, G. 2014. *Inside Roman Libraries. Book Collections and their Management in Antiquity*. Chapel Hill, NC.
Hutchinson, G. 2006. *Propertius. Elegies Book 4*. Cambridge.
Janan, M. 2009. *Reflections in a Serpent's Eye: Thebes in Ovid's* Metamorphoses. Oxford/New York.
Labate, M. 1987. 'Elegia triste ed elegia lieta. Un caso di riconversione letteraria.' *MD* 19, 91–129.
La Bua, G. 1999. *L'inno nella letteratura poetica latina*. San Severo.
Luck, G. 1977. *P. Ovidius Naso: Tristia Band II: Kommentar*. Heidelberg.
Mac Góráin, F. 2009. 'Tragedy and the Dionysiac in Virgil's *Aeneid*.' DPhil. thesis. Oxford.
Mac Góráin, F. 2013. 'Virgil's Bacchus and the Roman Republic.' In *Augustan Poetry and the Roman Republic*, edited by D. Nelis and J. Farrell. Oxford, 124–45.
McGowan, M. 2009. *Ovid in Exile: Power and Poetic Redress in the* Tristia *and* Epistulae ex Ponto. Leiden.
Miller, J.F. 2002. 'Ovid's Liberalia.' In *Ovid's* Fasti. *Historical Readings at its Bimillennium*, edited by G. Herbert-Brown. Oxford, 199–224.
Miller, J.F. 2009. *Apollo, Augustus, and the Poets*. Cambridge.
Miller, J.F. 2014. 'Virgil's Salian hymn to Hercules.' *CJ* 109, 439–63.
Miller, J.F. 2016. 'Ovid's Bacchic helmsman and Homeric Hymn 7.' In *The Reception of the Homeric Hymns*, edited by A. Faulkner, A. Vergados, and A. Schwab. Oxford, 95–108.
Myers, K.S. 2014. 'Ovid, *Epistulae ex Ponto* 4.8, Germanicus, and the *Fasti*.' *CQ* 64, 725–34.

Nagle, B.R. 1980. *The Poetics of Exile. Program and Polemic in the* Tristia *and* Epistulae ex Ponto *of Ovid*. Brussels.
Nisbet, R.G.M. and M. Hubbard. 1978. *A Commentary on Horace Odes Book II*. Oxford.
Norden, E. 1913. *Agnostos Theos*. Leipzig/Berlin.
Oliensis, E. 1997. 'Return to sender: the rhetoric of *nomina* in Ovid's *Tristia*.' *Ramus* 26, 172–93.
Radke, G. 1965. *Die Götter Altitaliens*. Münster.
Simon, E. 1990. *Die Götter der Römer*. Munich.
Waltzing, J.P. 1895–1900. *Étude historique sur les corporations professionnelles chez les romains*. 4 vols. Louvain.
Williams, G.D. 1994. *Banished Voices. Readings in Ovid's Exile Poetry*. Cambridge.
Wiseman, T.P. 2000. 'Liber. Myth, drama and ideology in republican Rome.' In *The Roman Middle Republic: Politics, Religion, and Historiography, c. 400–133 B.C.* (Papers from a Conference at the Institutum Romanum Finlandiae, September 11–12, 1998), edited by C. Bruun. Rome, 265–99, repr. in id. *Unwritten Rome*. Exeter, 84–139.

Alessandro Schiesaro
Alius furor. Statius' *Thebaid* and the metamorphoses of Bacchus

Abstract: The centrality of Bacchus' role in Statius' *Thebaid* is unprecedented in the epic tradition. Of Statius' predecessors, only Ovid had accorded him a significant on-stage role, while others, such as Virgil, made him important in indirect ways that are associated with the creative energies that drive the narrative. Statius responds to his predecessors mainly by subverting the traditional Bacchic imaginary. The god emerges as largely ineffectual, neither a fully-fledged culture hero, nor a terrible punisher of hybris. As if to work athwart the god's traditional role as 'most terrible but also most sweet to mankind' (Eur. *Ba*. 861) or 'a mediator of peace but midmost in the fight' (Hor. *Odes* 2.19.27–28), the poem oscillates between war and peace, between deferral and continuation of its own action. This chapter examines the presentation of Bacchus in the *Thebaid* and some of the implications of this presentation for the poem's poetic and ideological texture. There is particular discussion of Bacchus' main interventions: in book 4 to forestall the Argive alliance's assault on Thebes; and again in book 7 when he upbraids Jupiter for his complacency in allowing Thebes to be attacked, in both of which Bacchus emerges as unwarlike relative to his models and antagonists. Bacchic manoeuvres proliferate: Venus encroaches on the territory of Bacchus by staging her own Bacchae in the Lemnian episode of book 5; Statius' *matrona* (4.377–405) replays Lucan's sibyl (1.679–95) in her Bacchic enthusiasm, which in the revised version signals the furor of civil war, and yet remains ineffective as a plot-motivator. Leaving aside Virgil and Ovid, Statius takes most closely after the sublime Dionysian furor of Lucan and Seneca, and yet what we find in the *Thebaid* is an attenuated Bacchus, metamorphosed into the antithesis of the sublime aesthetic, a reduction of which the poem at several points shows metapoetic awareness. The chapter brings together the different strands of its argument by examining the role of Bacchus in the conclusion of the *Thebaid*.

1

Bacchus enters the realm of Flavian epic endowed with a rich and varied metapoetic history and a wealth of cultural and political associations, the symbol of a particular brand of tragic or epic inspiration. Dionysiac themes form a recurrent and important thread in Virgil's *Aeneid*, and Ovid in his *Metamorphoses* gives

Bacchus a palpable presence on stage when he deals with the vicissitudes of his fateful city. Seneca's plays, too, offer a striking instantiation of the force of 'Bacchic poetics,' and, as they endow extraordinary characters such as Atreus with Bacchic features, they systematically blur the boundary between the political and the poetic. Statius grants this multifaceted, naturally plural,[1] and traditionally metapoetic god a central role in the *Thebaid*, but while he builds on the tradition of Bacchus' symbolic associations, he also strives to subvert it. In this paper I intend to explore what this new representation of Bacchus implies for the poetics of the *Thebaid*, and also, given the long-standing association of Dionysus and Bacchus with ruler-figures, for the poem's ideological texture.[2]

The diffraction and reorganisation of the theological landscape of the *Thebaid* is matched by the poem's structural ambivalence and hesitations. This is a poem of contradictions and extended self-denial, where delay replaces action as the paradoxical driving force of the narrative, in a plastic embodiment of the tragic tensions at the heart of the two brothers' tale. Comparison with its most influential predecessor, Virgil's *Aeneid*, only places into sharper relief the drastic differences which characterize the dominating divine forces in the two poems. There are no surprises in the cast of divine characters, except that all of them — and Jupiter first of all — do not follow the scripts they inherit: they retain the outward appearance and, in principle, the received position of their traditional incarnations, but with radical differences in psychological complexion and in the nature of their actions.[3] There is paradox, yet again, in this unexpected behaviour: the tragedy awaiting Thebes and Argos, two cities opposed on the surface,[4] but deeply similar to one another, is inscribed in their destiny (the *fatum* guaranteed by Jupiter), and encoded in a quasi-Aeschylean predictability of *genus*,[5] so

---

1 Pairs and doubles feature prominently in the *Thebaid*, as Braund 2006, 270 discusses, twice in connection with Bacchus (a Bacchante sees the two brothers as two bulls at 4.397–400; the two tigers in book 7, later p. 211). On 'Dionysiac doublings' see Hardie 2002, 170–71.
2 See now Rebeggiani 2018 for a sophisticated discussion of these issues. For the association between Dionysus and rulers, see Mac Góráin, pp. 20–21; Wyler, pp. 97–98; and Massa, pp. 229–30, in this volume. For Dionysus as a god of poetic inspiration, see esp. Miller in this volume.
3 Feeney 1991, 337–91 and Criado 2000 are the indispensable starting points for the theology of the *Thebaid*.
4 The 'Argive proem' which occupies the second part of book 1 underscores the symmetrical relationship between the two cities. Cf. Schiesaro (forthcoming).
5 The *Thebaid* promotes an immutable view of human destiny, encapsulated by the early reference to *gentilis ... furor* (1.126). People do not change their minds (1.227 *mens cunctis imposta manet*) and their actions and reactions are therefore deeply motivated and easily predictable. A key articulation of this concept centres on the use of the word *semen*, at the same time 'genealogy', 'cause' and 'pretext', which turns upside-down Lucretian physics as well as Seneca's optimistic

much so that gods can largely relinquish their directive role and explore new territories at the expense of each other. The god's past, however, remains always readable, if under erasure, and the interplay between his models and the novelties Statius introduces sustains the dialectical patterns of the poem as a whole.

Although Bacchus plays a much more extensive role in the *Thebaid*, what is striking is that his ability to influence, let alone determine, the course of events, is severely limited. Overall, the actions and emotions of this Bacchus are at odds with the models prevailing in the literary texts which constitute Statius' key points of reference. He is, or at least appears to be, ineffectual at best, yet he also fails to emerge as either a fully-fledged cultural hero, generous in his benevolence, or as a fearsome divinity intent on punishing those who belittle his might.[6] His diffracted and shifting overall image – in contrast to the traditional representation of Dionysus/Bacchus as both terrible and soothing, 'most terrifying, but also most sweet to mankind',[7] 'a mediator of peace but midmost in the fight'[8] – mirrors the poem's deferral of a clear-cut choice between war and peace, or between its own existence and oblivion.[9]

Early on, the *Thebaid* forces us to confront the fact that its divine characters are bound to subvert expectations,[10] and are particularly adept at encroaching on the attributes and features of their fellow gods. Jupiter's appropriation of the foundational function of Virgil's Juno at the beginning of the poem sets the tone with a reversal of roles which goes far beyond, for instance, the ambivalent message Venus delivers early on in the Aeneid as she appears in Diana-esque disguise. Statius' own Venus and Mars, as well as Diana and Apollo, like to ignore their colleagues' prerogatives. Venus' behaviour in the Lemnian episode told by Hypsipyle (5.48–498) is a case in point: a warlike, vengeful and cruel figure, she unleashes the aggressive potential always latent in the *furor* of erotic passion when she spurs the women of Lemnos to slaughter all their menfolk.[11] But it is

---

omnium honestarum rerum semina animi gerunt (ep. 94.28–29). *Semina* are of course at the heart of the Theban Spartoi myth: *uipereo sparsi per humum, noua semina, dentes* (Ov. *Met.* 4.573).
6 Zeitlin 1993 offers a fundamental treatment of Dionysus' polymorphic image.
7 Eur. *Ba.* 861.
8 Hor. *carm.* 2.19.27–28 *sed idem | pacis eras mediusque belli*, with Nisbet and Hubbard *ad loc.*
9 Bacchus is not new to a revision of his status and reputation: see Smith 2007 for a convincing treatment of the 'taming of Bacchus' in the *Georgics*, following his dangerous association with Mark Antony's excesses; cf. also Cucchiarelli 2011. The topic is now further developed by Mac Góráin 2014, who teases out the interaction between positive and negative aspects of the god.
10 Feeney 1991, 337–64.
11 As Rosati 2005 shows, Statius fully exploits in this episode the association between love and war developed by Lucretius in book 4 of *De rerum natura*.

Bacchus who really defies preconceptions, flexible and accommodating as they may be in the case of a naturally polymorphous, fluid and metamorphic god. At stake here is the assumption, which emerges in different forms in Roman epic and tragedy from Virgil to Seneca, that the force of Dionysiac/Bacchic inspiration is inextricable from a poem's very coming into being. While Statius flaunts his engagement with these influential models, his Bacchus undergoes a remarkable metamorphosis and goes on to tell a different story.

2

Bacchus intervenes directly in the epic action of the *Thebaid* at two crucial junctures in the development of the plot: first in book 4, when he attempts, and very briefly manages, to forestall the Argives' attack on Thebes, and later on, in book 7, as he confronts Jupiter about his lack of sympathy for the city.[12]

By the end of book 4 the Argives have occupied the plain of Nemea and are bursting with martial ardour (*iam Sidonias auertere praedas, | sternere, ferre domos ardent instantque*, 4.648–49). The threat to Thebes is now tangible and imminent, but we are warned even before Bacchus enters the fray that the delaying tactics adopted so far will continue to carry the day. The narrator announces as much in a brief prologue which, whilst ostensibly announcing the imminent arrival of Bacchus, appeals to Apollo as guarantor of the correct retelling of events long past: he will explain the origin of both *morae* and *error*, and how their *irae* have been deflected (4.649–51). As he returns after his two-year victorious campaign against Thrace and the Getae, Bacchus, in what is almost certainly a Statian innovation, comes onto the scene overshadowed by Apollo's unquestioned authority,[13] blurring boundaries between the two gods and the poetics they traditionally embody. At the same time, his appearance at the beginning of Hypsipyle's Lemnian narrative signals that the *Thebaid* will now engage directly with

---

[12] On 'Bacchus and the outbreak of war' see the excellent treatment by Ganiban 2007, 96–110, to which I am much indebted.
[13] Vessey 1970, 49; Parkes 2012 on 652–79. Note, however, that lines 653–57 emphasise Bacchus' role in diverting the *armiferi Getae* towards non-bellicose pursuits.

tragic themes.[14] His presentation is subtle: the rare adjective *marcidus*[15] opens line 4.652 in strong hyperbaton with Liber, delayed until the following line. He is more than merely 'drunk', for Statius is likely developing a suggestion he found in Seneca's *Medea* (69–70), where Hymen is addressed in terms which are also suitable for his father Bacchus,[16] and evoke both his propensity to feisty drunkenness and his ambivalent, languorous sensuality:[17] *huc incede gradu marcidus ebrio | praecingens roseo tempora uinculo*.[18] Bacchus' retinue looks familiar at first, as it includes lynxes and tigers, as well as Bacchantes carrying the limbs of slaughtered beasts, but the Satyrs and Silens we would normally expect are replaced by the personifications of Anger, Madness, Fear, Valour and Passion (*Ira, Furor, Metus, Virtus, Ardor*), the latter *numquam sobrius* (4.662)[19] and unsteady on his feet. This is an impressive line-up, which, in spite of *marcidus*, raises the expectation of an all-powerful Bacchus, active in both war and peace, in both the emotional and the social sphere: this retinue is far from powerless (4.661 *nec comitatus iners*). Indeed *Ira, Furor* and *Virtus*, for instance, are traditionally better suited to flanking Mars rather than Bacchus, and *Metus*, too, will be found among Mars' guards at 7.49.[20] All of this would still be in keeping with the dualistic nature of Dionysus/Bacchus, god of revelry and battles alike. Remarkably, however,

---

14 The 'Bacchic frame' to Statius' own Hypsipyle, which opens here and closes with the reference to Bacchus at 5.729–30, directly engages Euripides' homonymous play, as Soerink 2014, 177–83 well shows (I have not been able to consult Brown 1994, which according to Soerink also makes the point that Bacchus' arrival signals the beginning of closer engagement with tragedy). The Dionysus of the *Hypsipyle* is very different from his counterpart in *Bacchae*, showing his benign, positive aspect, and engineering the liberation of his grandchild: cf. Collard, Cropp and Gibert 2004, 173–76, and Zeitlin 1993, 171–77.
15 Statius uses *marcidus* 4x in the *Thebaid*, always in connection with Bacchus, and once in the *Siluae* (1.6.33 *marcida uina*, 'languorous wine' [transl. D.A. Slater]). The adjective carries marked negative connotations in Luc. *BC* 1.628 (of rotten entrails) and fares no better in Pliny's *NH* and in both Senecas (with moral overtones).
16 Cf. 110 *candida thyrsigeri proles generosa Lyaei*, with *digitis marcentibus* at 112. The genealogy is attested among others by Servius on *Aen.* 4.127.
17 Masterson 2005 offers a valuable discussion, mainly focussed on Amphiaraus, of the construction of manhood in the poem and its relationship with contemporary reality.
18 Seneca in turn develops an effete and feminine image of Bacchus in the footsteps of Catullus 61 (see Costa on *Med.* 69), which may have been favoured by Ovid's 'Catullan' imagery at *Met.* 10.192 (Hyacinthus dies and falls like flowers which are abruptly cut: *marcida demittant subito caput illa grauatum*, cf. Cat. 61.91–93 and 193–95, provocatively reticent).
19 See Soerink 2015, 7 for an interesting discussion of *Ardor* in this section of the poem.
20 Cf. Criado 2000, 65–66 for a comparison between the two lists of personifications; Zeitlin 1993, 159 points out that his 'positioning ... between the two antithetical forces of an Ares and an Aphrodite ... seems to typify the workings of Dionysus in the tragic theater of Thebes.'

although he can rely on such an impressive cortège, and is fresh from a stunning victory, Bacchus' preoccupation for the future of his beloved city does not push him to resort to any of those forces, and to repel the Argives' military ardour with *Ardor*, which would aptly mirror the *calor* of Statius' inspiration (1.3).[21] Rather, he will limit himself to causing a further delay, and not a very substantial one at that, in the confrontation between the two armies: this he will accomplish, as he crisply announces at 4.677, by weaving delays through deceit (*nectam fraude moras*).

Although we cannot point with any degree of certainty to a precedent where Bacchus is responsible for the delay about to occur in Nemea,[22] Bacchus' actions here are clearly modelled on those of Juno in books 1 and 7 of the *Aeneid*. In book 1, which in turn harks back to *Odyssey* 5 and Poseidon's rage against Odysseus, the goddess succeeds, as her Homeric counterpart had done, in almost annihilating the object of her anger, and at any rate in throwing him off course; she thus opens up, in principle, a possible alternative to the plot sanctioned by Jupiter. This delaying strategy will become explicit over the course of the next few books, especially in book 4, even before Juno spells it out in her second programmatic intervention at the beginning of book 7, when she declares that since the decrees of fate cannot be altered, at least she can still 'drag things along and cause delays to such momentous events' (*Aen.* 7.315 *trahere atque moras tantis licet addere rebus*). *Morae* carry a gendered connotation: they are the evasive steps associated with Penelope's feminine guile, and the use of the verb *nectere*, more pointed than Virgil's *trahere*, reinforces the point.

The intertextual parallel with Virgil's Juno, however, highlights by contrast the ineffectiveness, at this stage, of Statius' Bacchus, who manages to cause only a brief delay, and even proceeds to engineer its reversal in the near future, since he specifically prepares (746 *ipse pararat*) the encounter between the Argives and Hypsipyle, who will come to their rescue by pointing to the one surviving source of water that saves them from certain death.

In the course of a few lines, and just one scene, both traditional and contextual expectations about the god have been subverted. He arrives basking in military glory, surrounded by a retinue which would not embarrass Mars himself, but he shows no sign of his fierce and often violent behaviour, nor indeed of his inebriating, liberating influence. This is neither the Bacchus who punished Pentheus, nor even the one who managed to escape the pirates, let alone the generous benefactor who bestowed the gift of wine. We wonder how, on this form, he

---

21 On the Bacchic connotation of *calor* at 1.3 see Briguglio 2017, 108–9.
22 Criado 2000, 58.

could have accomplished his oriental campaigns at all.[23] The god associated with speed and thrust now adopts *morae* and *error* (4.650) in order to avert the looming crisis, following in the footsteps of his archenemy, Juno, but with much more limited results.

Bacchus' apparent conversion to peaceful means is not the only marker of his metamorphosis. Two more aspects deserve mention. Just as he avoids anger and violence, he also promises the water nymphs, whose help he needs to enlist, that they will be shielded from the sexual attentions of Fauns and Satyrs, whose lustful nature is part and parcel of their traditional characterization. In a final twist, Bacchus reveals that his plan to stop the incoming army relies not, as in Juno's and Poseidon's case, on unleashing a major storm, but on the drying up of all the sources of water. Again, this is a gesture towards inaction rather than action, stillness rather than movement, a message which is hammered out at 4.730–40 by a string of negatives and a series of words which insist on the absence of motion.[24]

The Argives are not vanquished or pushed back, they simply lose the energy to fight (4.730–32 *nec... sufficiunt*; cf. 4.743 *sedent*), while Bacchic *furor* affects only the horses, thus rendering them useless.[25] Adrastus barely manages to bring his appeal to Hypsipyle to an end before dehydration causes him to collapse (4.772–75).[26] Crucially, in order to achieve his goal, Bacchus here disclaims his traditional association with all the liquids which testify to Nature's vitality and exuberance, water, wine,[27] milk, semen, sap, blood, the 'whole wet element in nature', as Plutarch puts it.[28] When he orders 'let water abandon Nemea from deep down' (4.689 *ex alto fugiat liquor*) he pointedly subverts[29] one of the causes for praise which his fellow Thebans had emphasised in the *populare carmen* at the centre of Seneca's *Oedipus*: *pumice ex sicco | fluxit Nyctelius latex; | garruli*

---

23 The contrast between military success abroad and the experience of civil war at home – which Bacchus strives to delay with his actions on book 4 – may actually mirror historical reality: as Ash 2015, 220 points out, foreign campaigns were the emperor's preserve, whilst 'for most Roman aristocrats, civil war is a far more likely sphere in which they will see military action.'
24 Negatives: 730 (2x), 732, 736, 739. Cf. *artos | ... nexus* (730–31), *angustisque ... | faucibus* (732–33), *gelant* (734), *adhaeret* (734), *catenatas* (738).
25 4.739–40 *nec legem dominosue pati, sed perfurit aruis | flammatum pecus.*
26 4.772–75 *dixit, et orantis media inter anhelitus ardens | uerba rapit, cursuque animae labat arida lingua; | idem omnes pallorque uiros flatusque soluti | oris habet.*
27 At *Silv.* 4.3.11–12 Statius praises Domitian for actually limiting the expansion of vines: *quis castae Cereri diu negata | reddit iugera sobriasque terras.*
28 *Moralia* 365 a.
29 In a further twist, Mars will provide rich, if macabre, sources of liquid nourishment: *sanguineis mixtum ceu fontibus ignem | hausissent belli magnasque in proelia mentes* (5.5–6).

gramen secuere riui, | *conbibit dulces humus alta sucos* | *niueique lactis candidos fontes* | *et mixta odoro Lesbia cum thymo* (491–96).[30]

3

Even for a god with a multifaceted and shifting personality, the Bacchus of book 4 appears too idiosyncratic for comfort, and his return to the fore in book 7 (lines 145–65) does nothing to allay puzzlement. Once again, his intervention is set in motion by the realisation that the Argives are on the verge of attacking. His distressed appearance attests that a metamorphosis has already taken place, as the description by negation at lines 149–50 conveys: the thyrsus has slipped from his hands, grapes have fallen from his horns, his usual rubicund complexion is marred by anxiety. Deprived of his decorum (7.151 *inhonorus*), Bacchus pleads with Jupiter for the salvation of Thebes in terms which are directly modelled on Venus' appeal in *Aeneid* 1, but naturally this second intervention also recalls Juno's actions in *Aeneid* 7: Statius' Bacchus appears to be torn between two competing models, both female ones, but starkly opposed to each other in the Virgilian mastertext. His dualistic nature morphs here into a synchronic conjunction of opposites, as if he were trying to promote, at one and the same time, action and inaction, progression and delay.

Bacchus is convinced that Jupiter, forgetful of his deep bonds with the city, plans to destroy Thebes at the behest of his *saeua coniunx*, in a replay of the cruel punishment which Juno had demanded of Jupiter against Semele. Then, as Bacchus concedes, he had been forced to act, his feelings notwithstanding (7.158 *inuitum*); this time Jupiter's direct responsibility would be greater, because he is not bound by an oath, and there is greater scope, or so he appears to believe, for reversing his decision.

While Virgil's Venus frames her case in favour of Aeneas and the Trojans in compelling theological and geopolitical terms (the fates have decreed the demise of Troy but have also guaranteed the eventual rise of Rome: *Aen.* 1.238–39), Bacchus relies almost exclusively on emotional considerations absent in the Virgilian model. Unlike Venus, who is temporarily worried about the latest misfortunes

---

30 This metapoetic *carmen* is an important precedent for Statius' own take on Bacchus, which is markedly different. In this case Lucan may also have provided a suggestion: at 9.433–34 Bacchus (here a metonymy) is listed among the victims of the excessive heat that characterizes the coast along the Syrtis.

befalling her protégé but is after all on the winning side of Fate's masterplot, Bacchus confronts the same unmovable Jovian determination which Juno herself had already attempted in vain to deflect.[31] All he can do is to remind Jupiter of the fact that he has brought him to term in his own body after his mother's death, and that the destruction of Thebes would deprive him (Bacchus) of his due honours and would force him into exile. Amplifying a rhetorical move already exploited by Venus, who reminds her father that Antenor had been allowed to settle in Italy unscathed, Bacchus lists instances of other gods, including his brother Apollo, who have secured the protection of their favoured localities. In the *Aeneid*, Jupiter does not pick up in his reply the corroborating example presented by Venus, while Statius has Jupiter focus on Bacchus' incidental, and scarcely believable, disclaimer that he is not speaking out of jealousy for his brother (7.183 *nec inuideo*) and laughs away his son's whole tirade as an outburst of *inuidia* (7.193 *inuidiam risit pater*).

The predominance of the personal over the political is most evident in the argument Bacchus deploys in defence of the Thebans at 7.168–74. They are an indolent, unwarlike people,[32] who can at best engage in the *proelia* typical of Bacchus (7.169) and live in fear of the Bacchic rites in which their women traditionally engage, *thyrsos nuptarum et proelia matrum* (7.168–71). Contrast Venus' reminder that the descendants of the Trojans have been promised unlimited power over land and sea (*Aen.* 1.236), and Jupiter's reassurance that Aeneas will successfully fight a *bellum ingens* against fierce opponents (*Aen.* 1.263). Bacchus had been introduced in the poem as a victorious army leader returning from a campaign, but the subsequent narratives underscore his weakness and emphasize his 'feminine', side, which he also, unsuccessfully, attempts to bring out in Jupiter.

The father of the god has different ideas in mind (7.208–14):

> scis ipse (ut crimina mittam
> Dorica) quam promptae superos incessere Thebae;
> te quoque...sed, quoniam uetus excidit ira, silebo.
> non tamen aut patrio respersus sanguine Pentheus,

---

31 1.248–82. Jupiter's reply is unequivocal: *horrendos etenim latices, Stygia aequora fratris, | obtestor, mansurum et non reuocabile uerbum, | nil fore quod dictis flectar* (1.290–92). Juno takes note, and promptly disappears from the scene for much of the poem. Cf. the same peremptory reply to Bacchus at 7.197–98: *immoto deducimur orbe | fatorum; ueteres seraeque in proelia causae.*

32 Bacchus deploys as a defence the very set of accusations that Ovid's Pentheus had voiced against him: *at nunc a puero Thebae capientur inermi, | quem neque bella iuuant nec tela nec usus equorum, | sed madidus murra crinis mollesque coronae | purpuraque et pictis intextum uestibus aurum* (*Met.* 3.553–56).

> aut matrem scelerasse toris aut crimine fratres
> progenuisse reus, lacero tua lustra repleuit
> funere: ubi hi fletus, ubi tunc ars tanta precandi?

He not only dismisses all of Bacchus' emotional arguments, arguing that the Thebans have always been ready to challenge divine authority (7.209), but he also comments polemically on his remarkable change of heart *vis-à-vis* his previous dealings with them. Jupiter sums up Bacchus' metamorphosis with pithy effectiveness: *uetus excidit ira* (7.210).[33] His traditional wrath having 'fallen away' just like his thyrsus and the grapes, Bacchus is no longer the god of the *Bacchae*, trailing his tragic *syrma* as in Seneca's *Oedipus* (423),[34] who had exacted a furious revenge on Pentheus for a crime which pales in comparison to Oedipus' *nefas*. This Bacchus has truly heeded Virgil's invocation, at the beginning of *Georgics* 2,[35] to 'take off his buskins' and contribute to the georgic project in a milder, non-tragic guise.[36] The Thebans are his descendants, *Oedipodionidae* (7.216), and *pietas, fides* and the very laws of Nature and of the Eumenides, guarantors of family order, demand – Jupiter states – that they be punished.

A number of loose ends complicate Jupiter's speech, and his assessment of the relationship between his own powers and those of fate is especially debatable (7.195–98). In this context, however, it is worth stressing the fact that he not only remarks explicitly on Bacchus' unexpected metamorphosis, but also that he calls into question, to a degree, its very motives and its veracity: the aposiopesis at 7.210 shows that Jupiter is puzzled by his son's behaviour.[37]

Bacchus' reaction to Jupiter's words is no less surprising. Although his father's final remark is far from reassuring – he declares that at this time he is not prepared to destroy Thebes, then adding ominously that 'more dangerous days and other avengers will come in the future' (7.219–21) – Bacchus soon returns to his old self (7.222 *mentemque habitumque recepit*), his *honos* suddenly comes back (7.225), and he is compared to a rosebush restored by a breeze after suffering under the sun and a strong wind. Yet this is not the most martial of similes, and

---

[33] Clearly Bacchus' wrath, not Jupiter's, whose hostile feelings against Thebes are alive and well (cf. 1.227–32): see Smolenaars 1994 *ad loc.*
[34] As well as in *HF*. 475; the word's lineage goes back to Afr. 64 R.² and the one extant line of Valerius' mime *Phormio* (R.²)
[35] *Geo.* 2.7–8 *huc, pater o Lenaee, ueni, nudataque musto | tinge nouo mecum dereptis crura coturnis*, with *nouo* signalling the suggested shift in function and attitude. Cf. Mac Góráin 2014, 6.
[36] Or at least according to a very different style of tragedy, see above n. 14
[37] Bacchus will turn Jupiter's question to him back at 10.888–89: *nunc ubi saeua manus, meaque heu cunabula flammae? | fulmen, io ubi fulmen?*

even after he regains his more usual aspect, this is nothing like the fierce and fiery Bacchus of old. Nor is he the Bacchus who figures in *Aeneid* 6.804–5 as a paradigm of warlike success, or the possible source of inspiration for Lucan in his proem (1.65–66). All this is in his past.

The series of actions inaugurated by Bacchus' display of rhetorical weakness and ineffectiveness finds a revealing parallel later in the same book. Eunaeus is the god's double: he is his priest (7.650), and his beloved (7.684), and when Capaneus swiftly dispatches him he hopes that Bacchus himself could appear to face the same fate (7.678–79).[38] The young man's age, clothing, appearance and weapons are all unsuitable for the fight ahead: they are redolent of oriental luxury and effeminacy and provide direct confirmation of the Thebans' lack of military prowess, which Bacchus had pointed out to Jupiter earlier in the book.[39] Even the narrator regards Eunaeus' decision to abandon the god's sacred groves as a *furor* different from, but comparable to, Bacchic enthusiasm (7.651). The question he addresses to Eunaeus inevitably involves Bacchus, too: 'Whom do you think you can frighten?', *quem terrere queas*? (7.652).[40] Comparable attacks that foreground the opponents' effeminacy often end up revealing a fatal underestimation of their danger: Virgil's Trojans, repeatedly berated along these lines, ultimately succeed; Ovid's Pentheus[41] is foolishly confident that the 'weaponless boy' (*Met.* 3.553 *puero ... inermi*) who holds Thebes in thrall, uninterested in martial endeavours (3.554 *quem neque bella iuuant nec tela nec usus equorum*), his hair wet with perfumes (3.555 *madidus murra crinis*), can be quickly made to confess his lies and be defeated; Seneca's Bacchus may sport a long tunic as he progresses on his lion-driven chariot in India, but he does so as a conqueror.[42] In Statius, however, Eunaeus – and by implication Bacchus himself – are portrayed as implausible

---

[38] As Bernstein 2013, 233, n. 1 remarks, Capaneus kills Eunaeus just as the latter is extolling the sacred nature of the Thebans: *gens sacrata sumus* (7.666).
[39] The connection is underscored by the similarity between 7.169–70 *mea tantum proelia norunt*, [sc. Thebans] | *nectere fronde comas...* and 7.652–53 (Eunaeus' attire) *clipei penetrabile textum* | *pallentes hederae Nysaeaque serta coronat*. It is significant that when Bacchus' intervention is described as effective – Hypsipyle says that he does succeed in saving Thoas from the slaughter on Lemnos (5.265–95) – he has dispensed with his usual attire and appearance (5.268–70). Hypsipyle's claim, however, is part of a narrative whose truth-value has been called into question, cf. n. 46.
[40] Capaneus will taunt Bacchus (who limits himself to complaining to Juppiter, 10.886–89) in similar terms: '*nullane pro trepidis*', *clamabat*, '*numina Thebis* | *statis? ubi infandae segnes telluris alumni,* | *Bacchus et Alcides? piget instigare minores* (10.899–901).
[41] Ov. *Met.* 3.553–58.
[42] Sen. *Oed.* 424–28 *uidit aurato residere curru* | *ueste cum longa regere et leones* | *omnis Eoae plaga uasta terrae,* | *qui bibit Gangen, niueumque quisquis* | *frangit Araxen.*

warriors, and so they are. Indeed, already in book 2.661–68 Tydeus had poured scorn on the Thebans by pointing out that the furor of war has nothing to do with the excesses of Bacchic rites: *hic aliae caedes, alius furor* (2.667). Eunaeus is surely not a Bacchic force to be reckoned with, a real threat to the serious business of war as embodied here by no less a fighter that Capaneus himself, who descends upon the young man as a lion attacking a doe or a young bullock (2.672). The traditional comparison of a menacing warrior with a lion is here brought into sharper relief by the fact that Eunaeus' attire recalls the association of Bacchus with wild beasts, but only insofar as he also wears the gilded skin of a lynx among his many fashionable accessories (7.661 *aurata lynce*). As we will see shortly, this is a telling, almost parodic symbol of his, and his master's, new-found tameness, which cannot stand up to the real world of conflict and war in which Capaneus wallows.

4

Venus encroaches on Bacchus' traditional prerogatives by staging in Lemnos her own version of the *Bacchae*, as told by Hypsipyle in an extended rhesis at 5.48–498. The goddess resolves to punish the island for foolishly neglecting her cult, mirroring Dionysus' motivation for punishing Pentheus. As Hypsipyle remarks, gods, or at least the gods of the *Thebaid*, are prone to taking revenge, *Poena*, when they are slighted or hurt (5.57–60).[43] As she prepares to fulfil this novel role, Venus signals her metamorphosis by abandoning her previous aspect (5.62 *nec uultu nec crine prior*) and dismissing the Idalian doves (5.63), a process which evokes Bacchus' own metamorphosis and paves the way for the goddess' appropriation of his role: this is indeed a topsy-turvy world, where traditional expectations about divine behaviour do not hold true.[44] Indeed, Bacchus himself declares his surprise when faced with Venus' violence: *unde manus, unde haec Mauortia diuae | pectora?* (5.282–83). When Love relinquishes Lemnos for good, Polyxo,

---

[43] This is made very clear at an early stage in the poem, when Adrastus explains the background to the festivities in honour of Apollo. The god had, inter alia, sent a monstrum (*Poena*) to avenge the killing of his former lover Psamathe: *sero memor thalami maestae solacia morti, | Phoebe, paras monstrum* (1.596–97). But *poena* is already signalled as a Leitmotif in this poem of revenge in the initial speeches by Oedipus (1.56–57; 1.71; 1.79–81) and Jupiter (1.216–18; 1.224; 1.245–46). Note especially Oedipus' programmatic aim to 'set out to punish all his descendants' (*totos in poenam ordire nepotes*), as he asks Tisiphone to do at 1.81.

[44] Cf. Rosati 2005 on inversion as the defining characteristic of the Lemnos episode.

seized by an unaccustomed *furor*, plays Agave to Venus' Bacchus: *insueta* (5.91) is the first of several textual markers referencing the novelty and oddity of the plot which is about to unfold, a novelty which the subsequent comparison with traditional Bacchic enthusiasm only emphasizes (5.92–94).[45] Polyxo may well recall a Bacchant *rapta deo*, but we should not forget that she is actually *rapta dea*. It was one of Pentheus' fatal errors of judgment to assume that the women of Thebes had left their homes and rushed to Mount Cithaeron[46] in order to please Aphrodite rather than Bacchus (Ba. 225 τὴν δ' Ἀφροδίτην πρόσθ' ἄγειν τοῦ Βακχίου).[47] While she urges her fellow Lemnians to take revenge on the men who abandoned them, Polyxo clearly signals her key role model by extolling Procne's revenge (she is the *Rhodopeia coniunx* of 5.121) with an urgency which recalls Atreus' own reference to her crimes in Seneca's *Thyestes*.[48] Under the unexpected banner of Aphrodite, here Statius does compete with Seneca in the same field in which his predecessor had confronted Ovid's legacy. If in Thyestes Atreus will have to surpass Procne's *Thracium ... nefas* (56) by slaughtering more victims, *maiore numero* (57), here Polyxo offers her own take on the *maius*-motif as she kills not just one or two, but as many as four children (5.125).[49] The contact between the two narratives extends to the very logic of Polyxo's and Atreus' motivations. The king consistently regards himself as the wronged party, able to survive simply because he shrewdly takes the initiative instead of waiting for Thyestes' attack.[50] Polyxo remarks that all the women of Lemnos are already widows because their husbands have deserted them: the proleptic vocative *o uiduae* at 5.105 signals the paradoxical atmosphere of inversion which dominates the episode as a whole, where women take on the role of men and Venus appears in Polyxo's dream holding a sword as the presiding deity of an oxymoronic *dulce*

---

[45] Cf. 5.159–60 *nec de more cruor: natum Charopeia coniunx | obtulit*, referencing novelty while subtly subverting Atreus' obsession for ritual appropriateness in the context of his perverse sacrifice: *seruatur omnis ordo, ne tantum nefas | non rite fiat* (Sen. Th. 689–90).
[46] Cf. *Ba.* γυναῖκας ἡμῖν δώματ' ἐκλελοιπέναι with 5.100–1 *erumpunt tectis, summasque ad Pallados arces | impetus*.
[47] Pentheus will be put right on this point by the messenger at 686–88.
[48] Cf. 5.120 *at nos uulgus iners?* with the beginning of Atreus' self-address at Th. 176 *ignaue, iners, eneruis...* He will explicitly invoke Procne at 275–76 *animum Daulis inspira parens | sororque*. A further point of contact between the tragic action of Thyestes and this section of the *Thebaid* is the reference to the perverse course of the sun and of time at 5.177–85 (cf. Sen. Th. 990–95).
[49] Note the emphatic *quattuor* at the beginning of the line.
[50] As Atreus plainly puts it at the beginning and the end of his revenge plot: *non poterat capi, | nisi capere uellet. regna nunc sperat mea* (288–89); *scio quid queraris: scelere praerepto doles* (1104).

nefas (5.162).[51] Here Polyxo may overturn Procne's admission that *scelus est pietas in coniuge Tereo* (Ov. *Met.* 6.635), but is also echoing the *dulce periculum* inspired by Bacchus which seduces Horace in *carm.* 3.25.18:[52] the oxymoron perfectly captures the bewildering combination of pleasure and fright provoked by *enthousiasmos*.[53]

Thus Venus infects her followers (or victims) with the power of Bacchus, who enters Hypsipyle's narrative only at the very end, with the limited aim of rescuing his son Thoas.[54] He appears suddenly in a flood of light (5.267 *et multa subitus cum luce refulsit*) and yet, as befits a god who has lost his power to influence actions, he is dishevelled[55] and uncharacteristically sad (5.270 *nubilus indignumque oculis liquentibus imbrem*). Venus has been granted by her father 'an unspeakable honour', *infandum ... honorem* (5.277) while he, the god of Bacchic revelry, is relegated to the role of a mourner.

5

Where has the Bacchus of old gone? Or, as Jupiter puts it, where has his old tragic *ira* ended up? And why? In the divine economy of the *Thebaid*, as we have already mentioned, no god is safe from the drive to rupture tradition, and the interaction among the gods is often novel and unexpected. Even so, this apparently tame, weak, almost gullible Bacchus is so far removed from his prevailing characterization that we cannot simply attribute his metamorphosis to a general restructuring of the theological landscape of the poem.

Let us turn in search of an answer to a passage which precedes Bacchus' actions in book 4, and involves him explicitly, if in absentia, the possession scene at 4.377–405, where a woman, the 'queen of the sylvan choir' (4.379), is suddenly overwhelmed by the god and addresses him in words which combine invocation,

---

51 Cf. Rosati 2005, 151. Venus holding a sword is also without parallel.
52 Cf. also the *iunctura dulce ... | pondus* at 7.165–66, where Bacchus reminds Jupiter that he has brought him to term (cf. p. 201), a further inversion of roles between the goddess of love and Bacchus. *dulce onus* is a more common *iunctura*, esp. in Ovid (see McKeown on *Am.* 2.16.29–30), but *dulci ... pondere recurs* at Mart. 14.151.1.
53 See Nisbet and Rudd *ad loc.* Statius has *dulce periculum* at *Silv.* 4.5.25.
54 Or so Hypsipyle avers. But how far can we trust her self-exculpatory version of the events at this juncture? Nugent 1996 and Casali 2003 are skeptical; according to Herodotus (6.138) Thoas, too, died alongside all the men of Lemnos.
55 Note the repeated negatives at 268–69: *non ille quidem turgentia sertis | tempora nec flaua crinem distinxerat uua.*

reproach and prophecy (4.383–405). The maenad runs down from Mount Cithaeron, symbolically occupied by the advancing Argive army,[56] brandishing a pine torch lit by three flames, and starts off by accusing Bacchus of forgetting Thebes and his people.[57] The contrast between what Bacchus is actually doing and what he should rather do is emphasized in both spatial and chronological terms. He reserves all his military might for his Oriental campaigns (4.389 *perfuris*), not for Thebes, and he has cast aside his customary love for his people (4.383–84 *cui gentis auitae | pridem lapsus amor*). The woman is horrified at the new scenario in which the once-peaceful city protected by Bacchus is now turned into a battlefield, and asks the god to rush her away to the slopes of Aetna or to the Caucasus, rather than being forced to utter her prophecy about the final outcome of the civil war.[58]

In her request for displacement – she would rather be dragged to Aetna or Caucasus than witness Thebes' demise[59] – the woman resorts to the traditional Bacchic imagery of *oreibasia* and selects terms which are often associated with the god's intervention, such as the verbs *fero* and *urgueo* (4.395–96), but in doing so she underlines the god's inability to perform his traditional duties. She also testifies to the prophetic power inspired in his followers by Bacchus, whom Tiresias himself labels a μάντις in Euripides' *Bacchae* (298).[60] The association with prophecy represents a distinctive, if marginal aspect of the representation of both Dionysus and Bacchus, which, alongside other factors, goes partly to explain the intricate relationship between him and Apollo.[61] Here the prophetess distinguishes between the mantic *furor*, or μανία, which Bacchus is now provoking, and a different kind of *furor*, *alium ... furorem* (4.396),[62] evidently more positive,

---

56 Th. 4.370–31.
57 Cf. Gibson 2013, 141–42 for an analysis of the unusual hymnic features of the invocation. As he rightly remarks, '[e]ven though Bacchus is behind the inspiration of the Bacchant, his status as a god is not enhanced but diminished' by the matron's speech.
58 Cf. Ganiban 2007, 62–65.
59 Note the contrastive *potius/quam* at 393–95.
60 Dodds 1951, 86 n. 30; Padel 1995, 87.
61 A similar syncretistic approach is explicitly mentioned by Lucan in connection with Thebes at 5.72–74: *cardine Parnasos gemino petit aethera colle, | mons Phoebo Bromioque sacer, cui numine mixto | Delphica Thebanae referunt trieterica Bacchae*. On the kinship of Bacchus and Apollo, see Miller, p. 190, in this volume.
62 396–400 *en urgues (alium tibi, Bacche, furorem | iuraui): similes uideo concurrere tauros; | idem ambobus honos unusque ab origine sanguis; | ardua conlatis obnixi cornua miscent | frontibus alternaque truces moriuntur in ira.*

which she had hoped for as she was initiated into his mysteries.[63] It is also worth noting, incidentally, that the bull imagery chosen to convey the prophecy is distinctly Bacchic, not just because there are other instances of people seeing bulls under the influence of the god, but because the bull is one of the traditional symbols of Bacchus.[64] This element of ambiguity will of course play a relevant role at the very end of the poem.[65]

The direct model for this scene is the matron's prophecy in Lucan's *Pharsalia* 1.678–95, with which it shares numerous points of detail, including the keynote use of *feror* in the first line. Lucan explicitly mixes Apollinian and Dionysiac influences: the woman is *plena Lyaeo* (1.675), but she addresses Paean and Phoebus in the midst of her prophetic trance, during which she foresees some of the main events of the conflict. The similarities between the two passages highlight their very different implications. Lucan's *matrona* is in the grip of Bacchic frenzy, the source and means of her inspiration,[66] and the points of contact between these lines and Horace's *Ode* 3.25, one of the mastertexts of Horace's 'Bacchic poetics',[67] seal the metapoetic implications of the passage. Lucan's Bacchus – with Apollo's cooperation – carries the *matrona* to the very end of the world, both horizontally and vertically, in a quest for a sublime poetic experience which, emphatically positioned at the very end of the first book, amounts to a major programmatic statement.[68]

Statius' take on the same scene is different. His *matrona*, for one thing, displays a degree of self-consciousness which the full force of Bacchic *ekstasis* denied her predecessor. She is *entheos*, but is also aware of being so, and aware of the problematic nature of this particular instance of possession. She is able to reproach Bacchus for not being there, at Thebes, but also for failing to carry her away to the remote regions which Lucan's character feels she is being dragged to. This *furor*, as we have seen, is different from the usual Bacchic *furor* which she

---

[63] On *alius furor* see also 7.649–87 and 2.661–68 (667 *hic aliae caedes, alius furor*), with Hershkowitz 1998, 46 and n. 189.
[64] On Dionysus and the bull, see Kerényi 1976, 115–18; Burkert 1985, 64.
[65] Parkes 2012, 212 (on lines 397-404) quotes Orpheus at Aesch. *Bassarides* fr. 23 Sommerstein and Pentheus at *Ba.* 618–22 and 920–22. See also Parkes 2012, 84–85 (on lines 69–73).
[66] This is all the more significant because, as Feeney 1991, 275–76 rightly remarks, Bacchus and Apollo had pointedly been omitted as possible source of inspiration in Lucan's proem, where their place is taken over by Nero.
[67] Cf. Schiesaro 2009.
[68] On Lucan's *matrona* and her metapoetic implications see Hardie 1993, 107; Hershkowitz 1998, 45–46; Taisne 1994, 191–92; Day 2013, 95–100.

had been entitled to expect, and different from the overpowering, totalizing experience of the *matrona* who, in the *Bellum Ciuile*, reveals the true nature of the poem's poetics of the sublime: her *furor* is the *furor* of the civil war itself.

Further confirmation of the different nature and impact of the *Thebaid's* scene as compared to its Lucanian model is offered by comparison with another possible intertext. As she rushes down from the mountain, the frenzied woman carries a torch with three flames. This is a standard complement for a maenad, but the combination of this detail with the mention of Fama just a few lines earlier (4.369) may point to a text which is also active elsewhere in the *Thebaid*, Amata's possession scene in *Aeneid* 7, a connection potentially enhanced by the fact that the *matrona* is here called *regina chori* (4.379). The pervasive programmatic and metapoetic import of Virgil's scene have been thoroughly investigated:[69] Virgil launches into the Iliadic half of his poem with a bold move. He envisages an alliance between an upper goddess, Juno, and her chthonic acolyte, Allecto, in order to replicate in the human world, between Latinus and Amata, the dualistic tension between the opposing principles and objectives which set Juno apart from Jupiter. Crucially, this operation is carried out in the name of and through the force of Bacchic frenzy, which combines the strength of inspiration with that of revenge. This is technically incorrect at first – Amata is Juno's victim, not Bacchus' – but we rapidly realize that the Bacchic dimension of Amata's fury is authentic.

Not so in the *Thebaid*: the *matrona* does not set anything in motion. Statius' possession scene raises the expectation of metapoetic engagement, but fails to provide a blueprint for a poetics of sublimity which its Lucanian counterpart had offered. It largely amounts to a statement in the negative: Bacchus is not present, his power to shape the poem is not perceptible, at least not yet, and not in this manner.

Compared with the Virgilian, and especially the Lucanian model, the intervention of Statius' own *regina chori* is almost a *recusatio* – a choice of poetics which is articulated as a rejection of its alternative. The Bacchic poetics of Virgil, and of Lucan, are an available option, but not one which Statius appears eager to embrace. In the *Thebaid*, Bacchus dries up that particular brand of inspiration together with (almost) all the sources of water in the plain of Nemea.[70] His intervention literally deprives men of words: their tongues are parched, their *flatus* is weak and uncertain (4.772–75). The rushing waters of epic poetry thin out and

---

[69] Bocciolini Palagi 2007 and Mac Góráin 2013 are especially valuable on this topic.
[70] On the possible Callimachean implications of this move on Statius' part cf. McNelis 2007, 87 and n. 31.

cease to be heard. A no less catastrophic thirst had beleaguered Afranius' troops in book 4 of the *Pharsalia*. There, however, Caesar, generous in victory, allows them to reach the restoring waters from which he had until then barred them (4.262–66).[71] He is *facilis uultuque sereno* (4.363), a smiling, life-giving Dionysus, and a most determined agent in the pursuit of epic action.

6

To a degree, Bacchus' unusual behaviour in the *Thebaid* is about setting a poetic agenda. Leaving aside for a moment Virgil and Ovid, Lucan and Seneca had offered major models, in two different genres, of the productive force of a Dionysiac sublime, which is embodied by 'inspired' characters such as Caesar, Atreus, Medea,[72] or even Pompey,[73] who transcend their human limitations and are driven by the epistemic and aesthetic power of furor. In Statius, paradigmatically, Capaneus embodies an aesthetic of the sublime which leaves him an isolated and ultimately failed figure.[74] As he develops the logic of *maius*, Statius strains to breaking point the strategic option suggested by his most immediate and imposing models,[75] and assigns an expanded metapoetic role directly to the Furies,[76] Pluto[77] and Tisiphone. In letting go of vengeful *ira* and in dropping his thyrsus, the Bacchus of the *Thebaid* relinquishes his role as the god of tragedy, and is no more capable of imposing his own brand of Dionysiac poetic sublimity than he is of acting decisively in the war between Thebans and Argives. He is the necessarily ambivalent signifier of an author who competes with his predecessors by, paradoxically, choosing to play down rather than amplify the volume of the Bacchic sublime. The logic of *maius*[78] becomes an impossible option for the poem as a

---

71 As Bacchus promises the nymphs as a reward: 4.693–94.
72 Cf. esp. the nurse's description of Medea at Sen. *Med.* 382–86.
73 On Pompey's sublimity see Day 2013, 174–233.
74 On Capaneus cf. esp. Delarue 2000, 83–85; Leigh 2006.
75 See Hardie 2013. As Hardie 2013, 135 puts it, the freedom inscribed in the striving for sublimity takes the form, in the Flavian authors, of 'an attempt to break free of the shackles of intertextuality.'
76 At the expense of the Muses, in yet another display of tension between traditional expectations of poetics and Statius' innovative approach: Rosati 2002.
77 His monologue at the beginning of book 8, coming shortly after Bacchus' ineffectual performance in book 7, is closely modelled on Atreus' and Medea's programmatic speeches in Seneca (see esp. 8.65–83).
78 On the poetics of *maius* in the *Thebaid* see esp. Bessone 2011, 87–94.

whole, and new paths must be attempted. In his proem, Statius includes Bacchus' *graues irae* (1.11) against his own city among the subjects that fall outside the scope of his project, for it would take too long to go as far back as that in retelling the story of Oedipus' family (and, as Jupiter will point out at 7.210, Bacchus 'old wrath' is no longer in evidence). This *praeteritio* is a thinly disguised judgement of poetic value: Bacchus' anger has been dealt with already, and more than once – *omnia iam uulgata*.[79] As Laius says when he finally brings to an end what until then has been an elaborate pageant of intertextual models with next to no value in terms of understanding the future, *satis est meminisse priorum*, 'enough remembering the past' (4.628). This time an *alius furor*, and another Bacchus, will set the tone and provide a blueprint.

The metamorphosis of Bacchus is remarked upon more than once in the *Thebaid* itself, almost with glee. Jupiter, we noted, comments on it with a mixture of surprise and incredulity, before moving to capitalise on it, in a display of metapoetic awareness. Later in the same book another densely intertextual episode elaborates on the point when the Erinys attempts to bring the armies closer to war (7.564–81). Here the place of Silvia's stag[80] is taken by two tigers, who had once (7.565 *quondam*) wreaked havoc under Bacchus' command in his eastern campaigns, but have recently (7.566 *nuper*) been set free by the god in recognition of their good service. Mirroring their master's transformation, they have forgotten the taste of blood (7.569 *sanguinis oblitas*) and roam the countryside or even enter town peacefully (7.576–77 *benigno | ... gradu*), an object of care and veneration for the locals. Indeed, they act as a double for Bacchus in his more peaceful, civilised aspect: homes and temples are warmed up by sacrifices as if the god himself had appeared. After Tisiphone infects them with *furor*, they turn back into 'their prior spirit' (7.580 *animum ... priorem*), and at a speed compared to lightning (7.582) they kill a number of Argive soldiers before being wounded by Aconteus and returning to die as they lean against the city walls. The Thebans, shocked at the tigers' fate, resolve to fight.

Tisiphone pours *furor* into the tigers by touching them three times with a 'snakey rod' (7.579 *uipereo ... flagello*), a detail which echoes Allecto's seizing of Amata in *Aeneid* 7, and, more importantly, evokes the actual initiation rites of the Bacchic cult. Here, however, fury and revenge are no longer Bacchus' own province, and (albeit metonymically) he turns into an object rather than an agent of possession. His tigers have lost the fearsome sublimity that used to characterize

---

[79] Or, as Adrastus tells Polynices, *quid nota recondis? | scimus* (1.682–83). His story is well known even at the extreme boundaries of the world (1.684–88).
[80] On the Bacchic connotations of the stag scene see Bocciolini Palagi 2007, 131–37.

them. Now that they are adorned with ribbons by the god's priests, they embody the enfeebled and gilded lion,[81] *languidus* and *bratteatus*, which Seneca's *Epistle* 41.6 compares unfavourably to the lion who is *incultus* but fearsome. The latter is *speciosus ex horrido*, attractive because of its sublime strength, whereas the former's lack of energy is aesthetically unsatisfactory.[82] Statius reworks the image, and its implications, in *Achilleid* 1, when Achilles, excited at the prospect of fighting at Troy, drops the disguise he had adopted at Thetis' urging (incidentally, quoting Bacchus as a precedent: 1.260–63),[83] and is compared to a tamed lion suddenly finding his old self (1.858–63).[84] We were told at the beginning what Achilles' true nature, uneasily repressed for a while, is like: a triumph of epic sublimity, which Charon conveys with an almost verbatim quotation of Propertius' excitement at the birth of the *Aeneid* (1.147–48 *nescio quid magnum – nec me patria omina fallunt – | uis festina parat tenuesque superuenit annos*), combined with a suggestive nod to Atreus' own self-presentation as a sublime tyrant (*Th.* 267–78 *nescio quid animus maius et solito amplius | supraque fines moris humani tumet*).[85] In the *Thebaid*, Statius deconstructs the Lucanian-Senecan compact of Dionysiac inspiration and sublimity, promoting deferral and displacement as the motivating forces of his epic. He achieves this by presenting a (momentarily) unthreatening Bacchus, and channelling some of his energy into other characters.

Shorn of the implications that had turned him into such an iconic advocate of *furor* and *nefas*, Bacchus is ready to be recruited, at the end of the poem,[86] as an appropriate term of comparison for the victorious, and yet generous and mild, Theseus (12.782–96).[87] He enters Thebes as, by now, a *hospes*, and the enthusiasm

---

81 On lion similes see Kytzler 1962, 150–52.
82 *aliter leo aurata iuba mittitur, dum contractatur et ad patientiam recipiendi ornamenti cogitur fatigatus, aliter incultus, integri spiritus: hic scilicet impetu acer, qualem illum natura esse voluit, speciosus ex horrido, cuius hic decor est, non sine timore aspici, praefertur illi languido et bratteato.* On this passage and its implications in terms of poetics cf. Schiesaro 2003, 127–28.
83 For the episode see Sen. *Oed.* 418–21.
84 *ut leo, materno cum raptus ab ubere mores | accepit pectique iubas hominemque uereri | edidicit nullasque rapi nisi iussus in iras, | si semel aduerso radiauit lumine ferrum, | eiurata fides domitorque inimicus, in illum | prima fames, timidoque pudet seruisse magistro.*
85 Pluto's orders to Tisiphone at 8.65–68 are also directly connected with Atreus' self-exhortation.
86 On the end of the poem see Braund 1996; Hardie 1997, 151–58; Lovatt 1999.
87 Hercules is also redefined along similar lines; see Rebeggiani 2018, 150–51.

of the local women matches the one India had displayed towards Bacchus' conquest – the repetition of *marcidus* seals the connection between the two scenes.[88] This positive recasting of Bacchus is in keeping with the association between Dionysus/Osiris and the emperor which recurs with some frequency in the *Silvae*, where the god shines as the culture hero of Flavian Rome, a suitable point of comparison for the virtues of the ruler, but also a reminder that he can display strength when needed.[89]

Yet such a soothing conclusion to the vicissitudes of Thebes, and to the *Thebaid*'s valiant attempts to chart a new path in narrative epic, is, however, more easily announced than realised, especially given the glaring absence of divine agency at this juncture in the plot.[90] The acquiescence and growing warmth which the Thebans display towards Theseus, conveyed by the comparison with Bacchus' Indian subjects, is immediately contrasted by the turmoil of the Argive women's frenzy, who, in the throes of maenadic possession, wander on the hills and look as if they have just committed or plan to commit a *magnum nefas* (792–93).[91] The two contrasting sides of Bacchus' personality and influence are set side by side, *ecce* at 789 emphasizing the contrast. Now it is the Argive women's turn to indulge in the same behaviour Jupiter had listed in 1.227–32 as the reason for his decision to punish Thebes and set the *Thebaid* in motion, as they, too, threaten a re-enactment of the archetypical *sparagmos* of the Bacchae.[92] Now, however, the act of following the impetus of the Argives' despair, which is described with sublime overtones, would demand of the poet a *furor* which he emphatically disclaims: *uix nouus ista furor ueniensque implesset Apollo, | et mea iam longo meruit ratis aequore portum* (808–9). There is no room, at least at this time, for a continuation of the poem in the name of *nefas*, fuelled by the boundless energy of Bacchic inspiration and, again, under Apollo's tutelage,[93] as the narra-

---

[88] Theseus's return to Athens after his victory over the Amazons already alludes to the pattern of Bacchus' return in book 4 (12.519–22).
[89] Rebeggiani 2018, 265, with further bibliography; see also Rebeggiani 2018, 46 and *passim* on the ideology of the *mitis princeps*. On the contrary, Dominik 2015, 278–79 stresses the 'disturbing aspect' of the representation of Theseus as a just ruler.
[90] Feeney 1991, 357.
[91] Argos is also involved in the worship of Bacchus: *et Argos | praesente Bacchum coluit nouerca* (Sen. *Oed.* 486–87).
[92] 1.229–30 *mala gaudia matrum | erroresque feros nemorum*, which is better taken as a specific reference to Pentheus' demise than to the generic sinfulness of the Theban mothers (cf. Briguglio 2017, 283). The sins of the Argives are more summarily dealt with at 1.245–47.
[93] Henderson 1998, 216–17.

tor adopts once again the stance of *praeteritio* and tiredness that he had advertised in the proem (1.16 *praeteriisse sinam*)[94] and extended, for instance, to Hypsipyle (5.38 *hoc memorasse sat est*), or metaphorically encoded in Polynices' wanderings.[95] According to Jupiter, Bacchus, too, could have said more in defence, of Thebes, but didn't.[96]

And yet it is Bacchus, after all, who has the last word. As these final phases of the narrative and its abrupt ending with an aposiopesis go to show, the untameable strength of the god's double nature cannot be restrained forever, neither in Thebes nor in Rome.[97] He may have been dressed as a woman, like Achilles in the *Achilleid*, but he is always ready to return to the fray. He may have momentarily stopped the Argives' advance on the plain of Nemea, but at the price of destroying a *locus amoenus*.[98] Again, he has shown himself as a more sober source of ecstasy in book 2, when the Bacchae roam mount Cithaeron 'sound of mind' (2.79 *sanas*) prodded by 'a better Bacchus' (2.80 *meliore Baccho*) momentarily oblivious of his *ueteres irae* (1.11).[99] But we need only think of Juno, who at the end of the *Aeneid* supposedly lets go of her hatred,[100] and in Ovid's *Metamorphoses* 14 finally brings her *ueteres ... irae* to an end.[101] We can no more trust these happy endings than we can believe that Bacchic furor is tamed for once and for all.[102]

---

[94] This passage is well discussed by Criado 2000, 237–38.
[95] Among the places he crosses, the narrator lists *pingues Baccheo sanguine colles* (1.329).
[96] 1.287–89 *neque me, detur si copia, fallit | multa super Thebis Bacchum ausuramque Dionen | dicere, sed nostri reuerentia ponderis obstat.*
[97] On the complex tension and the tragic models which enliven the end of the poem see Hardie 1993, 46–48; Bessone 2011, 128–99; and Heslin 2008.
[98] As Soerink 2015 shows. I agree with Soerink that an idealised (and overly Callimachean) reading of the Nemean episode is unwarranted, although I place more emphasis than he does on the (at least momentarily) taming of Bacchus' martial ardour.
[99] The following simile (2.81–88), which refers to the flesh-eating Thracians at a banquet, immediately qualifies the atmosphere.
[100] Significantly, when he admits his reluctant acquiescence to Jupiter's plan in book 7 (178 *cedo equidem*), Bacchus takes a leaf from Juno's book at *Aeneid* 12.818: *cedo equidem pugnasque exosa relinquo.*
[101] *Met.* 14.581–82 *iamque deos omnes ipsamque Aeneia uirtus | Iunonem ueteres finire coegerat iras.*
[102] I am grateful to Fiachra Mac Góráin for organising a stimulating (if sober) conference and shepherding the volume, and this paper, to publication with his usual combination of good-humoured tact and sharp insight. Thanks are also due to Federica Bessone, Antonino Pittà, Ludovico Pontiggia, Victoria Rimell and Stefano Rebeggiani, as well as the anonymous referees for the press, who read earlier drafts and offered very useful suggestions.

Bibliography

Ash, R. 2015. '"War came in disarray ..." (*Thebaid* 7.616): Statius and the depiction of battle'. In Dominik, Newlands and Gervais, 207–20.
Augoustakis, A., ed. 2013. *Ritual and Religion in Flavian Epic*. Oxford.
Augoustakis, A., ed. 2014. *Flavian Poetry and its Greek Past*. Leiden/Boston.
Bernstein, N. 2013. 'Ritual murder and suicide in the Thebaid.' In Augoustakis, 233–48.
Bessone, F. 2011. *La Tebaide di Stazio. Epica e potere*. Pisa.
Bocciolini Palagi, L. 2007. *La trottola di Dioniso. Motivi dionisiaci nel VII libro dell'*Eneide. Bologna.
Braund, S.M. 1996. 'Ending epic: Statius, Theseus and a merciful release.' *PCPS* 42, 1–23.
Braund, S.M. 2006. 'A tale of two cities: Statius, Thebes, and Rome.' *Phoenix* 60, 259–73.
Briguglio, S. 2017. *Fraternas acies. Saggio di commento a Stazio, Tebaide, 1, 1–389*. Alessandria.
Brown, J. 1994. *Into the Woods: Narrative Studies in the Thebaid of Statius with Special Reference to books IV–VI*, diss. Cambridge.
Burkert, W. 1985 [1977]. *Greek Religion*. Translated by J. Raffan. Cambridge, MA.
Carpenter, T.H. and C. Faraone, eds. 1993. *Masks of Dionysus*. Ithaca/London.
Casali, S. 2003. '*Impius Aeneas, impia Hypsipyle*: narrazioni menzognere dall'*Eneide* alla Tebaide di Stazio.' *Scholia* 12, 60–68.
Collard, C., M.J. Cropp, and J. Gibert, eds. 2004. *Euripides. Selected Fragmentary Plays*, Vol. II. Oxford.
Costa, C.D.N. 1989. *Seneca. Medea*. Oxford.
Criado, C. 2000. *La teología de la "Tebaida" estaciana: el anti-virgilianismo de un clasicista*. New York.
Cucchiarelli, A. 2011. 'Virgilio e l'invenzione dell' 'età augustea'. (Modelli divini e linguaggio politico dale *Bucoliche* alle *Georgiche*).' *Lexis* 29, 229–274.
Day, H.J.M. 2013. *Lucan and the Sublime. Power, Representation and Aesthetic Experience*. Cambridge.
Delarue, F. 2000. *Stace, poète épique: originalité et cohérence*. Louvain.
Dodds, E.R. 1951. *The Greeks and the Irrational*, 2nd edn. Berkeley, CA.
Dominik, W. 2015. 'Similes and their programmatic role in the *Thebaid*.' In Dominik, Newlands and Gervais, 266–90.
Dominik, W., C.E. Newlands, and K. Gervais, eds. 2015. *Brill's Companion to Statius*. Leiden/Boston.
Feeney, D.C. 1991. *The Gods in Epic*. Oxford.
Ganiban, R.T. 2007. *Statius and Virgil. The* Thebaid *and the Reinterpretation of the* Aeneid. Cambridge.
Gibson, B. 2013. 'Hymnic features in Statian epic and the *Siluae*.' In Augoustakis, 127–44.
Hardie, P. 1993. *The Epic Successors of Virgil. A Study in the Dynamics of a Tradition*. Cambridge.
Hardie, P. 1997. 'Closure in Latin epic.' In *Classical Closure: Reading the End in Greek and Latin Literature*, edited by D.H. Roberts, F.M. Dunn and D. Fowler. Princeton, 139–62.
Hardie, P. 2002. *Ovid's Poetics of Illusion*. Cambridge.
Hardie, P. 2013. 'Flavian epic and the sublime.' In *Flavian Epic Interactions*, edited by G. Manuwald and A. Voigt. Berlin/Boston, 125–38.

Henderson, J. 1998. *Fighting for Rome. Poets and Caesars, History and Civil War*. Cambridge.
Hershkowitz, D. 1998. *The Madness of Epic. Reading Insanity from Homer to Statius*. Oxford.
Heslin, P. 2008. 'Statius and the Greek tragedians on Athens, Thebes and Rome.' In Smolenaars, van Dam and Nauta, 111–28.
Hill, D.E. 2008. 'Jupiter in *Thebaid* 1 again.' In Smolenaars, van Dam and Nauta, 129–41.
Kerényi, C. 1976. *Dionysos. Archetypal Image of Indestructible Life*. Translated from the German by R. Mannheim. London.
Kytzler, B. 1962. 'Gleichnisgruppen in der *Thebais* des Statius.' *WS* 75, 141–60.
Leigh, M. 2006. 'Statius and the sublimity of Capaneus.' In *Epic Interactions*, edited by M.K. Clarke, B.G.F. Currie and R.O.A.M. Lyne. Oxford, 217–42.
Lovatt, H. 1999. 'Competing endings: re-reading the end of Statius' *Thebaid* through Lucan.' *Ramus* 28, 126–51.
Mac Góráin, F. 2013. 'Virgil's Bacchus and the Roman Republic.' In *Augustan Poetry and the Roman Republic*, edited by J. Farrell and D. Nelis. Oxford, 124–45.
Mac Góráin, F. 2014. 'The mixed blessings of Bacchus in Virgil's *Georgics*.' *Dictynna* 11.
McKeown, J.C. 1998. *Ovid:* Amores. Text, Prolegomena and Commentary in Four Volumes. Volume 3. A Commentary on Book Two. Leeds.
Masterson, M. 2005. 'Statius' *Thebaid* and the realization of Roman manhood.' *Phoenix* 59, 288–315.
McNelis, C. 2007. *Statius'* Thebaid *and the Poetics of Civil War*. Cambridge.
Nisbet, R.G.M. and M. Hubbard 1978. *A Commentary on Horace: Odes*, Book II. Oxford.
Nisbet, R.G.M. and N. Rudd 2004. *A Commentary on Horace: Odes*, Book III. Oxford.
Nugent, G. 1996. 'Statius' Hypsipyle: following in the footsteps of the *Aeneid*.' *Scholia* 5, 46–71.
Padel, R. 1995. *Whom Gods Destroy: Elements of Greek and Tragic Madness*. Princeton.
Parkes, R., ed. 2012. Statius *Thebaid* 4. Oxford.
Rebeggiani, S. 2018. *The Fragility of Power. Statius, Domitian, and the Politics of the* Thebaid. Oxford.
Rosati, G. 2002. 'Muse and power in the poetry of Statius.' In Spentzou and Fowler, 229–51.
Rosati, G. 2005. 'Il "dolce delitto" di Lemno. Lucrezio e l'amore-guerra nell'Ipsipile di Stazio.' In *Vicende di Ipsipile da Erodoto a Metastasio*, edited by R. Raffaelli, R.M. Danese, M.R. Falivene and L. Lomiento. Urbino, 142–67.
Schiesaro, A. 2003. *The Passions in Play. Thyestes and the Dynamics of Senecan Drama*. Cambridge.
Schiesaro, A. 2009. 'Horace's Bacchic poetics.' In *Perceptions of Horace*, edited by L.B.T. Houghton and M. Wyke. Cambridge, 61–79.
Schiesaro, A. Forthcoming. 'Il proemio argivo della Tebaide.' In *Studi in onore di A. De Vivo*, edited by G. Polara. Naples.
Smith, R.A. 2007. '*In vino civitas*: the rehabilitation of Bacchus in Vergil's *Georgics*.' *Vergilius* 53, 52–86.
Smolenaars, J.J.L., ed. 2008. Statius Thebaid VII: A Commentary. Leiden.
Smolenaars, J.J.L., H.J. van Dam, R.R. Nauta, eds. 2008. *The Poetry of Statius*. Leiden.
Soerink, J. 2014. 'Tragic/epic: Statius' *Thebaid* and Euripides' *Hypsipyle*.' In Augoustakis, 171–91.
Soerink, J. 2015. 'Statius' Nemea / paradise lost.' *Dictynna* 12.
Spentzou, E. and D. Fowler, eds., 2002. *Cultivating the Muse. Struggles for Power and Inspiration in Classical Literature*. Oxford.

Taisne, A.-M. 1994. *L'esthétique de Stace: la peinture des correspondances*. Paris.
Vessey, D.W.T.C. 1970. 'Notes on the Hypsipyle episode in Statius, *Thebaid* 4–6.' *BICS* 17, 44–54.
Vessey, D.W.T.C. 1973. *Statius and the* Thebaid. Cambridge.
Zeitlin, F.I. 1993. 'Staging Dionysus between Thebes and Athens.' In Carpenter and Faraone, 147–82.

Francesco Massa
The shadow of Bacchus: Liber and Dionysus in Christian Latin literature (2nd–4th centuries)

Abstract: This chapter proposes to analyse the role of Dionysus and Liber in the Christian Latin literature, from the end of the second century up until the second half of the fourth century. It aims not only to clarify how Christian authors wrote about Dionysus and Liber, but also to bring to light the differences that exist between the Greek Dionysus and the Roman Liber and between the originally Greek Dionysian *koine* attested in texts and images, and a distinctly Roman trait stemming from their ritual practices. The chapter will focus on some Christian works, in particular the *Apologeticum* by Tertullian, the *Adversus nationes* by Arnobius, the *Institutiones divinae* by Lactantius and the *De errore profanarum religionum* by Firmicus Maternus.

The Greek Dionysus and the Roman Liber: Christian views

In the complex process of the construction of ancient Christian identities, Christian authors are constantly confronted with the polytheistic world. The divinities of the Empire's traditional religions were often protagonists in (and targets of) apologetic treatises and Christian polemics; these intellectuals' pages drew out the conflict between the Christians' unique god and the disorderly multitude of the Greek and Roman gods. The Roman Empire's multi-religious world forced Christians, on the one hand to take a stand against previous religious traditions, and on the other, to find their place within the Roman political and cultural systems.[1]

In this context, the Roman Liber and the Greek Dionysus have an ongoing presence in Christian writings in the first centuries of our era. Of course, Dionysus

---

I would like to thank Fiachra Mac Góráin and the reviewers for their valuable comments on my paper. All remaining shortcomings are mine.

[1] For the construction of religious identities, see e.g. Frakes, DePalma Digeser 2006 and Belayche, Mimouni 2009. For Christianity as a religion of the Roman Empire, see Rüpke 2009.

is not the only divinity who is in competition with Christianity in the Roman Empire. Several divine figures (for example, Mithras, Orpheus and Heracles) were compared to Christ, as Justin shows in his *Apology* and as Celsus underlines in his *On the true doctrine*.[2] Nevertheless, the literary, epigraphic and iconographic evidence of the Imperial period confirms the great importance of Dionysus in most of the territories of the Roman Empire, partly as a traditional deity of Greek and Roman religion, and partly assimilated to local deities.[3] That is why, as it began to spread, Christianity confronted Dionysian myths and ritual practices described in a number of literary texts as well as on monuments, coinage, mosaics, frescos and sarcophagi. The Christian authors could simply not avoid engaging with this world with its Dionysian traditions.[4]

This chapter analyses the role of Dionysus and Liber in the Christian literature of the Latin language, from the end of the second century up until the second half of the fourth century. What interests us is not only to clarify how Christian authors spoke about Dionysus and Liber, but also to bring to light the differences that exist between the Greek Dionysus and the Roman Liber and between the originally Greek Dionysian *koine* attested in texts and images, and distinctly Roman characteristics stemming from Roman ritual practices. Christian Latin literature is a body of sources that is often neglected by scholars of ancient religions.

In a previous article, I have highlighted that studies of the Latin Liber often argue that, starting with the Republican era, the overlap between Greek Dionysus and Roman Liber excluded all differences between the two deities.[5] More recently some scholars have attempted to emphasize the discrepancies between the two deities by focusing almost exclusively on Archaic and Republican Rome.[6] Notably, they have highlighted two areas where there is no overlap between Liber's and Dionysus' respective spheres of influence: the wine festivals and dramatic

---

[2] For example, Justin, *Apol.* 1.65.3 and Cels. 7.3. The relationship between Jesus and the various divine figures of the pagan world have been studied in numerous essays: on Heracles, see Simon 1955; on Mithras, see Simon 1978, Martin 1989 and Mastrocinque 2009, 111–14; on the Mother of the gods, see Fear 1996 and Borgeaud 1996, 135–42; on Asclepius, see Magri 2007 and dal Covolo 2008. More generally see Alvar 2008, 383–421 and Massa 2014, 20–26.
[3] On Dionysus in the Imperial Age, see Nilsson 1957; Turcan 1989, 290 and Jaccottet 2003, II, 14.
[4] For an overview on the role of Dionysus in Christian evidence, see Massa 2014.
[5] Massa 2016; cf. Bruhl 1953, 13: 'il n'est pas surprenant que nous soyons peu renseignés sur ses attributions et son culte [*scil.* Liber Pater], car son assimilation au fils de Zeus et Sémélé s'était faite dans des temps relativement reculés et d'une manière si complète que les écrivains de l'époque classique disaient indifféremment Liber ou Bacchus quand ils voulaient parler de Dionysos'. See also Jeanmaire 1951, 453 and Le Bonniec 1958, 297. Scholars have rendered a similar judgment even more recently: see *e.g.* Pailler 1995, 14.
[6] Cf. Montanari 1988, 103–10. See also Mastrocinque 1988, 245–66.

competitions. In Rome, the public holidays connected with wine, the *Vinalia* on April 23 and August 19, are dedicated to Jupiter and Venus, not to Liber Pater, as Robert Schilling and subsequently Olivier de Cazanove have clearly demonstrated.[7] As for the theatre, in Rome Liber was not the only patron god of the festivals: theatrical performances were also part of the *ludi* in honour of the Magna Mater and/or Apollo, and the actors' guilds were not under Liber's tutelage.[8]

In order to clarify and interpret the identities of Dionysus and Liber, it is necessary to distinguish between two different planes. First, it is necessary to acknowledge that poetry and images since the Archaic era had portrayed Liber with substantially the same features as the Greek Dionysus, though often with local inflections.[9] The expansion of the Dionysian cult and its imagery in the Mediterranean world allowed Liber to assume a Greek identity in iconographic and literary representation. Nonetheless, certain differences do appear to persist between the Roman and the Greek divinity, especially within the ritual domain. With this in mind, the equivalence between Liber and Dionysus is not in fact comparable to that between Dionysus and Osiris, say, or Dionysus and Sabazios.[10] Rather, it is played out within the construction of the Roman Liber's identity, a hybrid identity comprising various cultural traditions and clearly encompassing the Greek Dionysus among other figures. The Roman Liber, as our rare Archaic sources present him, appears from the outset to be the result of contact between various cultures. Unlike the relationship between Dionysus and Osiris, for example, we cannot isolate among our sources a Liber that is entirely independent of the Greek Dionysus.[11]

Christian Latin literature fits perfectly within this context since, in drawing on themes that are derived from the Dionysian literary and iconographic *koine*, authors also reference more specifically Roman ritual practices. In the following

---

[7] See in particular Schilling 1955, 146–47 and Cazanove 1988, 245: 'Jupiter patronne l'obtention du vin sacrificiel (*uinum inferium*), Liber celle du vin profane, impropre à la libation parce qu'impur (*uinum spurcum*). Liber intervient au moment du pressurage parce que le moût, dont il reçoit les prémices, est un liquide temporairement impur et qui, pour partie, par les opérations de frelatage, va le devenir, irrévocablement'. See also Cazanove 1991.

[8] Cf. Mastrocinque 1988, 248.

[9] Cf. Gasparri 1986. On the Roman archaic poetry, see Rousselle 1987 and Wiseman 2000. On Virgil, see Mac Góráin 2013; see further the Introduction to this volume.

[10] Dionysus was identified with Osiris in Egypt, with Dusares in Arabia, with Atargatis in Hierapolis/Bambyke, etc. On this subject, see Turcan 1989, 290.

[11] For an important analysis of the analogies and differences between Greek and Roman divinities, see Bonnet, Pirenne-Delforge, Pironti 2016.

pages, I will analyse, without aiming at exhaustiveness, some examples of the utilization of the figure of Dionysus and Liber in Christian Latin literature.

Liber and Dionysus *versus* Jesus

Faced with this Dionysian presence, the Christian authors developed two different cultural responses in order to respond to the possible analogies between Dionysus and Christ. First of all, a process of selection of those elements that could be reinterpreted and adapted to the realities of Christianity. This involved adopting and transforming certain Dionysian scenarios from a Christian point of view, a valuable example of which is given in the works of Clement of Alexandria; in *Stromata* for example, Clement uses the words of the Euripidean Dionysus of the second episode of Euripides' *Bacchae* to explain the transmission of Christian doctrines.[12] A second response involved the construction of a negative representation of Dionysus based in part on the common anti-Dionysian polemic: this representation was ranged against the diffusion and popularity of the god during the first centuries of our era.[13]

For the representation of the 'clash' between the Greek and Roman divinities and the new Christian god, Latin apologists relied on the traditional repertoire of Greek mythology. A first important example is that of Tertullian, the first Christian author to use Latin as a literary language. In his *Apologeticum*, most likely written in 197, the author affirms his desire to address the judges of the city of Carthage, following legal trials in which Christians had been condemned.[14] Having dedicated an important section of the work to the *refutatio* of accusations against the followers of Christ, and having discussed the nature of the relationship between Jews and Christians, Tertullian presents the figure of Christ as a god (*necesse est igitur pauca de Christo ut Deo*). Christ is then the *filius Dei*. However, what is implied in Tertullian's discourse is that Christ cannot be assimilated to or superimposed onto the numerous sons of Zeus/Jupiter, evoked in the Greek and

---

[12] Clement of Alexandria, *Strom.* 4.162.2–4. On the intellectual constructions of Clement of Alexandria, see Herrero 2010; Jourdan 2010, 195–220 and Massa 2014, 157–99. For Clement's use of Euripides' *Bacchae*, see Mac Góráin and Perris in this volume, with further references at pp. 63–66.

[13] For anti-Dionysian polemic, see Mac Góráin in this volume.

[14] According to Price 1999, 109 Tertullian refers 'specifically to Roman governors, and not, as has been suggested, also to local, civic magistrates.' More generally, see Fredouille 2005.

Roman mythical tales. Here we are some distance from the rhetorical and narrative strategies employed by Christian authors writing in Greek, such as, for example, Justin, who developed the theory of *imitatio diabolica* in order to explain pagan myths and their analogies with Christian accounts.[15] Tertullian pursues his discourse in specifying that the birth of Christ is not the result of a shameful action:

> Not as the result of incestuous intercourse or the violation of another's wife has he a god for his Father – a god covered with scales, or horned, or feathered (*squamatum aut cornutum aut plumatum*), or a lover, for his vile ends transmuting himself into the gold of Danaus. They are your divinities upon whom these base deeds of Jupiter were done (*Iovis ista sunt humana vestra*). But the Son of God has no mother in any sense that involves the violation of her purity; in fact, she who is regarded as his mother had not married. First, however, let me discuss his nature; then the manner of his birth will be understood.[16]

The reference to the mythical tales of the sexual unions of Jupiter, which were well known in a cosmopolitan city such as Carthage, where Tertullian lived, is very clear in this passage of the *Apologeticum*.[17] The father of gods turns into a serpent (*squamatus*) to unite with Persephone/Proserpina and engender Dionysus/Liber; into a bull (*cornutus*) for Europa; into a swan (*plumatus*) for Leda; into a shower of golden rain (*in auro*) for Danaë. In what is an apologetic construct, Tertullian opposes the respectability of the human birth of Christ to the criminal and animal birth of the sons of Zeus. Among these unions that are against nature, Tertullian includes also Liber. Christian authors were familiar with various mythological tales concerning the birth of Dionysus. If the Theban tale in which Dionysus is the son of Zeus and Semele is well attested in Christian literature, the version of Zeus' union with his daughter Persephone is equally present.[18] The latter allowed Christian polemicists to highlight the incestuous and monstrous aspects of the birth of Dionysus: Athenagoras of Athens, for instance, in his *Embassy for the Christians*, speaks of the double union of Zeus, in the form of a serpent, first with his mother Rhea (or Demeter) and subsequently with his daughter Persephone, which led to the conception of Dionysus. It was perhaps

---

15 On Justin and the god Dionysus, see Massa 2014, 86–99. More generally on Justin, see Munnich 2012.
16 Tertullian, *Apol.* 21.8–9: transl. R.D. Sider, modified.
17 On Carthage during the second and third centuries see Barnes 1971, esp. 67–71, and Rebillard 2012, 9–33.
18 See for example Athenagoras, *Suppl.* 20.3 and Clement of Alexandria, *Protr.* 2.16.1. Diodorus, 3.64.1 and 4.4.1 evoke the birth of Dionysus from Zeus and Persephone without going into detail. On this version of the Dionysian myth, see Massa 2010.

the potentially negative aspects of this version which led Tertullian to cite it in his list of sexual unions with Zeus.[19]

In Tertullian's text, we encounter one of the most important problems in Christian apologetic literature from the first centuries of our era, namely the distinction between 'real' and 'false' discourses. During the history of the Empire, Christians authors developed their own reflections on myths, ritual practices and images through which Greek and Roman religions expressed themselves, in order to lay bare the deceit and lies which lay at their heart. The distinction and comparison between true and false, between the original Christian truth and its diabolical copy, the tension between the reality claimed for Christian beliefs and its supposed deformation at the hands of Pagans – all of these elements were essential for the formation of Christian identity.

Moreover, this is why the *Apologeticum* opens with a reflection on the primacy of the Christian truth and presenting the earth as a place of falsehood, as opposed to the heavens, the only residence of the truth.[20] The lexicon and rhetoric of truth contained in the work of Tertullian clearly show that the analogies between the biography of Christ and of the divinities of the Greek and Roman worlds had already entered the religious debates of the time.[21] To take a single example, according to Celsus' *On the True Doctrine*, the biographies of mythical figures presented several analogies with sacred Christian tales: Heracles, Asclepius, Dionysus, Orpheus, Mithras, Apollonius of Tyana, all of these figures, whether heroic or divine, were interpreted as rivals of Jesus, notably because of their birth from a woman, or their death and return to life.[22]

Tertullian's procedure is representative of a tendency that does not seem to change much throughout the centuries: although we advance from the end of the second century up until the fourth century, in a period in which Christianity, although – locally – limited by imperial power, had gained a certain diffusion throughout the Empire, the rhetorical strategies of Christian writers remain the same. A valuable testimony to this tendency is the *Adversus nationes* of Arnobius, a rhetorician in Sicca, Numidia, who presents an opposition between Pagan and

---

19 There are several references to Liber in the *Apologeticum*, but these are somewhat conventional: *Apol.* 11.6 and 8 where Tertullian says, adopting a Euhemeristic perspective, that Liber cannot be considered a god simply because he gave wine to men; 12.4 where he alludes to the link between Liber and beasts; 42.5 where he refers to Dionysian rituals in the streets.
20 See Tertullian, *Apol.* 1.2.
21 On religious competition in the Roman Empire see Rosenblum, Young, DesRosiers 2014, Engels, Van Nuffelen 2014, DesRosiers, Vuong 2016, and Naerebout 2016.
22 See Origen, *C. Cel.* 3.41–42 and 7.53.

Christian beliefs and practices.[23] The first book is divided into two main sections that appear to be the most apologetic parts of the entire work: the first aims to respond to the accusation levelled against Christians that they were the reason for the gods' anger and the punishments that were imposed upon men; the second, by contrast, concentrates on the problem of the human nature of Christ, which had been used as a basis to accuse Christians of venerating a mortal man. In this section, Arnobius recalls that Christians were accused of considering as a god an individual who was killed on the cross, 'something infamous for miserable people' (*quod personis infame est uilibus*). The author responds by proposing some of the others divine figures that had shared the same type of mortal birth: he evokes, amongst others, Liber Pater, 'thrust out of his mother's womb by a bolt of lightning' (*ex genitalibus matris... fulmine praecipitatus*).[24] Arnobius' ultimate goal is explicitly declared in this paragraph:

> But if, while you know that they were born in the womb, and that they lived on the produce of the earth, you nevertheless upbraid us with the worship of one born like ourselves, you act with great injustice, in regarding that as worthy of condemnation in us which you yourselves habitually do; or what you allow to be lawful for you, you are unwilling to be in like manner lawful for others.[25]

This part of the first book pursues the same arguments: some other parallelisms between Christ and the Pagan divinities are outlined. As the gods are venerated for their blessings towards men, Christians therefore considered Christ a divinity for what he had done for men. Arnobius cites also, amongst other things, Liber as the god who discovered wine and who taught men how to produce it, a clear statement of position in relation to Euhemerism.[26] Finally, we can cite a final analogy between Christ and Liber, concerning the matter of violent death. Arnobius complains that his Pagan addressees scoff at Christians because of Christ's crucifixion:

> And yet, O ye who laugh because we worship one who died an ignominious death, do not ye too, by consecrating shrines to him, honour Father Liber, who was torn limb from limb

---

[23] For an overview of Arnobius' work, see Le Bonniec 1982.
[24] Arnobius, *Adv. nat.* 1.36.1 and 3.
[25] Arnobius, *Adv. nat.* 1.37.4: transl. H. Bryce and H. Campbell.
[26] Cf. Arnobius, *Adv. nat.* 1.38.2: *Liberum, quod usum reppererit uini*. On wine as a subject of dispute between Pagans and Christians, see Massa 2014, 203–49. For Christian interpretations of Liber according to Euhemerism, see also Tertullian, *Apol.* 11.6 and 8 and Minucius Felix, *Oct.* 21.2. For Euhemerism in Christian texts, see Roubekas 2017, 115–38 and Borgeaud 2017.

by the Titans? (*nonne Liberum et uos patrem membratim ab Titanis dissipatum fanorum consecratione mactatis?*).[27]

Before launching an attack on Pagan cults and beliefs towards the middle of book 5, Arnobius establishes a series of parallels between the biography of Christ and those of the Greek and Roman divinities. The goal is to show that the Christian religion is not absurd in comparison to traditional cults and that it could therefore be included in the religious repertory of the Empire.

From myth to rite?

Arnobius' *Adversus nationes* also offers a basis for analysing how Christian authors thought about the relationship between mythical tales and ritual practices.[28] But first it is necessary to highlight that *Adversus nationes* offers a reflection on the existence of many gods with the same name and that Arnobius pokes fun at the plurality of divine figures in the Greco-Roman world:

> And lest it appear long-winded and fastidious to go through them [*scil.* the pagan gods] one by one (*minutatim velle capita ire per singula*), the theologians (*theologi*) themselves say that there are four Vulcans and three Dianas, as many Asclepiuses and five Dionysuses, two times three Herculeses and four Venuses, three categories of Castors and as many of the Muses, a triplet of winged Cupids and four Apollonian denominations, for whom they list both fathers and mothers, as well as their places of birth, and they explain the origin of each with their lineages [...]. We cannot be hard to influence if only something worthy of the conception of so great a name be shown us. Show us Mercury, but only one; give us Liber, but only one; a single Venus and likewise a single Diana.[29]

The Greco-Roman world of the gods is, Arnobius suggests, but a chaotic collective where the gods lose their identities. This presentation of the pagan gods by a Christian writer is of course a caricature, and seeks to emphasize the ridiculous aspect of the traditional cults scattered throughout the Empire. But it also reflects a particular phenomenon of the imperial era, namely the intensification of a process of equivalence between the names of the gods, which led to the formation of

---

[27] Arnobius, *Adv. nat.* 1.41.1.
[28] For an analysis of Arnobius' text in the context of religious competition see Simmons 1995.
[29] Arnobius, *Adv. nat.* 4.15.1 and 17.35: my translation.

a plurality of divine powers: the practice of *interpretatio*.[30] Dionysus is at the centre of this intellectual tendency. Cicero had already, in his *De natura deorum*, evoked the existence of several Dionysuses. One of the characters in this dialogue, Caius Cotta, *pontifex* and supporter of the principles of Aristotelian philosophy, proposed an example of equivalence and of an overlapping between divinities in order to critique Stoic theories in this regard. He also affirms that *Dionysos multos habemus* ('we have many Dionysuses'), by giving the list of five Dionysuses along with their genealogies.[31] From a similar perspective but in the fourth century, an epigram by the Latin poet Ausonius enumerates the multiple names of the god Dionysus according to the customs of several ancient peoples.

> Ogygiadae me Bacchum vocant,
> Osirin Aegypti putant,
> Mysi Phanacen nominant,
> Dionyson Indi existimant,
> Romana sacra Liberum,
> Arabica gens Adoneum,
> Lucaniacus Pantheum.

> The sons of Ogyges call me Bacchus, Egyptians think me Osiris, Mysians name me Phanaces, Indians regard me as Dionysos, Roman rites make me Liber, the Arab race thinks me Adoneus, Lucaniacus the Universal God.[32]

This text gives a good indication of the intellectual tendency that read into the names of honoured divinities, found in different places, a single divine power ultimately acknowledged to be the 'Pantheon' or universal divinity. The practice of translating divine names allows Greek and Roman intellectuals not only to reflect on the unity of the divine world, but also to view the entire world in a single uniform manner, even on the cultic and cultural planes. The translation of divine names is very much an integral part of the theological interpretations of this epoch.

From a Christian perspective, it was not acceptable to venerate multiple divinities who carried the same name, as Christianity held that the divinities' denominations could not be interchangeable depending on people's language. The *Contra Celsum* by Origen, a demolition of the work by Celsus written in the middle

---

30 For Christian attitudes to Greek and Roman *interpretatio*, cf. Arnobius, *Adv. nat.* 3.32; Origen, *C. Cels.* 1.24 and 5.46. On *interpretatio* see Hartog 1980; Borgeaud 2004, 71–72; Ando 2008, 43–58; Albert, Belayche, Bonnet, Borgeaud 2012; Bettini 2016.
31 Cf. Cicero, *De nat. deor.* 3.23.58.
32 Ausonius, *Epigr.* 32: transl. H.G.E. White.

of the third century, demonstrates this principle in argument. Origen deplores the Greeks' attitudes towards the translation of divine names and refutes the idea of the Pagan Celsus, according to whom it barely matters if the supreme God is called Zeus Most High, Zen, Adonai, Sabaoth, Amon, etc. Two main considerations are advanced in Origen's discourse: on the one hand, the divine names Adonai and Sabaoth are given after a 'divine science that is attributed to the Creator of the universe',[33] and, so, they cannot simply be the result of a translation; on the other hand, the translation between Pagan divinities and the supreme God is possible because Zeus, Amon, and the other gods, are, in the Christian conception, demons who do not have divine status and who are enemies of the true God.[34] The only means of translating the name of God permitted by the Christian religion is, obviously, through the generic term that indicates 'god'.

The Christian Latin authors rehearse the main topics of the relevant Greek god's mythology: thus, in Dionysus' case, the invention of wine, the love affair with Ariadne, and the death of the god at the hands of the Titans. Christian authors make a point of integrating these traditional stories into Roman forms and categories. In the *Adversus nationes*, Arnobius relates the myth of the dissection of Dionysus and defines it as a *bacchanal*, but at the same time, however, he affirms that the Greek term for *bacchanal* is *omophagia*:

> We shall pass by the wild bacchanalia also, which are named in Greek *Omophagia*, in which with seeming frenzy and the loss of your senses you twine snakes about you; and, to show yourselves full of the divinity and majesty of the god, tear in pieces with gory mouths the flesh of loudly-bleating goats [...].

> But those other bacchanalia also we refuse to proclaim, in which there is revealed and taught to the initiated a secret not to be spoken; how Liber, when taken up with boyish sports, was torn asunder by the Titans; how he was cut up limb by limb by them also, and thrown into pots that he might be cooked; how Jupiter, allured by the sweet savour, rushed unbidden to the meal, and discovering what had been done, overwhelmed the revellers with his terrible thunder, and hurled them to the lowest part of Tartarus. As evidence and proof of which, the Thracian bard handed down in his poems the dice, mirror, tops, hoops, and smooth balls, and golden apples taken from the virgin Hesperides.[35]

---

33 Origen, *C. Cels.* 1.24.
34 Origen, *C. Cels.* 5.46.
35 Arnobius, *Adv. nat.* 5.19: transl. H. Bryce and H. Campbell.

Arnobius plays with the Dionysian literary tradition. His view of ritual Bacchic omophagy no doubt derives from a long literary tradition at least as old as Euripides' *Bacchae*.[36] But it is possible that the *Protrepticus to the Greeks*, by Clement of Alexandria, a late second-century CE exhortation to convert to Christianity, also played a role in Arnobius' construction of Dionysian imagery.[37] The second part of the *Adversus nationes* refers to mythical and poetic traditions according to which Thracian Orpheus was the initiator of the Dionysian mysteries, and Clement had indeed devoted important passages of his work to condemning the myth of Dionysus and the Titans.[38] In Arnobius, the application of the Roman label *bacchanalia* attests to the attempt at Romanizing Greek rituals. Anyway we must not forget that the Roman literary tradition was influenced by the events of 186 BCE. Through Livy's account,[39] the memory of the Roman *bacchanalia* is imposed in Latin literature as a noble paradigm of the conduct of the *res publica* of Rome to the extent that the *senatus consultum* on the *bacchanalia* already addressed most of the legal and organizational aspects that an association should possess in order to be recognized by the Roman state. From this perspective, then, Jean-Marie Pailler has approached the utilization of the *bacchanalia* by Christian authors, from Tertullian to Arnobius, in order to show how the paradigm of the *bacchanalia* represented an enduring point of reference and source of inspiration for the following epochs.[40]

Between gods and emperors

The persistence of Roman traits in the construction of Dionysus/Liber is also evident in another context. Numerous studies have shown how, in the context of military campaigns in the east, imperial power appropriated the motif of Dionysus as leader of an army of maenads and satyrs and as conqueror of the Indians.

---

36 See Bocciolini Palagi 2007.
37 On Christian texts concerning omophagy and its relations with the Eucharist, see Herrero 2006.
38 Many scholars have considered Arnobius' passage on the mysteries a paraphrase, if not a translation, of Clement's *Protr.* 2.17.2–18.2: see Röhricht 1893 and Rapisarda 1939. More recently, the same interpretation was proposed by Le Bonniec 1982, 58–59 and Herrero 2010, 154–155. Whether or not it is in fact a translation, comparison of the two texts shows that Arnobius was familiar with the *Protrepticus*.
39 Livy 39.8–22; see Steinhauer in this volume on the organizational aspects of the cult.
40 Pailler 1988, 759–75. For Tertullian's reference to the *senatus consultum de bacchanalibus* see *Apol.* 6.7; for Arnobius, see *Adv. nat.* 5.19, even if the reference is not explicit.

Liber Pater received some attention from Roman emperors eager to be assimilated to the god, and the various guises of Dionysus, as of the myths involving him, were the object of important reinterpretations by figures of imperial authority. Roman propaganda since Mark Antony had many related motifs at its disposal: the account of the Dionysian conquest, the assimilation of Alexander to Dionysus, Dionysus' triumphal procession upon his return from India. This latter motif also found support within the Roman literary tradition, which placed the origins of the triumph in a Dionysian context: according to Ovid, Pliny the Elder, and Tertullian, it was Liber Pater who had invented the triumph.[41]

This Roman tradition is also attested in epigraphic texts. Inscriptions from the imperial era form a connection between Roman religion and the Bacchic thiasus, which was often portrayed in mythic accounts as an army, and often indeed appeared as such in the plastic arts as well (notably on sarcophagi and in mosaics).[42] Sarcophagi from the time of Severus, for example, clearly feature the 'Indian triumph' motif, conceived as a Roman adaptation of Hellenistic iconography and contributing to the construction of an imperial ideology.[43] The image of a victorious Dionysus who has returned from India could be interpreted as a parallel for the generals of the Roman army, and, consequently, for the *imperator* as well.

The diffusion of this Roman image of Dionysus/Liber is also confirmed by its presence in a Christian source from the beginning of the fourth century, a passage from Lactantius' *Institutiones divinae*. This testimony of a military representation of Liber is interesting in that it reveals the supposed otherness of the god *vis-à-vis* Greek myth. Before the anti-Christian persecutions of Galerius end in 312, Lactantius, master of rhetoric, writes the *Institutiones divinae* with the purpose of creating a corpus of Christian knowledge that might replace the traditional cult beliefs of the empire. The systematization and classification of 'Paganism' in the first three books of this work are remarkable.[44] The author presents the Greek and Roman myths and rites, not only in order to mock them, but also in order to understand and explain religious history.[45]

In the first book, while listing the pagan divinities and their human, non-divine origins, Lactantius offers the following portrait of Liber:

---

[41] See Ovid, *Fast.* 3.729–32; Pliny, *HN* 7.191 and 14.144. See also Varro, *De ling. lat.* 6.68.
[42] *CIL* III, 6150; *ILS* 4060. See Jaccottet 2003, II, 138–40 (n° 68).
[43] On this subject, see Turcan 1966, 459–65. On the triumph, see Versnel 1970, Buccino 2013 and Rutherford 2013.
[44] See, for example, Lactantius, *Div. inst.* 1.8–20, on the Christian refutation of the Pagan pantheon, or 1.21 on sacrifices. For an analysis of Lactantius' attitudes toward religions see Schott 2008, 79–109 and Colot 2016.
[45] See Fredouille 1978, 237–52 and Massa 2019.

> Of supreme authority in the senate of the gods, with right to speak first in debate, must be father Bacchus, the only one of them all, Jupiter apart, to win a triumph, after leading his army to victory in India. Yet our invincible general (*invictus ille imperator*), *Indicus* the greatest (*Indicus maximus*), became the shameful victim of passion and lust.[46]

The Christian Latin writers very often evoke Liber through the most famous episodes of Greek myth. They mention his birth from a mortal woman, his invention of wine, and so forth. In the above passage, however, Liber is a very Roman god: he is authorized to speak first in the senate of the gods (*in senatu deorum*) by virtue of his military successes. Liber is the only one, apart from Jupiter, to have benefited from triumphal honours, due to his victory against the Indians. Lactantius plays with the imperial titles: the epithets *invictus imperator* and *Indicus maximus* recall the traditional honorific titles of imperial ideology.[47] Nonetheless, the end of the passage also questions Liber's 'Romanness': the god that had never experienced a military defeat is conquered by *amor* and *libido*. Our Christian author also mentions Liber's arrival on Crete, where he finds a 'debauched woman' (*impudica mulier*): 'he gave her the name Libera and ascended to heaven in her company' (*Liberam fecit, et cum ea pariter ascendit in coelum*).[48]

The Christian setting obviously has a polemical purpose: it aims to emphasize Liber's human character by mentioning his deeds as *imperator* and his weakness for women. But the goal is also to criticize those Roman emperors who associated their personal image with a deity so lacking in dignity.[49] In the *Institutiones divinae* Lactantius is aware of two facets of Liber, the one related to Roman imperial tradition and the other derived from traditional Greek myth. The close association of these two facets with each other allows Lactantius to present what is a complex und multifaceted divine world as a unified whole. He wishes to offer a unitary view of 'Paganism', one where Greek and Roman beliefs mingle.

Liber and the Devil

In the decade after 340, another author concentrates his attention on Liber/Dionysus. In his treatise against pagan cults (especially mystery cults of oriental provenance) addressed to the sons of Constantine, Firmicus Maternus devotes

---

46 Lactantius, *Div. inst.* 1.10.8: trans. by A. Bowen and P. Garnsey.
47 Also Tertullian refers to Liber 'as the God of triumphs' (*ut deo triumphorum*): see *De cor.* 12.1.
48 Lactantius, *Div. inst.* 1.10.9: my translation.
49 Lactantius also proceeds to scoff at Jupiter's title of *Optimus Maximus*: see *Div. inst.* 1.10.10.

one chapter to the Bacchic mysteries.[50] He rehearses from a euhemerist perspective – as had many other Christian writers before him – the myth of how Dionysus was killed by the Titans. But by way of introducing this myth, he evokes Liber and Libera:

> Thus, Most Holy Emperors, have the elements been deified by the children of perdition. But there are still other superstitions (*adhuc supersunt aliae superstitiones*) whose secrets must be revealed (*secreta pandenda sunt*): those of Liber and Libera, whose whole story in detail must be made known to your sacred intelligence, to make you aware that in these pagan religions again (*et in istis profanis religionibus*) it is the deaths of human beings that have been hallowed by worship. Well then, Liber was the son of Jupiter...[51]

The reference to Liber and Libera together is not repeated in the following paragraphs, which focus on the myth of Liber. Nor is there any mention of Persephone, who might have been associated with Liber/Dionysus in the context of the mystery cults. Libera does not appear in Firmicus Maternus' account of Greek myth, but she is mentioned elsewhere due to her traditional presence in Roman ritual practice. Her presence next to Liber in the mystery cults is also mentioned in the Servian *Commentary* on Virgil's *Georgics*, a text from the fourth century.[52]

The *De errore profanarum religionum* of Firmicus Maternus is also important because he witnesses the development of a new phenomenon. Gradually over the course of the work, a change becomes evidence in the representations of the gods Liber and Dionysus: their image starts to evolve away from traditional mythical references and towards a progressive assimilation with demonic powers. Of course, since the beginning of Christian literature, Dionysus had been the target of ferocious attacks by the Christians. Based on a negative Dionysian stereotype that was already present in Greek literature from Euripides' *Bacchae* and in Roman literature at least since Livy, Christian authors often highlighted both the god's aggressive madness and his sexuality.[53] To Christian eyes, the sexual fury and excitation that inhabits Dionysus also permeates the ceremonies; the sacred

---

50 On the condemnation of Dionysian cults in Firmicus Maternus, see Massa 2010, 250–56; On Firmicus' specific attention to the cults of the East, see Praet 2011 and Massa 2013, 493–99.
51 Firmicus Maternus, *Err. prof. rel.* 6.1: transl. by C.A. Forbes.
52 Cf. Servius, Comm. Verg. Georg. 1.166: *Nonnulli Liberum patrem apud Graecos λικμητὴν dici adserunt: uallus autem apud eos λικμὸς nuncupatur... Alii 'mysticam' sic accipiunt, ut uannun uas uimineum latum dicant, in quod ipsam propter capacitatem congerere rustici primitias frugum soleant et Libero et Liberae sacrum facere: inde 'mystica'.* On the relationships between Liber and Libera, see Massa 2016, 124–27.
53 Cf. Clement of Alexandria, *Protr.* 2.12.2.

Bacchic (ὄργια) rituals derive then from the perverse nature of the god that presides over them.

Nevertheless, throughout the fourth century, a change came about in Christian authors' representations of the god Dionysus. At this time, it was as if the Bacchic imaginary had started to also nourish the representations of the devil and of his accomplices. Firmicus Maternus, in his *De errore profanarum religionum*, describes the Dionysian procession as evil, a *scelerum pompa*. Having recounted the origins and development of the cults of Liber, the author depicts a scene in which a group of Dionysus' followers appears:

> There, amidst the drunken young women and old men (*inter ebrias puellas et uinolentos senes*), he was always preceded by a wicked procession (*scelerum pompa*): one whose black fur gave him a repulsive aspect; another, grasping a serpent in a horrid display (*alter nigro amictu taeter, alter ostenso angue terribilis*); yet another, gore running from his mouth which he used to rend asunder the limbs of a living beast (*alter cruentus ore dum uiua pecodis* [sic] *membra discerpit*).[54]

Young women and drunken old men clad in black (or perhaps simply hirsute), serpents in hand, bloody from the raw flesh of the living animals they have dismembered: this is how a Dionysian procession appeared in the eyes of a Christian author in the fourth century CE. Even the term *pompa* (κῶμος in Greek), often describing the followers of Dionysus, was used widely in ancient Christianity to indicate diabolical encounters. The expression *pompa diaboli* is already found in Tertullian, in which it indicates 'les cultes des idoles qui accompagnent les différentes manifestations de la vie de la cité païenne'.[55] Firmicus Maternus' testimony seems to develop the stereotype that was already present in Livy, especially if we bear in mind that Firmicus was familiar with Livy's account of the *Bacchanalia*, and that he considers it an *exemplum* to be followed in the repression and elimination of Pagan cults.[56]

On the other hand, in *De errore profanarum religionum*, Firmicus entertains an explicit assimilation between Dionysus and the Devil: in connection with a formula used in the mysterious initiations in honour of Dionysus, Firmicus declares:

> He is the basilisk and the scorpion (*Ipse est basiliscus et scorpio*), who is stepped on by the sure footstep of the believers; this evil reptile (*ipse malitiosus anguis*), whose head mortals

---

54 Firmicus Maternus, *Err. prof. rel.* 6.8: transl. by C.A. Forbes. For a commentary on this text, see Turcan 2002 *ad loc.*
55 Daniélou 1978, 329. See also Tertullian, *De spect.* 4.12 and 24.12; *De idol.* 18.8.
56 Cf. Firmicus Maternus, *Err. prof. rel.* 6.9.

seek to stroke; that sinuous dragon (*ipse tortuosus draco*), who is led along by a fish hook, who is captured and imprisoned.[57]

The figure of Dionysus is superimposed onto the image of the Christian demons.[58] Firmicus Maternus' strategy is a response to the new political context. The historical situation after the death of Constantine in 337 and the laws enacted by his sons, Constans and Constantine II, prompt this rather servile author to ask the new emperors to eradicate the Pagan cults and to destroy their temples.[59] The sons of Constantine not only maintained and indeed intensified the distribution of benefits to Christian churches; they also imposed curbs on the empire's traditional cults: in 341, they condemn *superstitio* and *insania sacrificiorum*, and in 346 order the closing down of temples as well as the abolition of sacrifices.[60] To be sure, these legislative resolutions, included in the *Codex Theodosianus*, do not amount to a complete prohibition on Pagan practices, but they do bear witness to the intensification of a phenomenon that will lead to the recognition of a form of Christianity as a state religion in 380, and to the official prohibition of Paganism in 391–392.[61] In an explicit fashion, then, Firmicus derives the origins of the parallelisms between Pagan rituals and Christian beliefs from the Devil, laying the basis for 'demonizing' the 'Paganism' that justifies the Christian desire to permanently eradicate Pagan cult practices.[62]

Conclusions

The Christian writers discussed here avail themselves of literary traditions when writing polemically about Dionysian myth and ritual. Even when writing about ritual contexts they use the generic representational norms of older literature without referring to the actual ritual practices throughout the Empire. It thus becomes difficult to find any signs of regional or geographical cultic features in the texts. From a literary and iconographic point of view, the Dionysian *koine* also includes Liber. It is only occasionally that Liber's specific traits emerge from the

---

57 Cf. Firmicus Maternus, *Err. prof. rel.* 21.2: my translation.
58 See Monaci Castagno 1996.
59 Cf. Firmicus Maternus, *Err. prof. rel.* 28.6 and 29.1–4. On the relationship between Firmicus Maternus and Roman legislation, see Drake 1998. On the violence against Pagans in Firmicus' *De errore profanarum religionum*, see Barnard 1990 and Kahlos 2009.
60 Cf. *CTheod.* 16.10.2 and 16.10.4. See Bonamente 2010.
61 Cf. *CTheod.* 16.1.2 and 16.10.10.
62 On the construction of 'Paganism' in Firmicus Maternus, see Massa 2013.

sources. And the polemical goals of Christian Latin writers help us identify this phenomenon.

Images of Liber and Dionysos are used by Christian Latin authors for different purposes: to deny the comparison between the Pagan god and Christ, to explain that Pagan rituals are simply the imitations of Pagan myths, to assimilate Liber to the Devil, or to criticize Pagan emperors.

The testimony of Christian Latin authors is not only useful in order to study the narrative strategies used to represent the divine Pagan world and to fight against the Empire's traditional religions. The Christian outlook also provides us with an original point of view on myths and on Greek and Roman cults. We are thus able to identify the differences that still existed in the imperial epoch between the Greek Dionysus and the Roman Liber, which shows the importance of Christian sources from our era's first centuries in the study of ancient religions.

Bibliography

Albert, J.-P., Belayche, N., Bonnet, C., Borgeaud, Ph. 2012. 'Conclusions.' In *Les représentations des dieux des autres*, edited by C. Bonnet, A. Declercq and I. Slobodzianek, *Mythos* Suppl. 2, 239–51.

Alvar, J. 2008. *Romanising Oriental Gods. Myth, Salvation and Ethics in the Cults of Cybele, Isis and Mithras*. Leiden/Boston.

Ando, C. 2008. *The Matter of Gods. Religion and the Roman Empire*. Berkeley/Los Angeles/London.

Barnard, L.W. 1990. 'L'intolleranza negli apologisti cristiani con speciale riguardo a Firmico Materno', in *L'intolleranza cristiana nei confronti dei pagani*, ed. P.F. Beatrice. Bologna, 79–99.

Barnes, T.D. 1971. *Tertullian. A Historical and Literary Study*. Oxford.

Belayche, N. and Mimouni, S.C. (eds.) 2009. *Entre lignes de partage et territoires de passage. Les identités religieuses dans les mondes grecs et romains. «Paganisme», «judaïsme», «christianisme»*. Paris/Louvain/Walpole, MA.

Berti, F. ed., 1991. *Dionysos. Mito e mistero. Atti del convegno internazionale*. Comacchio 3–5 novembre 1989. Comacchio.

Bettini, M. 2016. '*Interpretatio romana*: Category or Conjecture?' In Bonnet, Pirenne-Delforge and Pironti, 17–36.

Bocciolini Palagi, L. 2007. *La trottola di Dioniso*. Bologna.

Bonamente, G. 2010. 'Sviluppo e discontinuità nella legislazione antipagana: da Costantino il Grande ai figli.' In *Istituzioni, carismi ed esercizio del potere (IV-VI secolo d.C.).*, edited by G. Bonamente, R. Lizzi Testa. Bari, 61–76.

C. Bonnet, V. Pirenne-Delforge and G. Pironti (eds.) 2016. *Dieux des Grecs, dieux des Romains. Panthéons en dialogue à travers l'histoire et l'historiographie*. Rome.

Borgeaud, P. 1996. *La Mère des dieux. De Cybèle à la Vierge Marie*. Paris.

Borgeaud, P. 2004. *Aux origines de l'histoire des religions*. Paris.

Borgeaud, P. 2017. 'Variations évhéméristes.' In Les discours sur la religion dans l'Empire romain: regards croisés entre 'païens', 'juifs' et 'chrétiens', *RHR* 234.4, 593–612.

Bruhl, A. 1953. *Liber Pater. Origine et expansion du culte de Dionysos à Rome et dans le monde romain*. Paris.

Buccino, L. 2013. *Dioniso trionfatore. Percorsi e interpretazione del mito del trionfo indiano nelle fonti e nell'iconografia antiche*. Rome.

Cazanove, O. de 1988. 'Jupiter, Liber et le vin latin.' *RHR* 205.3, 245–65.

Cazanove, O. de. 1991. 'Θεὸς ἐν ἀσκῷ. Osservazioni sui meccanismi di trasmissione della figura di Dionysos all'Italia centrale arcaica.' In Berti, 171–84.

Colot, B. 2016. *Lactance. Penser la conversion de Rome au temps de Constantin*. Florence.

dal Covolo, E. 2008. 'Asclepio/Esculapio nella letteratura cristiana antica (secc. II-IV).' In *Cristo e Asclepio. Culti terapeutici e taumaturgici nel mondo mediterraneo antico fra cristiani e pagani*, edited by E. dal Covolo and G. Sfameni Gasparro. Rome, 103–12.

Daniélou, J. 1978. *Histoire des doctrines chrétiennes avant Nicée*, vol. III, *Les origines du christianisme latin*. Paris.

DesRosiers, N.P., Vuong, L.C. (eds.) 2016. *Religious Competition in the Graeco-Roman World*. Atlanta.

Drake, H.A. 1998. 'Firmicus Maternus and the Politics of Conversion', in *Qui miscuit utile dulci. Festschrift Essays for Paul Lachlan MacKendrick*, edited by G. Schmeling and J.D. Mikalson. Wauconda, vol. III, 133–49.

Engels, D., Van Nuffelen, P. (eds.) 2014. *Religion and Competition in Antiquity*. Brussels.

Fear, A.T. 1996. 'Cybele and Christ.' In *Cybele, Attis & Related Cults. Essays in Memory of M.J. Vermaseren*, edited by E.N. Lane. Leiden, 37–50.

Frakes, R.M. and DePalma Digeser, E. (eds.) 2006. *Religious Identity in Late Antiquity*. Toronto.

Fredouille, J.-C. 1978. 'Lactance historien des religions.' In *Lactance et son temps. Recherches actuelles*, edited by J. Fontaine and M. Perrin. Paris, 237–52.

Fredouille, J.-C. 2005. 'L'apologétique latine pré-constantinienne (Tertullien, Minucius Felix, Cyprien). Essai de typologie.' In *L'apologétique chrétienne gréco-latine à l'époque pré-nicénienne*. Geneva, 39–67.

Gasparri, C. 1986. 'Dionysos/Bacchus.' In *LIMC* III, 1, 514–66 & III, 2, 428–56.

Hartog, F. 1980. *Le miroir d'Hérodote. Essai sur la représentation de l'autre*. Paris.

Herrero, M. 2006. 'Dionysos mi-cuit: l'étymologie de Mésatis et le festin inachevé des Titans.' *RHR* 223.4, 389–416.

Herrero, M. 2010. *Orphism and Christianity in Late Antiquity*. Berlin/New York.

Jaccottet, A.-F. 2003. *Choisir Dionysos. Les associations dionysiaques ou la face cachée du dionysisme*. Zürich.

Jeanmaire, H. 1951. *Dionysos. Histoire du culte de Bacchus*. Paris.

Jourdan, F. 2010. *Orphée et les chrétiens, La réception du mythe d'Orphée dans la littérature chrétienne grecque des cinq premiers siècles*, vol. I, *Orphée, du repoussoir au préfigurateur du Christ*. Paris.

Kahlos, M. 2009. 'The Rhetoric of Tolerance and Intolerance: From Lactantius to Firmicus Maternus'. In *Continuity and Discontinuity in Early Christian Apologetics*, edited by J. Ulrich, A.-C. Jacobsen and M. Kahlos. Frankfurt am Main, 79–95.

Le Bonniec, H. 1958. *Le culte de Cérès à Rome. Des origines à la fin de la République*. Paris.

Le Bonniec, H. 1982. Arnobe, *Contre les gentils*, livre I, texte établi, traduit et commenté par H. Le Bonniec. Paris.

Mac Góráin, F. 2013. 'Virgil's Bacchus and the Roman Republic.' In *Augustan Poetry and the Roman Republic*, edited by J. Farrell and D.P. Nelis. Oxford, 124–45.

Magri, A. 2007. 'Le serpent guérisseur et l'origine de la gnose ophite.' *RHR* 224.4, 395–434.

Martin, L.H. 1989. 'Roman Mithraism and Christianity.' *Numen* 36, 2–15.

Massa, F. 2010. 'In forma di serpente: incesti, mostri e diavoli nella condanna cristiana dei culti dionisiaci.' In *Come bestie? Forme e paradossi della violenza tra mondo antico e disagio contemporaneo*, edited by N. Cusumano and V. Andò. Caltanissetta/Rome, 235–56.

Massa, F. 2013. 'Confrontare per distruggere: Firmico Materno e l'origine diabolica dei culti orientali.' *SMSR* 79.2, 493–509.

Massa, F. 2014. *Tra la vigna e la croce. Dioniso nei discorsi letterari e figurative cristiani (II–IV secolo)*. Stuttgart.

Massa, F. 2016. 'Liber face à Dionysos: une assimilation sans écarts ? *Koinè* dionysiaque et pratiques rituelles romaines.' In Bonnet, Pirenne-Delforge and Pironti, 117–29.

Massa, F. 2019. 'Lactance, le paganisme, les dieux: construire l'image de la religion des autres au début du IVᵉ siècle.' In *La vertu des Païens*, Actes du Colloque international transdisciplinaire (Paris, 17–18 juin 2013), edited by S. Taussig, Paris, 341–62.

Mastrocinque, A. 1988. *Lucio Giunio Bruto. Ricerche di storia, religione e diritto sulle origini della repubblica romana*. Trento.

Monaci Castagno, A. 1996. *Il diavolo e i suoi angeli. Testi e tradizioni*. Florence.

Montanari, E. 1988. *Identità culturale e conflitti religiosi nella Roma repubblicana*. Rome.

Munnich, O. 2012. 'La place de l'hellénisme dans l'autodéfinition du christianisme. L'*Apologie de Justin*.' In *Les chrétiens et l'hellénisme. Identités religieuses et cultures grecque dans l'Antiquité tardive*, edited by A. Perrot. Paris, 61–122.

Naerebout, F.G. 2016. 'Religious Competition: Is It a Useful Concept?', *Entangled Religions* 3, BJ–CC.

Nilsson, M. 1957. *The Dionysiac Mysteries in the Hellenistic and Roman Age*. Lund.

Pailler, J.-M. 1988. *Bacchanalia. La répression de 186 av. J.-C. à Rome et en Italie : vestiges, images, tradition*. Rome.

Pailler, J.-M. 1995. *Bacchus. Figures et pouvoirs*. Paris.

Praet, D. 2011. 'Franz Cumont, the Oriental Religions, and Christianity in the Roman Empire: A Hegelian View on the Evolution of Religion, Politics, and Science.' In *American Academy of Religion (San Francisco Conference 2011), Papers of the Nineteenth Century Theology Group*, edited by T. Gooch, D. De Vries and A. Molendijk. Oregon, 133–58.

Price, S. 1999. 'Christian Latin Apologetics: Minucius Felix, Tertullian, and Cyprian.' In *Apologetics in the Roman Empire. Pagans, Jews and Christians*, edited by M. Edwards, M. Goodman and S. Price. Oxford, 105–29.

Rapisarda, E. 1939. *Clemente fonte di Arnobio*. Turin.

Rebillard, É. 2012. *Christians and their Many Identities in Late Antiquity, North Africa, 200–450 CE*. Ithaca, NY/London.

Röhricht, A. 1893. *De Clemente Alexandrino Arnobii in irridendo gentilium cultu deorum auctore*. Hamburg.

Rosenblum, J.D., Young, L.C., DesRosiers, N.P. (eds.) 2014. *Religious Competition in the Third Century CE: Jews, Christians, and the Graeco-Roman World*. Göttingen.

Roubekas, N.P. 2017. *An Ancient Theory of Religion: Euhemerism from Antiquity to the Present*. London.

Rousselle, R. 1987. 'Liber-Dionysos in Early Roman Drama.' *CJ* 82, 193–98.

Rüpke, J. 2009. 'Early Christianity out of, and in, Context.' *JRS* 99, 182–93.

Rutherford, I. 2013. '*Dithyrambos, Thriambos, Triumphus*. Dionysiac Discourse at Rome.' In *Dithyramb in Context*, edited by P. Wilson and B. Kowalzig. Oxford, 409–23.

Schilling, R. 1955. *La religion romaine de Vénus: depuis les origines jusqu'au temps d'Auguste*. Paris.

Schott, J.M. 2008. *Christianity, Empire, and the Making of Religion in Late Antiquity*. Philadelphia.

Simon, M. 1955. *Hercule et le christianisme*. Paris.

Simon, M. 1978. 'Mithra, rival du Christ?' In *Études mithriaques*, Actes du IIe Congres international (Téhéran, du 1er au 8 septembre 1975). Tehran/Liège/Leiden, 457–78.

Simmons, M.B. 1995. *Arnobius of Sicca. Religious Conflict and Competitions in the Age of Diocletian*. Oxford.

Turcan, R. 1966. *Les sarcophages romains à représentations dionysiaques. Essai de chronologie et d'histoire religieuse*. Paris.

Turcan, R. 1982. *Les cultes orientaux dans le monde romain*. Paris.

Turcan, R. 2002. Firmicus Maternus, *L'erreur des religions païennes*, texte établi, traduit et commenté par R. Turcan. Paris.

Wiseman, T.P. 2000. 'Liber. Myth, Drama and Ideology in Republican Rome.' In *The Roman Middle Republic: Politics, Religion, and Historiography, c. 400–133 B.C.* (Papers from a Conference at the Institutum Romanum Finlandiae, September 11–12, 1998), edited by C. Bruun. Rome, 265–99, repr. in id. *Unwritten Rome*. Exeter, 84–139.

Versnel, H.S. 1970. *Triumphus. An Inquiry into the Origin, Development and Meaning of the Roman Triumph*. Leiden.

Index rerum et nominum

Accius 9, 44, 70, 71, 94, 159
acculturation 85, 86
Actium 21, 23, 182
Acts of the Apostles 60, 61
Adoneus 227
Adonis/Atunis 118
Adrastus 199, 204, 211
Aequitas (divinity) 118
Aeschylus 42, 43, 56
Aesculapius 10, 93, 161, 163
Agave 42, 46, 47, 49, 51, 53–59, 65, 71–74, 77, 205
Ager Teuranus, Calabria 138
Alcibiades 97
Alexander Comicus 70
Alexander the Great 68
Alexandria 21, 39, 43, 60, 69, 74, 82, 83, 105
Alkamenes 98
Allecto 209, 211
Amata 23, 106, 209, 211
Amycus 97
Anchises 23
anger/*ira* 53, 184, 186, 197, 198, 199, 201, 202, 206, 207, 210, 211, 225
Antipater of Thessalonica 48, 69
Aphrodite 15, 25, 105, 118, 120, 122, 197, 205
Apollo/Apulu 1, 20, 23, 24, 26, 91, 93, 116, 118, 125, 177, 182, 183, 190, 195, 196, 201, 204, 207, 208, 213, 221, 226
Ps.-Apollodorus 74
Apollonius of Tyana 224
Apulia 68, 137, 153
Ara Pacis Augustae 8, 28
Ares 126, 197
Argonauts 73, 96
Argos 194, 213
Ariadne/Ariatha 11, 88–90, 105, 120, 122, 127, 129, 167, 228
Aristides (painter) 11, 20
Aristides (orator) 74
Aristippus (philosopher) 45, 46, 67
Aristodemus, tyrant of Cumae 136

Aristophanes 42, 66
Arnobius 26, 219, 225–29
Artapanus 60, 64
Artavasdes II, King of Armenia 46
Artemis/Artamis, see also Diana 121, 122, 128
associations, see also *collegia* 5, 7, 25, 106, 127, 133–56, 165, 193, 194, 237
Athena Lindia 117
Athenagoras of Athens 224
Athens 2, 9, 39–45, 67, 89, 98, 105, 122, 136, 160, 164, 213
Atreus 24, 73, 194, 205, 210, 212
Atticus, Titus Pomponius 17, 18, 22, 164, 167, 172
Attis 9
Augustine of Hippo 12, 13
Augustus/Octavian 11, 21–24, 48, 87, 98, 101, 104, 106, 147, 177–79, 182–90
Aulus Postumius Albinus (cos. 151 BCE) 11
Aulus Postumius Albus Regillensis (cos. 496 BCE) 10, 157
Ausonius 227
Aventine Hill 10, 90, 92, 157, 158, 161, 178, 190

Bacchanalia 1, 3, 4, 7, 9, 13–19, 25, 26, 47, 51, 114, 130, 139, 143, 146, 148, 149, 153, 164, 167, 228, 229, 233
Basil of Caesarea 75
beard 92–95, 98
Bendis 9
bull 53, 54, 208, 223
bulla 95–97
buskins 50, 202

Cadmus 18, 40, 48, 49, 53, 58
Caesar (Gaius Iulius Caesar) 22, 98, 172–74, 188, 210
Callimachus 43, 44, 68, 209, 214
Callisthenes 43, 75
Campania 8, 11, 15, 114, 134, 147, 149, 150
Campus Martius 177

Capaneus 186, 187, 203, 204, 210
Carmenta 89
Carrhae 46
Cassius (Spurius Cassius Viscellinus, cos. 493 BCE) 11, 90
Cassius Dio 21, 105, 174
Catullus 70, 105, 106
Celsus 60, 62, 63, 75, 220, 224, 228
Cerealia 7, 11
Ceres, see also Demeter 1, 6, 7, 11–13, 16, 17, 19, 21, 85, 90, 118, 138, 148, 150, 157, 161, 166, 174, 178, 190
Chaeremon 67
Chania 2
Charon 212
Christ/Christianity 3, 5, 25, 26, 39, 60, 62–65, 219–38
Christus Patiens 23, 39, 59, 60, 64, 78
Cicero 3, 11, 17–19, 22, 90, 93, 94, 99, 112, 148, 157–74, 227
Cithaeron 42, 54, 63, 101, 205, 207, 214
Claudius (Emperor) 50
Clement of Alexandria 26, 60, 63, 64, 66, 75, 222, 224, 229, 233
Cleopatra 105
Codex Theodosianus 234
collegia, see also associations 134, 139, 142, 152
collegium poetarum 178
Constans 234
Constantine I 232, 234
Constantine II 234
Corinth 11, 20, 51
Crassus (Marcus Licinius Crassus) 46, 47, 49, 70
Cumae 136, 143

Damophilos 11, 90
Danaë 223
Demeter, see also Ceres 10, 136, 138, 158, 224
Derveni papyrus 149
Devil 26, 232–35
Diana, see also Artemis 91, 125, 126, 195, 227
Dido 23
Dii Consentes 94

Dindia Macolmia 97
Dio Chrysostom 60, 74
Diogenes Laertius 45
Dionysius II of Syracuse 45, 67
Dionysius of Halicarnassus 10, 11
Dioscuri 93, 160

Eleusis/Eleusinian mysteries 11, 19, 90, 125, 164
Eleuthereus 12, 98
Ennius 9, 93, 94, 162, 164
enthousiasmos 206
Ephesus 21, 105, 174
Ephialtes 126
Erotes 101, 105
Esia 121, 122
Etruria 9, 15, 89, 90, 111, 114, 115, 117, 120, 123, 128, 148, 149, 168
Euhemerism 57, 226
Eumenides 202
Eunaeus 203, 204
Euripides 2, 3, 9, 14, 15, 18, 20, 23, 24, 26, 39–84, 141, 197, 207, 222, 229, 233
– *Bacchae* 2, 3, 9, 14, 15, 18, 20, 23–26, 39–84, 141, 197, 202, 207, 213, 214, 222, 229, 233
Euripides the Younger 42
Europa 223
Eusebius 64
evocatio 10
Exathres/Pomaxathres 47
Ezekiel 60, 69

fate 23, 24, 52, 181, 184, 185–87, 198, 202, 203, 211
Favorinus 75
Firmicus Maternus 26, 60, 76, 219, 232, 233, 234
Fortuna 89, 91, 124, 125
Forum Boarium 85, 87, 90, 99
Fufluns/Fuflunus 5, 7–9, 92, 111, 114–22, 125, 127, 128, 129
furor/μανία 24, 106, 169, 193–95, 197, 199, 203–205, 207–14

Gabii 6
Gellius, Aulus 75

Index rerum et nominum — **241**

gender of worshippers / female worship, see also women as worshippers of Bacchus 14, 57, 116, 133, 140, 141, 142, 147–49
genealogy 19, 157, 167, 173, 194, 197
George Cedrenus 77
Getae 177, 183, 185, 186, 196
Golden Age 43, 106
Gorgasos 11, 90
Gregory of Nazianzus 64, 65

Heracles/Hercules 89, 91, 93, 97, 161, 162, 127, 125, 185, 186, 212, 220, 224, 226
Hiaco/Hiacos, see also Iacchus/Iakchos 92, 111, 124, 125, 128, 129
Hipponion 6, 137, 138, 143
Hispala Faecenia 15, 41, 147–50
Hölderlin, Friedrich 2, 60
Homer 1, 44, 71, 160, 198
Horace 2, 21–23, 60, 71, 104, 105, 185, 206
hospitality 9, 10
hybridization 113
hybris 21, 57, 193
Hyginus 10, 71, 94
Hypsipyle 195, 197–99, 203, 204, 206, 214
Hyrodes II, King of Parthia 46

Iacchus/Iakchos, see also Hiaco/Hiacos 11, 17–19, 85, 90, 92, 105, 112, 127, 129, 163, 164, 180
Illyria 6
India 71, 179, 180, 185, 203, 213, 230, 231
Ino 51, 56, 71, 89, 99, 100
interpretatio Romana 6
Ioannes Antiochenus 77
Ioannes Lydus 77
Ioannes Malalas 77
Ioannes Tzetzes 77
Iophon 67
Isis 10, 105
Isodaites 9
ivy 13, 50, 115, 183, 184, 187

Janus 93
Jason of Tralles 46, 47
Julian 75
Juno 10, 91, 125, 158, 195, 198–201, 209, 214
Jupiter 7, 25, 91, 94, 112, 125, 157, 158, 160, 161, 163, 184, 186, 193, 194, 196, 198, 200–204, 206, 209, 211, 213, 214, 221, 223, 229, 231, 232
Justin (Martyr) 60, 220, 223
Juvenal 16, 25, 73

kalokagathia 97
Koré, see also Libera 10, 136, 158

Laconia 89
Lactantius 26, 93, 219, 230, 231
Lanuvium 85, 98, 99, 101
Latium 5, 6, 89, 111, 114, 115, 145, 152
Lavinium 12, 13
Leda 223
Lemnos/Lemnians 25, 195, 203–206
Leucothea 89, 99
Lex Iulia et Papia 147
Lex Oppia 147
Libera, see also Koré 1, 7, 11–13, 16, 17, 19, 21, 85, 88, 90, 97, 138, 157, 158, 161, 163, 178, 190, 231, 232
Liberalia 1, 7, 11–13, 16, 17, 24, 86, 90, 92, 97, 127, 157, 158, 172, 173, 177, 178, 181–84, 188–90
Libertas/libertas 12, 22, 172
Linear B 2, 4
Livy 10, 13–16, 23, 71, 90, 94, 114, 133, 134, 139, 146–52, 229, 233
Loufir 6, 115
Lucan 24, 193, 200, 203, 207–10
Lucian 51, 59, 74
Lucretius 22, 195
lucus 99, 100
Luke (evangelist) 61, 62
Lycophron 68
Lycurgus 8–10, 14, 42, 44, 58, 59, 67, 179–81, 188

Maccabees 64, 72
Macedonia 45

Magna Mater/Cybele 10, 16, 175, 221
Marius 21, 22, 98
Mark Antony 21, 51, 85, 87, 94, 98, 105, 169–74, 230
Mars 91, 93, 125, 126, 128, 195, 197–99
Mater Matuta 5, 89, 99
Matralia 89, 99
Medea 59, 64, 65, 73, 197, 210
Melicertes 89
Mercury 91, 126, 127
Mesopotamia 113
Messalina 50, 72
metonymy 166, 184, 200
Minerva/Menerva 89, 91, 125–29, 157
Minyades 179
Mithras 220, 224
mora 196, 198, 199
Mummius (Lucius Mummius Achaicus, cos. 146 BCE) 11
Muses/Pierides 43, 171, 183, 210, 226
mysteries 4, 8, 15–19, 24, 57, 60, 76, 87, 97, 101, 106, 128, 134, 136, 151, 161, 164, 168, 208, 229, 232

Naevius 8, 9, 12, 158
Naxos 101
Nemea 196, 198, 199, 209, 214
Neo-Attic art 95
Neos Dionysos 20, 21, 87, 94, 98, 106
Neptune 93, 166
Nero 72, 208
Nietzsche, Friedrich 1, 2, 26, 27
Nonnus of Panopolis 5, 10, 24, 56–60, 65, 76
Nouios Plautios Romai 96

Oedipus 73, 199, 202, 204, 211
Olympias (mother of Alexander) 43
omophagia 228, 229
Ps.-Oppian 24, 53, 75
oreibasia 101, 207
Origen 60, 61, 63, 75, 225, 227, 228
Orpheus 97, 106, 208, 220, 224, 229
Orphic golden leaves 6
Osiris 20, 213, 221, 222, 227
Otus 126

Ovid 3, 7, 12, 24, 55, 58, 72, 85, 89, 92, 93, 105, 177–92, 193, 206, 210, 230

Pacorus, Prince of Parthia 46
Paculla Annia 15, 114, 147–50
Pacuvius 9, 55, 69
Palaemon 89
Palatine Hill 94, 95, 178, 190
Papposilenus 97
Parcae 185
Parnassus 101
Paul 61, 62
Pausanias 67, 98
Penelope 198
Penthesileia painter 115
Pentheus 9, 15, 18, 24–26, 40–43, 45–59, 63–76, 180, 181, 187, 188, 198, 201, 202, 204, 205, 208, 213
Perugia 120
phallophoria 13
Phanaces 227
Pherecydes of Athens 122
Philo of Alexandria 60, 63
Philodamus of Scarphaea 67
philosophy 46, 112, 227
pietas 104, 202, 206
Plato 45, 48, 67, 149
Plautus 9, 68, 144, 148, 159
Pliny the Elder 11, 21, 90, 91, 94, 97, 101, 102, 151, 197, 230
Plutarch 13, 20, 21, 39, 43, 46, 47, 49, 66, 73, 97, 105, 174, 199
Pluto 210, 212
Pollux 97, 161, 185
Polynices 211, 214
polytheism 5, 112
Polyxo 204–206
Pompeii 7, 8, 87, 97, 100, 105, 115, 151
Pompey (Gnaeus Pompeius Magnus) 210
Porta Maggiore 72
Portunus 89
Poseidon 198, 199
Praeneste 91, 92, 111, 115, 120–29
Procne 73, 205, 206
Propertius 23, 70, 178, 182, 183, 190, 212
Puteoli 145, 152, 185
Pylades of Cilicia 47, 48

Index rerum et nominum — **243**

Pylos 2
Pythagoras 97

Quirinus 93, 161, 185

Rabelais, François 26
Rhea 224
Rohde, Erwin 1
Romulus 93, 161, 162, 185

Sabazios 9, 112, 221
sacro-idyllic landscape 22, 85, 86, 102, 103
Samuel (Book of) 64
Sant'Abbondio 7
Sant'Omobono 85, 87–89, 92, 106
Satricum 5
Saturn 93
Scipio Barbatus, Lucius Cornelius (cos. 298 BCE) 97
Semele/Semela/Semla 19, 42, 52, 53, 57, 58, 89, 112, 118–20, 125, 127–29, 160–62, 179, 186, 187, 200, 220, 223
Senate 9, 13, 14, 18, 19, 40, 59, 133, 134, 138, 139, 141–44, 146, 147, 150–52, 158, 167, 172, 174, 231
Senatus consultum de Bacchanalibus 14, 17, 133, 134, 138–46, 148, 151, 152, 158, 229
Seneca the Elder 105
Seneca the Younger 24, 73, 193, 194, 196, 197, 199, 202, 203, 205, 210, 212
Servius 94, 173, 197, 232
Sibylline books 10, 157
Sicily 11, 120
Silenos 102, 105, 116
Silius (Gaius Silius) 50
Social War 20
Solomon 60, 64
sparagmos 41, 51, 52, 54, 55, 56, 59, 73–75, 219
Spurius Postumius Albinus (consul 186 BCE) 14
Statius 3, 13, 24, 25, 73, 193–214
 – *Achilleid* 24, 73, 212, 214
 – *Silvae* 213
Strabo 11, 71

Studius (or Ludius) 101
Suda 42, 66
Sumeria 113
symposium 8, 23, 105, 106, 178, 182, 183
Synesius 76

Tacitus 6, 11, 49, 50, 51
Tarquinia 120
Tarsus 105
Technitai Dionysou (Artists of Dionysus) 144
Tertullian 26, 119, 222–24, 226, 229–31, 233
Thebes 25, 48, 52, 57–59, 73, 74, 76, 186, 193, 194, 196, 197, 200–203, 205, 207, 208, 212–14
Theocritus 24, 51–54, 59, 60, 66, 68
Theodoretus 76
theology 18, 39, 157–59, 173, 194, 200, 206, 228
thiasos 21, 25, 40, 64, 135, 145, 152
Thoas 203, 206
Thrace 1, 106, 196, 214, 229
thunderbolt 179, 187–89
thyrsus 50, 68, 98, 101–103, 125, 127, 200, 202, 210
Tibullus 20, 22, 104
Tigers 194, 197, 211
Timotheus of Gaza 76
Tiresias 13, 15, 18, 40, 43, 45, 55, 63, 187, 207
Tiriolo 13, 114
Tisiphone 204, 210–12
toga libera 12, 93, 96, 182
Tomis 177, 178, 181, 183, 186, 188
Torre Nova 5, 145, 152
translation 2, 4, 6, 7, 57, 69, 70, 93, 94, 111, 112, 113–15, 117, 125, 127–29, 133, 149, 164, 187, 227, 228, 229, 231, 234
Triptolemus 11
triumph 7, 20, 23, 24, 86, 90, 127, 177, 212, 230, 231
Troy 3, 200, 201, 203, 212
Turan (Aphrodite) 118
Turnu (Eros) 118

Valerius Flaccus 73, 202
Valerius Maximus 21
Varro 10–13, 16, 90, 94, 148, 158, 167, 168, 170, 179, 230
Veii 10
Venus 25, 117, 120, 163, 166, 167, 193, 195, 200, 201, 204–206, 221, 227,
Verres 162, 163, 166, 167
Vesuvius 8, 151
Vettius Valens 50
Victoria 56, 91, 125, 127, 214
Villa della Farnesina 20, 85, 102, 103, 105, 151
Villa of Mysteries 8, 87, 151
Vinalia 7, 221
Virgil 21–24, 44, 55, 56, 71, 104, 106, 193–96, 198, 200, 202, 203, 209, 210, 221, 232

viticulture 106, 157
Vitruvius 11, 91, 94
Vulcanus 118
Vulci 111, 115–20, 125, 127–29

wall-painting 8, 21, 22, 67, 98–105
Wilamowitz-Moellendorf, Ulrich von 1
women as worshippers of Bacchus, see also gender of worshippers 14, 15, 25, 46, 50, 52, 54, 57, 63, 70, 103, 134, 140–42, 144, 146–50, 152, 153, 201, 205, 213, 233

Xenophon of Smyrna 48

Index locorum

Acc. *Trag.* 204–05 R.²	94	Cic. *Tusc.* 1.28	99, 160, 162
Acc., *Stasiastae* vel		Cic. *Verr.* 2.4.128	162
Tropaeum Liberi	9	Cic. *Verr.* 2.4.135	163
Acts 5:39	61	Cic. *Verr.* 2.5.27	167
Acts 26:14	61	Clem. Alex. *Protr.* 12	63
Anth. Pal. 16.289	48, 69	Clem. Alex. *Strom.* 4	222
Anth. Pal. 16.290	48, 69	Diog. Laert. 2.78	45
Aristophanes, *Thesm.* 140	70	Dio 48.39	105
Arnob. *Adv. nat.* 1.36	225	Dio 50.25	21
Arnob. *Adv. nat.* 1.37	225	Dio 50.4–5	105
Arnob. *Adv. nat.* 1.41	226	Dion. Hal. 6.13	90
Arnob. *Adv. nat.* 4.15–17	227	Dion. Hal. 6.17	90
Arnob. *Adv. nat.* 5.19	230	Dion. Hal. 6.94.3	90, 157
Aug. *Civ.* 7.21	13	Dion. Hal. 7.79	90
August. *RG* 20	21	Enn. *Trag.* 128–32 R²	9, 94
Auson. *Ep.* 32	227	Eur. *Ba.* 78–82	16
Call. *Ep.* 48 Pf. = *AP* 6.310	43, 68	Eur. *Ba.* 225	25
Cat. 64.144	106	Eur. *Ba.* 234	15
Cat. 64.251–62	106, 164	Eur. *Ba.* 257	15
Cic. *Att.* 14.10	172	Eur. *Ba.* 278–85	13
Cic. *Att.* 14.14.2–5	22, 173	Eur. *Ba.* 485–88	15
Cic. *Balb.* 55	11	Firm. Mat. *Err. prof. rel.* 6.1	222
Cic. *Brut.* 276	170	Firm. Mat. *Err. prof. rel.* 6.8	233
Cic. *Cat.* 1.26	169	Hom. *Il.* 5.385–98	126
Cic. *Cat.* 4.11	169	Hom. *Il.* 6.123–32	10
Cic. *De or.* 3.167	166	Hom. *Od.* 11.321–25	122
Cic. *Div.* 1.80	168	Hor. *Epist.* 1.16	60
Cic. *Fam.* 7.23	22, 171	Hor. *Epist.* 2.1.156	20
Cic. *Fin.* 3.66	162	Hor. *Od.* 1.27	105
Cic. *Flacc.* 60	94	Hor. *Od.* 2.19	2, 71, 193, 195
Cic. *Har. resp.* 39	169		
Cic. *Leg.* 2.35–37	164	Hor. *Od.* 3.3.9–16	185
Cic. *Nat. D.* 1.119	93	Hor. *Od.* 3.25	2, 45, 206, 208
Cic. *Nat. D.* 2.60	165		
Cic. *Nat. D.* 2.62	160, 161	John Malalas,	
Cic. *Nat. D.* 3.21	90	*Chronographia* 31.7–12	58
Cic. *Nat. D.* 3.35	19	John the Lydian,	
Cic. *Nat. D.* 3.41	166	*Mens.* 4.51	112
Cic. *Nat. D.* 3.45	93	Juv. 2.1–3	25
Cic. *Nat. D.* 3.53	159, 160	Lact. *Div. inst.* 1.10	231
Cic. *Nat. D.* 3.58	160	Lact. *Div. Inst.* 1.11	93
Cic. *Orat.* 99	170	Liv. 2.20	90
Cic. *Phil.* 2.104	170	Liv. 2.41	90

Liv. 39.8	13, 15, 147, 148, 150, 167, 229
Liv. 39.13	15, 146–48
Liv. 39.15	15, 17, 144, 147, 148
Lucil. fr. 24–27 Warmington	93
Naev. *com.* 112 R²	12
Naev., *Lycurgus*	8, 9
Nonn. *Dionys.* 44–46	56
Ps.-Opp. *Cyn.* 4.230–353	53
Orig. *Cels.* 2.34	61
Ov. *Fast.* 3.771–78	93
Ov. *Fast.* 3.459–516	89
Ov. *Fast.* 3.713–26	178
Ov. *Fast.* 6.473–568	89
Ov. *Met.* 3.511–733	54, 72
Ov. *Met.* 4.11–17	85, 158
Ov. *Met.* 4.11–30	180
Ov. *Met.* 15.871–79	186
Ov. *Tr.* 5.3	177–90
Pacuv., *Pentheus*	9, 55, 69
Paus. 1.20.3	67, 98
Plin. the Elder, *NH* 34.15	90
Plin. the Elder, *NH* 34.26	97
Plin. the Elder, *NH* 35.116–17	102
Plin. the Elder, *NH* 35.154	90
Plut. *Ant.* 24	105
Plut. *Ant.* 26	105
Plut. *Ant.* 75	21
Plut. *Crass.* 33	46
Plut. *Num.* 8.20	97
Prop. 4.6.75–76	182
Sen. the Elder, *Suas.* 1.6	105
Serv. Virg. *Aen.* 3.19	93
Serv. Virg. *E.* 5.30	94
Tac. *Ann.* 11.31	50
Tertullian, *Apol.* 21.8–9	223
Theocr. 26, 25–26	52
Theocr. 26, 27–38	54
Varro, *ARD* 262 [42] Cardauns	13
Varro, *Rust.* 1.1.5	94
Vell. Pat. 2.82	105
Virg. *Aen.* 7.374–405	106
Vitr. *Arch.* 3.3.5	11

Index of inscriptions and visual artefacts

Inscriptions

CIE 10985	116
CIE 11073	116
CIE 11101	116
CIE 11110	116
CIE 8079	6
CIL 1².561 = *ILLRP* 1197 = *ILS* 8562	96
CIL 1².563	85
CIL 6.1285	97
CIL 1² 2.581 = *ILLRP* 511 = *ILS* 18 (*SC de Bacchanalibus*)	14, 17, 133, 134, 138–46, 148, 151, 152, 158, 229
CSE DDR 1, 5	118
CSE Italia 1, I, 10	122
CSE Italia 6, 83 = *CIL* 1² 2498	125
IGUR I 160	135, 152
SEG 4.92	6
*SIG*³ 648B	46, 69

Visual artefacts

Apulian phiale (BM F133)	68
Ara Pacis Augustae	8, 28
BCM Athens 376	98
Berlin, Charlottenburg, inv. Misc. 6239	85
Cista Ficoroni	96, 97
Copenhagen, Ny Carlsberg Glyptotek, inv. HIN 26	87
Lanuvium, Museo Civico, fresco fragment	98, 99
Naples, Museo Archeologico Nazionale, inv. 100019	100
Pompeii, House of the Centaur (VI.9.3–5)	100
Pompeii, Villa of the Mysteries	8, 87, 97, 151
Rome, Musei Capitolini, Antiquarium Comunale, statue fragments	87, 89
Rome, Museo Nazionale Etrusco di Villa Giulia, inv. 24787	96
Rome, Museo Nazionale Romano, inv. 1037, 1071, 1072	102, 103
Rome, Museo Palatino, inv. 601 and 614	94
Rome, Villa della Farnesina	20, 85, 102, 103, 105, 151
Rome, Villa Doria Pamphili	103, 104
Saint Petersburg, Hermitage Museum, inv. 18.832	98

www.ingramcontent.com/pod-product-compliance
Lightning Source LLC
Chambersburg PA
CBHW070758230426
43665CB00017B/2412